FOOD FOR WAR–FOOD FOR PEACE

FOOD FOR WAR-FOOD FOR PEACE
United States Food Aid in a Global Context

Mitchel B. Wallerstein

The MIT Press
Cambridge, Massachusetts, and London, England

This book was set in Compugraphic Palatino by A&B Typesetters, Incorporated and printed and bound by The Alpine Press Inc. in the United States of America.

Library of Congress Cataloging in Publication Data

Wallerstein, Mitchel B
  Food for war–food for peace.

  Bibliography: p.
  Includes index.
  1. Food relief, American. I. Title. HV696.F6W34   363.8'8   80-18417
ISBN 0-262-23106-9

For S.E.P., QTP

This book is dedicated to the memory of Hubert Horatio Humphrey, the late Senator and Vice-President of the United States, who died during the final stages of this study. More than any other American, Hubert Humphrey had the capacity to see the larger potential inherent in US food aid and the influence and energy to make that vision a reality. He will be missed.

Contents

Preface

The task faced at the outset of this project was formidable. Although much had been written on the general issue of food aid, no comprehensive analysis had been conducted regarding the political considerations, interests, and objectives that have shaped global food assistance efforts, both bilateral and multilateral, since World War II. This study attempts to fill that gap.

An investigation of the politics of food aid is complicated by the fact that there are, in reality, two discrete but intersecting sets of issues involved: those relating to the donor and those relating to the recipient. A basic decision was made at the outset, therefore, to concentrate only on the *donor* side of the aid relationship in order to keep the size of the study within reasonable limits. This is not to imply that issues pertaining to the uses and impact of food aid within recipient countries are any less important or worthy of attention. But, in order to deal adequately with such complex matters as the political and economic disincentive effects of food aid on recipients' agricultural development, a separate and equally exhaustive research effort would be required.

Even with the boundaries of the topic defined in terms of the food aid policies of donor countries, the difficulties involved in obtaining and analyzing information—particularly with regard to the more political (and, therefore, more controversial) aspects of the topic—were substantial. As a result, data for this study have been marshalled from a variety of sources, including (1) primary documents housed in the National Archives and the Kennedy and Johnson Presidential Libraries; (2) previously restricted government documents obtained through the Freedom of

Information Act; (3) secondary source material of all types; and (4) extensive personal interviews with policymakers—both past and present—in the United States, Europe, Japan, and Australia, as well as at the United Nations in Rome.

One more caveat must be added. Due to the currency of the topic, and to its obvious national security aspects, it was impossible in many cases to gain access to primary documents concerning events in the United States occurring after 1969. This raised certain methodological difficulties which were further complicated by the court-ordered impoundment during the period of research of all documents from the Nixon administration. It was necessary, therefore, to rely primarily on secondary source material and personal interviews in order to reconstruct events during this period. In these situations, however, a special effort was made to seek additional sources of corroboration wherever possible.

Yet another difficulty raised by the currency of the topic is that some of the issues addressed herein have undergone further development since this book entered into production. Although this is inevitable, I feel obligated to bring the more important of these changes to the reader's attention. With reference to the Food Aid Conventions discussed in chapter 5, it should be noted that the terms of a new, expanded agreement have now been accepted by all of the major parties. It also should be pointed out with regard to the discussion in chapter 6 of the uses of food power in foreign policy that the Carter administration's decision to employ the "food weapon" once again in response to the Soviet invasion of Afghanistan has now been countermanded by the Reagan administration. And one final point: due to the dire urgency of the present food situation in Kampuchea (Cambodia), the United States has removed its prohibition on the shipment of PL 480 food aid to that country. Beyond these modifications, it is hoped that this work proves both relevant and useful.

Cambridge, Mass.

June 1981

Acknowledgments

Many people contributed generously of their time, opinions, and recollections during the course of this research; so much so, in fact, that they are too numerous to mention individually by name. Nevertheless, they have my sincere thanks and appreciation. My work was also aided substantially by information and cooperation I received from officials of the UN–FAO World Food Programme, the UN World Food Council, the International Wheat Council, and the Commission of the European Communities, as well as from the appropriate ministries in each of the countries whose food aid programs are addressed herein. It must be emphasized, however, that information derived from these sources was not necessarily given by the interviewees acting in an official capacity. Moreover, the author, of course, remains solely responsible for all the views expressed.

The actual execution of the research was aided greatly by the assistance of three individuals: Janice Baker (Research Analyst, Congressional Research Service, Library of Congress); E. William Johnson (Senior Archivist, John F. Kennedy Presidential Library); and Linda Hanson (Archivist, Lyndon B. Johnson Presidential Library). I want, in addition, to express my gratitude to the two foundations that provided the funds to underwrite the two years of research and travel expenses. The bulk of my support was derived from two successive fellowships awarded by the Institute for the Study of World Politics (formerly, the University Consortium for World Order Studies), while additional assistance was provided by the Josephine de Karman Fellowship Trust.

Special mention is also due of the invaluable support, guidance, and criticism provided by Eugene B. Skolnikoff, Director of the Center for International Studies at MIT, John O. Field of Tufts University, and James E. Austin of Harvard University. Thanks are extended in a similar vein to Thérèse Belot and to D. John Shaw, who graciously consented to review several chapters, for which they were uniquely qualified by experience, and to Martin McLaughlin and Raymond Hopkins, who gave particularly insightful criticism. Lois Gabriel and Diane Peterson performed invaluably, in quickly and accurately retyping the manuscript. Finally, the completion of this study was aided beyond measure by the support and patience of my wife, Susan E. Perlik. Her special gifts are what help me to maintain a healthy perspective on my work, and they continue to be essential to whatever success I achieve.

Introduction

Food is unique as a natural resource. Like other human necessities such as air and water, it is essential for existence. Yet, unlike the air and—to a lesser extent—the water, food is *not* ubiquitous; that is, it cannot be produced in the same quantity or with the same quality in all geographic locations. As a result, since Biblical times nations have bought, borrowed, begged, stolen, and fought for additional food resources possessed by their more abundantly blessed neighbors.

This study concerns one particular aspect of this international relationship: how the process of giving and obtaining food has been translated, in modern political terms, into an organized international capacity to deliver food assistance; and, more specifically, how the United States, as the single most abundantly blessed actor within this particular global context has allocated its available food resources. Inasmuch as food assistance is a major component of the larger effort to transfer economic resources from rich countries to poor countries, this study also examines the relationship between food and foreign aid and analyzes the impact of these linkages in terms of US foreign policy.

When the United States first inaugurated a formal foreign assistance program at the close of World War II, few but the most farsighted policymakers conceived of the effort as anything other than a limited, short-term response to the critical social, economic, and political situation prevailing in Europe and elsewhere at the time. The rapid increase in East–West tension during the next six years, caused by competition over spheres of political and economic influence, quickly ended any such expectations. The role and importance of foreign aid did not diminish as the Western European countries recovered. Instead, the aid targets simply shifted to other parts of the globe, particularly to the so-called Third World, where attention to pressing human needs became an increasingly important element of the East–West ideological struggle.

The burden of responding to the developing world fell squarely upon the United States since its principal European allies were preoccupied with their own economic and social reconstruction. As a result, the conception of foreign aid as an instrument for meeting the "Communist challenge" and for promoting the global security interests of the "free world" largely dominated US strategic thinking during most of the next two decades (1950–1970). By the early seventies, however, many of the factors that had helped shape this view of the world had changed dramatically. The realities of new international political relationships among raw material supply, energy supply, and foreign markets had left the United States nearly as dependent upon the developing world as were they upon the United States. Under these altered economic and political circumstances, many developing countries no longer viewed aid as a privilege so much as a *right* derived from this mutual dependency. Some, in fact, took the notion one step further—as embodied in the doctrine of the New International Economic Order—by arguing that foreign economic assistance was the *obligation* of the developed countries. Aid was viewed, in fact, as a form of compensation both for past exploitation and for the correction of existing economic inequities.

At the same time that pressures on US foreign aid have been increasing, however, the total value of capital assistance appropriations authorized by Congress has been declining in real dollars. While it is undeniable that the overwhelming majority of the aid contributed by the United States since World War II has been in the form of capital loans and grants,[1] a significant percentage of US official development assistance (ODA) has nevertheless been made available in the form of food (approximately 28 percent of the total US ODA during the period from 1946 to 1976 was given as food aid).[2] The reliance on food as a form of foreign assistance is, of course, a matter of particular concern in this study, but the most basic explanation for this aid strategy is the fact that the United States produces a far greater volume of food than is required to meet domestic requirements. Thus, at least until recently, food has been a relatively "free good," with a low opportunity cost for use as aid in comparison to the opportunity cost of capital. As budgetary pressures have increased in the United States, the food resource has become increasingly attractive as a foreign aid alternative.

The importance of food as a foreign aid resource has, in turn, resulted in its inevitable involvement in the continuing debate over the proper objectives for US foreign assistance. Indeed, the evolution of food aid policy provides useful and important insights into the overall priorities and objectives of American foreign policy during the past twenty-five years. For example, much can be learned from the study of food aid regarding the US response to increased global interdependence and to new Third World political and economic demands. Examination of the manner in which food aid is channeled through or coordinated within the multilateral context also illuminates US foreign policy regarding efforts to increase aid burden-sharing by donors from among the developed countries. Finally, an analysis of the political benefits sought by the United States through the selective allocation of its food assistance helps to illustrate the role of food assistance as a bilateral American foreign policy instrument.

Due to the nature of the topic, however, it is not possible to test directly the strength of the relationship between food aid and American foreign policy. In fact, many of the factors which may account for a particular decision—or complex of decisions—are rarely explicit or even isolable, and there are frequently too many intervening and complicating variables, extending over too long a period of time, to permit the substantiation of such hypotheses. Instead, the methodology adopted here has been to construct a model that attempts to account for the apparent links between US food assistance and foreign aid doctrine. This conceptualization of US food aid policy, expressed in terms of its objectives, its beneficiaries, and its putative links with overall US foreign aid policy, is presented in the accompanying figure.

The model initially disaggregates US food aid policy into two major areas: the promotion of domestic agriculture and the promotion of foreign policy. Under these two broad rubrics, six general policy objectives are identified, of which two relate to the former goal and four to the latter. Each of these general objectives has, in turn, a specific, instrumental intent that flows from it. Moreover, each objective also has associated with it a discrete set of actors and an obvious group of beneficiaries. The model attempts to identify the apparent links between food aid and the overall objectives of US foreign policy as well as the most common delivery channel through which each goal is normally pursued.

Initial examination of the model leads to at least three preliminary observations regarding the trend in US food aid policy:

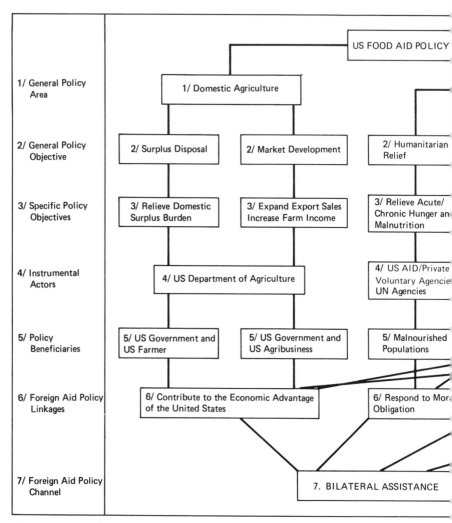

A conceptual model of US food aid policy.

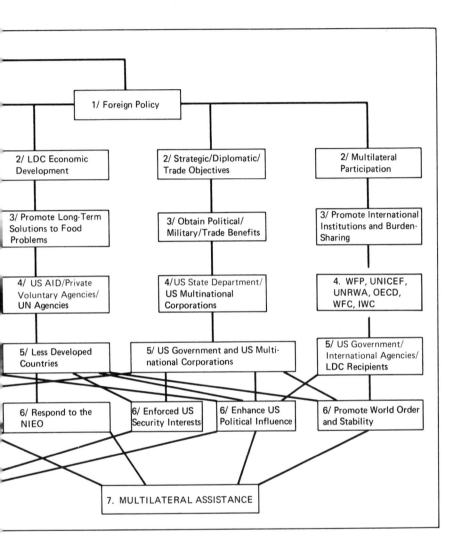

1. All six major objectives must compete for a limited supply of food commodities. As a result, the emphasis accorded to any one area—as measured in terms of total resources committed to it—would probably depend on the relative strength of the interest group supporting it and on the priorities of US foreign and domestic policy prevailing at the time.

2. A significant portion of the benefits resulting from the distribution of US food aid appear to accrue to the aid *donor* rather than to the aid *recipient*. If so, this would suggest that food aid is more a pragmatic function of US foreign policy than an altruistic extension of US values and social philosophy.

3. In comparison with the benefits obtainable through the bilateral aid channel, the multilateral delivery of food aid seems to be only a second-best alternative. Under these circumstances, the United States would be likely to expand its multilateral participation only when it could derive additional foreign (or domestic) policy benefits in the process or when no other suitable means of delivery was available.

The study itself is divided into four parts. Part I examines the evolution of the US food aid program. It juxtaposes the evolution of American agricultural policy with similar shifts in food aid policy, and it establishes the role of the PL 480 program both as a response to world food shortages and as an outlet for US food commodities during periods of surplus. The advantages and disadvantages of food as a form of foreign aid are then considered as well as the specific mix of foreign policy objectives fulfilled by food aid. Finally, the development of the PL 480 food aid program is examined, beginning with its direct antecedents at the close of World War II and following through until the end of the Ford administration in 1976.

Part II establishes the scope of the international food aid framework in which the US program is clearly the dominant factor. The individual bilateral aid efforts undertaken by the other major donor countries are considered briefly and special attention is given to the unique bilateral-multilateral character of the program operated by the European Economic Community. Multilateral food aid mechanisms are then examined, including the effectiveness of major international food aid agencies such as the UN–FAO World Food Programme.

Part III narrows the focus and time frame of the investigation substantially. Based on the international frame of reference provided in the previous section, the impact of specific foreign policy objectives manifest in American food assistance programs are assessed primarily during the period from 1961 through 1976. Specific case examples are examined under foreign policy rubrics: food aid used as an instrument of *diplomatic leverage;* as a means of promoting US interests in *international trade;* as part of an explicit strategy to expand international food aid *burden-sharing;* and as a flexible instrument of *presidential initiative.* The section concludes by reintegrating the four principal foreign policy threads in order to identify the nature, setting, and outcome of the various food aid applications considered in the previous chapters. The use of food aid as a bilateral foreign policy instrument is contrasted with its use as a means to fulfill US responsibilities within the larger global context.

In part IV, the arguments both favoring and opposing the wider multilateralization of international food aid are analyzed and the realistic capabilities of the multilateral aid delivery channel are set forth. This, in turn, leads to an evaluation of the wider implications for the international food aid framework, including the impact of food aid policies adopted by each of the major donor countries—particularly the United States. The study concludes by speculating on the nature of a rational, global food security arrangement and the most likely (and fortuitous) mix of bilateral and multilateral food aid programming.

A variety of factors combine to make this undertaking important and timely. In the period since the 1974 World Food Conference, a great amount of public attention and debate has been devoted to the question of the proper role of food aid in addressing the immediate needs of the so-called "food priority countries."[3] In the course of this international debate, much has been made of the ethical and political considerations inherent in the notion of food assistance.[4] It has been argued, in fact, that traditional motivations for giving food aid, such as surplus commodity disposal, agricultural market development, and strategic–diplomatic foreign policy leverage, may no longer be appropriate or acceptable in view of the serious global dimensions of the hunger problem. Moreover, the requisites of the New International Economic Order, which include demands for a greater sharing and transfer of resources from rich nations to poorer nations, has made multilateral food aid an increasingly attractive alternative for donors to the traditional bilateral approach.

Due also to the enhanced role and importance of food trade in the United States as a means of coping with the deteriorating balance of payments situations, food is no longer the virtually "free good" of a decade ago. As a result, donor willingness to expand food assistance levels is now far from automatic. This has, in turn, reopened the entire question of the most appropriate vehicle (or vehicles) for meeting world food needs and has sparked renewed interest in international aid burden-sharing.

Finally, a unique confluence of events at the end of the 1970s encouraged a critical reexamination of food aid policy within the United States and in other donor countries as well. A series of bountiful world harvests provided a fleeting respite from the ongoing Malthusian struggle between population and available food supplies. During this interlude the nature of world food problems could be considered apart from the "crisis atmosphere" that typified food policy formation during most of the decade. The current opportunity is also enhanced by indications of interest in some quarters in a reassessment of American foreign aid priorities and the role of the United States within multilateral organizations. In this context, a sharpened appreciation for the problems and characteristics of international food aid should contribute not only to the development of a more appropriate American food policy but also to a more effective and equitable global approach to what is perhaps humanity's oldest quest: the freedom from hunger.

PART I
THE EVOLUTION OF THE UNITED STATES
FOOD AID PROGRAM

Chapter 1
Food Aid in the Context of Agricultural Shortage and Surplus

An assessment of US food aid policy must begin by establishing clearly both the historical precedents for the program and the policy priorities that have shaped it. These priorities have related specifically to the shifting relationship between donor supply and recipient demand. Indeed, the thesis of this chapter is that US policy can be understood adequately only through close examination of the intersecting relationship between the requirements of domestic agriculture and the imperatives of US foreign policy.

Food aid is, perhaps, unique as a policy instrument in its capacity to act as a flexible buffer mechanism between these two powerful, and often competing forces. As agricultural and political conditions have changed both at home and abroad, so too has the relative emphasis accorded each of the policy objectives embodied in the food aid program: surplus disposal, market development, humanitarian relief, economic development, and foreign policy. This constant tension has rearranged these priorities many times, but it has also resulted in a multifaceted program which has been capable of surviving nearly continuous amendment and alteration for twenty-five years under the same basic enabling legislation: PL 480, the Agricultural Trade Development and Assistance Act of 1954.

EARLY PRECEDENTS FOR THE USE OF US FOOD AID

During the 1920s, the two major objectives of US food assistance were the relief of periodic famines abroad and steadily mounting food sur-

pluses at home. Franklin D. Roosevelt assumed the presidency under extremely bleak economic and agricultural conditions promising both to
resolve the devastating economic and social crisis which gripped the nation and to address himself to agricultural price and supply problems.
Accordingly, Roosevelt proposed, and congress passed, the Agricultural
Adjustment Act of 1933. The major feature of this legislation was an
innovative combination of "parity price" supports and production controls, the former to be a political quid pro quo for the farmers' acceptance of the latter. Although the act of 1933 was successful in raising the
average farmer's income substantially, it did little to limit the problem of
surplus accumulation.[1]

The only international food initiative at this time was the passage in
1935 of PL 74-320, which amended the Agriculture Adjustment Act of
1933. Section 33 of the new law later became the basis for surplus
commodity disposal; it authorized the use of import tax revenues to
subsidize agricultural exports as well as to encourage domestic consumption. Thus, the end of the period between the world wars was
characterized by mounting domestic agricultural surpluses and generally ineffective efforts to develop an organized policy or programmatic
capacity to dispose of this surplus either through domestic programs
or through international trade or aid channels.

The outbreak of World War II thrust the United States once again into
the role of residual food supplier, providing vital support for the maintenance of the Allied war effort. Under these terms of the Lend-Lease Act
of 1941, slightly over $6 billion in agriculture commodities were shipped
to the European allies. [US Congress HCIR (1977, p. 22)].

ORIGINS OF THE POSTWAR SURPLUS PROBLEM

After the end of World War II, US wheat shipped under the European
Recovery Program (or the Marshall Plan) became a major component in
US international export trade.[2] The massive influx of American food
resources fed the populations engaged in rebuilding war-torn Europe,
but they also proved to be a boon to US domestic agriculture. Marshall
Plan aid provided a guaranteed export market for US farm output at the
very time when high levels of peacetime production were resumed.

Harry S. Truman had campaigned on a promise *not* to abolish the
wartime price support program, despite the fact that large grain surpluses were then building in the Midwest. To make good on his campaign promise, the newly elected President supported the agricultural

acts of 1948 and 1949, both of which extended support prices at between 80 and 90 percent of parity. Fortunately for Truman—and also for the farmers—the outbreak of another military conflict turned the growing surplus burden once again into a major US asset.

The Korean War (1950–1953) made heavy demands on US agricultural output, but it also promoted new domestic political support for food assistance by demonstrating its usefulness in winning the "hearts and minds" of people caught up in the conflict between Communist and Western ideologies—a fact that would once again become significant in the context of Southeast Asia. Marshall Plan aid to Europe had also been designed to check the spread of communism, but it was intended to have only a *limited* lifetime and a *specified* purpose: the short-term rebuilding of the shattered European economies. Thus the recognition at the end of the Korean War that food aid could serve *long-term* foreign policy, as well as surplus disposal, objectives marked the first shift in the ordering of priorities motivating the program.[3]

The major agricultural issue at the conclusion of the Korean War was, once again, the troublesome—and growing—problem of surplus production.[4] Within this context it is useful to review the mix of political, economic, and social factors which then prevailed in order to gain an understanding of the factors which motivated the creation of the US food aid program. Congress and the White House had been locked into annual support of artificially high levels of production long after changes in postwar demand for US farm products had indicated the need for a major adjustment in national agricultural policies. The balance of supply and demand was disrupted further in the early 1950s by a virtual explosion in the scale and pace of technological advance in agriculture, leading Benedict and Bauer [Benedict and Bauer (1960, pp. 60–61)] to conclude that the surplus problem under Truman probably only aggravated a problem that would have existed *anyway* due to the extreme rapidity of technological advance in agriculture during the decade.

It can be argued that, given the powerful combination of economic and social forces driving the continued production of agricultural surpluses in the early 1950s, the United States needed to develop an expanded food aid program as one mechanism for relieving economic pressures. Stated food aid goals of humanitarianism or economic development were, in this sense, merely useful and convenient by-products of a pragmatic policy designed to accomplish a single objective: to ease the political and economic problems stemming from the accumulation of unmarketable surpluses being held at government expense.

THE ERA OF SURPLUS DISPOSAL

The surplus legacy of the Truman era was inherited in 1952 by the new Republican president, Dwight D. Eisenhower, and by his Secretary of Agriculture, Ezra Taft Benson. Benson's policy was largely in keeping with the historical Republican position that the role of government should be to help ease agriculture through periods of transition rather than to support the continuation of the strongly interventionist agrarian policies of the New Deal. Price supports were thus maintained at high levels, but were viewed as only a transitory phenomenon. By 1954, however, it had become apparent that some additional action would have to be taken to deal with the surplus problem, which was already serious and growing worse with each harvest.[5]

It was in this agricultural context that the Agricultural Trade Development and Assistance Act of 1954, PL 480, was conceived, debated, and approved. As the title of the PL 480 act suggests, the promotion of agricultural trade (and the disposal of existing surpluses) was the dominant motivation, overwhelming other, more humanitarian and/or developmental purposes also present in the original legislation. Under the auspices of PL 480, the United States was able to expand its export of agricultural commodities from $449 million in 1952 to $1.9 billion by 1957, possibly saving farmers from complete disaster in the late 1950s. [Cochrane and Ryan (1976, p. 77)].

At about the same time that the United States was establishing the PL 480 food aid program, serious concern arose in the international community over the continued dumping of surplus commodities on the world market at concessional prices. As a result, the Seventh FAO Conference in November–December 1953 directed its Committee on Commodity Problems (CCP) to establish a consultative subcommittee to deal specifically with the surplus disposal problem. The tangible result of the subcommittee's work was the so-called Principles of Surplus Disposal,[6] a set of guidelines which specified the conditions under which agricultural commodities should be given or sold concessionally so as not to compete or conflict with normal commercial trading patterns.

In 1954, the consultative Subcommittee on Surplus Disposal (CSD) was formally established with the principal responsibility "to keep under review developments in the disposal of agricultural surpluses, and to assist FAO Member Nations in developing suitable means of surplus disposal . . . in light of the principles recommended by the Seventh Session of the FAO conference." [FAO (1972, p. 21)]. The net result of the

CSD's initiatives was to provide the basis for constraining the US disposal policy and for encouraging more responsible behavior by all exporters in their aid and trade decisions.[7]

Efforts to reduce surplus production through control programs continued through most of the Eisenhower years but were more or less abandoned in 1959 and 1960. The burden of disposing of unwanted surpluses thus fell primarily on the PL 480 program. But there was also a growing recognition at the end of the Eisenhower period that entirely new approaches would have to be developed rather than continuing to rely on food aid as a mechanism for surplus disposal.[8]

It may strike the reader as curious that virtually the entire discussion of US food aid policy up to this point has been concerned only with the problems of the ever mounting *domestic* agricultural surpluses, with little or no mention of American response to global food needs. United States policymakers remained preoccupied, however, with the need to employ food aid as a safety valve for the domestic agricultural crisis, and they apparently overlooked or ignored its potential as a legitimate development resource. In fact, not only was the government preoccupied with the domestic food problem, but policymakers really had not yet made the conceptual leap to considering the possible use of American food for other purposes.

SHIFT IN AID-AND-TRADE POLICY

Despite the preoccupation of the Eisenhower administration with surplus disposal and market development, President John F. Kennedy and his Secretary of Agriculture, Orville L. Freeman, were confronted in 1961 with the largest wheat and feedgrain carry-over in the nation's history: 115.2 million metric tons.[9] They were also faced with a number of additional factors. First, there had been a demographic shift in the United States caused by the continuing outflow of farm population in search of higher-paying urban jobs. The out-migration of rural voters, and later the historic "one man–one vote" ruling[10] of the US Supreme Court, resulted in a shift of power within the House which, according to Rosenfeld, "broke the back" of the politically dominant farm bloc [Rosenfeld (1974, p. 19)]. Kennedy and Freeman soon recognized that an increasingly urbanized society would not support the growth of farm programs indefinitely, nor would they tolerate government policies which led to rising food prices.

Finally, influential foreign policy advisers to the new President had convinced him of the necessity of rethinking and restructuring the programmatic framework and organizational structure of US foreign assistance. Kennedy had been persuaded further that the PL 480 program could play a major role in this new foreign aid posture. As a consequence, the mix of policies adopted by the Kennedy administration demonstrated a dual agenda: to expand demand for US agricultural products and to meet the domestic and overseas responsibilities of the United States in the alleviation of hunger and malnutrition.

Despite the unwillingness of farmers to abide by acreage quotas,[11] the Kennedy–Freeman policies of expanding demand and limiting production began slowly to pay off. A study of the data reveals that total wheat and feedgrain carry-over continued to decline with each successive crop year.[12] At the same time, commercial export sales and PL 480 assistance were both expanding. Substantial progress had thus been made by the time of John Kennedy's death in shifting the orientation of PL 480 from a mechanism purely for the disposal of surplus to a mix of policy objectives that also included humanitarianism, development, and foreign policy.

INCREASING DEMANDS ON US FOOD RESOURCES

Immediately after the election of Lyndon B. Johnson to a full term of office in November 1964, Secretary of Agriculture Orville Freeman prepared a memorandum for the President articulating the interests of US agricultural trade and aid policy within the international context. Regarding trade, Freeman urged the following:

1. Firm adherence to our policy of insistence on constructive gains in agriculture as part of our negotiations in the Kennedy Round [of the GATT].
2. Continued and enhanced activities . . . in the development and expansion of markets for American products abroad.
3. Concern for economic development and higher standards of living in the developing nations in order that they may become future dollar customers for American farm products.[13]

Regarding food aid, Freeman counseled that the program should move away from its heavy surplus disposal orientation and toward "gearing our Food for Peace program more constructively toward providing food most seriously needed, and by operating that program in a manner that will best promote economic development in recipient countries." [Freeman (1964, p. 1)] Indeed, Lyndon Johnson and his Secretary of Agriculture must be given much of the credit for the profound changes that did take place in the orientation and programmatic structure of PL 480 in 1964 and 1966.

By 1965, the overall US agricultural situation had also begun to change. Carry-over stocks of wheat and feedgrains were declining, while the aid-and-trade demand for US food commodities was climbing steadily, driven by rapidly expanding populations and rising incomes in the Third World. This new global trend to higher export demand and lower carry-over is reflected in figure 1.1. In addition, passage of the Food and Agriculture Act of 1965 signified the end of an evolutionary shift in US agricultural policy which had begun in 1961. Mandatory production controls were removed and were replaced by a system of voluntary restraint, low levels of price support, and limited, direct government payments to producers.

Under these altered agricultural conditions, Secretary Freeman had proposed, as early as January 1966, that the United States should create a reserve of agricultural commodities in order to supplement and support the Food for Peace Program and to protect US consumers from unstable supplies and high prices. He noted,

We have been able to avoid the reserve question so far because our surpluses have exceeded reserve needs. *This situation has about run its course* [emphasis in the original].[14]

Figure 1.1
World wheat carry-over and exports in major exporting countries, 1953–1967. Source: Freeman (1966c, p. 10).

We must be prepared not only to feed our own people, but: 1) to maintain dollar markets, 2) to meet our foreign commitments, and 3) *to take advantage of expected agricultural failures in Communist countries* [emphasis in the original]. . . . Willingness to carry reserves *does not* amount to a determination to feed the world at all costs. We should, in fact, invite others to join us in this endeavor . . .. [Freeman (1966, p. 2)]

We may note here an illustration of the double-edged sword of US agricultural policy, used both to stabilize domestic food prices and to respond to humanitarian and foreign policy objectives, which was also reflected in the Food for Peace Act of 1966.

Such a double-edged sword is not always easy to wield, however. In 1967, when US farmers produced another record-breaking harvest at the same time that good harvests were reported in other exporting countries, discussions were resumed concerning the need for a strategic reserve to strengthen farm prices.[15] At the same time that Freeman was again urging Johnson to act on this concept in 1967, he was also warning of the difficulties inherent in the use of PL 480 to stabilize farm prices:

World political events may make it difficult, if not impossible, to move as much grain under these programs as in recent years. Since movement under the Food for Freedom [PL 480] program is at this time a "rather blunt instrument" to use in stabilizing farm prices, the added authority of a reserve policy including the possibility of buying grain to put in stocks, to help carry out our commitment to farmers becomes most timely.[16]

In any event, during the middle of the decade, the cumulative effect of acute and chronic food import needs in the developing world kept US agricultural commodities moving briskly both on commercial and concessional terms. Indeed, India had suffered disastrous harvests in 1965, and again in 1966, and President Johnson had responded by requesting that Congress enact a special joint resolution in support of a massive US campaign to meet India's pressing food deficit. In fiscal year 1966 alone, fully one-fifth of the US wheat crop was shipped to India.

Famines precipitated by the failure of harvest were not the only cause of the growing shortage situation. The failure of most developing countries to expand agricultural output adequately in order to keep pace with their burgeoning population growth rates and higher per capita incomes forced an increasing reliance on food imports. It is possible, under the circumstances, to appreciate why the Johnson administration felt compelled to institute the food aid policy of "agricultural self-help," which ultimately required a reorientation of resource allocation priorities among less developed countries (LDCs) toward agriculture development if aid flows were to continue.

SHIFT TO A "FREE MARKET" POLICY

The change of administrations in 1969 signaled the beginning of a major shift in virtually all aspects of US agricultural policy, both domestic and international. By the end of the first Nixon term, in fact, rising inflation and a series of poor harvests had changed economic and food production conditions so drastically that the impact of other traditional objectives of food aid, such as surplus disposal and market development, had been largely neutralized.

Richard Nixon's choice to replace his first Secretary of Agriculture, Clifford Hardin, was Earl L. Butz, a man of strong and often abrasive leadership style, who possessed a deep and abiding faith in the value of free market agriculture.[17] Butz was aided immeasurably, however, in the implementation of his philosophical approach by the prevailing agricultural and economic climate of global shortage.

Under these circumstances, the export of US agricultural commodities had obtained an enhanced importance in balance of trade considerations. At the same time, serious domestic inflation, which the Nixon administration had tried futilely to reduce during the first term, had resulted in a devaluation of the dollar. One immediate effect was that US agricultural commodities became substantially more attractive on world markets.

Another factor motivating the movement toward a free market policy was the mounting cost to the United States of avoiding, carrying and/or disposing of agricultural surpluses. By 1971, the cost of diverting acres from production of feedgrains had reached 136 percent of the cost of export under PL 480, while the diversion cost of wheat had climbed to 111 percent of the export cost.[18] Moreover, the cost of storing and maintaining grains under the control of the Commodity Credit Corporation, while reduced substantially from the heavy surplus period of the early 1960s, continued to be significant (see table 1.1).

Unquestionably, however, the most important factor leading to a "free market" shift in US international agricultural policy was the series of interrelated events during the period from 1972 to 1974, which caused severe regional food shortages and unprecedented commercial demand for US agricultural exports. Table 1.1 also reveals the precipitous rise in US wheat exports from 1971 to 1973, almost doubling within the course of two years. Under these circumstances, Secretary Butz promoted the adoption of the Agriculture and Consumer Protection Act of 1973, which represented, he claimed, the most important and sweeping change

Table 1.1
US Wheat: Acreage, Production, Utilization, and Stocks (1948–1973)

Crop year (July–June)	Acreage (in millions) Planted	Diverted under programs[a]	Production (in million bushels)	Utilization (in million bushels) Total[b]	Export	Stocks: end of year carryover (in million bushels) Total[c]	Government owned
1948	78.3		1,294.9	1,185.0	503.6	307.3	227.2
1949	83.9		1,098.4	983.2	302.9	424.7	327.7
1950	71.3		1,019.3	1,055.7	365.9	399.9	196.4
1951	78.5		998.2	1,163.6	475.0	256.0	143.3
1952	78.6		1,306.4	978.5	317.5	605.5	470.0
1953	78.9		1,173.1	850.6	216.7	933.5	774.6
1954	62.5		983.9	885.4	274.0	1,036.2	975.9
1955	58.2		937.1	949.7	346.0	1,033.5	950.7
1956	60.6	5.7	1,005.4	1,137.8	549.1	908.8	823.9
1957	49.8	12.8	955.7	993.9	402.3	881.4	834.9
1958	56.0	5.3	1,457.4	1,051.4	442.8	1,295.1	1,146.6
1959	56.7		1,117.7	1,106.7	509.8	1,313.4	1,195.4
1960	54.9		1,354.7	1,264.9	661.5	1,411.3	1,242.5
1961	55.7		1,232.4	1,327.4	719.4	1,322.0	1,096.6
1962	49.3	10.7	1,092.0	1,224.2	643.8	1,195.2	1,082.5
1963	53.4	7.2	1,146.8	1,444.5	856.1	901.4	828.9
1964	55.7	5.1	1,283.4	1,368.6	725.0	817.3	646.0

1965	57.4	7.2	1,315.6	1,598.6	867.4	535.2	340.0
1966	54.4	8.3	1,311.7	1,423.6	744.3	425.0	124.0
1967	67.8		1,522.4	1,408.9	761.1	539.4	102.0
1968	62.5	11.1	1,570.4	1,298.1	544.2	818.6	162.7
1969	54.3	15.7	1,460.2	1,378.0	606.1	884.7	301.2
1970	49.5	13.5	1,378.5	1,506.0	738.0	730.2	369.9
1971	53.8	20.1	1,639.5	1,487.0	632.0	865.3	366.5
1972	54.9		1,544.8	1,970.9	1,186.3	438.4	209.2
1973	59.0	7.2	1,705.2	1,900.0	1,148.7	247.4	18.9

Source: adapted from Cochrane and Ryan (1976, p. 203.)

a. There were no acreage diversion programs in 1948–1955, 1959–1961, and 1967–1968.
b. Including exports.
c. Including government owned and under loan to the government.

in US agricultural policy since the passage of the Agricultural Adjustment Act of 1933.[19]

The net effect of the new agricultural policies was profound. As revealed in table 1.1, in the course of a single year (1972–1973), government-owned wheat stocks plummeted from 209 million bushels to just 18.9 million bushels. In addition, total acreage diverted from production dropped from an all-time high in 1972 of 20.1 million acres to just 7.2 million acres in 1973 (and to nearly zero in 1974), while the per bushel price received by the farmers more than doubled during this same, single-year period.

THE WORLD FOOD "CRISIS" PERIOD

While US agricultural policy was encouraging this tremendous expansion in the export of commodities on straight commercial terms, total world food production was declining for the first time in twenty years. The world wheat crop, for example, declined by 5 percent, due largely to the poor harvest in the Soviet Union, and rice production dropped by a similar percentage as a result of short-falls in key Asian countries. Concurrently, the anchovetta, the primary source of protein for animal feed worldwide, disappeared suddenly off the coast of Peru, resulting in a severe and unexpected increase in the demand for soybeans, which were used as an alternative animal protein source. The net impact of all these events was that importers among the major developed countries, such as Japan and the Soviet Union, reacted by making large food and feedgrain purchases within US markets,[20] which in turn, resulted in severe upward pressure on international grain prices.

As serious as these compound problems were in the normal channels of international trade, they were many times more severe for the poorest food importing nations. The cumulative effect of poor domestic harvests, the quadrupling of OPEC oil prices between 1972 and 1974 (petroleum desperately needed by the LDCs in order to produce fertilizers and pesticides), continued high inflation (meaning that less food could be purchased abroad with the resources available), rising domestic food prices, and the reduced availability of food aid in the face of competition with commercial exports provided the conditions for a supply crisis in food of global proportions.

As a result of these events, there was a substantial reduction in the role of PL 480 as a channel for US agricultural exports and a virtual explosion in the volume of commercial sales. The total volume of commodities exported under PL 480 had been declining since 1965, and, whereas PL 480 had financed 33 percent of US agricultural exports in 1957, the proportion had slipped to 20 percent in 1966, 13 percent in 1972, 7 percent in 1973, and only a meager 4 percent in 1974. While cereal food aid volumes were dropping from 317 to 57 million bushels from 1971 to 1974, commercial sales mushroomed from 316 million to 1,092 billion bushels during this same period.[21]

Beyond the matter of "free market" competition between the demands of aid and trade for increasingly scarce US food resources were two additional problems within the aid program itself. Inflation had taken its toll on the food aid program in the United States, as well as in the developing world, primarily because US food aid allocations are budgeted in *dollars* rather than by commodity volumes. Thus, whereas in fiscal year 1971, $655 million budgeted for PL 480 bought about 9.1 million metric tons of grain, the $727 million budgeted for fiscal year 1974 bought only 3.4 million tons [USDA (1974, pp. 7–8, 16–18)]. Particularly hard hit by this sudden drop in commodity availability were the humanitarian feeding programs operated by the US voluntary agencies that were maintained by the donation of free PL 480 food aid.

The Nixon administration also chose to employ the flexibility available to it in the concessional credit sales of the PL 480 program in order to circumvent congressionally imposed limitations on military assistance to South Vietnam and Cambodia. During fiscal 1974, more than two-thirds of all Title I resources, or almost half the commodities shipped under PL 480 for that year, were allocated to these two countries alone [Saylor (1977, p. 203)]. Thus, at the peak of the worst food shortage period since World War II, US foreign policy priorities assumed major prominence in the allocation of scarce food resources.

The United States did propose, however, before the UN General Assembly that a World Food Conference be convened during 1974.[22] The proposal was accepted and the conference arranged for November of the following year. But, in the intervening period, the United States suffered some of the worst drought conditions in nearly twenty years. As a result, total world grain production for 1974–1975 declined by nearly 5 percent from the previous year.[23]

By the time of the opening of the World Food conference, the US food policy was caught between four competing pressures: (1) the available supply of grain export was limited by the reduced size of the US crop and depleted government-owned reserves; (2) a World Hunger Action Coalition was demanding that the US *increase* its food aid contributions;

(3) growers and exporters were exerting heavy pressure on the administration to avoid at all costs any further restrictions on free market trade
similar to the temporary and controversial imposition of export controls
on soybeans in 1973; and (4) continuing inflation had caused consumers
to be vocal in their demands that the administration hold the line on further food price increases. Under these circumstances, domestic considerations once again became predominant and US food aid levels were not
increased, despite the fact that the World Food conference had been
called at US initiative.[24]

RETURN TO FOOD ABUNDANCE

The US decision *not* to increase its international food aid contribution
toward the goal set by the World Food conference of 10 million metric
tons per year was widely criticized both at home and abroad. On 4
December 1974, Senator Mark Hatfield decried on the Senate floor a
"food aid policy" where "preserving puppet regimes is more important
. . . than preserving the lives of millions of people."[25] Shortly thereafter,
Congress enacted a provision as part of the Foreign Assistance Act of
1974 that limited to 30 percent of total annual programming the proportion of Title I commodities which could be allocated to countries *not* appearing on the UN list of countries "most seriously affected" by the
current economic crisis. The net effect of this precedent-setting change in
the terms of PL 480 was to increase the emphasis on the humanitarian
and developmental objectives of US assistance and to limit the total
amount of aid that could be employed for short-term political or quasi-
military purposes.

In early 1975, the international price and supply pressures began to
ease. As a result, Secretary Butz was able to announce in February that
the United States would increase its food aid contribution to a total of
$1.6 billion, which, even when discounted for inflation, was still the
largest dollar amount programmed since 1968. The United States also
began to consider various means by which an international structure
could be created in order to prevent the recurrence of the extreme fluctuations in commodity prices experienced between 1972 and 1974.[26]

As the presidency of Gerald R. Ford drew to a close in 1976, certain
significant contrasts became discernible between the current US policy
posture and the situation of a decade earlier. Two successive bumper
harvests were in hand and a third was predicted. Surpluses were once
again beginning to accumulate, although this time in private grain eleva-

tors rather than at government expense. With the easing of the supply situation, priority attention reverted once again to the use of food aid in pursuit of humanitarian and developmental objectives. But the most spectacular contrast between 1976 and 1966 was the fact that, whereas in the 1960s the great US food reserve potential was *in the land* (i.e., in the form of idled prime acreage, production controls, and surplus holdings), in 1976 all prime acreage had been returned to production and price supports and acreage allotments had been removed.

The cycle of shortage and surplus thus had come full circle with the passage of the Food and Agriculture Act of 1977. The new act placed a 20 percent set aside on wheat and a 10 percent reduction on feedgrain acreage, primarily in order to enhance the market price received by farmers. Once again, domestic political pressures caused by the heavy surplus buildup and low world market prices had forced the administration to impose production controls similar to those of the previous decade.

A RECAPITULATION: THE SHIFT FROM SHORTAGE TO SURPLUS

Throughout the preceding pages, one theme constantly has been in evidence: the close relationship between the level of agricultural production and the evolution of US food aid policy. That is, since the organization of a discrete food aid capacity, the manipulation of the objectives of food assistance has occupied a pivotal role between two traditional—and often conflicting—relationships: food shortage versus food surplus and the primacy of domestic agricultural policy versus foreign policy. Figure 1.2 provides an illustration of the patterns resulting from this dynamic interaction for each administration since 1948.

During the Truman and early Eisenhower periods, the emphasis of food aid policy was clearly on meeting the urgent needs of domestic agriculture, that is, the location of the upper left hand of Figure 1.2. Massive domestic food surpluses and continuing postwar agricultural adjustment problems dictated that heavy priority be accorded to the objectives of surplus disposal and market development. Toward the end of the second Eisenhower term, however, the foreign policy possibilities inherent in food aid were first recognized, prompting movement away from purely domestic agricultural concerns.

The beginning of the Kennedy era brought with it a major rethinking of the role of foreign aid within the foreign policy framework and an alteration in the ordering of food aid priorities. Kennedy perceived the

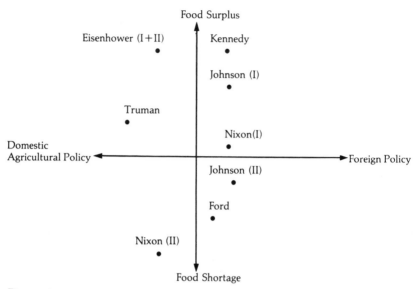

Figure 1.2

foreign policy value of the humanitarian aspects of US food and, toward
the end of his life, he had also begun to place more emphasis on the use
of food aid in economic development. As a result, the locus of food aid
policy shifted (on the axes of figure 1.2) toward foreign policy considerations, although the tremendous government-owned surplus burden was
also a major policy consideration.

While fulfilling the remainder of Kennedy's term, Lyndon Johnson
struggled with the same combination of factors confronted by his predecessor. During Johnson's own elected term, however, the priorities of
food aid policy changed once again as a result of a series of disastrous
harvests on the Indian subcontinent, which created tremendous demand
for the export of US food and feedgrains; the impact of US agricultural
policy, which had finally begun to reduce the volume of surplus food
commodities under government control; an alteration in the prevailing
philosophy of foreign assistance, which now emphasized the need to
employ food aid to encourage "self-help" in the expansion of LDC agriculture; and the ever growing US involvement in Southeast Asia, which
brought with it further reliance on food as an adjunct to the massive
military assistance already flowing to that region. With food surplus
stocks drawn down and a variety of political and economic foreign assistance goals heavily emphasized by the Johnson administration, the locus
of policy thus began to move for the first time toward the food *shortage*

end of the continuum and also more substantially in the direction of foreign policy primacy.

The early years of the Nixon presidency changed the balance of these forces very little, except perhaps for the fact that the overall food commodity supply situation improved somewhat both in the United States and abroad. The war in Southeast Asia continued apace, and with it the reliance on food aid as a principal component of foreign policy. Moreover, certain new foreign policy uses of food were developed, for example, the withdrawal of food aid in retaliation for uncompensated expropriation of US property. But, by the end of the decade, domestic inflation and a worsening balance of payments situation had again produced a reevaluation of the priorities of US food policy.

The second Nixon term brought with it the full ascendence of a market-oriented agriculture secretary, Earl L. Butz, and a radical shift in the locus of food policy. For one thing, the commercial export of food emerged as one of the principal US responses to the petrodollar drain. There was also a fundamental change in domestic agricultural policy, resulting in the conscious depletion of all government-held surplus stocks and in purposeful movement toward a relatively free market for international agricultural trade. These policies were manifested in a heavy new commitment to export US agricultural resources through commercial channels at precisely the time when serious crop failures were severely affecting many parts of the developing world.

It was at this point that the conflict in policy priorities was, perhaps, most clearly in evidence. While agricultural interests clamored for continued government non-interference in food exports, the unprecedented size of the Soviet grain purchase forced the imposition of temporary export controls. At the same time, pressures mounted both from within and outside the government for an increased commitment of US resources as food aid.

Thus, at the premature end of the Nixon presidency, US food aid policy was suspended in a conflict between two competing forces: one urging that food resources remain available for export on commercial terms and the other demanding that a larger proportion be allocated for humanitarian, strategic, and developmental purposes. The immediate result of this confrontation was disappointing for those advocating increased food assistance, but actions resulting from it have had a major effect on food aid policy in the ensuing years.

Gerald Ford's food aid options were, in some respects, far less flexible than those of his predecessors, due to new congressional restrictions on aid allocation criteria. However, under the influence of Henry Kissinger and other senior advisers, Ford did consider briefly alternative means of achieving foreign policy objectives utilizing food, including the viability of using "food power" as a diplomatic and economic lever in a manner analogous to OPEC's use of "petropower."

Once again, the food aid policy debate resulted in changes in the focus of food policy. Food power arguments were rejected as unworkable and deleterious to domestic agriculture. Instead, proposals for a nationally-held but internationally regulated food reserve were developed to deal with the long-term fluctuations in price caused by variations in food supply. With signs pointing to a reemergence of substantial domestic surpluses, the policy process was again activated at the end of the Ford administration in order to create a new structural equilibrium among the various food aid objectives.

In many respects, the food aid program operated by the United States is unique. This is the case not only when the US effort is compared to other bilateral and multilateral programs, but also when the PL 480 program is compared to most other major programmatic initiatives undertaken by the federal government. In few other undertakings have so many independent objectives been addressed simultaneously and in even fewer have policy priorities been altered successfully so many times to reflect prevailing economic and political conditions.

In many respects, it can be argued that the use of food as a form of foreign aid began essentially as a useful adjunct to other, more urgent policy objectives. As noted in chapter 1, overseas food distribution in the period after the European recovery was intended primarily to move the ever increasing volumes of US agricultural surpluses. The fact that the food might also serve certain humanitarian functions in relieving hunger and/or foreign policy objectives in aiding nations sympathetic to the United States was considered, under the circumstances, to be only a useful, secondary benefit.

This approach may be explained by the fact that the PL 480 program was conceived and promoted originally by US agricultural interests rather than by individuals or groups concerned with foreign policy. Moreover, due to the size and newness of the food aid program, foreign policymakers had comparatively little experience with the use of food as a foreign aid instrument. In fact, it was not really until the intensification of the Cold War that official thinking about the foreign policy possibilities inherent in food aid began to evolve beyond simplistic notions of surplus disposal and humanitarian relief.

The expansion of the Cold War, with its competition for spheres of political and economic influence, provides yet another explanation for the narrow conception of early US food aid. As foreign assistance came to be viewed increasingly as an instrument of influence in the global ideological struggle, new efforts were made to improve the political leverage obtainable through *all* forms of nonmilitary aid: capital, technical, and food.

This diversifying trend reached a watershed of sorts during the Kennedy administration with recognition of the fact that the negative attitude of the Congress toward foreign aid would mean growing shortfalls in capital assistance appropriations. Moreover, it had also become apparent that public interest in moving the steadily mounting grain surpluses being stored at government expense remained undiminished and, if anything, had increased. The next logical step in the evolution of aid policy was then obvious: if capital assistance was likely to be in chronically short supply, why not substitute food resources, to the extent practicable, in its place? Food was abundant and its political and economic opportunity cost was comparatively low. On the other hand, the scarcity of capital meant that its cost as aid was high relative to other demands for its use within the federal budget.

PROBLEMS WITH THE USE OF FOOD AS AID

Rogers, Mayer, and Heady (1972, p. vi) contend that "food aid can substitute for capital on a dollar-for-dollar basis up to the amount of additional demand for food which will be generated by development investments." They also suggest that "food aid should be a near perfect substitute for capital on a project that is composed entirely of labor inputs and employing previously unemployed personnel."[Rogers, Mayer, and Heady (1972, p. vii)]. Yet, even in the so-called food-for-work type food aid projects, labor rarely—if ever—constitutes the sum of all project inputs or costs. Such projects normally also include the need for other types of supplies and equipment, which have to be purchased with cash. Moreover, even if labor does represent 100 percent of investment costs, the marginal preference of the consumer is usually such that additional food demand will not exhaust wages. In this case, part of the surplus food used to finance a given project finds its way into the market system and is likely to create a depressing impact on market prices.

The fact that food is not completely substitutable for capital assistance is an issue which has often tended to be of far greater interest to development economists than to policymakers in either donor or recipient governments. Often, if the choice is between accepting food aid versus receiving *no* aid (although rarely are the choices ever so completely black and white), the decision in most cases usually will be to opt for the former. More recently, with the increasing focus on aid as an instrument of development [Field and Wallerstein (1977, p. 242)], the tradeoffs involved in giving and accepting food assistance have been subject to more careful scrutiny—particularly with regard to the possibility that such aid may act as an agricultural disincentive.[1] The fact of the matter is that the disincentive effects of food aid appear to be highly "country specific": in some cases, the injection of additional commodities may indeed discourage local producers; in others, it may actually help small farmers by serving as a "risk reducer" while they are shifting to more modern agronomic practices.

It is undeniable, however, that where large volumes of food have been dumped indiscriminately on LDC markets through the concessional credit sales provisions of PL 480, the profitability of indigenous agriculture has been reduced at least to some extent. The principal adverse effects of food aid under these circumstances are twofold. Increasing the supply of food on the local market reduces (or maintains at a low level) the price obtained by the local farmer, which destroys his incentive to increase production. Furthermore, the availability of cheap (or free) food may permit the recipient government to ignore, or postpone attention to, agrarian reform and other rural development programs.

A second, related problem with the use of food as aid has been that, unlike capital assistance, food is *consumed* by people. Consequently, while shipping surplus wheat to a country of rice eaters may make sense from the perspective of the surplus producer, it will have a highly disruptive effect on local dietary practices. Such actions occurred frequently in the early years of US food assistance and still happen occasionally even at present. Of more serious consequence, however, is the fact that the long-term flow of imported food at concessional prices has occasionally resulted in wholesale changes in LDC food preferences and eating habits.[2] The long-term impact of such a change is to increase consumer demand for imports and, ultimately, to place additional strain on the recipient country's balance of payments position. Ironically, this is one of the key problems that food aid is intended ostensibly to relieve.

A third difficulty pertaining to the use of food as aid relates to the fact that *all* aid, almost by definition, necessitates the continuing involvement of the donor in the internal affairs of the recipient. Bilateral food aid is rarely (if ever) given without some conditions attached since, at the very least, the donor will want to monitor and evaluate the use of its assistance. But food aid raises special difficulties from a foreign policy perspective because it is far more difficult to "turn off" a food aid relationship once it has been initiated. Thus, donor initiatives to attach conditions or "strings" on food aid will surely be resented by the recipient and may well place the donor in a long-term situation from which it will be difficult to extricate itself. Such aid dependency relationships might seem attractive in terms of immediate political payoffs; but in the longer term, they may actually *reduce* political leverage by limiting the donor's bargaining options. Long-term aid relationships also tend to constitute a substantial economic burden on the donor's economy.

ADVANTAGES OF THE USE OF FOOD AS AID

Arrayed against this rather compelling set of critical arguments against the use of food as aid are some major factors favoring food assistance. Once again, it must be emphasized that food remains cheaper and relatively more available than other forms of aid. Moreover, as Field and Wallerstein have noted, poor people cannot eat capital loans and grants [Field and Wallerstein (1977, p. 242)]. Reference here is to the fact that since capital assistance must be employed first in projects or programs (unless used directly to purchase food), the most deprived sectors of recipient population often benefit only very slowly and indirectly through what has been called the "trickle-down effect" of economic development. Food aid, on the other hand, is "double barreled" in that, when properly programmed, it can alleviate hunger and malnutrition directly while also facilitating other kinds of social and economic development activities. This is the conceptual basis for the so-called food-for-work projects which utilize food as payment in kind for recipient labor on development-oriented projects such as irrigation canals, farm-to-market roads, rural electrification, and so on.

In more explicit political terms, the capacity of food aid to serve multiple policy objectives simultaneously continues to set this form of assistance apart from capital grants and loans. Even efforts to develop methods of tying capital aid to purchases in the donor country, known as source-tieing, have not resulted in the same degree of enthusiastic domestic support for capital assistance that the shipment of food overseas has generated among US agricultural interests. The reason, of course, is that the domestic benefits of source-tied capital aid are minuscule when compared to aggregate size of U.S. wheat crop available for export.[3]

From the perspective of the executive branch, food aid offers another unique and important advantage. Owing to the bureaucratic mechanism through which the PL 480 program is funded, that is, the Commodity Credit Corporation, food aid is the only major form of US foreign assistance that is more or less free from the annual scrutiny and funding revisions that are characteristic of the congressional appropriations process. As a result, if appropriated funds in a particular fiscal year are insufficient to meet desired programming objectives (or in the event of a sudden foreign policy crisis), the administration may simply draw on its CCC borrowing authority to make up the difference. Although the budgetary flexibility of the PL 480 program has been somewhat reduced recently by specific congressional limitations on use, either by category or by country, the basic capacity of food assistance to offset or circumvent congressionally imposed reductions in foreign aid programming remains in force.

Congress, for its part, has consistently found it more expedient politically to agree to the continuation of food aid at levels generally commensurate with—or sometimes even exceeding—White House budget requests than to approve increases in the capital aid budget. This contrast may be accounted for by the lack of a strong and easily identifiable *domestic* constituency for capital and technical aid. Foreign capital assistance is often a difficult and remote concept for the average, taxpaying constituent to grasp, while the need to feed the "starving children" (or, at times, to aid the US farmer) draws instant public understanding and empathy. The result has been that food assistance accounted for about 40 percent of all US economic assistance from fiscal 1955 through 1976.[4]

TYPES OF US FOOD AID MECHANISMS

Much discussion has focused on the various means of using food in order to avoid agricultural disincentive effects while also promoting effective economic development. Two distinct types of food aid have evolved as a result of this concern: project aid and program aid. *Program* food aid, which is the type of assistance given by the United States under Title I of PL 480, is sold to the recipient government on concessional credit terms. The recipient, in turn, sells the food either in the open market or through some form of government "ration" or "fair price" shop system. The funds generated from market sales are used as a means to support a wide variety of economic development programs. *Project* food aid, by contrast, which is given by the United States under Title II of PL 480, is provided totally on a grant basis; that is, there is never any repayment requirement.

Project aid may *not* be sold by the recipient, except under limited and unusual circumstances. Rather, project aid must be utilized *directly* as food, supplementing that which would otherwise be available. The intent of the project approach is to ensure that a maximum volume of aid actually reaches those in need, while also facilitating the launching or completion of specific development projects.

The concept of project aid was also developed specifically in order to respond to the agricultural disincentive issue by focusing the assistance directly on the humanitarian and development needs of the recipients and by avoiding sale through agricultural markets. But the annual volume of project aid has been limited due to the traditional policy priorities of the United States; the government obviously finds it preferable to promote commercial market development if at all possible rather than simply to give the food away. Moreover, the overall developmental impact of project-type aid is more limited than program assistance, since the latter facilitates the generation of badly needed cash for use by recipient governments and functions, therefore, as an indirect capital resource transfer.

The Congress and the executive branch have become increasingly sensitive to the need to encourage a greater developmental impact from program-type food assistance, which now accounts for almost 70 percent of food aid allocations. For example, Title I of PL 480 previously contained over twenty categories (under Section 104) through which the local currencies generated from the sale of the food could be used to promote economic development.[5] More recently, the so-called forgiveness provisions, added as Title III of PL 480, have made it possible for recipients to be absolved of the need to repay a certain portion of the debt to the extent that proceeds from the sale of the food are used for specified developmental purposes.

THE HISTORICAL ANTECEDENTS OF US FOOD AID

As noted previously, the motivation to provide overseas assistance in the form of food is, by no means, a recent manifestation in American foreign affairs. In fact, as early as 1812 the US Congress is known to have appropriated some $50,000 in order to provide food for shipment to the victims of a Venezuelan earthquake [McGovern (1964a, p. 12)]. Other precedents for US bilateral food aid also existed long before domestic agricultural surpluses had become a problem of major proportions. Most early efforts were organized and funded by private charitable organizations such as the American Red Cross. Food was made available in this manner to the victims of the great Russian famine of

1891 and to those affected by the severe civil disturbances which racked Turkey between 1893 and 1894 [McGovern (1964, p. 12)].

In 1902, the eruption of Mount Pelé on the island of Martinique again motivated the Congress to appropriate $200,000 for the provision of food and other relief supplies [McGovern (1964a, p. 13)], and this action was repeated, albeit with a new twist, in 1908: President Theodore Roosevelt, upon learning of the Sicilian earthquake disaster of 28 December 1908, immediately dispatched government supply ships, "confident," he informed Congress, "of your approval," [McGovern (1964a, p. 13)]. As may be apparent, most (if not all) of the food aid provided during this early period was of a purely humanitarian nature— to be used for the relief of famines and other natural disasters.

With the outbreak of World War I in August 1914, the pattern of ad hoc US food aid responses came to an end, although the prevailing interest continued to be in humanitarian operations. Despite the fact that the United States did not formally declare war until 1917, America's involvement in providing food aid to Europe actually began shortly after the initiation of hostilities. Herbert Hoover, soon to be US Food Administrator (and later, of course, President), happened to be in England at the outbreak of the war in the capacity of a private businessman. When war was declared, Hoover was asked by President Woodrow Wilson to help organize the evacuation of the 200,000 Americans who were trapped on the Continent. After successfully completing this task, and just as he himself was about to embark for the United States, Hoover was convinced by certain European leaders to remain in England in order to organize and direct a food relief effort for Belgium and northern France, where an estimated ten million people faced imminent starvation due to the disruption of normal food supply channels. Hoover subsequently launched the Commission for the Relief of Belgium (CRB), utilizing American food commodities to supply European food needs.

With the formal entry of the United States into the war on 6 April 1917, Hoover was called home by President Wilson to assume the post of American Food Administrator, while retaining his position as Chairman of the CRB. Total US food aid contributions during the course of World War I (1914–1918) amounted ultimately to more than 28 million metric tons.[6] At the war's end, Hoover was again enlisted by President Wilson to return to Europe, this time in the post of Allied Director-General of Relief and Rehabilitation.

Hoover arrived in Europe armed with a congressional appropriation of $100 million, authorized under the Relief in Europe Act of 1919. At Wilson's direction, Hoover proceeded to form the American Relief Administration (ARA), which was active in food aid efforts until the formal signing of the armistice at Versailles on 28 June 1919. Upon the conclusion of the armistice, and with the good harvest of 1919, Hoover then proposed that the remaining US food commodities, plus any additional private charitable contributions, should be turned over to a new organization created to assist the thousands of destitute children in Europe. This new agency, which became known as the ARA European Children's Fund, was operated on a private, charitable basis throughout the reconstruction period, terminating with a massive operation in relief of another severe Russian famine in 1922–1923.

The US relief program during World War I, while clearly humanitarian, was still far from apolitical. In fact, more than 72 percent of the total assistance went to just three countries: Britain, France, and Italy [Surface and Bland (1931, p. 5)]. Cohen has suggested that Hoover was among the first to take note of the Communist "threat" in Europe, and he viewed food assistance as a possible deterrent [Cohen (1974, p. 153)].

If Cohen's information is correct,[7] such manipulation of food aid by the American "food czar" in Europe represents, perhaps, the earliest known precedent for the use of food aid as a means of political influence and leverage. For example, Cohen reports that in Hungary the power of Hoover's food leverage caused the overthrow of two successive governments unfriendly to US interests, while in Poland Hoover allegedly was able to employ the threat to withdraw food as a means to place his friend, Paderewski, in power [Cohen (1974, p. 154)]. Finally, Hoover, reportedly recommended that the Allies tie food assistance to the Soviet Union to certain political concessions: the Soviets were "to cease all militant action across certain defined boundaries and cease their subsidizing of disturbances abroad." Ultimately, however, French opposition to the plan apparently ended any further discussion of an Allied relief program for the Soviets [Cohen (1974, p. 155)].

Little of significance concerning food aid occurred in the hiatus between the world wars, as America, like the rest of the Western World, struggled to overcome its massive economic (and agricultural) problems. With the outbreak of World War II, however, the United States was once again thrust into the role of food quartermaster for the Allied war effort. Under the Lend Lease Act of 1941, over $6 billion in food commodities were shipped from the United States to Europe. (The now ex-

President) Herbert Hoover attempted once again to organize a food aid effort similar to that mounted during and after the previous conflict. Although without any official title or office, Hoover proposed that the Allies begin food aid operations in Greece, Poland, Scandinavia, and the Low Countries. But his plans met with firm opposition from British Prime Minister Winston Churchill, who apparently saw the provision of food aid during hostilities as playing directly into the hands of the Nazis.

After the United States entered the war, the Allies created the Government and Relief in Occupied Areas program (GARIOA) in 1942 in order to forestall widespread starvation in the liberated areas. The GARIOA program was part of the Department of the Army until 1947, and it was responsible for providing food and other types of relief for all areas secured under Allied control. A year later, on 9 November 1943, forty-three countries met in Washington, DC, to sign an agreement which established the first multilateral food aid operation, known as the United Nations Relief and Rehabilitation Administration (UNRRA). UNRRA was established in order to plan, coordinate, and administer aid measures for victims of the war, including food, clothing, health care, and housing. The aid was "not to be used as a political weapon, and no discrimination was to be made in distribution for racial, religious, or political reasons."[8]

Unlike the Lend-Lease Act, UNRRA was a grant program with the United States contributing fully 73 percent of the agency's $2.9 billion total resources. Food stuffs comprised over $1.2 billion of the US input [US Congress HCIR (1977, pp. 22–23)]. Both GARIOA and UNRRA food aid proved critical at the end of the war, particularly during the devastating winter of 1946–1947, when the United States alone shipped over 8.5 million tons of grain to forestall massive famine in war-ravaged Western Europe. It is interesting to note that India, which had experienced a severe famine during 1943 that reportedly killed three to four million people, did not receive allied food aid under these programs. India was also unable to obtain assistance in 1945–1946, when a second food crisis developed, despite the pleas of such internationally known figures as Albert Einstein and Pearl Buck.[9]

United States food aid efforts at the end of World War II commenced with the European Recovery Program of 1948, more commonly known as the Marshall Plan. These developments are covered fully in chapter 3 since they formed the direct programmatic precedents for the creation of a formal US food aid program. It is significant , however, that the preeminence of the United States in the provision of foreign assistance—

both as food and as capital loans and grants—had its origin in the unique and fortuitous position of America as one of the few Western powers whose economy and agricultural productive capacity had been spared the direct ravages of the war. The United States was, in short, the only producer then capable of feeding an increasingly hungry world.

Chapter 3
The United States Food Aid Program

If a study of international food aid had been undertaken twenty years ago, its character and content would have been far different from that which is necessary today. For all intents and purposes, to study US food aid policies and programs at that time was to be fully knowledgeable about the sum of international food aid. Now, of course, the food aid burden is shared much more widely; yet the fact remains that the present US food aid program dwarfs those of all other bilateral donors and outstrips the UN multilateral program as well. For example, US cereal aid for 1977–1978 totaled 6,310 thousand tons, while cereal aid from the next largest donors, the EEC and Canada, were 1,287 thousand and 1,000 thousand tons, respectively [FAO (1978, p. 10)]. Because America has effectively functioned as the world's residual food supplier since World War II, food aid contributions by all other donors have been *predicated* upon the existence of a reliable US supply. This chapter will consider how the United States came to establish a formal food mechanism in 1954 and how this mechanism has evolved in succeeding years.

PROGRAM ANTECEDENTS

The two previous chapters documented the earliest examples of US involvement in food assistance. One characteristic was common to these initiatives through the end of World War II: the food aid was conceptualized and packaged as an ad hoc, limited-duration response to sudden and acute crisis situations. Moreover, there was generally little or no attempt made to institutionalize the assistance as a regular government function. But, with the advent of the European Recovery Program at the close of the war (i.e., the so-called Marshall Plan), all of this changed. While short-term humanitarianism and surplus agricultural disposal remained as principal motivating features, the United States became committed for the first time to a continuing responsibility for the supply of food aid to Europe—albeit only for the duration of the European reconstruction. Of the $4.2 billion in aid furnished during the first year and a half of the Marshall Plan, fully 39 percent consisted of food, feed, and fertilizers. During the entire program period, 29 percent of a total aid package of $13.5 billion was committed to these three aid resources [US Congress HCIR (1977, p. 23)].

The Marshall Plan also became a precedent for the program-type food aid incorporated later as Title I of PL 480. Commodities supplied by the United States to the European countries were contributed directly to recipient governments, which then sold the food for their own local currency through regular market channels. Not only did this policy help swiftly to reestablish disrupted food marketing systems, but it also represented one of the earliest attempts to utilize food aid to avoid the foreign exchange bottleneck so common in countries lacking hard currency.[1]

In 1950, and again in 1951, emergency food aid was also made available as Congress passed legislation to earmark funds for two major relief efforts. The first was the Yugoslav Emergency Relief Assistance Act of 1950 (PL 81–897), which authorized $50 million to avert a famine caused in part by Yugoslavia's political schism with the Soviet Union. Among other departures from the Marshall Plan was the Indian Emergency Food Act of 1951 (PL 82–48), necessitated by a series of disastrous floods and droughts which had resulted in major famines.[2] President Truman originally had requested that the Indian food aid, which totalled $190 million, should be given entirely in the grant form, but Congress balked and, ultimately, the funds could only be loaned to India.[3]

The European recovery period also marked the emergence of certain private voluntary organizations whose sole function was the delivery of food aid. Former President Herbert Hoover, who, it will be recalled, had directed food aid efforts during and after World War I, brought together representatives from twenty-seven civic, religious, charitable, and farm groups, and formed the Cooperative for American Remittances to Europe (original name), now known simply as CARE, Inc.

CARE later broadened its scope of operations substantially to include the needy of the developing world, changing its name in the process to the Cooperative for American Relief Everywhere. CARE was the first of a growing number of American voluntary agencies that took principal responsibility for lobbying for and distributing the grant-type food commodities that later became Title II of PL 480. Interestingly, the private voluntary organizations also functioned on some occasions as "neutral" conduits through which the US government could furnish aid to (the mostly Communist) countries, such as Poland and Yugoslavia, with whom it wished to curry favor but which it could not, for domestic political reasons, assist more directly.

The other major program precedent for the formal institutionalization of US food aid was the authorization of the Mutual Security Act (MSA) of 1951 (PL 82–165), which emphasized the use of economic and military aid to maintain the security of the non-Communist world. A new aid category was developed under this rubric known as "defense-supporting assistance," which provided yet another programmatic outlet for food aid. While the MSAs of 1951 and 1952 set important precedents for the use of surplus agricultural commodities for defense-related purposes, Congress added a special new section to the MSA of 1953 (Section 550), which authorized the Secretary of Agriculture to earmark up to $280 million in resources for the sale of surplus commodities. These commodities could be purchased by friendly governments for their own local currency, which was then deposited to the credit of the US government in local banks for use as aid and for other purposes. This provision was expanded in the MSA of 1954, which repealed the previous acts (1951–1953) and authorized $350 million for the export and concessional sale of surplus agricultural commodities. Taken together, the four-year evolution of the MSA established a firm precedent for concessional credit sales of food aid for local, nonconvertible currencies, which later became a keystone of Title I of the PL 480 program.

The final antecedents to the establishment of PL 480 were two bills passed during the summer of 1953. The first, PL 83–77, provided President Eisenhower with authority to make a grant to Pakistan of 1 million tons of surplus wheat in order to avert a famine. The second, PL 83–216, authorized the President to grant $100 million worth of surplus commodities for famine relief out of funds already appropriated for the MSA program.

THE AGRICULTURAL TRADE DEVELOPMENT
AND ASSISTANCE ACT

In the face of such numerous precedents for US food aid, it may well be asked why Congress delayed the establishment of a formal US food aid program until 1954? One overly simplistic answer is that, up to the end of the Korean War, world food shortages—like US agricultural surpluses—were still considered to be isolated and temporary occurrences. By the end of the Korean conflict, it had become apparent, however, that neither situation was likely to end in the foreseeable future. But certain other factors must also be taken into account: surpluses were once again mounting rapidly as demand from a now fully recovered Europe declined sharply; and the emphasis in foreign aid had shifted to a military-oriented program that was generally unsuited to moving large volumes of surplus commodities [Anderson (1970, p. 84)].

It was ultimately the support of the US agricultural community—as embodied by its principal lobbying group, the American Farm Bureau Federation (AFBF)—that assured the eventual passage of PL 480. McClellan has traced the origin of the PL 480 concept to the 1952 AFBF National Conference in Seattle, Washington, where the AFBF adopted a resolution urging the government to expand the utilization of agricultural surpluses by selling them for foreign currencies [McClellan (1964, p. 4)]. The rationale for the proposal was that many developing countries having dollar surpluses needed to use their hard currency for capital purchases but would be willing to buy US agricultural products for local, nonconvertible currencies. The attractiveness of the plan was that it would increase local economic demand while reducing the US surplus burden through a disguised form of aid. Thus, the 1952 resolution provided AFBF President Allan Kline with a mandate for employing a former official of the European Recovery Program, Gwynn Garnett,[4] to begin drafting a legislative proposal that eventually became PL 480.

The Republican party controlled both Congress and the White House at the time and support for the concept of an institutionalized food aid program was considered uneven at best. Moreover, a crucial ally, Secretary of Agriculture Ezra Taft Benson, still clung to the belief that the surplus problem was only temporary and could, in any case, be handled through the MSA. Benson therefore refused to seek Eisenhower's support for the AFBF concept. At the other end of Pennsylvania Avenue, farm state congressmen were also wary of (or opposed to) the AFBF draft. By mid-1953, however, government-owned agricultural surpluses had passed the $5 billion mark, thereby spurring the Senate at least to take action on the measure.

Hearings were held in the upper chamber during July 1953 on a bill (S 2249) which, although given approval, failed to win passage in the House or to gain the support of the administration. But, in the period between the congressional sessions, the skyrocketing surplus stocks apparently had a sobering influence on many of the skeptics, including Secretary Benson. Substitute versions of the bill were introduced in the second session of the 83rd Congress and different versions were passed by both the House and Senate with virtually no substantive debate. A conference committee was convened in late June, and on 10 July 1954 President Eisenhower signed PL 83–480 into law, commenting that the program would "lay the basis for a permanent expansion of our exports of agricultural products, with lasting benefits to ourselves and to people of other lands" [*Congressional Quarterly Almanac* (1954, p. 121)].

The available evidence would tend to indicate that the reversal of congressional and White House positions on the food aid program, and its swift subsequent passage, may be ascribed to three factors. First, there was a realization that the domestic surplus problem was the result of fundamental systemic difficulties within US agriculture and were *not* temporary, passing phenomena. As a result, Benson and many congressional leaders had finally recognized that some sort of new institutional mechanism was required. Second, the State Department was reluctant to move greater volumes of surpluses through the MSA, fearing that it would antagonize other agricultural exporters by dumping commodities on Third World markets. This angered farm state legislators, who reacted by supporting an even *more* aggressive surplus disposal program. Third, the intense pressure of farm interest groups for relief from the avalanche of surpluses was responsible for the transferral of the food aid legislation to the exclusive jurisdiction of the respective congressional agricultural committees. In retrospect, avoiding the foreign affairs committees aided passage of the bill significantly because of the entrenched opposition of a significant portion of the foreign policy community [McClellan (1964, p. 7)].

As the title suggests, the Agricultural Trade Development and Assistance Act of 1954 (PL 83–480) was passed with two specific purposes: to move domestic agricultural surpluses and to make food available on grant and concessional credit terms to food deficient nations. Other goals set forth in the act included developing new markets for American farm products, disposing of surplus agricultural stocks, combatting

hunger and malnutrition, encouraging the economic development of recipient countries, and promoting the foreign policy of the United States.[5]
The specific means for carrying out these policy objectives were contained in three separate titles (or sections) of the law, which are outlined
briefly below [US Congress SCAF (1976a, pp. 5–6)].

The original configuration of PL 480 (as passed in July 1954)
1. *Title I*—authorized the President to use, with the agreement of the
recipient government, foreign currencies earned from the sale of US agricultural commodities for eight different purposes: LDC economic development, US agricultural market development, payment of US obligations, international educational exchange, procurement of military supplies, carrying out programs of US government agencies, purchase of
goods and services from other countries, and purchase of strategic
materials. Ten percent of the local currencies were to be subject to congressional appropriation.
2. *Title II* —provided for the use of food commodities on a strictly grant
basis for famine relief and/or other foreign emergency purposes.
3. *Title III*—authorized the Commodity Credit Corporation to make
commodities available to private voluntary organizations (e.g., CARE,
etc.) for distribution in the US and abroad. It also permitted the President to barter food commodities for strategic material and goods not
produced in the US.

THE SURPLUS DISPOSAL YEARS

Whether or not all of the executive branch agencies had reached unani-
mity of opinion on the value of PL 480 soon became immaterial once it
became apparent that the US farmer was benefiting dramatically from
the program. Secretary Benson reported that, during the course of a single crop year, US agricultural exports had climbed fully 33 percent over
the previous year.[6] This news quite naturally pleased Congress, especially those legislators from the farm states. On the executive side, President Eisenhower signed Executive Order No. 10560 on 9 September
1954, dividing authority for the administration of PL 480 among a
number of relevant federal agencies, thereby giving each an operating
stake in the successful implementation of the program.

By 1956, a substantial change had occurred in executive and legislative
attitudes toward the use and value of PL 480. The State Department no
longer feared the disruptive potential of food aid on foreign markets and
came increasingly to view PL 480 as a major instrument for feeding the
world's hungry and for limiting Communist expansion in the developing
world. The food commodities supplied under PL 480 also served in a
sense as a free form of foreign aid since the costs were at that time charged

to the budget of the Commodity Credit Corporation rather than to the State Department. But this set the stage for a new conflict with Congress because most legislators had never envisaged PL 480 as anything *other* than a means of surplus disposal [McClellan (1964, p. 27)].

The State Department was thus confronted with a dilemma: if it wished to continue using food aid as a foreign policy instrument, it would have to convince Congress of the validity of this policy; but if it wished to avoid LDC charges of economic imperialism, it had to find some way to avoid (and reduce) the embarrassingly high levels of US-owned foreign currencies which it had acquired under the terms of Title I of PL 480.[7] The decision ultimately was made to opt for the latter course of action, and it was therefore proposed that the "maintenance of value" clause,[8] which was obstructing the reloan of US-owned local currencies, be dropped from PL 480. As McClellan correctly points out, no foreign government would be willing to borrow its own currency at its original value *plus interest* when it could just as easily print additional money for nothing [McClellan (1964, p. 28)].

Although a number of prominent farm state legislators resisted this change in PL 480, the problematic maintenance of value clause was eventually eliminated. Despite the change, however, local currencies continued to be amassed in countries such as India and Yugoslavia in volumes far beyond the capacity of the US government either to spend them for its own purposes or to reloan them to the recipient government.

During the summer of 1957, Representative Harold D. Cooley, Chairman of the House Agriculture Committee, was successful in amending Section 104(e) of Title I PL 480 to set aside 25 percent of the local currencies from each food aid transaction for loans to private business firms wishing to invest in countries where the United States held large currency surpluses. These so-called Cooley loans were made available until 1972, *both* to local entrepreneurs as well as to US businessmen, and they became a source of largesse for US multinational corporations and their overseas affiliates, which received 90 percent of the funds loaned [McClellan (1964, p. 29)]. But the Cooley amendment also failed to stem the tide of US foreign currency accumulation. Ultimately, the State Department was forced to enpanel an outside group of experts, headed by Harvard economist Edward S. Mason, to review the entire problem. The Mason Report stated that local currencies already held by the United States in Spain, Yugoslavia, Israel, Pakistan, and India and other countries had reached the point where they could not possibly be utilized, at current rates, before the year 2000.[9] The conclusions of the Mason Committee also paralleled closely those reached by a growing number of congressmen, including Senator Hubert H. Humphrey.

THE CREATION OF FOOD FOR PEACE

Hubert Humphrey, along with a small group of colleagues in the House and Senate, had been attempting since 1954 to transform the PL 480 program from a surplus disposal orientation to a comprehensive foreign aid program. Agricultural surpluses, Humphrey argued, should not be considered a burden to be disposed of but a valuable American aid resource. In 1956, Humphrey was commissioned by the Senate Committee on Agriculture and Forestry to make an extensive study of the goals of the PL 480 program; his report, entitled "Food and Fiber as a Force for Freedom," was submitted to the Committee in February 1958. It called for a multiyear extension of the food aid program and the creation of a Peace Food Administrator at the White House level.

The report was received rather coolly by both Congress and the administration; but Humphrey, in characteristic fashion, proceeded anyway to introduce a bill (S 1711) on 16 April 1959 entitled, "A Bill to promote the foreign policy of the United States and help essential world conditions of peace by the more effective use of United States agricultural commodities for the relief of human hunger, and for promoting economic and social development in less developed countries" [McClellan (1964, p. 71)]. Hearings on the Humphrey bill were held during the summer of 1959 and the proposal received wide-ranging criticism. The Foreign Relations Committee reported the bill favorably in early August, albeit with the addition of some major amendments.

At this point, Humphrey's frontal assault on the underlying philosophy of the PL 480 program ran headlong into two other powerful sets of forces, each with its own view of the proper role for, and use of, US food aid. Toma describes the ensuing three-way struggle as a debate between the Humphrey faction wanting to strengthen the foreign policy aspect of PL 480; the Eisenhower administration wanting to change the name of the program without changing its surplus disposal orientation; and a group of farm state congressmen wishing to retain *only* the surplus disposal objective [Toma (1967, p. 60)]. In the meantime, the State Department had hired a former USDA Assistant Secretary, John Davis, to conduct a review of PL 480 and other foreign agricultural programs which related to foreign policy.

Davis recommended a comprehensive, five-year program that could be made "an integral part of a food and fiber policy, which might be called the Food for Peace program, to be announced by the President and designed to utilize and adapt our agricultural productive capacity for the benefit of the U.S. and the advancement of peace in the free world" [Peterson (1975, p. 309)]. But the Davis plan was rejected due to opposition from within the administration. Secretary Benson apparently feared that it would result in a series of "permanent relief clients" and that the Republican Eisenhower administration would be criticized for adopting a proposal sponsored by Hubert Humphrey and the Democrats.

Ezra Taft Benson, the most influential advisor to the President on these matters, began almost immediately to have second thoughts about the Davis concept, however. Knowing that the Humphrey bill was then in preparation, Benson urged Eisenhower in January 1959 to include a reference to the subject in his special farm message.[10] Although it soon became apparent that this was a last-minute grandstand play by the administration, the Humphrey forces had, in effect, been outmaneuvered. Humphrey himself later termed the President's proposal "a tragic failure of executive responsibility" [Peterson (1975, pp. 376–377)], but it did at least represent an admission by the administration that the time had come for a fundamental restructuring of the program's objectives.

The existence of surpluses was to remain a burdensome agricultural problem well into the next decade, but the 1959 revisions in PL 480 marked a major turning point in the orientation of US food aid. As Humphrey had urged, the short title of the law was changed to the Food for Peace program. Titles I and II were extended for two years and a new Title IV was added authorizing ten-year supply contracts to friendly nations with repayment over twenty years, at interest rates well below commercial terms.

Republican leaders also encouraged the President to follow up the legislative changes by appointing a Food for Peace coordinator to give the accomplishments of the program increased visibility in the upcoming election year. Eisenhower reacted favorably, requesting Secretary Benson's special assistant, Don Paarlberg, to work out the organizational details. Paarlberg recommended that a new White House office be created with a director acting as an expeditor rather than as an operational administrator. Paarlberg suggested a number of prestigious names as candidates for the new position, but Secretary Benson urged, and Eisenhower agreed, that Paarlberg himself be given the job since he had been involved with the concept from the beginning [Peterson (1975, p. 378)].

The Paarlberg appointment was acceptable to the relevant operating agencies and on 13 April 1960 the Office of Food for Peace and the position of Food for Peace Coordinator were both established by the President. According to Peterson [Peterson (1975, p. 378)], Paarlberg concentrated on three particular problems in the short time remaining in the Eisenhower term:

1. The balance between dollar aid moving through the US foreign aid agency, the International Cooperation Administration (ICA), and food moving under PL 480.
2. The difficulties which had occurred in the voluntary agency food aid programs due to conflict between the ICA and the USDA.
3. A publicity venture aimed at gaining UN support for the US Food for Peace program.

Taken in sum, the Eisenhower food policy changes represented more of an effort to repackage old concepts in a new format than the kind of fundamental reconceptualization of the program urged so energetically by Hubert Humphrey.

KENNEDY: CHANGES IN THE CONCEPTION OF US FOOD AID

From the early days of the 1960 campaign, it was apparent that John F. Kennedy was far more attuned to the use of food in international relations than he was to the needs or problems of domestic agriculture. While agricultural speeches tended to bore both the candidate and his audiences, Kennedy was able to speak at length extemporaneously about his plans for the use of American food aid. For example, during a campaign swing through South Dakota, Kennedy stated,

I don't regard the existence of . . . agricultural surpluses as a problem. I regard it as an opportunity. . . . I think the farmers can bring more credit, more lasting good will, more chance for peace, than almost any other group of Americans in the next ten years, if we recognize that food is strength, and food is peace and food is freedom, and food is a helping hand to people around the world whose good will and friendship we want. [*The New York Times*, 30 January (1959, p. 1)]

Also during the campaign, Kennedy announced the appointment of a "committee of distinguished citizens" (including the man he had defeated, Hubert Humphrey), to formulate recommendations for his new administration "to transfer the 'food for peace' slogan into a truly effective long-range use of our food abundance."[11]

The candidate proposed a six-point program designed to transform the slogan into action:

1. Change the surplus emphasis of the program into the use of food as a "long-range investment in progress."
2. Centralize responsibility for all phases of overseas distribution of US foods.
3. Increase substantially the annual amount of food and fiber to be distributed overseas by the voluntary relief agencies.
4. Continue and improve government-to-government assistance in the case of sudden disasters.
5. Hold a second International Conference on Food and Agriculture, similar to the one convened at Hot Springs, Virginia by Franklin Roosevelt, "to deal on a constructive multilateral basis with the food needs of the world."
6. Pending such a conference and creation of "a world food agency," negotiate long-term agreements for donor countries to supply food commodities for food-for-work schemes [John F. Kennedy (1960, pp. 2–3)].

It seems reasonable to suggest on the basis of this evidence that the new President *was* committed to a fundamental change in the objectives of US food policy and in the manner in which the aid was distributed.

After his inauguration, Kennedy moved swiftly to implement his new conception of food aid policy by establishing the Office of Food for Peace within the Executive Office of the President (as his second Executive Order on 24 January 1961) and by naming his friend and campaign supporter, George McGovern, as it first director.[12] The concept of food aid seemed well suited to Kennedy's New Frontier image, with its emphasis on social and technological optimism. This optimism was characterized by the belief that all problems were solvable with the appropriate combination of money, technology, and expertise.[13]

The food aid policy of the new Secretary of Agriculture, Orville Freeman, was even a step ahead of the President's own conception. The Secretary of Agriculture, who was to become the linchpin of subsequent efforts under Kennedy (and later Lyndon Johnson) to expand the developmental impact of Food for Peace, urged the President to formalize the US commitment to *eradicate* (not simply relieve) worldwide malnutrition by submitting to the Congress a USDA evaluation of the total resources required and then by making a "very bold statement in connection with the percentage of the deficiency that we as a nation are willing to meet." Freeman proposed that we would then go about producing the things needed to meet that deficiency.[14] A policy of cons-

ciously planned production was indeed a radical departure from the surplus disposal mentality of the previous decade, requiring that food aid
be allocated henceforth on the basis of recipient need rather than simply
as a result of commodity availability.

Freeman marshaled three arguments favoring such a fundamental
alteration of US policy. First, it would be consistent with the traditional
US philosophy and policy of sharing its agricultural abundance. Second,
it would represent a great and dramatic step which would bring to the
attention of the world the fact that the United States was no longer
dumping its surpluses willy-nilly, but was instead producing food for
human use. (This would, Freeman suggested, also pose a direct challenge
to the Soviet Union and to other, Free World exporters.) Finally, it
would be part of a long-term effort to expand markets for the product
of US agriculture [Freeman (1961a)].

But the evolution of policy in other agencies was not proceeding at
quite the same speed as in the USDA. Many career civil servants in the
State Department were still reluctant to use the PL 480 program as an
expanded instrument of US foreign aid, fearing that it would damage the
markets of other exporters considered friendly to the United States.
There is some amount of disagreement as to the actual intensity of this
antifood aid sentiment,[15] but it is clear that State Department policy was
being "pulled" from the White House far more than it was being
"pushed" from high levels within the agency itself.

Other foreign policy initiatives involving food aid were also emerging from the White House in 1961–1962. For example, at the behest of
George McGovern, Kennedy approved US participation in the three-
year experimental multilateral food aid undertaking which eventually
became the UN–FAO World Food Programme.[16] Once again, it is significant that such initiatives neither originated with nor were promoted
by the State Department.

JOHNSON: FOOD AID FOR ECONOMIC DEVELOPMENT

As early as July 1974, Lyndon Johnson had begun to express privately to
Orville Freeman his growing disillusionment with "pouring food around
the world to countries that were progressively ignoring their own agriculture [which] was a dead end policy."[17] Johnson informed Freeman
that he intended US food policy to include the principle of self-help, and
these sentiments later became embodied in Johnson's 1966 Food for Free-

dom proposal (discussed below). In the interim, however, PL 480 underwent a major congressional scrutiny in 1964.

The most controversial issue addressed during the debate on PL 480 was the question of preventing the allocation of aid to unfriendly (read: Communist) nations. An amendment was adopted prohibiting the sale of Title I commodities to Communist-controlled governments, countries trading with Cuba, or countries involved in military aggression against nations with which the United States had diplomatic ties. This restriction held significant implications for the foreign policy aspects of Food for Peace, and the President expressed his annoyance with the provision, stating that it would inhibit "our ability to deal selectively with countries that may demonstrate a tendency toward political and economic independence from communism" [Toma (1967, p. 129)].

Lyndon Johnson's unhappiness over the "bottomless-pit" characteristic (i.e., the fact that huge amounts of food continued to be programmed through the PL 480 with little tangible developmental impact) of the Food for Peace program continued to increase and, by 1965, White House staffers had set to work on a comprehensive reexamination of US food aid policy. In September of that year, Richard Reuter, who had replaced George McGovern as Director of the White House Office of Food for Peace, presented Johnson with a memorandum outlining a dramatic appeal for a "war against hunger" under presidential leadership.

This proposal was enlarged upon in discussions during November 1965 involving Senior Presidential Advisor McGeorge Bundy and Budget Director Charles L. Shultze. Bundy and Shultze outlined a three-point plan designed to help control the size of the US food aid burden:

1. "A strong emphasis is given to self-help measures by recipient countries to *increase their own food production*. Food shipments *will not* be used as a mere "hand out" keeping these countries dependent on U.S. gifts [emphasis in the original].
2. Food aid and other economic assistance are to be tied together and made *conditional on such self-help measures* [emphasis in the original].
3. Food aid will gradually be shifted away from sales for useless local currency to long-term dollar repayable loans.[18]

These three concepts won vigorous presidential approval, paralleling as they did a number of other initiatives of the Great Society (e.g., the War on Poverty). Johnson also favored the plan because it proposed to use food aid as an instrumental lever through which tangible, self-sustaining results could be achieved—a concept which Johnson, the consummate politician, both understood and endorsed.

By the beginning of 1966, there were essentially two food aid policy options under active consideration. With surplus food stocks largely depleted, the Food for Peace program could either be restructured to include self-help provisions as proposed in the President's war on hunger concept, or it could be reduced or even terminated. Oudes (1966, p. 121) suggests that the administration was dissuaded from adopting the latter course of action due to the likely objections of the farm interests. But Congress was also giving regular foreign aid proposals extremely close scrutiny and was unlikely to approve a further aid increase request to compensate for the elimination of PL 480. Food for Peace was actually serving as a second foreign aid source in two respects: the local currencies could be loaned back to recipient countries and the allocation of PL 480 resources could be undertaken through the CCC, thereby eliminating the need to go through the congressional appropriations process. Thus, a decision was made to proceed with the first option. PL 480 was to be repackaged as the so-called Food for Freedom program, representing the principal component of the President's war on hunger.

On 10 February 1966, President Johnson submitted a special message to Congress in which he proposed the most fundamental revisions in the US food aid program since its inception in 1954. The ensuing give-and-take between the White House and the congressional agriculture committees was lively, particularly concerning the issues of changing the short title of PL 480 from Food for Peace to Food for Freedom[19] and on adding restrictions on aid to countries exporting and/or shipping to Cuba or North Vietnam.[20]

As finally enacted, the Food for Peace Act (PL 89-808) of 1966—the name was *not* changed—did, in fact, represent a comprehensive restructuring of PL 480. Besides modifying the operational characteristics of the program and expanding the annual level of CCC authorizations to their highest point ever, the act also contained four critical changes affecting the use of US food aid as an instrument of foreign policy. First, the legislation eliminated at long last the need for the Secretary of Agriculture to designate food commodities as surplus before they could become eligible for use in the program.[21] This meant that the surplus disposal stigma was removed entirely and that commodities could now be produced (if necessary) specifically for export as aid.

Second, the sale of Title I commodities for local currencies was to be phased out progressively in favor of sales only for dollars or convertible currencies. This effectively removed the onerous local currency problem from the food aid relationship, although it also represented a hardening of the terms of PL 480. Third, self-help requirements were added making the continuation of food aid conditional, at least in theory,[22] on progress toward agricultural development.

Finally, the Congress expanded the scope of its political restrictions on the use of PL 480 beyond those added in 1964 to include an explicit ban on the provision of aid to countries furnishing anything but nonstrategic medical and agricultural supplies to Cuba or North Vietnam. This amendment eliminated any further food aid agreements with the Eastern European countries (many of whom traded extensively with Cuba) and it provided, in the opinion of some, a dangerous precedent for similar restrictions on future capital assistance appropriations.[23]

On 12 November 1966, Lyndon Johnson signed the Food for Freedom bill into law (he continued to use the term even though it had not been approved by the Congress), stating, "For six consecutive years world food consumption has exceeded production. A precarious balance has been maintained through our surplus stocks. Seventy million tons of surplus grain have been used since 1961. But today the surpluses are gone. . . . The only long-term solution is self-help."[24] The changes in US food aid policy enacted in 1966 ushered in a new, more activist period in the use of Food for Peace. While the size of the program remained close to its 1964 zenith in terms of total resources, (see table 3.1), the focus began to shift. No longer was food virtually a "free good" to be dumped indiscriminately on recipient countries; the program's cost effectiveness had become a major concern.

NIXON: FOOD AID POLITICIZED

Richard Nixon's conception of foreign aid was vastly different from that of his predecessor, Lyndon Johnson. As articulated in the so-called Nixon Doctrine, there was to be a general lowering of US overseas visibility and the Nixon food aid policy largely reflected this bias. Moreover, as Rothschild has concluded, US food aid policy from the outset of the Nixon years "recognized that PL 480 required real money, and that the United States itself had real problems with inflation and with its balance of payments" [Rothschild (1977c, p. 46]. In keeping with this Realpolitik, the role of the Office of Management and Budget (OMB), as it had been renamed under Nixon, now became paramount in PL 480 programming decisions. A 1968 federal budget ceiling, passed by the Congress at Nixon's request in order to check rising inflation, gave OMB the needed leverage over agency operations, and the USDA and the State Department were pushed for the first time to establish rigorous allocation criteria and program justifications. Moreover, the budget office demanded that an annual operating plan be formulated for the PL 480 program which was to include even food aid targeted for disaster relief.

The PL 480 legislation itself was revised modestly in 1968, primarily in order to reflect congressional concern over the need for adequate population control measures in the developing world and an even stricter prohibition on food aid that might indirectly benefit North Vietnam. For most of the remaining Nixon period (1968–1973), PL 480 remained largely unaltered, although the growing national preoccupation with the war in Southeast Asia also took its toll on the food aid program as well. As Lappé and Collins report, "Between 1968 and 1973, South Vietnam alone received twenty times the value of food aid that the five African countries most seriously affected by drought (i.e., the Sahelian region) received during that same period [Lappé and Collins (1977, p. 337)]. By 1973 almost half of all US food assistance was flowing to South Vietnam and Cambodia, as the Nixon administration attempted to circumvent the increasingly stringent congressional limitations on US assistance to the war effort in Southeast Asia.

The influence of the "free market" agricultural trade policy advocated by Secretary of Agriculture Earl L. Butz also had a significant impact on US food aid policy during the second term. Butz adopted the view that in a world short of food, the US farmer was entitled to obtain whatever the market would bear for his food commodities. Furthermore, Butz took the concept of food aid quite literally; that is, he felt that, as a form of *foreign* assistance, the cost of purchasing the commodities should come out of the budget of the State Department—not the Department of Agriculture.[25]

The Butz agricultural policy resulted in a precipitous decline in the levels of grain carry-over stocks held at government expense. Whereas, prior to 1972, the question of commodity availability had been relatively routine, serious questions now arose as to the US capability of meeting its food aid commitments. In order to alleviate the problem, the USDA relaxed its production controls (i.e., the regulations which held land out of production) for the 1973 crop year, and it removed them entirely in 1974. But an unforeseen series of events, which had begun in 1972 and which included the sudden and highly secretive purchase of US wheat by the Soviet Union, placed unprecedented demand on commercial agricultural exports and put US food aid in even greater jeopardy.

Comparing the food aid and trade figures for 1972 and 1975 provides an indication of the magnitude of the problem. In 1972, aid financed agricultural exports were worth $1.1 billion while commercial food exports were valued at $6.9 billion; but in 1975, while aid financed agricultural exports were again worth $1.1 billion, commercial food exports had nearly *quadrupled* to $21.8 billion.[26] The result was that during this so-called "world food crisis" period, available supplies of food commodities were insufficient to meet aggregate demand. For example, the AID proposal for a $300 million Title II food aid grant program for fiscal 1974 was slashed subsequently by the OMB to only $198 million. As a result, commodities made available under Title II to the voluntary agencies, the World Food Programme, and directly to governments declined from 2.3 million tons in 1973 to 1.5 million tons in 1974 (34-percent reduction). This shortfall forced an almost 50-percent reduction in voluntary agency and WFP programs, including the premature termination of twenty-six feeding programs in twenty-three countries [US GAO (1975, p. 16)].

Faced with the prospect of either reinstating controversial agricultural export controls (in order to limit domestic food price increases) or cutting the resources allocated to PL 480, an Assistant Secretary-level group formed to deal with the crisis urged President Nixon to adopt the latter option; the Title II donation program was clearly the more vulnerable. In the wake of the cutbacks, criteria for Title II food aid were established henceforth on a political basis, with priority given to Southeast Asia, general disaster relief, and other "overriding" political uses of the food. Officials of the private voluntary agencies and the World Food Programme were outraged by the commodity reductions, and they proceeded to take their case directly to the national media, to members of Congress, and to the general public. As noted below, these efforts were not long in producing results.

THE CONGRESSIONAL RESPONSE

There were actually two separate issues which sparked congressional concern for, and involvement in, US food aid policy. The first was the so-called use of "food for war," which actually had been part of policy since the early years of the Vietnamese involvement. The second issue which prompted congressional scrutiny was the food aid commodity shortages that occurred in 1973. The two were related in the fact that it was due partially to the massive programming of food aid to South Vietnam and Cambodia (during fiscal 1974, over 66 percent of Title I commodities went to these two countries alone) that insufficient resources were available to meet needs elsewhere.

By 1972, Congress and the American public were growing increasingly weary of, and antagonistic to, the long American involvement in Southeast Asia. This was reflected in more limited congressional military assistance appropriations for Southeast Asia, which, in turn, caused the administration to rely more and more on food aid as a form of "backdoor financing" for the war effort. When the actual extent of this practice finally became known to Congress, long-time food aid advocates such as Hubert Humphrey and George McGovern reacted strongly.

Their first effort was to amend in 1973 the Foreign Assistance Act, in order to prohibit the use of foreign currency proceeds from the sale of Title I commodities for "common defense" purposes without the express consent of Congress. This action effectively eliminated the common defense feature of Title I [Section 104(c)], although the impact on the offending US policy was practically nil since the proceeds from most Title I sales simply revert to the recipient's general treasury and thus become practically untraceable [Lappé and Collins (1977, p. 339)]. Opponents soon realized that they had been unsuccessful in deterring the Nixon administration from its "food for war" policy.

In 1974, a second attempt was made, this time using a different and more effective strategy. The Foreign Assistance Act of 1974 was amended to include a provision that for fiscal 1975 not more than 30 percent of Title I commodities could be allocated to countries other than those designated by the United Nations as "most seriously affected" by the current worldwide economic crisis, unless the President could demonstrate that the food assistance was to be used solely for humanitarian purposes. This action did finally begin to constrain executive branch flexibility, although it did nothing (nor was it intended) to respond to the supply crisis which had also developed at this time.

Rothschild has suggested that one of the reasons for the drastic reductions in Title II food aid during 1973–1974 was that people concerned about humanitarian questions, that is, the church groups and other private voluntary agencies, did not comprehend the full impact of what was happening until the supply crisis was almost over [Rothschild (1977c, p. 48)]. While this was no doubt true for those outside of the government, it does little to explain the congressional insensitivity to the problem. But the issue of adequate supply of food had never before been a problem for the United States, even in the midsixties, when the large carry-over stocks were drawn down by huge grain shipments to India. This fact may well provide the key to the lack of congressional awareness.

Thus, Secretary Butz's decision to liquidate all remaining publicly owned food stocks, combined with the sudden and unexpected explosion in world demand for US food commodities (both as aid and trade), confronted policymakers with the first situation in the more than twenty years of formal aid giving in which there was simply not enough food to meet all commitments. A decision ultimately was made by the USDA to give preference to commercial and concessional credit (Title I) sales *before* meeting Title II grant-type food aid commitments. The resulting congressional uproar over this pragmatic but morally insensitive decision was swift and substantial.

The breakdown of the Title II food aid pipeline helped to precipitate a full-scale review of the Food for Peace program by the staff of the Senate Committee on Agriculture and Forestry. The Senate committee's review also prompted Senators Humphrey and Clark to introduce a bill (S 1654) in May 1975, which represented the most comprehensive restructuring of the PL 480 legislation since the changes enacted in 1966.

As subsequently passed by the Congress, the International Development and Food Assistance Act of 1975 (PL 94-161) was designed to promote the humanitarian and agricultural development features of US food aid. Six important new provisions were included in the 1975 act:

1. The commodity supply problem regarding Title II was eliminated through the unprecedented addition of a 1.3-million-ton minimum "floor" on grant-type programming.

2. The 70:30 split of Title I commodity distribution was made even more stringent by revision so that not more than 25 percent (i.e., a 75:25 split) of such aid was to be allocated to countries having a per capita income of more than $300.

3. The President was empowered to waive repayment of up to 15 percent of total annual Title I concessional credit loans in cases where the recipient agreed to use the funds generated for population control and/ or increased food self-sufficiency.

4. The President was authorized to waive the ban on Title I sales to Cuba and North Vietnam if he found it in the national interest to do so.

5. The President was directed to seek an international agreement, subject to the approval of Congress, on a system of food reserves for emergency purposes.

6. The President was urged to maintain a significant US contribution toward the annual 10-million-ton food aid target established by the World Food Conference and to encourage other countries to do so as well.

The 1975 changes in PL 480 demonstrate that the values and priority interests of the Congress in the midseventies were vastly different from those of their colleagues two decades earlier when the food aid program was created. Gone was the preoccupation with surplus disposal and market development and, in its place, a new and growing interest in limiting the political use of food aid, meeting the continuing US responsibilities toward the world's hungry, and promoting LDC agricultural development. As with so many previous food aid program initiatives, high-sounding rhetoric tended to overshadow continuing obstacles, but the temporary supply and allocation problems which initially motivated congressional action may well turn out to have a positive long-term impact.

FORD: FOOD AID AS A SCARCE RESOURCE

When Gerald Ford was called upon unexpectedly in August 1974 to replace the disgraced Richard Nixon, US food aid policy was yet another unresolved headache inherited from the outgoing administration. At Secretary of State Kissinger's initiative, the United States had proposed that a World Food Conference be convened in November 1974. Thus, not only was there a need to resolve the supply issues facing the US food aid program, but the newly installed White House staff also had to contend with the final determination of a position for the Rome meeting.

The new President was caught squarely between farm interests demanding an end to government intervention in the export of agricultural commodities and humanitarian and international interests demanding that the United States meet its food aid responsibilities despite the existence of heavy commercial demand and short supply. Soon after assuming office, Budget Director Roy L. Ash presented Ford with a memorandum outlining his options regarding the level of Food for Peace operations[27] and offering the President three levels of funding options.

While urging fiscal restraint, the memorandum took note of the "strong foreign policy reasons" for increasing PL 480 funding for 1975. Ash cited the upcoming World Food Conference and Kissinger's UN speeches promising increased food aid. He also made note of the following fact: "Food aid is considered a vital part of our Mid East [sic] diplomacy; Israel and Egypt in particular have requested large programs.

Further, recent floods in Bangladesh have increased the need there, India will have a significant grain shortfall this year, and recipients like Korea, Indonesia, Chile and Pakistan expect commitments (even though conditional) to be made good" [Ash (1974, p. 3)].

The accessibility of this memorandum is particularly valuable when its recommendations are compared to the actual policy adopted by the administration; it reveals that the domestic concerns—especially the need for fiscal restraint—precluded a major expansion of the food aid program. Instead, Ford opted for announcing a modest increase for fiscal 1975 in *dollar* terms (i.e., not volume), but the release of a specific figure was deferred until December (1974), well after the end of the World Food Conference.

In early November, just prior to the start of the conference, Secretary Kissinger made a special appeal to the President seeking permission to announce an increase in the volume of US food aid; but senior advisors such as Treasury Secretary William Simon and Roy Ash convinced the President to authorize the Secretary of State to indicate only that the dollar level of aid would be expanded. The resulting US position at the meeting proved awkward for Secretary Kissinger, who was, after all, the initiator of the conference. At the same time, a coalition of liberal senators and private sector groups, known collectively as the World Hunger Action Coalition, worked through the media to bring public pressure to bear on the administration to announce an increase in its food aid programming. Matters went so far that the US delegation pressured Secretary Butz into calling the President from Rome to officially request an additional 1-million-ton aid commitment. But Ford chose ultimately to reject the request, citing his concern for the need to exercise restraint in order to "whip inflation."

Foreign demand for US food commodities waned during 1975, and the food aid issue soon began to lose its crisis orientation. Moreover, the Ford administration's policy flexibility was further constrained by the passage of the International Development and Food Assistance Act of 1975, which limited the amount of food aid available as a foreign policy instrument.[28] By the end of the Ford interregnum, a new US food aid policy had begun to emerge which was characterized by a growing interest in promoting long-term LDC food self-sufficiency. Moreover, the end of the Ford period also brought a new recognition—at the State Department and elsewhere—of the paramount importance of seeking *global* solutions to world food problems.[29]

US FOOD AID IN 1976

This chapter has documented the slow evolution of the PL 480 program
from an explicit mechanism of surplus disposal and market development
to a limited instrument of US foreign policy and development assistance.
The resources made available during this period (1955–1976) indeed
were substantial. Table 3.1 and 3.2 provide an indication of the dollar
value and commodity volume of US farm products actually shipped
under the two principal titles of PL 480: Title I, the concessional credit
sales program; and Title II, the outright grant program.

The data in these tables provide some interesting contrasts. Whereas
the zenith of PL 480 in terms of *dollar* value was reached in 1965, the
peak *volume* year actually occurred three years earlier, in 1962. This
may be accounted for by the often overlooked fact that PL 480 is budgeted in dollars, *not* by volume. Thus, the lower the farm prices at any
given time, the greater the buying power of the PL 480 program. Conversely, when agricultural prices rise, as they did quite dramatically in
the 1972–1974 period, food aid volume levels must decline. This relationship is apparent from the data: note the volume reduction beginning
in 1972 that continued, despite an *increase* in dollars budgeted to food
aid, for 1975–1976.

Another method of evaluating the resources of the Food for Peace
program is in terms of the gross costs of financing PL 480. Gross costs in
this case refer not only to the actual purchase price of the commodities,
but also to the cost of ocean transportation, interest, processing, and so
on. As might be expected, the data in table 3.3 indicate that the gross
costs of PL 480 are higher than the previous tabulations. It might be concluded on this basis that table 3.3 is most representative of the "true"
cost of maintaining a US food aid program. But, to actually derive a
true cost figure, it would also be necessary to account for the costs of
domestic agricultural support programs (which PL 480 operations help,
in part, to reduce) and for the reflow of funds under the long-term, soft
credit repayment provisions of Title I. Such an analysis would be likely
to indicate that the true cost of operating the PL 480 program is substantially *below* any of the statistical summaries presented here.

Another aspect of aggregate PL 480 resources which is of interest in
the context of overall US food aid policy concerns the commodity composition of the assistance shipped. These data are summarized in tables
3.4–3.6, covering the period from 1955 to 1977. Table 3.4 illustrates the
distribution of commodities within Title I, the largest part of the PL 480

Table 3.1
Value of US Farm Products Shipped under PL 480: Fiscal Years 1955–1977 (Thousands of US Dollars)

Year	Title I	Title II	Total
1955	197,584	186,841	384,425
1956	737,237	247,667	984,903
1957	1,308,283	216,779	1,525,062
1958	757,292	223,741	981,033
1959	856,402	160,884	1,017,286
1960	973,104	142,762	1,115,866
1961	1,095,449	220,917	1,316,366
1962	1,246,768	248,730	1,495,498
1963	1,192,805	263,464	1,456,269
1964	1,148,043	269,950	1,417,993
1965	1,331,739	238,748	1,570,487
1966	1,079,357	266,522	1,345,879
1967	1,003,450	267,368	1,270,818
1968	1,029,326	250,138	1,279,464
1969	773,853	264,737	1,038,590
1970	815,221	240,594	1,055,815
1971	743,018	279,945	1,022,963
1972	769,000	403,741	1,082,741
1973	667,400	289,961	957,361
1974	575,376	282,915	858,291
1975	763,620	334,437	1,098,057
1976 (est.)	983,000	376,147	1,359,147
1977 (est.)	866,000	365,000	1,231,000
Cumulative total	20,913,326	6,041,988	26,955,314

Source: US Congress SCAF (1976a, p. 33)

Table 3.2
PL 480 Commodity Volume Shipments: Fiscal Years 1955–1976 (Millions of Tons per Metric Ton Grain Equivalent)

Year	Title I	Title II	Total
1955	2,588	830	3,418
1956	9,045	1,025	10,070
1957	12,836	1,435	14,271
1958	7,460	1,768	9,228
1959	9,978	1,510	11,488
1960	12,724	1,601	14,325
1961	13,759	2,583	16,342
1962	15,851	2,927	18,778
1963	14,552	2,814	17,366
1964	14,016	2,760	16,776
1965	16,082	2,329	18,411
1966	15,454	2,703	18,157
1967	11,612	2,345	13,957
1968	12,396	2,183	14,579
1969	7,762	2,234	9,996
1970	8,727	2,211	10,938
1971	7,491	2,344	9,835
1972	7,167	2,738	9,905
1973	4,956	2,345	7,301
1974	1,773	1,503	3,276
1975	3,495	1,229	4,724
1976	3,370	987	4,357
Transitional quarter	1,836	250	2,086
Cumulative total	214,930	44,654	259,584

Source: US Congress SCANF (1977, p. 78).

program. Grain products have clearly dominated the commodity mix, accounting for approximately 85 percent of total deliveries. Within this category, wheat and wheat products represent fully 76 percent of the grain component, with feedgrains comprising another 16 percent of the total. Vegetable oil was the single largest commodity within the "nongrain" category, comprising 41 percent of Title I nongrains. But the most noteworthy factor here is the "other" category: in the years between 1955 and 1970, the United States was able to dispose of an average of 374,000 tons of surplus commodities under the Title I program, including such *nonedible* products as tobacco and cotton.

The second data compilation, table 3.5, provides a similar display for commodities shipped under Title II, grant-type food aid operations. It is important to reiterate that, whereas Title I commodities are most often sold directly by recipient governments in order to generate local resources, Title II commodities are allocated through the voluntary agencies, the UN World Food Programme, and directly government-to-government for emergency and institutional feeding purposes. As a result, nonedible commodities such as tobacco and cotton are of little value.

Perhaps the most striking fact about Title II commodity distribution, however, is its small aggregate size when compared with Title I. It is also interesting to note the inordinately large allocation of rice in 1972 which resulted from the US rice glut of that year. Rice was, in some cases, dumped under PL 480 in countries where the commodity had never before been programmed. In addition, two other special features characterize the grant-type program: the large volumes of nonfat dry milk shipped as aid and (after the 1966 revisions in PL 480) the use of so-called blended foods (e.g., corn–soy milk, and wheat–soy blend). Although the programming of nonfat dry milk has been on the decline in recent years, both products have played a substantial role in the institutional and emergency feeding programs.

Finally, table 3.6 indicates the total level of PL 480 commodity programming. Grain has accounted for fully 92 percent of all commodities utilized as aid, with the peak volume year occurring in 1962. Volumes have fallen off sharply since 1971, due to rising grain prices. At its low ebb in 1974, during the height of the world food supply "crisis" period, grain shipments were only 16 percent of their 1962 levels. Title II has also been affected by price and availability fluctuation, but the addition of the legislated minimum volume of 1.3 million tons per year has helped substantially to mitigate this problem.

Table 3.3
Gross Costs of Financing PL 480 Food Aid Programming: Fiscal Years 1954–1975 (Millions of US Dollars)

Fiscal year ending June 30	Title I		Title II, donations abroad		Title III	Total
	Sales for foreign currency	Long-term dollar and convertible foreign currency credit sales	Famine and other emergency relief	Voluntary agency programs	Bartered material for supplemental stockpile	
1955	129.5	–	86.9	214.5	–	430.9
1956	624.2	–	93.6	271.2	–	989.0
1957	1,396.4	–	124.9	234.1	217.3	1,972.7
1958	1,144.7	–	121.4	254.3	83.9	1,604.3
1959	1,113.3	–	97.9	178.7	314.7	1,704.6
1960	1,308.0	–	95.5	130.8	192.4	1,726.7
1961	1,557.3	–	198.6	169.3	200.5	2,125.7
1962	1,606.1	29.0	241.9	191.7	193.3	2,262.0
1963	1,739.4	80.3	215.6	238.8	99.7	2,373.8
1964	1,636.2	65.1	228.2	341.6	37.7	2,308.8
1965	1,505.8	211.0	147.2	174.6	40.6	2,079.2
1966	1,287.8	274.6	222.5	148.3	25.8	1,959.0
1967	1,067.8	221.7	335.9	34.2	32.5	1,692.1
1968	784.8	350.0	344.6	–	25.9	1,505.3
1969	373.0	495.4	364.2	–	1.7	1,234.3
1970	335.3	560.0	351.0	–	0.2	1,246.5
1971	225.2	625.9	395.7	–	0.1	1,246.9

1972	155.0	614.9	524.4	—	—	1,294.3
1973	8.2	736.3	396.1	—	—	1,140.6
1974	0.3	577.8	384.8	—	—	962.9
1975	4.6	767.9	460.4	—	—	1,227.7
Total	17,997.7[a]	6,609.9[b]	5,431.3[c]	2,582.1[d]	1,466.3[e]	33,087.3

Source: USDA (1977b, appendix, table 6).

a. Represents the gross cost to CCC of financing sales of US agricultural commodities for foreign currency. Includes commodity and other costs, ocean transportation costs, and interest costs.

b. Represents the gross cost to CCC of financing long-term dollar credit sales of US agricultural commodities. Includes commodity and other costs, ocean transportation costs, and interest costs. The export value of commodities financed and ocean transportation costs (except ocean freight differential) are repayable by the importing country or private trade entity.

c. Represents CCC's investment value in commodities made available for donation abroad under title II of 480, ocean transportation costs for such donations and for foreign currency for use in self-help activities. Also includes gross cost of foreign donations through nonprofit voluntary agencies beginning 1 January 1967.

d. Represents CCC's acquisition cost value, plus the cost of any processing and packaging performed after acquisition, for commodities donated through nonprofit voluntary agencies under authority in Section 416. Agricultural Act of 1949. This authority was repealed by the Food for Peace Act of 1966, PL 89-808, and such donations consolidated into new Title II of such act, effective 1 January 1967.

e. Represents the value at which barter materials were transferred to the supplemental stockpile.

Table 3.4

Annual Volume of PL 480, Title I Shipments by Commodity: Fiscal Years 1955–1977 (Metric Tons per Metric Ton Grain Equivalent)

Grains

Year	Wheat	Feedgrains	Rice	Total
1955–59 (cum.)	26,164,449	11,393,325	1,492,217	39,049,991
1060	8,945,858	2,660,787	484,898	12,091,543
1961	10,286,984	2,266,050	560,922	13,113,956
1962	11,991,169	2,765,968	400,075	15,157,212
1963	11,691,087	1,407,548	613,811	13,712,446
1964	11,563,364	1,032,145	674,321	13,269,830
1965	13,861,892	883,765	565,685	15,311,342
1966	12,833,194	1,838,173	359,388	15,030,755
1967	6,987,321	3,183,772	828,319	10,999,412
1968	9,392,327	1,595,044	734,605	11,721,976
1969	5,388,589	721,038	983,632	7,093,259
1970	6,152,320	1,068,756	939,542	8,160,618
1971	5,204,369	862,023	923,076	6,989,468
1972	4,797,553	1,212,774	813,577	6,823,904
1973	2,461,441	1,273,759	964,044	4,699,244
1974	716,304	378,286	605,620	1,700,210
1975	2,779,456	14,433	759,251	3,553,140
1976 (est.)	4,088,400	50,000	800,000	4,938,900
1977 (est.)	3,992,500	100,000	650,000	4,742,600
Cumulative total	159,299,077	34,707,646	14,155,083	208,161,806

Nongrains Year	Veg. oil	Nonfat dry milk	Blended foods	Other	Total
1955–59 (cum.)	1,154,339	66,887	–	1,634,169	2,855,395
1960	339,214	28,275	–	264,939	632,428
1961	280,384	22,230	–	342,336	644,950
1962	313,403	15,885		364,128	693,416
1963	251,158	19,988	–	568,661	839,807
1964	313,946	14,892	–	417,284	746,122
1965	366,005	10,561	–	394,593	771,159
1966	196,092	7,492	–	219,635	423,219
1967	219,358	1,196	–	392,529	613,083
1968	300,575	4,967	–	368,720	674,262
1969	290,278	8,675	–	370,361	669,314
1970	249,925	5,386	–	310,758	560,069
1971	292,932	9,182	–	199,093	501,207
1972	193,526	10,116	–	139,836	343,478
1973	106,225	1,954	–	148,837	257,016
1974	65,324	–	1,788	43,240	110,352
1975	29,355	–	–	15,572	44,927
1976 (est.)	87,500	–	5,000	43,240	150,000
1977 (est.)	125,000	–	–	50,400	175,400
Cumulative total	5,174,539	227,686	6,788	6,302,591	11,711,604

Source: US Congress SCAF (1976a, p. 35).

Table 3.5

Annual Volume of PL 480, Title II Shipments by Commodity: Fiscal Years 1955–1977 (Metric Tons per Metric Ton Grain Equivalent)

Grains

Year	Wheat	Feedgrains	Rice	Total
1955–1959 (cum.)	3,292,300	1,279,786	342,252	4,914,338
1960	979,325	383,700	88,905	1,451,930
1961	1,655,506	591,951	96,617	2,344,074
1962	1,679,223	828,973	21,194	2,520,390
1963	1,847,880	494,801	635	2,343,316
1964	1,862,523	505,573	–	2,368,096
1965	1,503,716	492,643	–	
1966	1,887,148	472,811	–	2,359,959
1967	1,339,895	655,170	–	1,995,056
1968	1,341,024	467,784	–	1,808,808
1969	1,502,722	306,353	9,452	1,818,527
1970	1,476,946	363,577	7,463	1,847,986
1971	1,415,550	522,940	–	1,938,490
1972	1,650,473	271,568	247,824	2,169,865
1973	1,489,776	315,556	32,906	1,938,238
1974	705,312	555,948	–	1,261,260
1975	655,934	307,750	4,000	967,284
1976 (est.)	614,200	473,000	–	1,087,200
1977 (est.)	730,000	270,000	–	1,000,000
Cumulative total	27,729,413	9,559,484	851,248	38,140,145

Nongrains Year	Veg. oil	Nonfat dry milk	Blended foods	Other	Total
1955–1959 (cum.)	35,962	1,076,577	–	542,985	1,655,584
1960	–	147,193	–	2,177	149,370
1961	3,675	220,670	–	14,745	239,090
1962	48,413	262,151	–	87,625	398,189
1963	47,051	315,060	–	108,897	471,008
1964	23,011	285,902	–	83,037	391,950
1965	106,201	198,675	–	27,296	332,172
1966	123,913	210,343	–	9,240	343,495
1967	123,495	136,715	87,936	1,451	349,597
1968	100,223	129,583	117,912	26,297	374,015
1969	77,459	133,980	187,824	16,095	415,338
1970	80,621	132,614	147,287	998	361,520
1971	86,069	141,352	178,251	–	405,672
1972	187,137	115,466	265,783	–	586,386
1973	111,513	25,683	269,314	–	406,510
1974	53,533	–	180,559	8.073	242,165
1975	41,353	44,334	182,800	–	258,487
1976 (est.)	52,208	25,900	180,250	7,000	265,358
1977 (est.)	55,000	70,000	230,000	–	355,000
Cumulative total	1,356,000	3,673,198	2,017,916	935,916	7,982,866

Source: US Congress SCAF (1976a, p. 36.)

Table 3.6

Annual Volume of Total PL 480 Shipments, Grains and NonGrains: Fiscal Years 1955–1977
(Metric Tons per Metric Ton Grain Equivalent)

Fiscal year	Grains	Nongrains	Total
1955	3,101,948	316,518	3,418,466
1956	9,207,440	863,128	10,070,568
1957	12,965,169	1,306,159	14,271,328
1958	8,253,259	975,320	9,228,579
1959	10,438,493	1,049,794	11,488,287
1960	13,543,473	781,793	14,325,271
1961	15,458,030	884,040	16,342,070
1962	17,686,602	1,091,605	18,778,207
1963	16,055,762	1,310,815	17,366,577
1964	15,637,926	1,318,072	16,775,998
1965	17,307,701	1,103,331	18,411,032
1966	17,390,714	766,714	18,157,428
1967	12,994,477	962,670	13,956,947
1968	13,503,784	1,048,277	14,552,061
1969	8,911,786	1,084,672	9,996,458
1970	10,008,604	929,589	10,938,193
1971	8,927,958	906,879	9,834,837
1972	8,993,769	911,864	9,905,633
1973	6,637,482	663,526	7,301,008
1974	2,916,470	352,517	3,268,987
1975	4,520,424	303,414	4,823,838
1976 (est.)	6,026,100	415,408	6,441,508
1977 (est.)	5,742,600	530,400	6,273,000
Cumulative total	246,301,951	19,696,510	265,998,461

Source: US Congress SCAF (1976a, p. 34.)

United States multilateral commitments are presented in table 3.7, including contributions made under Title II to the UN World Food Programme. In the early years of the UN program (1963–1968), the United States contributed fully 51 percent of the resources. But, as the concept of international burden-sharing gained increasing emphasis, the size of the US pledge was reduced successively. Ignoring an anomalous rise in 1971–1972 due to an overall WFP pledging shortfall, the US share has now stabilized at about 25 percent of total world contributions. Since countries may participate in the World Food Programme in the form of either commodity or *cash* contributions, the United States now computes its own WFP pledge according to the size of its *overall* UN contribution—which now represents about 25 percent of total UN resources—rather than in recognition of its continued dominance as an agricultural exporter.

The United States has also pledged 1.89 million metric tons of grain each year since 1967 under the multilateral Food Aid Convention.[30] This has represented more than 40 percent of the total aid contributed under the convention. Initially the United States was required to meet its commitments solely through Title II grant-type food aid. However, since 1971, a portion of Title I concessional credit sales have also been accepted. It should be emphasized, however, that the commodities provided by the United States under the Food Aid Convention do not represent a net addition to its total annual food aid contribution,[31] although they *have* represented another means of encouraging increased interna-

Table 3.7
US Share of Total Resources Pledged to the UN World Food Programme, 1963–1976 (Millions of US Dollars)

Pledge period	Target	Total pledged	US Share Amount	Percent
1963–1965	100	84.5	43.6	51.5
1966–1968	275	187.2	95.9	51.2
1969–1970	200	320.0	99.6	31.1
1971–1972	300	249.7	125.0	50.0
1973–1974	340	361.2	136.0	37.7
1975–1976	440	616.0	140.0	22.7
Cumulative total	1,655	1,818.6	640.1	35.2

Source: US GAO (1977, p. 4.)

tional food aid burden-sharing and of insuring a floor under US aid flows.

In recent years, some observers have suggested that the PL 480 concept may finally have reached the end of its programmatic lifetime and should, therefore, be abandoned or modified substantially.[32] It should be reiterated, however, that the long-term functional effectiveness of the Food for Peace program has been the result of a remarkable, and probably unique, confluence of domestic and foreign policy objectives, diverse interest group support, and enduring congressional favor. Although the need to modify or change the conception of US food aid is now recognized by many of those responsible for this alliance of interests, a substantial conceptual distance still remains between the *theoretical* recognition of what food aid could (or should) be and the *political* reality of what it now is. Bridging this paradigmatic gap may ultimately prove far more difficult than has heretofore been imagined.

PART II
THE FRAMEWORK OF INTERNATIONAL FOOD AID

In order to assess the objectives of US food aid policy within the global context, it is necessary first to delimit the framework of aid in which the US contribution is but one component. The most salient feature of international food assistance is the predominant role and influence of the United States both on the behavior of the other donors and on the effective functioning of the system itself. Although the imbalance between the US contribution and those of the other major donors has been reduced significantly in recent years, there can still be little doubt that the continued availability of large volumes of US commodities is essential to the success of the international food aid effort.

The historical record indicates that, since the early sixties, the United States has sought to use its aid as one means of convincing other food exporting nations (both developed and less developed) to become more deeply involved in providing such assistance. This policy of burden-sharing has resulted in two principal (and parallel) manifestations: a group of twenty countries which now make food commodities—or the cash to purchase same—available to selected recipients on a bilateral basis; and a small but growing number of institutional mechanisms which have been established to coordinate and implement multilateral programs of food assistance. In certain cases, bilateral and multilateral food aid overlap to such a degree that they become virtually indistinguishable. In others, however, the objectives and allocative criteria of the two types of programming are diametrically opposed.

It must also be emphasized that matters related to food obviously do not exist apart from the wider context of international relations. Food as a commodity has both economic and political implications, whether it is transferred in the form of aid or in commercial trade. A clear understanding of these factors is therefore critical to the explanation of the policies adopted by each donor regarding the volume, terms, and degree of participation in the framework of international food aid.

Due to the historically dominant position of the United States, the food aid contributions of other donor countries have often been overlooked or at least undervalued. As noted previously, overseas food assistance during the twenty-year period 1945–1965 following the close of World War II was, for all practical purposes, the exclusive domain of the United States. This situation was one which the United States accepted readily during the heavy surplus years of the forties, fifties, and early sixties. But as carry-over stocks dwindled and competing pressures on the use of food as an aid resource increased, the Johnson administration (then in office) began to insist on a wider degree of international food aid burden-sharing among the developed countries.

The data in table 4.1 reveal that, since 1963, when the US contribution of food aid represented fully 96 percent of available resources, the proportionate shares of the other donors have been rising while the US contribution has been declining. By 1975, the US share represented 58 percent of total food aid, a large but substantially reduced figure from the previous period, while food resources flowing from the European Economic Community (EEC) had grown impressively, representing 20 percent of total food aid in 1975. As a level of participation of other donor countries has increased, so too has the importance of this assistance in each country's total official development assistance (ODA). Table 4.2 provides a breakdown for the year 1977 of the share of each donor's food aid as a percentage of total food aid, as a percentage of each country's ODA, and in comparison with the total ODA of all types by each donor. It may be observed that the United States was still

Table 4.1
Share of Principal Donors in Total Bilateral and Multilateral Food Aid Contributions[a]

	1963		1966		1969		1972		1975	
	$m	%	$m	%	$m	%	$m	%	$m	%
United States	1,221	96	1,213	91	907	77	978	77	1,216	58
Canada	47	4	88	7	60	5	88	7	263	13
EEC countries	4	–	6	–	88	8	129	10	413	20
Japan	–	–	1	–	60	5	35	3	15	0.7
Others	5	–	21	2	64	5	46	3	171	8.3
Total	1,277	100	1,329	100	1,179	100	1,276	100	2,078	100

Sources: OECD (1974, p. 9) and OECD (1976, P. 149).
a. DAC figures.

Table 4.2
Share of Each DAC Country's Food Aid in Total DAC Food Aid and Total ODA,
Net Disbursements: 1977 (Millions of US Dollars)[a]

Countries	Food aid	Food aid as % of total	Food aid as % of each country's ODA	For comparison ODA	ODA as % of GNP
Australia	24.2	1.2	5.6	427	0.45
Austria	(1.9)	0.1	1.6	118	0.24
Belgium	23.0	1.1	6.2	371	0.46
Canada	184.9	9.1	18.6	991	0.51
Denmark	28.6	1.4	11.0	258	0.60
Finland	7.5	0.5	15.3	49	0.17
France	51.8	2.5	2.3	2,267	0.60
Germany	132.2	6.6	9.5	1,386	0.27
Italy	45.6	2.3	24.5	186	0.10
Japan	15.1	0.7	1.1	1,424	0.21
Netherlands	64.8	3.2	7.2	900	0.85
New Zealand	1.3	0.1	2.4	53	0.39
Norway	19.5	0.9	6.6	295	0.82
Sweden	38.5	1.9	4.9	779	0.99
Switzerland	16.5	0.8	13.9	119	0.19
United Kingdom	46.7	2.3	5.1	914	0.37
United States	1,312.0	65.1	31.5	4,159	0.22
Total DAC	2,014.5	100.0	13.7	14,696	0.31

Source: OECD (1978, pp. 202–203).
a. DAC figures.

clearly predominant both in absolute terms (65.1 percent of total food aid) and in terms of food as a percentage of its total ODA (31.5 percent of ODA).

This latter fact is particularly significant in that total US ODA for that year ($4,159 million) was almost *twice* the size of that offered by the next largest donor, France ($2,267 million). Food assistance thus accounted for an inordinately large share of US official development assistance. In fact, it is interesting to note that when aid is examined in terms of ODA as a percentage of each country's gross national product (GNP), which is the indicator considered by development economists to be most representative of a nation's real aid effort), those countries which compiled the most impressive overall statistics for 1977 in terms of ODA relative to GNP (e.g., Sweden, Norway, and the Netherlands) also demonstrated a marked tendency toward only *limited* use of food as an aid resource. This may be explained in part by the fact that, with the possible exception of Sweden, these countries have never had the agricultural capacity to make food a major component of their aid effort.

Finally, a sense of the net flow of food aid over time from the various donors may be gathered from tables 4.3 and 4.4. The trends inherent in this data offer interesting observations on the overall functioning of the system. First, as might be expected, there is a general pattern of rising contributions among all non-US donors. In some cases, however, there have also been substantial fluctuations in annual programming. For many of these donors the food aid contribution is made partly in the form of cash grants with which to purchase food elsewhere. As a result, during periods of fiscal austerity of balance of payments difficulties, food aid contributions may be among the first programs to be cut back. This suggests a fundamental distinction between donors who give food aid on the basis of available commodity surpluses (and/or their ability to produce needed commodities) and donors who are net food importers but who give aid on the basis of their perceived moral, economic, or political obligations as developed nations.

A second set of observations arising from the data is that, whereas the cash contributions from various donors increased fairly steadily over the ten-year period covered in table 4.3, the portion of the same period (1969–1977) included in table 4.3 (which concerns physical quantities of cereal[1] food aid) reveals a generally *declining* trend. Although the data in the tables do not represent an identical set of donors (one is drawn from OECD data and the other from the United Nations), there is sufficient congruence to validate the evidence observed.

The data indicate that between 1969 and 1977, total dollar contributions from all sources increased from $1,174 million in 1969 to $2,015 million in 1977. This apparent growth (in current dollars) of food aid resources includes some increases in contributions from Australia, Canada, France, Germany, Sweden, and the United Kingdom which came as a result of a major upward movement of world food prices during the 1972–1974 period. Yet, during this same period, the total volume of cereal aid was declining precipitously, reaching its nadir in the food-short year of 1973–1974 at 5.8 million tons before rising to 9.2 million tons in 1976–1977.[2] Thus, a 41-percent increase in dollar aid resources was accompanied by a *decrease* of more than 36 percent in the physical quantities of the most common type of food aid, cereal grains. Most of this seeming paradox may be attributed to the ravages of worldwide

Table 4.3
Total Bilateral and Multilateral Food Aid Contributions from DAC Countries, Net Disbursements: 1967–1977 (Millions of US Dollars)[a]

Countries	1967	1968	1969	1970	1971	1972	1973	1974	1975	1976	1977
Australia	15.6	8.8	15.1	20.9	12.6	18.5	19.6	75.2	61.0	35.8	24.2
Austria	1.0	0.6	0.5	0.5	0.7	0.8	(0.8)	0.6	1.1	1.1	1.9
Belgium	0.2	0.2	3.8	4.7	7.5	11.1	16.0	(28.3)	28.7	18.5	23.4
Canada	86.4	63.1	60.2	99.2	88.5	87.8	95.9	142.5	263.3	189.6	184.9
Denmark	1.6	2.5	9.4	6.7	7.3	8.0	13.9	20.9	20.0	22.5	28.6
Finland	NA[b]	NA	NA	NA	NA	NA	NA	NA	7.8	10.0	7.5
France	1.0	1.0	21.2	26.3	34.0	32.5	66.0	105.8	83.7	50.2	51.8
Germany	3.2	3.2	25.7	33.5	49.9	44.5	91.9	144.4	131.4	90.5	132.2
Italy	1.0	0.5	23.7	29.6	31.1	20.4	29.6	47.6	45.1	20.0	45.6
Japan	0.5	0.5	55.3	100.0	134.2	34.6	105.8	74.0	15.3	8.1	15.5
Netherlands	0.9	0.1	13.8	17.1	15.7	20.3	33.0	47.8	44.5	45.8	64.8
New Zealand	NA	NA	NA	NA	NA	NA	(1.2)	1.6	6.0	2.7	1.3
Norway	1.2	8.5	6.3	7.2	4.8	2.5	3.9	8.0	7.6	14.0	19.5
Sweden	2.9	4.2	8.0	7.4	9.4	6.6	11.2	35.2	75.4	25.0	38.5
Switzerland	1.3	4.1	6.8	6.4	4.1	7.6	8.5	10.0	12.5	13.7	16.5
United Kingdom	1.0	1.9	17.4	16.0	17.3	2.7	14.3	58.2	60.0	33.3	46.7
United States	1,007.0	1,060.0	907.0	888.0	800.0	978.0	618.0	(728.0)	1,361.0	1,288.0	1,312.0
Total DAC	1,124.8	1,159.2	1,174.0	1,257.3	1,217.1	1,276.0	1,129.7	1,502.5	2,224.4	1,868.2	2,014.5

Sources: OECD (1974, p. 90), OECD (1975, pp. 204–205), and OECD (1978, p. 202–203).
a. DAC figures: figures in brackets Secretariat's estimates.
b. Not available.

Table 4.4
Food Aid in Cereals from All Sources (Thousands of Tons)[a,b]

	1969/70	1970/71	1971/72	1972/73	1973/74	1974/75	1975/76	1976/77
Argentina	27	10	13	2	10	20	–	23
Australia	216	235	193	143	330	319	268	231
Canada	663	1,608	605	712	499	728	1,123	1,516
EEC	1,356	983	917	896	1,219	1,420	1,021	1,287
Finland	15	13	–	25	17	24	33	33
Japan	395	753	731	528	435	300	56	46
Norway	14	9	8	–	–	–	10	10
Sweden	38	65	8	56	45	263	65	122
Switzerland[c]	35	45	27	21	33	29	35	32
United States[d]	10,008	8,927	8,993	6,704	2,983	4,576	4,154[e]	–
Algeria	–	–	–	–	–	18[c]	–	6,197
Iraq	–	–	–	–	–	283[c]	–	–
Others[f]	–	10	291	547	311	390	126	137
Total	12,767	12,658	11,786	9,634	5,882[g]	8,370	6,891	9,244

Sources: WFC (1977, p. 3) and WFC (1979, p. 4).

a. FAO figures.
b. Figures relate to shipments during July–June for the period 1969/70–1976/77.
c. Quantities estimated from cash contributions.
d. Includes wheat and coarse grains products in grain equivalent, but does not include grain equivalent of blended foods.
e. Food aid in cereals for the period 1 July 1975 to 30 June 1976. Does not include US shipments for the "transitional quarter" (1 July to 30 September 1976), which amounted to 2.1 million tons of cereals.
f. Includes triangular transactions in rice, occasional food aid from various countries on a calendar year basis, and food aid provided through the United Nations Emergency Operation (UNEO) in 1974/75, and 1975/76 and by Saudi Arabia in 1975/76 and 1976/77 through cash contributions to the World Food Programme.
g. Excluding the Soviet Union food aid loan of 2 million tons of wheat to India, repayable in kind.

inflation, meaning that cash contributions from donors simply bought less food each year.

These conflicting trends were also the result of the powerful complex of market forces at work during this period which magnified the inflationary pressure. Specifically, when the poor harvests and other food source failures occurred during 1972–1974, the market value of food exports (notably food grains and rice) soared. The resulting impact on fixed line item budgets for food aid (by means of which the food was to be purchased) was devastating.

Finally, one general set of observations may be noted. Table 4.4, which includes all donor nations belonging to the United Nations, reveals a fact not evident in table 4.3, which contains only the data on OECD countries, namely, since the 1972–1974 crisis period, a number of *new* donors have appeared on the global scene. For example, certain OPEC nations such as Algeria, Iraq, and Saudi Arabia have begun to provide limited amounts of capital loans and grants, on a strictly ad hoc basis, for the purchase of food aid.

It should be pointed out that this analysis does not deal with food aid provided by countries which are considered in economic terms to be "less developed." Argentina is the prime example, having provided an average of 15,000 tons of cereal food aid annually between 1969 and 1977. Moreover, food aid offered irregularly and in limited quantities by the Soviet Union and other centrally planned economies has not been included or analyzed here, primarily due to the fact that data on aid from these sources are not readily available. Food allocations from the Communist countries have also tended to be too unpredictable and infrequent to form any basis for useful comparison.

CANADIAN FOOD AID

Canada has been providing food aid since the early 1950s, making its program one of the oldest next to that of the United States. Canada presently ranks third behind the United States and the combined program of the EEC in terms of total volume of aid committed. The factors that motivated the Canadian program were similar in many respects to those present in the US context since the problems of Canadian agriculture often parallel its larger neighbor to the south on a reduced scale. Thus, the need to move surplus agricultural commodities (particularly wheat) in the years following World War II largely motivated early Canadian initiatives.

More recently, Canada has redirected the focus of its food aid programming through the Canadian International Development Agency
(CIDA) in order to respond more effectively to the overall development
needs of recipient countries. The majority of Canadian food aid is bilateral,[3] while approximately 16–22 percent of the aid was directed through
multilateral channels in 1970–1974. During 1975 and 1976, however,
good harvests changed this situation dramatically: according to World
Food Council data, Canadian multilateral contributions rose to 44.8 percent of its total food aid effort.

In terms of geographic distribution, Canadian bilateral aid has a demonstrated concentration on countries in Asia, particularly Bangladesh
(which alone received fully 40 percent of Canadian bilateral aid in 1973),
Pakistan, and Indonesia. Since Canada does not have any past history
as a colonial power, the limited geographic distribution of its aid may be
accounted for by the country's association with the British Common-
wealth and also by an apparent government policy of focusing Canadian
resources where they might be utilized most effectively relative to the
aggregate level of food deficits. There is virtually no evidence that Canadian food aid has been allocated for political purposes, although there
may well be some relationship between the recipients of its bilateral assistance and the countries which are the focus of Canadian international
trade interests.

Canada currently lists three primary objectives for its food aid program: (1) improve nutrition; (2) facilitate economic and social development; and (3) provide emergency relief [CFA (1977, p. 10)]. All Canadian assistance is given in grant form (i.e., none is sold on concessional
credit terms as in the United States). Canada is obligated to supply
495,000 tons of wheat and flour under the Food Aid Convention (FAC)
of 1974, and it is also a major contributor to the UN–FAO World Food
Programme.

AUSTRALIAN FOOD AID

Food aid has played a role in Australia's overseas assistance programs
since its early involvement in the Colombo Plan, under which it made
contributions of wheat and flour to Sri Lanka, India, and Pakistan.
Given the country's geographic location, it is hardly surprising that the
bulk of Australian food aid has been directed toward recipient countries
in Asia and Oceania.

Since 1967, Australia has been committed under the FAC to provide a minimum annual contribution of 225,000 tons of wheat and flour. The vast majority of the aid (96.5 percent) has moved through bilateral channels, although Australia has been a steady and reliable contributor to the WFP since its creation (providing 2.8 percent of its total food aid since 1974).[4] The food is provided on straight grant terms, and it is directed primarily toward satisfying nutritional needs and providing emergency relief. It is significant that since reaching a peak of $75.2 million in the food-short year of 1974, Australian food aid has declined steadily.

JAPANESE FOOD AID

Despite the fact that Japan is one of the world's largest net agricultural importers, advances in production technology and shifting domestic consumption patterns since 1967 have resulted in an annual rice surplus of about 2 million tons. By 1970, this surplus accumulation had reached 7.2 million tons (which is about two-thirds of Japan's average domestic consumption), motivating the government to enact legislation that permitted the sale of rice to foreign governments on concessional terms. It is interesting to note the similarities between the Japanese and American programs. Like the United States, Japan's program has been motivated to a limited degree by the need to dispose of agricultural surpluses. Japan is also the only country other than the United States to offer a portion of its food on concessional credit terms rather than as outright grants.

As a result of the 1970 legislation, Japan became a major bilateral donor with net disbursements over the period of 1969–1974 totaling $503 million,[5] including $427 million of bilateral concessional credit loans for the purchase of Japanese rice. In 1974, Japan gave only 18.9 percent of its food aid on grant terms, although the government has apparently shifted all food aid onto a grant basis since 1975. Aid offered on a concessional credit basis has consisted of loans repayable either in kind or in currency with soft terms of thirty years maturity, ten years grace period, and interest rates ranging from 2 to 3 percent per year [CFA (1977, p. 10)].

Prior to the buildup of surplus rice stocks, Japan's food aid contributions had been rather modest and were channeled primarily through the WFP. Japan's multilateral pledge has been rising steadily, however, and it represented approximately 33 percent of its total food aid in 1977. Japan is also a signatory to the FACs of 1967 and 1971, under which it has pledged 225,000 tons of cereal aid or its cash equivalent.[6]

As an island nation, Japan has always emphasized the need for agricultural self-sufficiency. Likewise, the Japanese government has taken the view that LDC food problems are better handled through direct aid to increase domestic production rather than through food aid. Some critics have claimed that this policy is merely a means by which Japan can avoid carrying its full, proportionate share of the aid burden.[7] But the Japanese have set up an International Cooperation Corporation for LDC agricultural development, placing special emphasis on ensuring that what food aid they do provide neither acts as a disincentive to indigenous LDC agricultural production nor competes in traditional LDC export markets.

BRITISH FOOD AID

British efforts to respond to world food needs have been hampered by the fact that, like Japan, it is an island nation and a net food importer. It would be possible for Britain to overcome this fact by donating cash (along with a limited amount of commodities) as Japan does, except for the serious deterioration of the British economy and its international balance of payments. In spite of its problems, the United Kingdom became a signatory to the first FAC, pledging contributions equivalent in cash value to 225,000 metric tons of wheat annually for three years.[8] But at the expiration of the first FAC, Britain's skepticism concerning the impact of food aid on recipient country agriculture, plus the ever worsening condition of its economy, apparently caused it to withdraw from the second FAC in 1971. Upon gaining admission to the European Common Market in 1973, however, Britain automatically resumed its FAC food aid commitment.

British food aid has normally been in the form of cash which is then used to purchase wheat from other exporting countries. Before joining the EEC (under whose regulations triangular transactions are not permitted), Britain had made at least one attempt to use its cash to purchase its grain commitment from Argentina, a developing country food exporter. Surprisingly, British bilateral food is *not* concentrated geographically among its former colonial possessions nearly to the degree of French or Belgian aid. Significant amounts of food assistance were given to India and Ceylon between 1969 and 1971, but the level of aid to these countries has since diminished.

Until Britain joined the EEC in 1972, its multilateral food aid consisted solely of contributions to the WFP. British pledges to the multilateral program reached a peak between 1966 and 1968 at $6.2 million and then declined as a result of the government's displeasure over the difficulties encountered by the UN agency in calling forward the donor pledges. More recently, UK pledges to the WFP have increased once again to a level of $6.3 million for 1973–1974. For 1976, the WFP reported that it received 85.8 percent of the total British food aid contribution [CFA (1977, p. 13)].

FRENCH FOOD AID

France did not maintain a separate food aid program until 1968, preferring instead to make a rather inconsequential $1 million annual pledge to the WFP. A dramatic change in the level of French participation occurred in 1969, however—one which may not have been altogether voluntary on the part of the government.[9] In that year, the EEC countries were required to begin making food aid available under the terms of the FAC. France, as a member of the EEC, was therefore called upon to provide 320,000 tons of wheat annually, one-third to be distributed through the EEC and the other two-thirds to be allocated bilaterally. As a result, French food aid contributions increased by over $20 million in the course of a single fiscal year.

Since the initiation of the FAC, French food aid contributions have risen steadily, increasing dramatically once again in 1973 at the height of the world food "crisis" period. This doubling of resources committed to food assistance is linked directly to the fact that FAC commitments are in *volume* terms, requiring a vast increase in resources when world grain prices explode upward. Moreover, the French made major contributions to finance the cost of emergency aid to the Sahelian countries, many of which had formerly been under French domination.

The proportion of French aid moving multilaterally through EEC channels has also increased. By the 1973–1974 harvest year, French multilateral food aid accounted for about 63 percent of the country's total contributions (and by 1977, this figure had risen to 81 percent of total food aid). But, while France was expanding its involvement in EEC food aid, its contributions to the WFP were dropping sharply; since 1971, France has contributed on average only a token $100,000 per year to the UN program.

One particularly interesting aspect of French food aid is its geographic distribution. As a former colonial power, France continues to maintain a certain sphere of political and economic influence among French speaking countries, primarily in Africa, which is known commonly as a "franc zone." Prior to 1971, a majority of French bilateral food aid actually went to countries *outside* the franc zone, since the government at that time viewed such aid as one means of achieving better geographic distribution of its assistance. After the commencement of joint EEC food aid, however, when the French multilateral food aid commitment had increased to the point where the government no longer controlled the decision as to the destination of a majority of its food resources, the emphasis in its bilateral program was shifted consciously in favor of the franc zone countries—particularly in the Sahelian region.

WEST GERMAN FOOD AID

German food assistance demonstrates certain similarities and contrasts to that of its western neighbor, France. Like France, West German food aid prior to the FAC of 1967 consisted largely of multilateral contributions through the WFP, averaging $2.7 million per year between 1965 and 1968.[10] After accession to the FAC, Germany's average annual bilateral aid increased by over $14 million and multilateral food assistance by almost $20 million. This strong upward trend continued through 1974 and resulted in a further 400 percent increase in total resources over the 1969–1971 period. Since 1975, however, both forms of West German food aid gradually have been declining.

Since Germany no longer maintains a zone of overseas influence similar to that of France or Britain (although its international economic influence is nevertheless extensive), its bilateral contributions, although heavily concentrated, have been widely dispersed geographically, involving Bangladesh, Sri Lanka, Indonesia, Chile, and Egypt. From 1972 to 1974 approximately two-thirds of German food aid was distributed multilaterally, in line with the general EEC policy of increasing the proportion of European food aid given jointly (see later section of this chapter on the EEC program).

One particular feature of German aid is rather unique among donor nations. In response to recent changes in the conceptualization of food aid for development, donors have been urged to participate in "triangular transactions" whereby cash is provided by the developed country donor to purchase food commodities in a less developed agricultural exporting nation, such as Argentina, Thailand, or Brazil, for eventual shipment to a third country in need of food assistance. In 1976, the

Federal Republic of Germany purchased fully 25 percent of its aid through such triangular transactions.

DANISH FOOD AID

In contrast to the United States and most other European countries, the Danish government does not base its food aid allocations on domestic policy considerations such as surplus disposal. In fact, Denmark does not really favor the concept of food aid in general, preferring to limit its use to exceptional circumstances such as the recent Sahelian drought and famine. Where food assistance is clearly necessary, Denmark adheres to the following distributive principles: (1) aid is to be used only to bridge the gap between need and available commercial imports; (2) aid should not have an adverse impact on local production; and (3) aid should be given as project aid and should be accompanied by appropriate technical and infrastructural assistance.

Multilateralism is favored strongly over bilateral food aid distribution as a result of the firm Danish adherence to a depoliticized aid policy. In fact, Denmark actually withdrew in 1971 from the FAC, a multilateral agreement that is implemented on a bilateral basis, due to its reluctance to participate in bilateral food aid other than in acute emergencies. When Denmark joined the European Common Market in 1972, however, it was obliged in 1973 to rejoin the FAC since the EEC is a signatory.

In 1975, Denmark provided 67 percent of its aid to the WFP alone, while another 19 percent was contributed through the EEC multilateral program.[11] Denmark was thus providing fully 86 percent of its food aid multilaterally, all on a straight grant basis. As with a number of other donors we shall examine, rising world prices have meant that Danish aid buys less food, since the majority of its aid is provided in the form of a cash equivalent (i.e., not in commodities). Although this problem is not confined to Denmark, it is particularly serious because prices tend to fluctuate much more rapidly than national aid budgets are adjusted upward.

SWEDISH FOOD AID

In terms of meeting its responsibilities in the area of foreign aid, Sweden has often been referred to as "the conscience of the West."[12] Likewise, in terms of food aid, Sweden has been a reliable and generous contributor relative to its available resources. It favors especially the World Food Programme as the channel for the majority of its aid. With the exception of the years 1972 and 1974, virtually all of Swedish food has moved multilaterally, with approximately 60 percent allocated to the WFP alone.[13] During the 1972–1974 "crisis" period, Sweden did make a sizable amount of aid available on a bilateral basis, but it has not done so again. In 1973, Sweden created a grain fund to be administered by the Swedish International Development Agency (SIDA) for relief programs in famine areas. Sweden also participates in the FAC, but it channels its aid commitment under the convention through the WFP.

Like Denmark, Sweden seeks consciously to avoid politicization of its food aid. Sweden also shares the Danish concern that food aid should not act as a disincentive to local LDC production. In many respects, the Swedish food aid effort stands as a model for other donors: it has been generous with its cash contributions; it offers all of its aid on a straight grant basis; and it was among the first of the developed countries to set aside a portion of its agricultural output for use by the WFP in its emergency food reserve scheme.[14]

NORWEGIAN FOOD AID

Norway's food aid program, although small relative to that of the United States and certain other donors, presents some interesting and unique factors.[15] As a result of parliamentary debate, a special government committee was established in 1970 to study the entire issue of Norwegian participation in food assistance. Previous parliamentary action in 1966 and 1967 had emphasized Norway's commitment to reduce world food shortages and to utilize its fishery resources toward this end. But in 1970 two new principles were accepted by the government: (1) Norwegian food aid policy henceforth was no longer to be based on surplus disposal considerations or the objective of keeping the nation's fishing industry fully employed; and (2) Norwegian food aid was to be channeled multilaterally through the WFP, except in limited emergency situations [OECD (1974, p. 62)].

The result of this change in policy was that, as of 1971, Norway virtually discontinued its bilateral food aid programming and began to concentrate its efforts primarily on multilateral aid channeled through the WFP. In addition, Norway withdrew as a signatory to the FAC at the expiration of the first agreement in 1970. While the new policy no doubt encouraged greater attention to the developmental impact of

Norwegian food aid, no attempt was made until 1976 to compensate for the reduction in the country's bilateral contributions through concomitant increase in multilateral giving. But total Norwegian food aid in 1977 was triple that of 1975.

OTHER BILATERAL DONORS

We now turn attention briefly to the food aid programs of four additional European donors, Switzerland, Italy, Belgium, and the Netherlands, whose individual efforts are insignificant in comparison to that of the United States or Canada, but which nevertheless present some noteworthy features.[16] In the interest of brevity, however, the four programs shall be dealt with collectively.

Two features of the *Swiss* program merit special attention. First, unlike a number of other national programs mentioned previously, Switzerland has *not* abandoned its policy emphasis on surplus disposal. With a continuing surplus of dairy products, Switzerland has maintained a "dairy credit" within the federal budget in order to finance and promote the distribution of these agricultural products. Second, more than half of Swiss food aid still retains a distinctively humanitarian orientation, being targeted for emergency relief in natural or manmade disasters. Although the government has tried increasingly since 1968 to link food aid with development, such project-linked aid accounted only for 7 percent of Swiss food assistance in 1973.

Italy, on the other hand, is a net importer of food commodities. As a result, until the government acceded to the FAC of 1967, there was no bilateral food aid program to speak of. Italy's food aid involvement between 1963 and 1969 consisted solely of cash pledges through the WFP (which happens also to be headquartered in Rome). After 1969, Italy did begin to provide limited bilateral cereal aid as well as a few special loans to permit developing countries to purchase wheat on Italian markets. Italy's most significant food contribution, however, continues to be multilateral under the auspices of the EEC Community Food Aid Program.

Belgian food aid prior to 1969 consisted almost exclusively of cash contributions to the WFP; since then, its food aid commitments have increased substantially from $3.8 million to $28.3 million in 1974. What limited bilateral food aid Belgium does provide is directed specifically to countries with which it has special relations, either due to their former colonial status (e.g., Zaire, Rwanda and Burundi) or as the result of preexisting technical assistance agreements (e.g., Tunisia, Indonesia, Peru, or Chile). All Belgian aid is provided in purely grant form, and the government has indicated a preference for using its aid to assist countries suffering from balance of payments difficulties.

Even though the *Netherlands* has been a modest food exporter in recent years, its food aid program, like most of its other EEC partners, did not really commence on any significant scale until its accession to the FAC of 1967. The most notable feature of the Dutch program is the aid supplied via international private voluntary agencies through the government's cofinancing provisions. Under this scheme, the Dutch government will match—usually on a 75:25 basis—aid given for specific projects carried out by private voluntary agencies in the LDCs. The aid is normally supplied in the form of food commodities, which amounted to $1.9 million in 1973 and was used in projects in twenty different countries.

THE EUROPEAN ECONOMIC COMMUNITY PROGRAM

We come, finally, to the food aid program operated under the auspices of the Commission of the European Communities (CEC) on behalf of the nine member states of the European Economic Community (EEC), or Common Market. This program is unique in certain respects. It combines certain characteristics of a multilateral program such as the WFP (since the food commodities and/or cash are contributed by the member countries to a community budget and distributed according to policy guidelines also agreed upon jointly) with a capacity to function bilaterally outside of the European context, either by allocating EEC aid through *other* multilateral institutions such as the WFP and private international charitable organizations such as the International League of Red Cross Societies, or by offering the aid on behalf of the EEC directly to a recipient country in a manner similar to any other bilateral donor. In this sense, the CEC food aid program operated for the European countries is *both* bilateral and multilateral, depending on the frame of reference in which it is considered.

Noncereal food aid from the European Community historically has been a function of the continuing agricultural surpluses in Europe which have centered on particular products—most notably milk powder and butter oil. The existence of these surpluses is in itself significant, considering the fact that, in the aggregate, Europe is a net food importer. The origin of these commodity-specific agricultural surpluses can be traced to the historic Treaty of Rome in 1957 which created the EEC and which first stressed the need for a common agricultural policy (CAP) for the member nations.

At that time, the production policies of the European countries were widely divergent; but, in 1958, the treaty signatories convened at the so-called Stresa Conference in order to define the governing principles of the new CAP. A first draft of the policy was presented subsequently to the EEC Council of Ministers at the end of 1959, and final proposals were put forward to that body in June 1960. The council rejected certain aspects of the plan as overly ambitious and unworkable, but it ultimately accepted a CAP with three principal features: (1) *market and price policies*—which enabled agricultural produce to move freely throughout the EEC and which included a variable price levy. The levy, considered generally to be the root cause of EEC surpluses, is attached to foreign imports when world prices are below those of the EEC countries, and it is reversed if world market prices should remain above those of the Common Market. Because the latter situation has most often prevailed, European farmers have, in effect, been supported to produce commodities for which there is often no existing commercial market; (2) *external relations*—which concern the relationship of EEC agricultural production to international trade and aid both with developed and less developed countries. This aspect of the CAP provided the initial policy foundation for the creation of the food aid program; and (3) *structural issues*—which concern the attainment of a certain level of structural efficiency in agriculture between and among the member states.[17]

One of the principal results of the CAP, affecting the development of the EEC's food aid program, has been the existence of persistent surpluses of dairy products. In January 1970, the EEC variable price levy protection policy had resulted in a dairy product surplus of over 40,000 tons. As a result, the commission embarked upon an ambitious $900 million program, not too dissimilar to the original motivation for the US PL 480 program, designed to reduce its surplus stock levels by subsidizing commodity exports both in trade and as aid.

It is apparent that this overhanging surplus burden has been direct motivation for the expansion of EEC dairy-related food aid. But the policy formulated to relieve the surplus pressure has also made the EEC vulnerable to criticism that the composition of its food aid tends to shift in relation to whatever particular dairy commodity happens to be in oversupply at the time. Thus, in many respects, EEC food assistance policy—like that of the United States—has been developed more in response to the needs of its own agricultural producers than in order to meet the particular *food* needs of recipients.

Early European food aid contributions were very much an ad hoc affair, being solely dependent on the periodic contributions of the member states (i.e., those with surpluses of a particular commodity). A good indication of the surplus disposal orientation of the early EEC food aid effort is that, when a formal institutional food aid mechanism was created in order to meet the EEC's responsibilities under the FAC of 1967, the Agriculture Directorate of the Commission of the European Communities (CEC)—rather than the Development Directorate—was assigned responsibility for the program. As the concept of food aid gradually evolved away from straight surplus dumping toward the use of aid as an instrument of economic development, administration of the program has been shifted increasingly to the commission's Development Directorate.

Food aid programmed through the CEC is delivered both bilaterally and multilaterally.[18] In the case of bilateral assistance, the commission determines how its available supplies may best be allocated among requesting countries, and it then presents a formal proposal to the EEC Council of Ministers. Once the proposal is approved, a determination is made as to what proportion of the aid will be available through the CEC versus the proportion which must be supplied (if necessary) by the member states. All assistance is donated as outright grants, with a portion used directly for emergency and nutritional feeding purposes and the remainder used in a manner so as to promote the generation of local currency for nonstrategic (i.e., nonmilitary) development purposes. In 1976, 81 percent of CEC food aid was reportedly allocated to six of the "most seriously affected" countries and to the nations of Southeast Asia.[19]

Multilateral food aid offered by the CEC is channeled through a variety of mechanisms, including the WFP, UNRWA, UNICEF, and the International League of Red Cross Societies. Officials of the WFP have, on occasion, expressed a certain degree of frustration that the UN program does not receive a larger proportion of the EEC multilateral food aid allocation. The WFP has also been displeased by the fact that the CEC has frequently been as much as six months to a year late in delivering a commodity pledge.

In management terms, the problem of providing an adequate and efficient "call forward" of pledged aid, whereby the CEC may obtain in a timely fashion the volume of commodities to which each member state is committed, is probably the single most serious issue facing the EEC food aid program. Because the individual countries view their dairy aid contributions directly in relation to their current surplus stocks, they are unwilling to meet their commitments until after the full extent of the surplus is known. Consequently, the CEC has encountered serious and continuing delays in gaining access to commodities from the member states, commodities which the CEC, in turn, has already committed as aid.

At the other end of the pipeline, WFP operations officials have indicated that, due to these chronic call forward problems experienced by the CEC, it (the WFP) is unable to count on the availability of the EEC's food aid pledge for the first six months of any given operating year.[20] CEC officials, however, have expressed doubts of their own about the allocation criteria and managerial effectiveness of the WFP, and they have noted also that the other policy objected to by the WFP (i.e., EEC contributions to the *other* multilateral agencies) represents long-standing commitments that predate even the existence of CEC itself.[21] On the whole, it would appear that, on the basis of the difficulties so far encountered, the multilateral component of the EEC aid effort is unlikely to be expanded significantly in the foreseeable future.

Under the FAC of 1967, the EEC agreed to provide 1,035,000 metric tons of cereal grains per year as food aid. In fact, had it not been for the FAC, EEC food aid would more than likely have been confined to the provision of surplus dairy products on an ad hoc basis.[22] Until 1970, food assistance did continue to be financed by special contributions from member states, but it has come subsequently from the joint budget of the CEC. With the enlargement of the Common Market in the early seventies, the EEC cereal pledge under the 1971 FAC was expanded to 1,161,000 metric tons in 1972–1973 and to 1,287,000 metric tons in 1973–1974. Thus between 1968 and 1975, the EEC granted almost 1.4 billion ua (in 1975 EEC units of account were convertible into dollars at 1 ua = $1.30) as food aid to the Third World countries [CEC (1977, p. 14)].

EEC food aid[23] is distributed according to three principal objectives: operations for emergency assistance; operations to improve nutritional standards; and operations to promote economic development. Development criteria are further elaborated in terms of the recipient country's per capita income (average per capita not to exceed $520 per annum), prevailing food deficit, and overall balance of payments position. The use of that portion of European food aid flowing via the individual donor countries is, of course, up to the government of each nation.

However, the proportion of aid distributed multilaterally through the CEC (and thereby subject to the criteria suggested above), has grown from 30 percent of total European aid in 1973 to 44 percent in 1974 and now approaches 55 percent of total food aid given by the European countries.[24] While it is unlikely that the CEC will ever be responsible for all of the available food resources (since France and Germany—among other member states—continue to use a portion of their food aid for political and trade promotion purposes), the fact that the majority of the resources now flow jointly through the commission assures a certain degree of uniformity in EEC food aid programming.

Since 1974, the EEC has, according to its stated policy at least, been committed to a major reorientation of its food aid programming aimed at increasing its developmental impact. The reality of the situation, however, is that most of the recommendations presented in recent EEC policy documents,[25] and accepted by the EEC Council of Ministers, have bogged down consistently in negotiations between the CEC and the member states. As a result, little of substance has actually changed regarding either the manner in which EEC food aid is allocated or the total volume of the EEC's commitment. Thus, four common criticisms concerning EEC food aid remain generally accurate as of 1977:

1. Its modest size in relation to food aid requirements of the developing world, to food aid programs financed by other developed countries, and to the per capita GNP of the member states.
2. Its excessive dependence on surplus agricultural commodities—particularly dairy products—generated by the unrealistic pricing policies of the EEC Common Agricultural Policy.
3. Its lack of advance supply commitments, with the resulting difficulties for medium-term planning of supplies in the EEC and for their integration in the development policies and plans of the recipient countries.
4. Its serious management difficulties occurring between the CEC and the member governments which often result in major delays in calling forward aid commodities previously committed by the EEC. This problem is especially acute with regard to EEC pledges to the WFP.[26]

The principal argument which may be marshaled in rebuttal to this critique is the basic fact that, as a result of EEC commitments to succeeding FACs, total European food aid levels have increased so substantially since 1967 that the EEC is now the second-largest overall donor of international food assistance. There is also recent evidence of new thinking within the CEC itself concerning the proper uses of food aid, particularly in the context of development. In a food-short world, it is always easy to criticize nations (or groups of nations) for not giving enough or for giving for the wrong reasons (e.g., for surplus disposal). But the fact remains that EEC food aid has represented a net addition to the absolute amount of food assistance available worldwide, and this addition has been effected under difficult and ambiguous circumstances of pluralistic allocation and control.

CONCLUSIONS

This chapter has considered the bilateral food aid initiatives that have been undertaken by market-oriented, developed countries other than the United States—essentially, the other nations which constitute the OECD. Certain fundamental characteristics and trends in bilateral food aid become apparent from the evidence considered here. Clearly, the most basic distinction is between nations which are *net agricultural exporters*, who simply earmark food aid as one component of stocks in excess of domestic requirements (i.e., stocks used for carry-over, commercial export, etc.) versus nations which are *net agricultural importers*, who generally must allocate capital resources for the purchase of commodities from the former group.

Net importers, of necessity, base their decisions on the nature and volume of their food aid contributions on a different set of factors than do net exporters. In fact, it may be useful to divide further the exporting donors between those few nations (perhaps only the United States and Canada, and very recently the EEC) which produce agricultural commodities in such abundance that they have been concerned with the matter of surplus disposal and those nations (generally the individual European countries, Australia, and Japan) that produce limited volumes of food for export for which, under normal circumstances, there is a ready foreign commercial market. It is possible, on this basis, to identify three distinct but overlapping motivational constellations for donor participation in food aid.

The basic reasons why large food exporting countries such as the United States or Canada give food as aid have already been considered at length in chapters 1 through 3. There is little argument over the fact that the massive surpluses of the fifties and early sixties conditioned a view of food aid as primarily a commodity dumping operation. Food was available; it was a relatively "free good" in terms of its shadow cost of the donor, and it produced useful secondary results related to an improvement in the donor's foreign image. The surplus disposal rationale remained in effect until the midsixties, when a number of factors combined to change the policies of the large donors to conform more closely to those of the small food exporters.

Besides the reduction in the large volumes of surplus stocks held at government expense in the United States, another major new factor in 1967 was the creation of the Food Aid Convention as part of the International Grains Agreement (see chapter 5). As suggested previously, accession by a number of the donor countries to the FAC marked a fundamental alteration in the volume of their food aid commitments. For the large exporters—in this sense, really just the United States—the existence of the FAC meant that the long-sought goal of wider international aid burden-sharing had finally begun to be realized.

The smaller agricultural exporters derived a different set of benefits from the creation of the FAC, benefits which nevertheless provided them with a solid reason for participating in foreign food assistance. Many of the smaller exporters had long been supplying aid on an ad hoc basis, as their resources permitted, in response to specific food shortage situations. From the substantial size of the aid increases that many of these donors accepted under the FAC, however, it may be deduced that the added burden was considered to be a *quid pro quo* for other trade-related concessions contained in the International Grains Agreement (of which the FAC was only one component). Many of the smaller net exporting countries were particularly interested in the protocols that sought to normalize certain critical supply and price features of the international grain trade. Thus, in the process of acceding to the (not insignificant) pressures from the large exporters—and from the developing world as well—for a more significant commitment to provide a greater share of food aid commodities, the other agricultural exporters also sought to gain a greater measure of economic security in the form of an assured capacity to sell their agricultural produce (in this case, grain) on world markets.

Lastly, there are the motivations of the net food *importing* donor countries such as Italy or Great Britain. In this case as well, the negotiations of the International Grains Agreement had a significant influence, although here in the larger context of international trade. Since the net importers had little choice but to provide food aid in the form of cash with which to purchase the commodities from agricultural exporters, it cannot be stated that the aid in this case was being used as a bargaining chip for other, agricultural-related concessions. However, if the International Grains Agreement is viewed as only one part of the Kennedy Round negotiations under the General Agreement on Tariffs and Trade (GATT), then it may be argued that the importers *also* had a secondary bargaining agenda for their participation in the FAC.

Many of the nations in the importer category had, of course, long and respectable traditions of involvement and concern for the provision of foreign aid of all kinds (Britain is an especially good example). But it is also true that, if the wider range of international trade issues under negotiation in the Kennedy Round are included, most (if not all) of the food importing countries then become medium-to-large net *exporters*. It is thus plausible to suggest, particularly in view of the substantial cash contributions pledged by these countries, that a major motivation for the food importers in accepting this added burden on their international balance of payments may have been identified at least as much with the desire to improve their bargaining position regarding other trade and tariff issues as with a laudable but less likely shift in their foreign aid policies for purely altruistic reasons.

It should also be noted that many of the European food exporting and importing countries became party to the 1967 FAC more or less automatically as a result of their membership in the EEC. Once again, the larger array of economic benefits to be derived from participation in the Common Market overrode the disadvantages of the increased food aid commitment. (Britain is again an excellent example: the United Kingdom had actually withdrawn after the termination of the first FAC, but the powerful incentive of membership in the EEC caused it to reverse its policy after 1973). Thus, it is reasonable to conclude that, with the notable exception of the Scandinavian food aid programs in which altruism is truly a major motivating factor, much of the increased participation among non-US bilateral food aid donors may be explained in terms of the collateral economic benefits that they were able to capture in return for a rather inconsequential investment.

Lest the reader be misinformed, however, it should be emphasized that *all* bilateral food aid programs considered here have contained a strong and enduring element of altruism as well. Furthermore, whatever the ultimate nature of a donor's reasons for increasing its food aid contributions, the assistance nevertheless represents, in absolute terms, a net addition to the volume of aid previously available and a wider commitment by the developed countries toward meeting the urgent human needs of the developing world.

ANTECEDENTS TO MULTILATERAL FOOD AID

Two events occurred in 1943, at the height of World War II, which marked the beginning of modern multilateral food aid. The first was a conference convened by President Franklin D. Roosevelt at Hot Springs, Virginia, that laid the conceptual foundation for the establishment of the Food and Agriculture Organization (FAO) shortly thereafter. The second was an agreement signed in Washington, DC, in November of the same year which created the United Nations Relief and Rehabilitation Administration (UNRRA) to provide and administer a variety of different relief measures—including food—for the destitute populations of Europe. But the UNRRA program fell victim to the titanic ideological struggle that raged across Europe after the war, and the United States, as principal donor, became increasingly disillusioned with the overt efforts by the Communist bloc to influence the allocation of UNRRA aid for political purposes.

The United States objected particularly to the fact that it did not have a weighted vote in UNRRA proportionate to the $1.25 billion in food aid which it was responsible for providing. The United States also objected to the fact that the food was to be sold by recipient governments, rather than distributed free to needy individuals, with little guarantee that it would ever reach the millions of Europeans left destitute by the war. The government eventually came to believe in fact that it could obtain a more substantial political and humanitarian impact through the bilateral allocation of its food resources, and its participation in UNRRA program was therefore terminated in 1947. A small, supplementary food distribution scheme, financed by remaining UNRRA funds and by voluntary contributions from individuals and governments, was continued on a limited scale, but the year 1947 essentially marked the end of multilateral food aid until the early 1960s, when the concept was resurrected.

This is not meant to suggest that no new programmatic initiatives were proposed at this time. On the contrary, the Hot Springs Conference convened by Roosevelt was followed by an organizational meeting in San Francisco in 1945 which established the working mechanisms of the FAO. The founding meeting of the new institution was held in Quebec, Canada, that same year, where the respected agricultural expert Sir John Boyd-Orr was elected as the organization's first Director-General. At the first annual FAO conference, held in Copenhagen in 1946, the matter of multilateral action on food commodity supply issues was raised directly by Boyd-Orr. The concept was also strongly endorsed at the meeting by the outgoing Director-General of (the soon-to-be-terminated) UNRRA, Fiorello LaGuardia, who delivered an impassioned plea for the creation of a world food board or some other international commodity supply scheme.

Boyd-Orr's formal proposal was for the establishment of a World Food Board (WFB), which would unify some of the work of the FAO, the Economic and Social Council, and the World Bank.[1] Boyd-Orr recommended that the board be financed by governments diverting a greater portion of their current bilateral aid resources through the United Nations, a feature which later caused President Truman to withdraw US support.[2] Without the backing of the United States, the concept was clearly doomed, and a commission established to study the proposal recommended subsequently that an FAO Food Council[3] be created instead.

But the idea of a multilateral commodity mechanism was raised again at the 1947 and 1948 meetings of the International Federation of Agricultural Producers (IFAP), where resolutions were adopted calling for further study of the matter. The second FAO Director-General, Norris Dodd, was invited to attend the 1949 IFAP meeting in Canada in order to discuss the matter once again. The result was the creation of a *new* FAO study commission, which proposed the establishment of an International Commodity Clearinghouse (ICCH). The ICCH concept met with favorable reaction on the part of the US agricultural community, but it failed significantly to gain the support of Secretary of Agriculture Charles Brannan. The matter was again decided by President Truman, who, after some consideration, announced that he could not support the plan.

Consequently, the ICCH plan, like its predecessor, was not implemented, although a Committee on Commodity Problems was established to attempt to deal with international agricultural trade issues. It is significant from a political perspective that, in each case where the FAO membership was unable to agree upon the form or substance of a multilateral entity requiring the relinquishment of bilateral control over food resources, a new bureaucratic structure of a purely advisory and/or informational nature was created instead. These actions clearly evaded the underlying issue of multilateralism in operational areas, and ironically they also made the FAO vulnerable to charges (continuing to this day) of bureaucratic topheaviness. Moreover, as Ezekiel has remarked, "Both proposals (i.e., the WFB and the ICCH) . . . were in a sense premature. Both were based on the assumption that the chronic pressure of agricultural supplies on demand, so familiar as the 'farm problem' of the late '20s and the 'surplus problem' of the '30s, would reappear fairly promptly after World War II" [Ezekiel (1954, p. 403)].

What the FAO leadership could not know, however, was that they were essentially correct in their assumption—but their calculations were off by about four years. By 1953, however, both the United States and Canada had amassed large volumes of surplus agricultural commodities for which there was no ready market. In the United States, this situation led shortly to the enactment of the Agricultural Trade Development and Assistance Act of 1954 (PL 480), described in chapter 3. Within the international arena, it had two other effects. The first was a proposal to deal with emergency food shortages, known as the Three Circles Plan, [4] which also was not adopted by the FAO.

The second effect of the intensifying surplus crisis was the decision at the Seventh FAO Conference in 1954 to direct the FAO Committee on Commodity Problems to establish a standing subcommittee on surplus disposal to consider the best means of disposing of agricultural surpluses and safeguarding agricultural export markets. This later became the FAO Consultative Subcommittee on Surplus Disposal (CSD), which has remained the principal forum in which specific international food aid agreements are discussed (see the last section of this chapter).

Few other significant multilateral initiatives on food-related issues were proposed or undertaken during the remainder of the decade. The lack of additional action may be ascribed, in large measure, to continued US dominance of FAO and other international institutions. Seen in this context, the laissez faire agricultural policies of Secretary of Agriculture Ezra Taft Benson—and Dwight Eisenhower's own lack of interest generally in international institution building—meant that multilateral approaches to food and agricultural problems found little support in the United States.

THE UN-FAO WORLD FOOD PROGRAMME

Impetus for the creation of a new multilateral food aid program under UN auspices came from a variety of sources for which interest in wider use of agricultural surpluses had been growing since the late 1950s. But international action once again was clearly impossible without the active support and participation of the largest surplus commodity producer, the United States; and the Eisenhower administration had indicated little interest in such undertakings.

In September 1960, however, the United States introduced a resolution in the UN General Assembly calling for immediate research on the modalities for a multilateral food aid mechanism. The sudden change on American policy was motivated apparently by the need for another outlet to help reduce the steadily accumulating surplus commodities and by the desire to shed the solitary burden of responsibility for meeting the food needs of the developing world. The US proposal was referred to the UN Economic and Finance Committee of the General Assembly, which reported it favorably despite Soviet objections that the idea was "not new and, not urgent," and that there was "no need," on this basis, "to give it priority" [Peterson (1975, p. 386)].

On 20 October 1960, the General Assembly adopted a resolution calling upon the FAO "to establish without delay procedures . . . by which, with the assistance of the United Nations system, the largest practicable quantities of surplus food may be made available."[5] The FAO responded by authorizing the Director-General to undertake the study and to establish a thirteen-member advisory committee which met subsequently in Rome in April 1961. The US delegation, headed by George McGovern, made a bold and somewhat unpremeditated proposal at the meeting for a three-year, experimental program of $100 million, which was to include an initial US contribution of $40 million. In June, the study requested by the General Assembly, entitled *Development through Food* [FAO (1961)], was submitted and the entire matter was referred to the UN Economic and Social Council (ECOSOC).

On the basis of a positive action by ECOSOC, the General Assembly, and the FAO, the formation of World Food Programme was approved finally in late 1961. The General Assembly resolution reaffirmed that a joint UN–FAO cooperative effort would be undertaken on a three-year *experimental* basis with resources pledged voluntarily by member governments. The resolutions also provided for the creation of a twenty-member governing board, to be known as Intergovernmental Committee (IGC), which was to determine policy and to approve specific food aid projects. The IGC was to be elected equally by the ECOSOC and the FAO Council and to be composed equally of representatives from donor and recipient nations.

Operating principles and procedures for the World Food Programme (WFP) were drafted by the IGC in 1962. These general regulations required that assistance could be given only as so-called project grants in order not to compete with the larger program-type operations conducted by the bilateral donors. The regulations also provided a new and distinctive feature for WFP aid: delivery and management of the food was to become the sole responsibility of the *recipient* government upon its arrival at the country's port of entry. IGC decisionmaking on specific projects was to be made with no formal, weighted voting procedure such as that employed within the World Bank. This fact later became especially significant since, in the early years of the program, the United States alone provided more than half of the total resources.

The WFP's resources were to be derived solely from the voluntary biannual pledges and were to be composed ideally of one-third cash and two-thirds commodities. The initial WFP pledging conference was held in New York in 1962, and it succeeded in raising $84.6 million of the original target figure of $100 million—although almost half of the amount pledged had been committed previously by the United States.

The IGC established three basic priorities for the allocation of the food aid: *emergency needs,* both chronic and acute (for which 25 percent of annual resources were committed), *preschool and school-age institutional feeding;* and *experimental economic and social development projects.*

WFP food aid operations were scheduled to commence in 1963, but many of the recipient countries remained skeptical about the program and its capabilities. Some recipients apparently feared that an international aid agency would be harder to deal with than PL 480 and they had to be persuaded that multilateral aid would not reduce, or even replace, bilateral aid [Wightman (1968, p. 46)]. The WFP also suffered from the usual assortment of start-up difficulties exhibited by any new organization, plus an additional set of problems caused by the fact that this was an unprecedented venture into a new form of multilateralism.

Many problems were encountered because the WFP was seriously viewed as an experiment and recipients often were not even aware of the availability of aid or of the procedures for requesting assistance. When project requests *were* submitted, they were frequently of low quality. Moreover, the commodity shipping response by donors was slow and sometimes completely inadequate—especially by the United States, whose bureaucratic procedures were not well suited to the needs of the WFP. Additional start-up difficulties included lack of adequate cash resources to purchase commodities when necessary, commodity acceptance problems caused by religious and other cultural-related taboos, and transportation, storage, and handling difficulties within the recipient countries. Despite the obstacles encountered during the first three years, however, the program was judged generally successful both by ECOSOC and by the FAO conference and its continued operation was approved subsequently on an open-ended basis in 1965.

Types of Programming
WFP food aid was established from the outset on a straight grant basis, meaning that little or none of the commodities were to be sold on the open market. This was done primarily in order to avoid problems involving market displacement, agricultural disincentive, and resource diversion[6] encountered frequently with the program-type assistance. Generally speaking, WFP project aid has been of two major types: food aid for development projects and food aid for chronic and/or acute emergencies. Of the total resources made available to the program during the first ten years of its existence (1963–1972), roughly 66 percent was used for development projects, 16 percent for emergency assistance, and the remaining 19 percent for ocean transportation, administration, and other supporting services [WFP (1973a, p. 6)].

Within the development category, twenty different types of projects have been supported, and these are summarized in table 5.1. It is noteworthy that, of the five most frequently funded types of WFP development projects, only two relate *directly* to the relief of hunger and malnutrition; taken together, they account for only 23 percent of total resources committed to development projects.[7]

This situation may be explained partially by the fact that a large proportion of WFP development aid is utilized as food-for-work (FFW) schemes rather than as feeding programs for populations at nutritional

Table 5.1
Distribution of WFP Resources by Type of Project: 1963–1972

Category	Number of approved projects (as of 12/31/72)	Total resources ($ US millions)	Percentage of total WFP aid
Land development	62	234.0	16.0
Land settlement	57	120.1	9.0
Food reserve and price stabilization	7	38.6	3.0
Forestry	33	57.2	5.0
Fisheries	3	2.8	0.2
Animal and dairy development	45	141.6	12.0
Industry, mining, and power works	17	20.5	2.0
Housing, transport, and communications	37	83.0	7.0
Community development	34	82.8	7.0
Feeding vulnerable groups	47	263.0	23.0
Mother & preschool	22	91.0	8.0
School feeding	25	172.0	15.0
Hospital and public health projects	19	25.1	2.0
Education[a]	37	71.8	6.8
Training	25	52.7	4.0
Grand Total	470	1,457.2	100.0

Source: adapted from WFP (1973a, pp. 10–35).
a. Food to primary school groups included under vulnerable groups heading.

risk. The notion of FFW is that food rations may be employed as payment for labor in development projects such as the digging of irrigation and drainage facilities, the building of farm-to-market roads, and so on. Such schemes are especially attractive in the WFP context because they facilitate the use of food aid in highly rural, nonmonetized areas, as well as among populations characterized by high rates of un- or underemployment. While there are a number of unresolved problems with the FFW approach, relating to resource leakage and diversion, mismanagement, and the lack of adequate work incentives, the concept nevertheless provides a useful and generally less controversial means of promoting rural development.[8]

Responding to chronic and acute emergency situations has been the other major operational focus of WFP food aid. However, the multilateral channel—by definition—is difficult to employ for this purpose because it automatically adds an additional layer of bureaucracy (and delay) in responding to food crisis. That is, where bilateral donors can respond by shipping or airlifting food directly to a disaster area, the WFP must first receive an "official assessment" from the host government and then seek the necessary resources from the various donors. Thus, despite the fact that more than 10 percent of WFP resources are officially reserved for emergency use by the FAO Director-General,[9] average emergency response time has often amounted to weeks or even months. This problem was apparent even at the initiation of the WFP in 1963, and it caused Adoeke Boerma, the first Executive Director of the WFP, to suggest that the WFP might be more effective in "postemergency" situations for which the need for food continued but the crisis-induced interest of bilateral donors had diminished.[10]

Since October 1976, the WFP has maintained a separate Emergency Unit in its Project Management Division in order to deal with fast developing crises.[11] This has relieved to some extent the problem of inadequate or nonuniform emergency response, since these situations had been handled previously on an ad hoc basis by regular WFP country desk officers.

The WFP Emergency Unit is also intended to act as a focal point for the coordination of operations among various specialized agencies of the UN, nongovernmental organizations such as CARE and CRS, and even among the bilateral donors to some extent. Coordination of bilateral emergency relief efforts has been hampered, however, by the reluctance of some donors to produce the necessary data. A higher degree of success has been achieved with the nongovernmental food aid providers— most recently in the Angolan civil war—although interorganizational jealousies have caused problems here as well.

Within the UN system, the WFP has worked directly with the UN High Commission for Refugees (UNHCR), the UN Disaster Relief Office (UNDRO), the FAO Office of Special Relief Operations (OSRO), formed to deal with the Sahelian drought and famines, as well as UNICEF and UNRWA. The WFP clearly aspires to fill the role of global emergency food relief coordinator, but its efforts have so far been frustrated by the fact that general operational responsibility for disaster relief coordination lies elsewhere within the UN system (i.e., with UNDRO). Furthermore, most of the bilateral donors have not demonstrated any great interest or willingness to be coordinated.

As early as 1968, concern was expressed within the WFP about the growing number of situations which were neither acute emergencies nor specifically developmental in nature, but where food assistance was desperately needed to alleviate a growing crisis. Accordingly, the WFP Secretariat developed a third type of multilateral program option, known as the Quick Action Procedure (QAP). Under this scheme, the normally extensive project scrutiny procedures are bypassed, and aid is approved quickly, albeit only for a twelve-month duration. QAP projects may have a food cost of no more than $1 million and may be approved by the Executive Director on his own authority. The idea, of course, is to allow the program to respond quickly to a developing problem and then, in the interim, to create a more carefully developed plan of action.

A number of other features of WFP programming—both proposed and realized—deserve brief mention. The first is the question of shifting part of multilateral food aid to a program approach. As Wightman has suggested, "Donor countries prefer the project approach, because with it the benefits of food aid are more apparent and not dissipated through some obscure market mechanism. It gives greater assurance of tangible results. It also gives donor countries a better sense of control over the activities of the secretariat" [Wightman (1968, p. 53)].[12] But project aid tends to be more expensive and complicated to administer[13] than program assistance, and it requires that the recipient country have the financial and managerial wherewithal not only to get the food to the recipients but also to provide the necessary program support components. Particularly in the cases of countries characterized by the United Nations as *least* developed countries—or in countries where the center–periphery political gap is wide—such assumptions about resource availability may be seriously open to question.[14]

The WFP governing council has debated since the midsixties whether it should permit experiments with the program approach. In November 1965, a mission was sent to Jamaica—which had been selected on the basis of its size and comparatively advanced stage of development—in order to ascertain the viability of undertaking a program-type operation. The idea was to determine whether the WFP was capable of providing not only the commodities needed for a particular project but also the food resources needed to meet the country's food deficit. The study mission's report, however, concluded bluntly that "in the current and prospective circumstances of Jamaica and of current commodity pledges there is very little that WFP can do to help under a program approach. This does not mean, of course, that the food problem of Jamaica is not very serious, but simply that the resources available to the Program are not those required for solving it."[15] Although recipient countries have continued to maintain interest in the concept since the Jamaican case study, the lack of adequate resources has prevented any further action.

In lieu of shifting to a program approach, the WFP governing council has permitted the limited sale of commodities in situations where a project cannot otherwise be undertaken successfully. Member countries have demonstrated, however, extreme reluctance toward approving the sale of WFP food aid for local currency due to the continuing sensitivity about the price disincentive effects on local agriculture.[16] In view of the reluctance of the governing council to experiment with a full-scale program approach, there is little doubt that limited sales of WFP commodities will continue to be a necessary and useful adjunct to the normal food aid programming. Far from the feared negative impact, evidence accumulated to date suggests that the sales policy has facilitated projects in circumstances under which all assistance would otherwise have been impossible.

Yet another alternative to program aid is the so-called "multiproject" approach. This concept was developed primarily for use in remote, rural areas of Africa and Asia where widely and thinly scattered populations with varying food needs require the infusion of project food aid to be used for such unrelated purposes as road construction, housing, agricultural development, and the like. The idea is to simplify administration of the aid by lumping together many work sites[17] and types of projects within the context of the recipient's overall development plan. Clearly, capital or technical aid would be far less difficult to utilize in such remote areas than bulky food aid, but it is the *food* that remote, rural populations often lack.

The WFP has also drawn on the conceptual approach of program aid to establish food reserves for price stabilization in developing countries on both a seasonal and an annual basis. WFP commodities are employed in this context as a form of limited buffer stock which are released when food prices rise above certain predetermined levels and held back when prices fall too far in the other direction. The object of the buffer stock scheme is to ensure that local farmers have an incentive to produce and local consumers may obtain food at affordable prices. WFP experience with price stabilization schemes[18] has so far been limited by its own resource constraints and by donor reluctance to see WFP resources tied up in reserve stocks rather than applied directly as project aid.

Finally, it is important to give some recognition to a problem of growing importance in WFP programming, namely, the difficulties encountered in providing *nonfood* inputs in multilateral projects. Rarely (if ever) are food aid projects—even those involving FFW schemes—composed entirely of a labor component. But, due to existing limitations on the sale of WFP commodities, the WFP is legally precluded from assisting a recipient government to procure *other* types of infrastructure components (e.g., hand tools, trucks, seeds, etc.) that may also be necessary to operate a particular project. What the WFP has done, however, is to form a small liaison unit within its External Relations Division, whose task is to locate and coordinate the provision of public and private sector resources for such purposes. The problem of nonfood requirements in project aid may be mitigated to some degree by the newly created International Fund for Agricultural Development, but it currently remains a most vexing impediment to WFP food aid projects in many parts of the developing world.

Project Selection and Geographic Distribution

Three significant issues have been raised during the existence of the WFP regarding the manner in which projects are selected for support. The first is the basic dilemma in multilateralism regarding geopolitical balance in aid programming; the second concerns the question whether WFP aid should be focused only on the *least* developed countries or whether it should continue to be distributed in a more balanced fashion; and the third involves the availability of WFP food aid to liberation movements, political refugees, and countries not belonging to the United Nations. Since the first two issues are actually different aspects of the same problem, they may usefully be considered together. The third, however, is of a more ad hoc nature and has been handled by the WFP according to the prevailing political sentiment of the moment. For example, the WFP refused to allocate food aid to UNRWA to assist the Palestinian refugees, but it did subsequently offer food to the victims of the Angolan civil war. Because of the lack of a consistent policy, this topic will not be addressed further here, although it will be considered again in chapter 8 in relation to US multilateral food aid policy.

The question whether all geographical and political components of the United Nations are (or should be) receiving equal treatment is a perennial concern to both donor and recipient delegates. This problem has been somewhat less severe in the case of the WFP, due partially to the fact that the Communist bloc plays a very minor role in the program.[19] In fact, the concern in the WFP context is not so much with the political need to allocate equal shares to client states of each superpower as it is with the level of economic development of the countries to whom the food aid is distributed. In fact, it was really not until the advent of heightened political and economic sensibilities during the 1972–1974 food "crisis" period that the geopolitical distribution of aid was even questioned seriously.

The data presented in table 5.2 generally confirm that, up through 1972, WFP food aid was widely distributed on a geographic basis. The distribution of WFP aid to each region and country has nonetheless been subject to some criticism. There are those, for example, who contend that a disproportionate amount of the resources has been directed toward North Africa and the Near East because countries in these areas have been better equipped to handle the food (especially in the early days of the program). Similarly, it is argued that the areas of greatest population growth pressure, Latin America and the Asian–Pacific area, have been relatively shortchanged. The available evidence would appear to support this claim; the geographical balance of WFP aid commitments probably has *not* kept pace with changing global demographic trends. Much of this distribution imbalance grew out of allocation decisions made during the early "experimental" years of the program, when quick and positive results were necessary to ensure the WFP's continued existence. Recipient countries were sometimes chosen more on the basis of their capacity to absorb and handle aid quickly than because of their absolute food deficit.

During the experimental period of the program, there were no specific

Table 5.2
Total WFP Commitments by Region, 1963–1972

Region	Resource commitment ($ US millions)	Percentage of total aid
Africa (south of the Sahara)	218.8	16.6
Asia and the Pacific	367.0	27.9
Europe (southern)	20.5	1.6
Latin America and the Caribbean	175.3	13.3
North Africa and the Near East	534.4	40.6
Grand total	1,316.0	100.0

Source: WFP (1973, pp. 58–59).

geographical or economic criteria for aid allocation; the requesting country simply had to be classified economically in the developing category. But a new set of allocation criteria [WFP (1966b, p. 2)] was approved in 1965 which included a geographical criterion. The overall emphasis, however, remained on the efficient use of resources, and there continued to be no official policy regarding the distribution of resources in relation to the economic situations of the recipient countries.

These revised distribution criteria remained generally in effect until the onset of the worldwide economic crisis in 1972. At that point both the developed and developing countries became rapidly sensitized to the urgent need for a reorientation of aid priorities among *all* the UN agencies. In November 1971, the General Assembly had passed a resolution[20] calling for special measures to be taken throughout the UN system in favor of the so-called "least developed countries." Moreover, in October 1972 the government of Canada proposed that the WFP refocus its allocation criteria in a similar fashion.

The Canadian proposal recommended that the Executive Director be authorized to use WFP case resources in such situations to meet up to 50 percent of the costs involved in inland transportation, handling, storage and distribution of food, and that high priority should be accorded to channeling WFP aid to these countries [WFP (1973b)]. The Canadian proposal was accepted by the IGC in October 1973 and implemented immediately; some of the results of this policy are presented in table 5.3. It may be observed that, over the base year of 1972, there was an increase of 16 percent in aid to the least developed countries by 1974, and this percentage had nearly doubled by 1976.

There are problems with this new policy, however. For one thing, emphasis on the least developed means that other, more developed countries such as Egypt or Brazil (which still have pockets of poverty as severe as conditions anywhere in the world) have received less food aid, and some projects have had to be discontinued or ended prematurely. Moreover, there continue to be crippling management problems in these countries which the WFP, despite the use of its cash resources, is neither empowered to, nor capable of, resolving. Questions also remain concerning the wisdom and cost effectiveness of pumping large amounts of additional resources into countries lacking in nearly all other types of requisite development resources. It might be far more cost effective instead to channel the aid to more developed countries,[21] particularly those with well-conceived development plans and projects, in hopes of achieving a far greater long-term impact on the level of human welfare.

Table 5.3
Estimated Disbursements to the Least Developed Countries: 1972–1976 (Quantities in Metric Tons)

Country	1972	1973	1974	1975	1976
Haiti	609	573	1,743	5,238	6,300
Sudan	33,255	32,687	32,742	28,811	19,850
Yemen Arab Republic	5,382	5,560	5,866	6,711	9,400
Burundi	5,126	5,378	5,319	3,703	3,386
Chad	1,443	1,313	957	1,285	1,526
Dahomey	2,577	2,577	2,675	6,910	12,100
Guinea	6,824	5,915	6,673	6,500	5,101
Mali	411	622	1,848	2,720	2,720
Niger	869	1,013	2,490	3,687	3,642
Rwanda	–	–	1,140	1,770	3,500
Upper Volta	4,870	4,038	3,040	2,355	1,980
Botswana	5,785	9,760	9,459	11,159	14,472
Ethiopia	623	1,680	3,168	5,061	7,412
Lesotho	15,600	18,175	20,590	16,775	14,550
Malawi	1,353	1,493	1,110	1,230	2,879
Somalia	4,760	7,810	9,325	8,390	5,262
Tanzania	4,155	3,915	4,095	3,300	3,060
Afghanistan	16,465	10,588	14,337	20,240	17,111
Bhutan	–	–	100	1,000	1,800
Nepal	4,193	5,222	5,907	9,925	12,993
Total	114,193	118,265	132,584	146,770	149,101
Annual percentage rate of increase over 1972	—	+3.5	+16.0	+28.4	+30.4

Source: WFP (1973b, p. 5).

Program Resources

During the WFP's experimental years, the program was heavily dependent on the United States both for its political and fiscal vitality. As
table 5.4 indicates, the US contribution to the WFP during its first three
years was five times larger than that of the next largest donor, the
Federal Republic of Germany. A fivefold increase in the Canadian contribution (making it the second-largest donor) during the second biennial
pledge period reduced this ratio to just over 3:1, but the United States
has clearly remained the sustaining force in multilateral food aid.

The United States has not carried this burden lightly, however. Consequently, in an effort to promote an increased donor participation, the
United States announced at the conclusion of the three-year experimen-

tal period that its contributions would henceforth be made on a 50:50 matching basis with those of other donors. Under this arrangement the United States proposed to match on a one-to-one basis the total pledges of the other donors up to a stated dollar level. This policy remained in effect until 1971, when the United States attempted to place additional pressure on the other donors by further reducing its matching formula to 40:60. In the latter 1970s, the American matching contribution has generally been adjusted in relation to the level of overall UN contribution of 25 percent. Thus, it now matches only one-third of the resources allocated by all other WFP donor countries.

The US matching strategy has apparently had the desired result of increasing the pledges of other donors, although there is no way of ascertaining what these other pledges might have been in the *absence* of the US prod. According to the data presented in table 5.4, Canada has maintained its position as the second largest individual donor, while the European Economic Community has generally been the third largest in volume.

Two points of special interest may also be noted about this ranked list. First, Australia and Japan, both of whom have operated fairly substantial bilateral food aid programs over the last ten years, each failed frequently to be ranked among the top ten contributors to the WFP.[22] Second, a major *cash* contribution during the 1975–1976 pledging period catapulted Saudi Arabia from the status of a negligible donor to the position of fourth-largest contributor. While there is some doubt about the likelihood of other such commitments by OPEC nations,[23] the Saudi cash contribution represents the only major resource development of recent years.

Table 5.5 provides a comprehensive summary of the evolving WFP resource position since its inception in 1963. It reveals that the total volume of resources handled by the program has increased steadily. For the purposes of perspective, however, it is interesting to note that total WFP pledges for the entire period from 1963 to 1976 were only slightly larger than the total US food aid contribution for a *single* fiscal year. Nevertheless the increase in resources—pledged as food commodities, cash,[24] and services[25]—has been significant. The actual pledging target for the current biennium (1977–1978) was $750 million, with a proposed target for 1979–1980 of $950 million.[26]

The WFP resources position has been helped greatly since 1968 by the existence of succeeding Food Aid Conventions (FAC). The FAC contributions to the program amounted to $53,246,000 (727.6 thousand metric

Table 5.4
Ranking of Largest WFP Donors for Biannual Pledging Periods: 1963–1976

Country[b]	Resources pledged (millions of US dollars) and rank[a]					
	1963–1965[c]	1966–1968[c]	1969–1970	1971–1972	1973–1974	1975–1976
Australia	1.50(10)	2.25(9)	1.65(11)	1.65(11)	1.75(12)	1.85(12)
Canada	5.50(4)	28.43(2)	32.50(3)	32.58(2)	34.00(3)	194.22(2)
Denmark	1.81(8)	7.20(6)	9.00(6)	15.00(4)	27.68(4)	29.32(6)
EEC	–	3.04(9)?	91.53(2)	16.28(3)	65.44(2)	103.29(3)
France	3.00(5)	3.04(9)	–	–	–	–
Finland	–	–	–	2.85(10)	–	–
W. Germany	7.98(2)	7.98(5)	6.39(9)	9.10(7)	14.87(7)	23.03(9)
Italy	1.48(11)	–	–	–	–	–
Japan	–	1.63(11)	–	–	3.0(10)	6.0(11)
Netherlands	2.45(6)	10.36(3)	13.62(4)	12.41(5)	22.05(5)	30.24(5)
Norway	1.66(9)	6.86(7)	7.28(8)	8.51(8)	9.68(8)	24.83(7)
Saudi Arabia	–	–	–	–	–	50.00(4)
Sweden	2.00(7)	8.00(4)	8.00(7)	12.00(6)	19.09(6)	23.51(8)
Switzerland	–	1.69(10)	–	–	2.11(11)	–
United Kingdom	5.70(3)	6.20(8)	2.98(10)	3.77(9)	5.87(9)	19.04(10)
United States	43.56(1)	95.93(1)	99.60(1)	125.00(1)	136.00(1)	205.00(1)

Source: WFP (1973a, pp. 49–50) and WFP (1977a)
a. Rankings are listed in parentheses. Blanks indicate less substantial grants.
b. Data for countries listed only for years when ranking among top eleven.
c. Three year pledging period.

Table 5.5
Resources of the WFP—Commodities, Cash and Services, 1963–1976 ($US millions)

Pledging Period		Total	Commodities	Cash	Services
1963–1965	First	84.5	59.1	19.0	6.4
1966–1968	Second	187.2	126.2	35.1	25.9
1969–1970	Third	319.9	257.7	35.2	27.0
1971–1972	Fourth	243.2	180.3	34.1	28.8
1973–1974	Fifth	360.8	267.1	52.6	41.1
1975–1976	Sixth	673.6	487.1	145.8	40.7
Cumulative total		1,869.2	1,377.5	321.8	169.9

Source; WFP (1977, p. 8).

tons) under the 1967 FAC and has so far totaled $63,356,000 (455.8 thousand metric tons) under the extended protocols of the 1971 FAC.[27] Due to the difficult and somewhat unpredictable nature of the negotiations for a new convention, the program has chosen wisely to consider these resources as *additional* to its regularly pledged contributions. This policy also appears justified by the continuing difficulties encountered in obtaining resources pledged to the WFP under the FAC in a timely fashion.

From a resource perspective, one of the most glaring deficiencies in the multilateral food aid mechanism is the fact that donor pledges are made in terms of cash and/or commodity value equivalents rather than in terms of commodity *volumes*. As a result, when grain prices skyrocketed in the early seventies, the WFP found itself seriously overcommitted; that is, the value of resources pledged to the program were simply insufficient to provide the volume of food on which the project planning had been predicated. It must be emphasized, moreover, that the program is no less vulnerable to this problem today should there be another substantial jump in world grain prices.

Program Management
The quality and effectiveness of WFP management practices has been a matter of almost continual debate and controversy since its inception in 1963. In the early years, of course, the program labored under the need to prove itself quickly in order to ensure its existence and guarantee its access to resources; yet, without the benefit of an extensive foreign service already in place (similar to those maintained by the largest bilateral donors), an entirely new set of administrative procedures had to be conceived and a system of field operations developed.[28]

Through the early years, the WFP's operating practices were scrutinized carefully by the donors—particularly by the United States, which (as the largest contributor) had by far the largest stake in the program. The resulting modus operandi is that the United States, alone among all other donors, continues to insist on the right of prior scrutiny for each individual WFP project; this is the case despite the fact that US contributions now represent only 25 percent of the WFP's total resources.

At the same time, however, it must be noted that the US oversight policy—although now largely a vestige of past problems and practices—was formulated in reaction to *real* difficulties encountered by the WFP. In fact, there are actually three interactive sets of issues which account for the WFP's partially deserved reputation for management mediocrity: ad hocism in management practices and policies; the politics of the program's governing council; and the nature of the multilateral aid mechanism itself. A certain amount of ad hocism (i.e., handling each particular problem de novo rather than on the basis of preceding experience and an established procedure) is no doubt inherent in the development of any new organizational entity, often because many problems have never before been encountered. But the WFP has had to deal with more than its share of ad hoc decisionmaking. This has been due, in part, to the role of personality politics in its leadership, to the nature of the projects which it supports, and to the unpredictable volume and availability of its resources.

As Smethurst (1969, p. 207) has noted, the WFP has been administered since its creation by a succession of strong bureaucratic personalities, each of whom has had larger career aspirations (quite often the Director-Generalship of the FAO) and a powerful (and sometimes conflicting) sense of how the progam should be operated. Consequently, policies established by one Executive Director have, on occasion, been modified or contravened by his successors. But, whereas most other UN agencies operate—some would argue excessively—on the basis of intra-agency memoranda and discussions, the short time frame for food aid has meant that the process of problem resolution has remained largely uncodified, being communicated most often in verbal form on the basis of an individual's memory. The result in many cases has been the continual rediscovery of the wheel, much wasted energy, and duplication of effort.

A second type of management problem faced by the WFP relates to the politics and policies of its governing council, the Committee on Food Aid Policies and Programs (CFA). The CFA was established as a result

of action taken during the 1974 World Food Conference, which recommended that the old IGC be abolished and a new committee be formed
with greater LDC representation and expanded food aid policy responsibilities. As with many other UN political bodies, the work of the CFA
has been affected by the contentious political atmosphere that now characterize many international forums. Political problems within the CFA
have been mitigated somewhat, however, by the fact that the committee
has a specific, concrete task to perform (i.e., the approval of food aid
projects), although most decisions must still be reached by consensus
rather than through formal votes.[29]

The foregoing critique also points up the difficulties inherent in the
nature of food aid multilateralism.[30] Many of the problems encountered
by the WFP originate from the fact that donors basically remain unwilling to relinquish control over all but the most mundane operational aspects of the program. As a result, the CFA—as a governing body—is
forced to involve itself in matters with which it is ill equipped to deal.
Moreover, the charter of the WFP is structured in such a way as to make
many of these problems virtually unresolvable. For example, the
General Regulations of the WFP constrain it specifically from actually
managing the delivery of food aid once the commodities have been received by the recipient country. This constraint exists in spite of the
well-known fact that many host governments lack the necessary
management expertise and infrastructure to operate such projects
successfully.[31]

The WFP has been criticized also for its slow call forward of donor
pledges. Part of the difficulty here can be traced to late notification by
the donors of the specific mix of commodities which they intend to make
available (this is especially acute regarding the EEC food aid pledge). It
is due mainly, however, to the slow pace at which projects are developed and implemented by the WFP and recipient governments.

Project monitoring and evaluation is yet another type of management
difficulty. Although the effectiveness of the WFP's evaluation component has improved substantially in recent years, it remains understaffed
and continues to be prevented by the General Regulations from requiring that recipient countries open their records to formal audits. Where
evaluations are conducted, they are generally in the form of brief field
inspections (average duration two weeks) during which it is possible to
gather only limited information.[32] Where there is strong evidence of improper management or resource diversion, food aid projects can and
actually have been suspended; in some cases, they have even been ter-

minated. But problems with managerial incompetence and food loss through pilfering remain a significant factor in WFP projects.

In terms of its *external* relations, the WFP has had a poor record in relating to the private voluntary organizations (PVOs) such as CARE and Catholic Relief Services. Although both sides have made a conscious effort in recent years to improve matters, the PVOs raise a number of points in criticism of WFP operations—only some of which may be resolvable. For example, the PVOs—many of which are, of course, church sponsored—have complained that the WFP has an unfair advantage in non-Christian countries, where host governments fear the PVOs may try to proselytize. Moreover, the PVOs note that the WFP food aid basket, composed of the contributions of many donors, is more varied than they can possibly offer and is therefore more attractive to recipients. But the most serious complaint is that, as a result of the restrictions that the US AID places on the voluntary agencies (but which it is unable to enforce in the multilateral context), the food aid ration offered in WFP food-for-work projects is larger than that which can be offered by the PVOs.[33] Thus, recipients have, at times, been drawn away from the programs of the latter and toward those of the former.

The nature of these difficulties offers an interesting perspective on the positive side of aid multilateralism. It would seem that, under some circumstances, it is possible to accomplish certain aid objectives *more* effectively through the WFP than through bilateral programs. This fact does not in any way relieve the problems which have existed between the WFP and the PVOs, but it seems doubtful whether much more can be accomplished[34] in the future to relieve the situation. Furthermore, in the broader context of world food problems, this competition appears rather pointless and unnecessary given the overwhelming need for food aid in relation to the resources available.

Current Effectiveness
From its inception, the WFP has been largely a creature of its principal resource benefactors, the United States, Canada, and the EEC. Unlike some of the UN specialized agencies which, once established, have tended to assume a partially autonomous existence that transcends the expectations (and desires) of their supporters, the WFP has not been an empirebuilder. Thus, for example, unlike its parent organization, the FAO, the WFP has maintained a disciplined limit on the size of its Rome staff. Even the pressures of the New International Economic Order have not caused it to chart a radical new policy course divergent from the

wishes of the major donor members. The Realpolitik of multilateral food aid thus requires that, no matter what the true extent or nature of *recipients'* views on the proper uses of WFP aid, policy cannot deviate substantially from the wishes of the major donors for fear of losing aid resources. This is particularly true with regard to US participation, where the WFP lacks an effective and well-organized interest group constituency in Washington, which increases its vulnerability to funding reductions in both the legislative and executive branches.

If, in fact, the WFP can never be anything more than that which its major contributors permit it to be, then it becomes difficult to fathom the rationale behind many of the major donor criticisms of the program. In some respects, this criticism is simply a reflection on the donor's *own* multilateral food aid policies. Many of the WFP's managerial shortcomings are due also, of course, to conceptual difficulties inherent in the nature of multilateralism—difficulties which have proved highly resistant to resolution. But it is also true that the program has managed to surmount or to circumvent a remarkable number of these obstacles during the course of its existence. It would seem, therefore, that a substantial need exists for the principal donor countries to reevaluate their multilateral food aid policies in light of current global food needs and present WFP management capabilities.

OTHER UN FOOD AID AGENCIES

A number of UN agencies other than the WFP have also become involved from time to time in food relief operations. In some cases, these efforts have related closely to the agency's specific mandate; in others, they have only been one part of a broad and continuing area of responsibility (e.g., the UN Disaster Relief Office, UNDRO). It is important to add, however, that the WFP is the *only* UN agency employing food aid specifically as an instrument of development. In all other cases, food assistance has been used primarily as a *short-term* means of relieving chronic or acute hunger and malnutrition or as a means of facilitating other aspects of the agency's responsibilities.

For example, the United Nations International Children's Emergency Fund (UNICEF) has confronted few of the political or managerial difficulties which have beset the WFP, due in large part to its specific focus on maternal and child welfare. UNICEF has been in the business of providing food relief to these vulnerable groups since shortly after the end of World War II. By 1959, it was supplying nearly 50,000 metric tons of food commodities, although this figure began to decline as of 1960. The reduction in UNICEF food aid activities became even more pronounced after 1963 when WFP operations commenced. With the burden of direct child feeding removed, UNICEF refocused its policy after 1968 purely on emergency situations.

Even at its peak, UNICEF food aid has amounted to only one-tenth of the volume of food provided by the private voluntary organizations such as CARE and Catholic Relief Services.[35] With no direct responsibility for feeding programs per se, UNICEF has begun increasingly to use what food commodities it does command as a "come on" to attract women and children (especially in rural areas) to visit community health centers. Health maintenance activities are clearly its primary focus, and food aid is now employed primarily for its prophylactic value in terms of groups at risk in the recipient populations.

In June 1976, UNICEF and the WFP formalized their food aid relationship and mutual assistance procedures in a "memorandum of understanding" which set out the areas of responsibility of each agency.[36] As a result of this formal understanding, UNICEF food aid activities in 1976 amounted to only 30,000 metric tons, which was only 3 percent of total WFP operations for that year. With its focus on a specific and decidedly nonpolitical client group and its positive working relationships with the WFP, other UN agencies, and major donor nations, UNICEF has suffered few of the financial difficulties that have encumbered the food aid operations of other UN agencies. There is every indication that UNICEF's limited food aid operations will continue to supplement assistance provided through the main WFP multilateral channel.

THE FOOD AID CONVENTIONS

The concluding section of this chapter focuses on those international institutional mechanisms that do not distribute food aid *directly* but perform important political, economic, and coordinative functions with regard to bilateral food assistance. Of principal concern in this context are the Food Aid Conventions, which have been components of larger multination agreements on food and feed grains, the International Grains Arrangement of 1967, and its successor, the International Wheat Agreement of 1971. In fact, had it not been for the successful negotiation of the two grain agreements, it is likely that there would have been no food aid conventions either. That is, the notion of an international convention dealing specifically with grain to be given as food aid became ac-

ceptable to many exporting countries only because of *other* benefits
derived from joining in an international trade treaty. Without these
benefits, there would have been little or no incentive for the donors to
agree to new food aid commitments.

International agreements on the export of wheat had their origin in
1949 during the period of international economic and political activism
following World War II. Essentially the same basic agreement was renewed in 1953, and again in 1956. Also, in 1956, an International Wheat
Council (IWC) was established in London to coordinate the selling policies of the exporting nations. After the agreement was renewed once
more in 1959, the change in political leadership in the United States precipitated a major reevaluation of the terms and provisions of the treaty.
The 1962 renewal of the wheat agreement consequently was postponed
while discussions were held as part of the so-called Kennedy Round of
the General Agreement on Tariffs and Trade. It was at this point that
the direct linkage developed between the grain negotiations and food
aid.

The United States and Canada had been providing, of course, almost
all of the food aid delivered worldwide up to that date. But, with the decline in the level of surplus grain stocks in the midsixties, both donors
sought a wider level of international burden-sharing. As Wightman
concludes,

The Kennedy Round (of the GATT) was the chosen place because it
offered the maximum opportunity for across-the-board bargaining;
concessions received on some commodities would be paid for with concessions granted on others. The exporters had little or no hope of per-
suading the European importers to accept a larger share of the food aid
bill except as part of a wider bargain or package deal.
    To put it bluntly, the EEC, Britain and Japan heartily disliked the ex-
porter's proposal. The United States, for its part, made it plain that
without the food aid provisions there would be no grains agreement, and
that without the grains agreement it would offer few concessions on industrial products. Tough and tense negotiations ensued, neither side was
easily budged from its initial position. Only at the last possible moment,
in May 1967, was complete deadlock averted and the Kennedy Round
saved from ignominy. [Wightman (1968, p. 58)]

Thus, it is more accurate to state that the United States did not *seek*
wider food aid burden-sharing through the GATT negotiations, but *demanded* it as the price of its participation and of its specific commodity
concessions.

In any case, the specific provisions of the grain commodity aspects of
the Kennedy Round were finalized at an International Wheat Conference

in Rome during the summer of 1967. The terms of the International Grains Arrangement included two major provisions: a Wheat Trade Convention and a Food Aid Convention (FAC).[37]

The FAC of 1967 committed the United States and eleven other developing countries to provide 4.5 million tons of grain annually in the form of food aid. United States volume and percentage contributions dominate, but the US contribution was actually aid that it would have provided anyway, while the contributions of most other donors (e.g., the EEC) represented new or additional resources.[38] The grain was to be provided bilaterally on straight grant terms, with each donor choosing the individual recipients for its assistance.

A number of significant features were included as part of the FAC. First, a Food Aid Committee was created with the same membership as that of the convention and with responsibility for monitoring donor performance. While the operational aspects of coordination and monitoring are handled by the staff of the International Wheat Council in London, the Food Aid Committee functions as the forum in which donors discuss the fulfillment of outstanding obligations. Each country has an interest in monitoring the performance of its fellow participants, although the only sanction that the committee may impose on delinquent donors is a vote of censure. Such action forces countries into the somewhat embarrassing position of having to request a formal extension on their pledge. In all other respects, the committee's function is purely informational; it provides no food aid directly to recipients.

A second important feature of the FAC was that commitments were made in *quantitative* terms rather than by currency value. Consequently, in contrast to the WFP, whose resources are pledged by value, FAC contributors are obligated to provide a certain *volume* of grain no matter what the current level of international prices. This characteristic became particularly important during the volatile grain price increases of 1973–1974, when the WFP suffered severe resource reductions because of its lack of similar quantity guarantees. The WFP does benefit, however, from the existence of the FAC, since use of the multilateral program as a food aid delivery channel is officially encouraged.[39]

A third notable feature was the special provisions for participation by food *importing* donor countries. Special arrangements were made for these nations to substitute rice or coarse grains (or cash for the purchase of wheat), and a reference price for equivalent contributions (in 1967 dollars) was established in terms of wheat ($1.73 per bushel or $63 per ton).[40] Countries wishing to avail themselves of this feature can provide either the value equivalent in the form of another cereal grain or the cash equivalent to be used to purchase wheat from one of the exporters. Some donors have criticized this equivalency policy, however, because countries using the plan do not carry the same proportionate food aid burden when grain prices rise, since the conversion is expressed according to a fixed value of wheat in dollars per bushel.

Finally, the same article that facilitated the donation of cash in lieu of grain also specified that not less that 25 percent[41] of any cash contribution (or that portion needed to procure 200,000 metric tons of grain) was to be used specifically for the purchase of grain commodities from *developing* country exporters who were members of the FAC. The original intent was to entice additional LDC donors with the promise of increased agricultural export markets, but the only developing country which has actually joined the FAC is Argentina.

A new round of negotiations was conducted within the International Wheat Council at the end of 1971 concerning the renewal of the International Grains Arrangement. The terms of the FAC remained generally unaffected by the changes reflected in the renamed International Wheat Agreement (IWA) of 1971. The most significant alteration was that certain member countries—notably Denmark, Norway, and the United Kingdom—withdrew after the expiration of the 1967 agreement.[42] The 1971 FAC resulted in a net *decrease* of 526,000 tons in total donor pledges, or an 11.7-percent reduction from the 1967 accord.[43] The United States was once again the predominant donor (47.5 percent of total pledges) with the EEC (26.0 percent) and Canada (12.4 percent) retaining their same respective rankings.

The 1971 agreement was to remain in effect for three years. In 1973, however, the donors could not agree on the terms of a renewed IWA, and thus both the food aid and wheat trade conventions have been extended by protocol each year since 1974. New negotiations have only recently resulted in the successful conclusion of a new FAC, although the parties have been unable (as of this writing) to agree upon the terms of a new IWA.

There is little doubt that the net effect of succeeding FACs has been to increase the absolute volume of food resources available as aid. Their unique contribution is that they accomplish the fundamental goal of expanding the level of donor food aid participation while, at the same time, leaving the donors free to employ their food aid pledges bilaterally (within certain limits) in pursuit of their own particular political and economic foreign policy objectives (since each donor can continue to select the recipients of its aid). Although these agreements have applied exclusively to grains, such commodities have, in any case, comprised the bulk of the food resources shipped as aid to recipient countries. In view of the continuing reluctance of many of the largest donors to contribute a larger portion of their available food aid resources for outright multilateral distribution via the WFP, an internationally agreed upon volume commitment from each donor offers a viable alternative for reaching some—although certainly not all—of the same objectives.

FOOD AID COORDINATION WITHIN THE UN SYSTEM

It would be inappropriate to conclude this chapter without making brief mention of the numerous agencies, committees, and policy councils within the United Nations that deal on an ongoing—albeit sometimes indirect—basis with the issues of food aid. While a detailed consideration of the role and responsibilities of each organization is beyond the scope of this study, two UN institutions deserve limited attention here because of their central roles as multilateral coordinative mechanisms: the Consultative Subcommittee on Surplus Disposal (CSD) of the FAO Committee on Commodity Problems and the recently formed World Food Council (WFC).

It will be recalled that the CSD was formed in 1954 by the parent FAO Committee on Commodity Problems in order to administer the FAO Principles of Surplus Disposal, which had been formulated in response to the growing problem of surplus commodity dumping by the major agricultural exporters (notably the United States). Bard (1972, pp. 138–140)[44] suggests that the work of the CSD may be divided roughly into three phases: 1954–1957—during which time the committee functioned as a forum for developing surplus disposal proposals and for hearing grievances lodged primarily against the United States by the other agricultural exporters; 1956–1968—when the CSD began to raise its operational sights beyond merely protecting the markets of agricultural exporters against subcommercial transactions (i.e., food aid) toward improving the consultative procedures among the donor countries; and 1968–1976—when the CSD was forced to deal with a radically changed agricultural environment characterized by the elimination of large commodity surpluses and increased multilateral food aid burdensharing.

The work of the CSD has included consideration of acceptable methods of surplus disposal, suitable means for utilizing surpluses, gov-

ernment food aid policies and legislation, and individual food aid transactions. The subcommittee has met since its inception in Washington,
DC, which is partially a reflection of the dominant role of the United
States food aid and the time spent discussing PL 480 agreements. In fact,
although other donors have begun to report their food aid agreements
on a more regular basis since 1971, US transactions represented practically the sum total of CSD concern prior to that year. The CSD today
performs two basic functions: it provides a forum through which the
donors may notify each other of pending food aid agreements with a
particular recipient; and it offers the opportunity for donors to consult
on the manner in which their food assistance is made available.

Like the Food Aid Committee, which governs the FAC, there are no
formal penalties for donor noncompliance other than the vociferous pro-
tests of other CSD member countries. The United States has received a
disproportionate share of criticism within the CSD primarily because it
is the only donor to announce its annual surplus availability and because
it offers the largest total amount of food aid. In recent years, however,
the disappearance of agricultural surpluses has reduced the criticality of
CSD operations. Where once the subcommittee served a vital role in al-
laying exporter fears that the United States intended merely to impose
its will unilaterally by dumping its commodity surpluses, the CSD's
major function today is that of passing information between donors on
pending food aid agreements.

The UN World Food Council (WFC), on the other hand, is of much
more recent origin. Its creation was one of the principal results achieved
by the 1974 World Food Conference. Such an institutional mechanism
became necessary, in the view of conference delegates, because the FAO
had proved itself unable to coordinate the myriad of UN agencies dealing in some respect with food issues (e.g., WHO, WMO, UNIDO,
UNICEF, UNDP, PAG, World Bank, and the WFP). There was also
great dissatisfaction with the functioning of the FAO itself. The food
bureaucracy was perceived by many as having become too country
oriented and conservative in its policy approach. Moreover, FAO has
never been a fully representative body since neither the Soviet Union nor
the People's Republic of China are members.[45] Thus, over the active, but
futile, objections of the FAO leadership, the UN General Assembly
adopted Resolution XXII of the World Food Conference in December
1974,[46] thereby creating the WFC as a subsidiary organ reporting
through the Economic and Social Council.

The thirty-six-member WFC was envisioned originally as a sort of

"Security Council dealing with world food issues," in that it was to be the highest political forum in which urgent global food issues could be confronted and appropriate action taken. The WFC Secretariat was purposely kept small and elite since the intention is not for the council to become an operational agency but for it to function as a coordinative, persuasive, and mobilizing force. The WFC is not considered duplicative with the work of the FAO because it does not maintain any operational responsibilities in the food and nutrition fields. The council is constituted at the ministerial level; and, as such, it is designed to have the necessary power and breadth of responsibility to coordinate the food policies and programs of all the agencies within the UN system. At the same time, it functions as a forum for discussion of the most urgent priorities for individual nations.

The WFC is now the principal policy venue on major food aid issues. The council, in turn, relies upon the Committee on Food Aid Policies and Programs of the World Food Programme for follow-up action and monitoring. The WFC's most significant food aid policy initiative has been its efforts to urge the food donor countries swiftly to meet the 10 million metric ton per year food aid target established by the 1974 conference.[47] Other major food aid policy concerns monitored by the council include diversification of the international food aid basket to include noncereal items, greater specification of the food aid needs of individual recipient countries, wider utilization of food aid purchases from developing country exporters, increased allocation of food aid on straight grant or highly concessional terms, and greater forward planning of donor food aid allocation so that longer-term, better-planned development projects might be undertaken.

It may be noted that all of these issues would require a modification or change in current donor food aid policies. Yet, along with its lack of operational responsibilities, the WFC has not been assigned any specific enforcement powers. This fact clearly distinguishes the WFC from the UN Security Council which can act to enforce its decisions. Nevertheless, on matters concerning food aid (the other issue) the WFC functions primarily as a political forum. If the council does have any enforcement power, it is through the "peer pressure" applied by the WFC Secretariat to urge donors to adhere to approved WFC policies. The WFC Secretariat is also constrained in its actions by the need for a specific mandate from the council before proceeding on an issue. In fact, the secretariat cannot initiate *any* action on a problem, no matter how pressing or obvious the need, unless it has received the prior approval of the council

ministers. As a result, the majority of the secretariat's responsibility is
in the nature of follow-up on matters acted upon previously by the
council.

As in other UN forums the WFC has encountered difficulty in achieving consensus on policies defeated at the ministerial level. These matters
have a long and involved history that cannot be presented adequately
here, but they have mainly to do with the confused and contentious atmosphere under which the WFC was established. The net result of these
political difficulties has been, at least up until the Third Ministerial Session, a partial loss of support for the WFC by the developed country
donors and an inability to reach agreement on much of substance beyond the resolutions agreed upon at the 1974 World Food Conference.

The early faltering of the WFC has not affected any of the bilateral of
multilateral food aid operations significantly—except, perhaps, for the
rate at which the 10 million ton annual world aid target has been attained. Some signs of increased effectiveness have appeared since the
WFC's Third Ministerial Session,[48] but it is still uncertain whether the
council will ultimately be able to transcend its troubled beginnings and
internal problems in order to function as an effective, political mechanism for coordinating food aid and other food-related issues. It is apparent, however, that the WFC has promoted greater attention to the
need for and importance of international food assistance through both
bilateral and multilateral channels.

PART III
FOREIGN POLICY OBJECTIVES IN UNITED STATES
FOOD AID: 1961–1976

In the previous section, the general dimensions of the international food aid system were described and analyzed. There, the primary concern was to place the US food aid program within the context of efforts undertaken by other bilateral donors and through the multilateral system as well. It is now possible on this basis to focus the analysis more narrowly on the specific foreign policy objectives inherent in US food aid between 1961 and 1976. The objective is to assess the different applications in which the United States has employed its food aid resources as a means of facilitating the attainment of its global interests, both bilateral and multilateral.

A brief word is also in order concerning the historical time frame adopted here. With the exception of certain illustrative examples which date from the early years of the Cold War, all of the remaining cases examined in this section occurred during the years 1961–1976. This fifteen-year period is of particular salience for a number of reasons. It commences with the evolution of the Food for Peace concept from the surplus disposal era of the Eisenhower administration into a new, expanding role as an element of US foreign policy. At the same time, it spans four presidencies, two Democratic and two Republican, all of which recognized the foreign policy value of food aid and employed the resource accordingly. The period also encompasses the years since the creation of the UN–FAO World Food Programme in 1961. Finally, it embodies the fundamental transformation of US international agricultural policy from persistent surplus disposal, caused by chronic overproduction, to a new emphasis on commercial export sales, conditioned by changes in global food production and growing US balance of payments difficulties. Thus, in some respects, this is a discrete historical period which provides an opportunity to trace the evolution of US food aid policy through a process of maturation and development as a component of US international relations.

Since it became apparent that food aid would be more than a temporary expedient for rebuilding war-shattered Europe, the United States has sought to fulfill multiple foreign and domestic policy objectives through the allocation of its food resources. As food aid has become integrated with, and responsive to, the evolving perceptions of US foreign policy, increasingly it has come to exemplify the diplomatic and strategic applications of foreign aid as a whole. It will be argued here, in fact, that the availability of food as a foreign aid resource has played a pivotal role in the attainment of certain specific policy objectives that could not have been accomplished by means of other aid instruments.[1]

The chapter will thus consider four separate cases wherein food aid has been employed in support of US foreign policy objectives as an instrument of diplomatic and/or strategic leverage and the effectiveness of each application. It is, of course, impossible to include all of the diplomatic and strategic uses to which US food aid has been applied. Often, the allocation of food commodities has been simply one component of a larger package of foreign policy instruments that has, on occasion, included capital, technical, and/or military assistance, preferential trade access rights, and so on. But the intent here is to provide the reader with an informed sense of the scope of situations in which food aid has been utilized as a flexible instrument of US foreign policy.

COLD WAR CARROT-AND-STICK

The principal attraction of food aid as a foreign policy resource is its capacity to achieve political objectives through either of two opposing

strategies: offering food as an incentive to reinforce certain desirable behavior patterns on the part of the recipient country, or withdrawing (or
threatening to withdraw) food as a political sanction for behavior considered inimical to US interests. A number of examples from the early
years of the PL 480 program offer solid illustrations of these contrasting
applications.

Food Aid As Political Enticement

The strategy of employing food aid as a "carrot" in bilateral relations between the United States and Yugoslavia was a natural and logical response to the growing Cold War struggle in Europe. In this case, the
offer of food aid was to be used to attempt to coax the Tito regime further away from the Soviet sphere of influence by nurturing independent
political inclinations which already seemed to exist. But the provision of
food aid to a Communist country also forced the Eisenhower administration to defend this foreign policy in the face of generalized congressional displeasure over US aid to Communist bloc nations at the height
of the Cold War.

Initial US food assistance to Yugoslavia had grown out of the war relief operations during and immediately after World War II. As the boundaries of political hegemony solidified after the war, the United States—at
Soviet insistence—reduced its aid to Yugoslavia, which was administered primarily under the auspices of CARE, Inc.[2] But Tito's eventual
break with the Soviet Union prompted the continuation of US economic
assistance. On 5 January 1955, a food aid agreement (only the second
since the creation of PL 480 the year before) was signed providing $43
million in wheat and cotton commodities. United States relations with
Yugoslavia were not uniformly positive, however, due to Tito's erratic
policy toward the Soviet Union. Markovich reports, in fact, that the
United States slowed its aid shipments in May 1955 (the date of Khrush-
chev's visit to Belgrade) in order to demonstrate its fear that Yugoslavia
might be drifting back toward the Soviet orbit [Markovich (1968,
p. 101)].

Following Tito's pro-Soviet statements during his return visit to
Moscow in mid-1956, the Eisenhower administration actually suspended
all military and economic assistance, and the Congress attached new restrictions to the Mutual Security Act (the principal foreign aid legislation
at that time) regarding the conditions under which Yugoslavia could
continue to receive aid.[3] But the brutal Soviet suppression of the 1956
Hungarian uprising cast a new chill on Soviet–Yugoslav relations, and

US aid was resumed again, although this time on a short-term basis. Continued disruptions in relations occurred during 1957–1958, causing the United States to back away from the use of capital grants and toward the use of food aid and development loans. In March 1958, Secretary of State John Foster Dulles justified aid to Yugoslavia on the grounds that there was "no doubt that Yugoslavia is independent of Moscow and is zealously maintaining its independence" [US Congress SCFR (1958, p. 173)].

It was quickly apparent that the new Kennedy administration intended to continue the policy of using food and other aid to encourage a shift in the nature of Yugoslav relations with the Soviet Union. George Kennan, Ambassador-Designate to Yugoslavia, reiterated in March 1961 congressional hearings that the administration did not wish to become involved in Yugoslavia's domestic affairs but did expect that nation to maintain "true independence" and to conduct a foreign policy which would permit continued American cooperation [*The New York Times*, 7 March (1961, p. 29)]. But Yugoslavian relations with the United States in 1961 were not altogether positive. President Tito used the occasion of the Belgrade Conference of Non-Aligned Countries to express support for Soviet foreign policy and resumption of nuclear weapons testing. On the day following Tito's speech, Kennedy declared that "it is my belief that in the administration of these funds [i.e., foreign aid] we should give great attention and consideration to those nations who have our view of the world" [*The New York Times*, 15 November (1961, p. 11)], and he proceeded to postpone negotiations on the current Yugoslavian economic aid request.

By early 1962, however, the administration's desire to discourage pro-Soviet policies in the Tito regime resulted once again in growing interest in the use of food and other forms of economic assistance as a means of political leverage. Secretary of State Dean Rusk prepared a secret memorandum on US policy regarding Yugoslavia in which he argued, "US economic assistance has been one of the principal factors in enabling Yugoslavia to resist the effects of Soviet economic pressures and to complete its successful schism from the bloc."[4] Rusk outlined the US interest in the Yugoslavian separation from Soviet hegemony:

The separation of Yugoslavia . . . has brought major political advantages to the US and the Western countries in the world struggle against Sino–Soviet imperialism. Tito's assertion of independence set in train a series of developments bringing into question the basis on which the world Communist movement had previously functioned. . . . In a narrower, strategic sense Yugoslavia's assertion of national independence has afforded an obstacle to the advance of Soviet imperialism in Southeastern Europe and aided the restoration of political and economic stability in that area. [Rusk (1962, p. 4)]

Rusk urged the President to maintain the five-point policy of support for the Tito regime, which included technical assistance, development loans, food aid, military sales, and most favored nation trading status. President Kennedy apparently accepted Rusk's advice, although his support became increasingly difficult in the face of Tito's continued anti-United States pronouncements.

Frustration in the executive branch over the vacillating nature of Yugoslavian policies was mild, however, in comparison to that of Congress, which was already scrutinizing the US foreign aid program with mounting skepticism. In June 1962, Congress passed amendments to the 1962–1963 foreign aid bill prohibiting *any* assistance to Communist countries unless the President could certify that such aid would further American national security interests. Kennedy recognized clearly the limiting effect that this restriction would have on his policy of enticement toward marginal Communist regimes, but he also feared that to give his strong support to a continued aid program for Yugoslavia (and Poland) was to lay his administration open to partisan charges that he was soft on Communism. The President did, however, send both McGeorge Bundy and Dean Rusk to testify before Congress in support of continuing food aid. Moreover, in an insightful and revealing statement, Kennedy himself argued;

I understand very well the motives of the authors of these various amendments. . . . It would be easy for me, just as it would for a lot of other people, just to say: Sure, I'm for these amendments because I'm against Communism. But the fact is that this is not the real issue.
. . . It's a relatively simple thing to determine our economic policy towards the countries at the two ends of the ideological spectrum. . . . But there is a gray area inbetween where things get much more complicated. Our job here is to influence people in directions we think are conducive to world peace.
. . . To do this we have to be able to say "no" on certain occasions. Whoever deprives us of the possibility of saying either "yes" or "no" at the right time makes it impossible for us to operate at all in this [gray] area with any effectiveness; and this is precisely what these amendments would do.[5]

But the President's argument did not prevail, and the amendments were attached to the foreign aid bill, which Kennedy could not possibly veto on such geographically limited grounds. The Congress did modify the restrictions in order to give the President discretionary power to continue sales of Title I food commodities under PL 480 to Communist countries. At a press conference on June 7, Kennedy expressed his small pleasure at this limited reprieve:

The amendment will be helpful because the primary assistance that we have been giving, for example, to Poland, has been through food. . . . I suppose that people do get tired [of continuing such aid programs begun after World War II], but our adversaries are not tired. . . . We are not prepared to take military action to free them [i.e., the peoples of Eastern Europe] . . . but I don't think we should slam the door in their face.[6]

Food aid agreements between the United States and Yugoslavia continued through the end of the Kennedy administration and into the Johnson years, but new congressional restraints[7] neutralized much of the impact of the enticement strategy as outlined for the President by Dean Rusk in 1962. It may be concluded, however, that the US policy of using food aid in conjunction with other forms of economic assistance to strengthen the capacity of Yugoslavia and other Eastern European regimes to resist Soviet political and economic domination had demonstrated generally positive results, despite the vascillating, "love–hate" nature of relations with these countries.

Food Aid As Political Sanction

United States food assistance to Egypt began in early 1953 and was intended to fulfill both real humanitarian needs and strategic objectives regarding the allegiance of the Nasser regime. By 1956, Title I food aid deliveries had already reached $19 million. In that momentous year, the United States backed out of the Aswan Dam construction project, Nasser nationalized the Suez Canal, and the joint British–French–Israeli invasion of Egypt occurred, resulting in, among other things, a freeze on all US economic aid. By 1958, relations were improving with the newly formed United Arab Republic (UAR)—which had been established through the "merger" of Egypt and Syria in February 1958—despite American participation in the Lebanon–Jordan intervention. The Eisenhower administration sought to exploit this opportunity, and, by the end of the second term, three new PL 480 agreements had been signed totaling $164 million.

The Kennedy administration took office determined to develop further these tentative openings to the Arab world. Kennedy chose as his ambassador John Badeau, a respected Arabist, and instructed him to encourage moderation and conciliation in Nasser's foreign policy through a variety of means, including the selective use of economic assistance. This strategy was abetted by the withdrawal of Syria from the UAR in September 1961, which served to reinforce Nasser's own isolationist fears. At the same time, however, Dean Rusk was cautioning Kennedy against an overly aggressive US policy:

We . . . have no illusions that any broad understanding with Nasser is possible. We do feel, however, that modest assistance is useful to help the UAR meet its massive challenge of industrialization and over-population and to make it clear that there is a continuing alternative to full reliance on Communist Bloc assistance. . . . This position reflects our considered view that efforts to modify specific policies would only (a) make progress on such problems even more difficult than at present; (b) make it more difficult for the UAR to follow a genuine neutral course; and (c) afford new opportunities for Communist exploitation.[8]

Kennedy proceeded slowly but resolutely to improve relations, dispatching Chester Bowles, a high-level State Department official, to Cairo in February 1962 to underscore for Nasser his continued interest. In addition, as a result of Nasser's own request for development assistance, the President enlisted Harvard development economist Edward S. Mason to undertake a mission to the UAR in order to assess Egypt's development plans and overall need for foreign assistance. Mason concluded that Egypt's development plans were reasonable, albeit somewhat optimistic, and he noted regarding US food aid that "the continuation of the PL 480 program at somewhere near the current level is essential if the UAR is to have sufficient foreign exchange to meet its development requirements. Effective planning to meet these requirements would be greatly facilitated by a multi-year program on which, I understand, there have been initial discussions[9]." Mason also warned that US *failure* to act on the UAR's economic and social needs would be likely to result in political and social unrest, increased dependence on the Soviet Union, and further movement toward the Communist bloc [Mason (1962, pp. 10–11)].

On the basis of the Mason Report, plus the recommendations of Rusk, Bowles, and Badeau, the President decided to approve a $390 million multiyear PL 480 agreement as a part of a more comprehensive package of development assistance. This decision was not greeted with universal approval, especially in Congress where a good deal of anti-Nasser sentiment already existed. It is significant that, up through the signing of this 1962 agreement, the pattern of US–UAR relations involving food aid was actually more consistent with the strategy of enticement discussed earlier.

The tone of US policy changed quite suddenly, however, after Nasser's decision in September 1962 to intervene in Yemen after a coup d'etat by his friend Abdulah Sallal. As Presidential adviser Walt W. Rostow recalled, "From the American point of view, Nasser's decision was a setback in both the short run and the long run. Immediately, it raised the question of pressure on Saudi Arabia [an American ally]" [Rostow (1972, p. 199)]. The Yemeni intervention marked the end of direct US economic assistance to Egypt until 1967, although the US continued to meet its obligation to the multiyear food aid agreement.[10]

Much of the empathy was eliminated from relations between the US and the UAR with John Kennedy's death in 1963. Lyndon Johnson had neither the interest nor the inclination to maintain the kind of personal contact with Nasser established by his predecessor. In January 1964, Ambassador Badeau underscored for Johnson (just before he was replaced) the fact that US interest in the UAR was "to blunt Soviet penetration, to preserve Western access to sea and air routes and to Arab oil; and to promote peace and progress in the area." Badeau also warned the President bluntly that "the UAR remains heavily dependent on Soviet military aid, but Western aid—particularly PL 480—has helped preserve non-alignment. . . . Cessation of U.S. aid to the U.A.R. would not moderate their policies, would nullify the gains since 1956, and jeopardize our interests. *The guillotine can only be used once per subject*"[emphasis added].[11] But US economic and technical aid remained suspended, due to further provocation by Nasser during the Congolese crisis, and Johnson also ordered food aid shipments curtailed as a further indication of US displeasure.

Nasser again requested a new PL 480 agreement in September 1964, but a series of events late in the year induced a renewed deterioration in relations. On November 23, the USIA library in Cairo was burned and a private plane belonging to an American firm was shot down. President Johnson reacted by seizing upon Nasser's request for additional food aid as an opportunity to pressure the UAR to modify the anti-US aspects of its foreign policy. Nasser was reportedly furious upon learning of the President's demands, and he proclaimed in a speech at Port Said on December 23,

If the Americans think that by giving some aid they can dominate the UAR policy they are wrong. We are ready to reduce our consumption of tea, coffee, et cetera, to maintain our independence. . . . If they [the United States] don't like our behavior, they can "drink from the sea" [i.e., go jump in the lake]. We will not sell our independence. If anyone reproaches us, we shall "cut out his tongue."[12]

President Johnson, under heavy congressional pressure, reacted to Nasser's speech by ordering the further cessation of US economic aid.

Efforts were made in Congress during the early months of 1965 to legislate a compelte halt to PL 480 aid to Egypt. But, in lieu of tieing the President's hands completely, the Senate passed a measure leaving the final decision to his discretion. This action in part reflected administration concern that an open break with Nasser might conceivably endanger US and British Middle East interests, including military and civilian air rights, oil concessions, and passage through the Suez Canal.

Despite Nasser's inflammatory rhetoric, however, the UAR *was* seriously in need of continued American food shipments. Thus, in April, Nasser made a conciliatory gesture by discontinuing arms shipments to the (then) Belgian Congo. On this pretext, the US once again resumed food aid shipments in June 1965, while at the same time warning that any "untoward developments" would "limit Executive Branch capability to deal with Congressional critics."[13]

Nasser maintained his new policy of moderation through the end of 1965. He agreed, for example, to abide by a cease-fire in Yemen, to pay a $500,000 settlement for damages to the USIA library destroyed by the firebombing, and to reduce the stridency of anti-United States comments in the state controlled press. As a result, despite serious congressional misgivings, two new Title I agreements were concluded in January 1966 providing $56 million in food aid (as opposed to the $500 million requested by Nasser). But the terms of the aid were hardened substantially in that repayment was required in dollars rather than local currency, and the agreement was made applicable for only a *six-month* period— thereby indicating Washington's intention to make future aid contingent on a continuation of the UAR's moderate policy line.

During the first half of 1966, Nasser began to strain against the US "short tether." In July, after the six-month PL 480 agreement expired, his speeches resumed their defiant and contentious tone: "The freedom we have bought with our blood we shall not sell for wheat, for rice, or for anything [PL 480 had been stopped] because we spoke of Israel, and nuclear development, Saudi Arabia and China as we feel" [*The New York Times*, 28 July (1966, p. 4)]. Nasser's rhetorical hostility and other symbolic actions—for example, inviting the Viet Cong to open an office in Cairo—prompted the United States once again to refuse another UAR food aid request. By early 1967, Nasser saw little hope of obtaining any additional US aid, and he further increased his anti-US campaign, calling for the ouster of King Faissal of Saudi Arabia. Later in the year, of course, the entire matter was superseded by events as renewed Arab–Israeli hostility caused Egypt to break diplomatic relations entirely with the United States.

In retrospect, the strategy of using food aid as a form of political sanction in order to express displeasure with Egyptian policies and actions from 1962 to 1967 was an ill advised, but nonetheless unavoidable, response to political conditions at that time. The policy was ill advised in that it served only to confirm Nasser's own worst suspicions about US motivations in the Middle East and, in turn, to make him even more suspicious. Yet, given Nasser's unpredictable nature and the vehement anti-US tone of many of his public pronouncements, the White House had little choice but to react to the Egyptian insults in some fashion or risk a more drastic congressional response.

It is also true that, in the short term, the threat and application of US political sanctions *did* have a moderating influence on the Nasser regime, particularly when it was (1) in severe need of the food or (2) in a period of cool relations with Moscow. In fact, from a strategic perspective, the manipulation of US food aid probably left the United States in a slightly more advantageous position—or, at least, no worse off—than it would have been had it not used food as a political lever. Gamel Nasser, like his American counterpart, Lyndon Johnson, knew how to manipulate propaganda and foreign policy as it suited his purposes. He saw as clearly as anyone what the United States wanted in the Middle East, and he therefore chose at some times to acquiesce and at others to resist the short tether. Ultimately, the course of other Middle Eastern events in 1967 left the United States in a less advantageous diplomatic position relative to the UAR than had prevailed in 1961. But, in the intervening years, the United States had used its food aid successfully in order to promote its political interests and to provide the UAR with a viable alternative to continued, heavy reliance on Soviet economic support.

SUPPORT FOR US SECURITY INTERESTS

One of the key foreign policy functions that food aid has performed is that of economic support for regimes considered critical to US security interests. The lack of adequate food supplies, or supplies available at prices affordable by LDC populations, is often a principal cause of urban unrest and regime destabilization. Thus, the United States has found that timely food assistance can be an expeditious means of retaining in power those regimes which are favorable to its policies. Moreover, food aid has served frequently as an effective quid pro quo for the attainment of specific, US security needs such as military base rights or supporting military assistance. Of course, food aid was also a critical factor for years in the direct military involvement of the United States in Southeast Asia.

Beyond its obvious role in immediate food shortage situations, the question may well be asked, "On what basis can food aid be considered an attractive strategic instrument?" The answer is, in fact, that food is *not* superior in any respect to other forms of assistance; it is simply more available. This conclusion parallels that reached in a major White House food aid policy study in 1974. The study found that "with respect to security-related programs, food aid cannot be judged an inherently more effective form of assistance than grants of dollar aid. . . . Grants provide recipients with the greater economic flexibility which is normally desirable in security-related budget and balance of payments support programs" [CIEP (1974a, p. 1)]. But there are three particular features which do make food aid attractive from a strategic perspective: it can be allocated quickly and on easy credit terms; it does not require prior congressional approval; and it can be initiated or increased in a recipient country specifically to offset cutbacks in other aid or to meet contingencies (since there was no effective legislative limitation on the size of the annual PL 480 program until the early 1970s).

It would appear, therefore, that food aid is used for strategic purposes not because it is particularly well suited to the task but because its specific programmatic configuration offers the executive branch a more flexible policy instrument than most other options at its immediate disposal. The data in table 6.1 provide a good indication of the actual scope of the government's strategic use of the Title I food aid resource. For fiscal year 1973 alone, short-term security objectives accounted for about 30 percent of Title I commitments, while other related political interests accounted for approximately another 40 percent. Thus, if the strategic use of food aid is defined broadly to include both immediate security objectives and longer-term interests in encouraging a pro-US attitude among recipient governments, nearly 70 percent of Title I aid (which itself represents about 70 percent of total PL 480 resources) was committed in 1973 for such purposes. Under these circumstances, it may be useful to examine a few of the more representative types of strategic concerns that food aid has satisfied: support for regimes on the edge (or "rim")

Table 6.1
PL 480 Programs by Objective: Title I Programs Shown by Country (Millions of US Dollars)

Program Type	Actual				Proposed
	1970	1971	1972	1973	1974
Security–shorter-term political					
Indochina–Asia					
Cambodia	–	0.9	9.8	29.1	194.2
Thailand	–	–	–	2.9	28.1
Vietnam	124.0	117.2	108.4	176.9	304.2
Subtotal	124.0	118.1	118.2	208.9	526.5
Middle East					
Israel	41.0	50.7	49.8	45.7	39.4
Jordan	–	1.2	1.9	5.8	6.8
Lebanon	–	6.4	6.1	–	–
Subtotal	41.0	58.3	57.8	51.5	46.2
Base Rights					
Iceland	0.6	0.8	0.6	0.7	0.5
Portugal	–	–	–	17.9	10.4
Subtotal	0.6	0.8	0.6	18.6	10.9
Short-term Political					
Burma	1.9	–	–	–	–
Guinea	1.9	4.6	5.1	3.2	3.0
Guyana	0.1	0.3	–	0.2	–
Liberia	–	1.0	1.6	–	–
Sierra Leone	–	–	0.5	–	–
Taiwan	–	9.7	5.1	4.5	–
Zaire	2.3	1.1	2.3	0.3	–
Subtotal	6.2	16.7	14.6	8.2	3.0
Total security–STP	171.8	193.9	191.2	287.2	586.6
% of total PL 480	(15.8)	(17.6)	(17.4)	(29.4)	(57.9)
Commercial–Political					
Korea	–	130.8	151.2	149.4	6.0
% of total PL 480	–	(11.9)	(13.7)	(15.3)	(.6)
Humanitarian					
Title II	263.0	302.8	403.7	290.0	267.0
% of total PL 480	(24.2)	(27.5)	(36.7)	(29.7)	(26.3)
Economic development–Long-Term Political					
Afghanistan	3.0	3.0	6.3	1.8	–
Bangladesh	–	–	–	–	38.1
Bolivia	7.2	0.4	3.9	2.7	13.8
Chile	9.2	–	–	–	–
Colombia	5.2	8.1	5.2	3.6	12.1
Dominican Republic	6.2	8.9	12.4	0.1	0.5
Ecuador	2.1	–	4.7	5.6	1.2
Ghana	17.8	11.0	6.5	2.4	–
India	186.8	146.6	33.4	–	–
Indonesia	128.7	126.6	114.9	103.8	10.8
Jamaica	–	–	–	–	0.8
Korea	99.0	–	–	–	–
Morocco	2.9	17.5	24.8	1.2	9.3

Table 6.1 (continued)

	Actual				Proposed
	1970	1971	1972	1973	1974
Pakistan	85.4	63.6	67.2	70.6	30.1
Paraguay	1.5	2.7	1.6	–	–
Philippines	9.5	9.2	20.4	23.3	7.0
Sri Lanka	7.3	8.1	21.2	10.9	4.4
Sudan	–	–	–	1.1	5.0
Tunisia	16.8	12.1	14.1	3.5	8.6
Turkey	37.1	20.1	3.1	–	–
Total economic development–LTP	625.7	437.9	339.7	230.6	141.7
% of total PL 480	(57.6)	(39.7)	(30.8)	(23.4)	(14.0)
Market development	24.9	37.0	15.2	20.3	12.2
% of total PL 480	(2.3)	(3.4)	(1.4)	(2.1)	(1.2)
Total PL 480	1,085.4	1,102.4	1,101.0	977.5	1,013.5

Source: CIEP (1974a).

of the Soviet sphere of influence; contribution to direct US military operations; and payment for facilitating US security needs.

Regime Support

Food aid has long been a key factor in efforts to lend assistance to governments whose continued existence and viability are considered essential to the United States either because of their sensitive geopolitical location, i.e., on the rim of the Communist world, or due to their symbolic importance as a US ally. The long-standing US–India aid relationship represents a well-documented example of such strategic support, particularly with regard to the former category. India received its first shipment of US food commodities under the PL 480 program in 1956 in a three-year, $360 million Title I agreement. The food, intended to be utilized over a three-year period, was exhausted within two; the world was suddenly beginning to comprehend the enormity of India's impending food population problem. Over the next two years (1958–1960), the United States entered into three additional food aid agreements with the government of India totaling $535 million. In addition, as a result of President Eisenhower's successful visit to the subcontinent, a fifth agreement—the largest in the history of the PL 480 program up to that time—was signed in May 1960 for $1.3 billion in wheat and rice commodity aid over a four-year period.

By 1964, the shortage of domestically grown grain was the worst since India's independence in 1947 and hoarding by speculators had caused severe local shortages and inflationary pressures. The situation had become critical by the summer, with widespread demonstrations and riots in the food deficit states and attempted looting of food stores. Armed police intervention was required to restrain the demonstrators.

United States concern about the food situation in India increased substantially during the fall of 1964, as witnessed by internal memorandum prepared for Secretary of Agriculture Orville Freeman:

The situation in India is apparently very bad. The food crisis, the political crisis and the development crisis (which is first of all a long-run food crisis) are serious and inseparable. All are deteriorating rapidly if our observers are correct. The middle ground in the political spectrum . . . is fast disappearing as the various political factions polarize on the right and on the left. . . . Our efforts to alleviate the food crisis may be thwarted if the country does not hold together and if Shastri [the Prime Minister] is replaced by a left of center group.[14]

Accordingly, in September 1964 the United States provided another $398 million Title I aid.

In early 1965, however, a secret CIA report [CIA (1965, p. 2)] was predicting that renewed civil disturbances were likely to accompany the continuing Indian food shortages; these were considered potentially damaging to the position of the ruling Congress party for the upcoming state and national elections in 1967. Moreover, the report noted that a serious weakening of Congress party domination would end two decades of political stability and "would probably produce a formal shift in power from the center to the provincial and local governments." Finally, the assessment emphasized that "the Communists—both the Peiping- and Moscow-oriented wings—would be quick to try to exploit any general decline in India's political stability or civil order" [CIA (1965, pp. 3–5)]. The seriousness of these events from a strategic perspective is revealed by the fact that, beginning in 1965, Lyndon Johnson involved himself personally in the ongoing discussions about Indian food aid.[15]

India's food needs have generally been larger than those of most other recipients, rendering valid cross-national comparisons somewhat spurious. The United States has also provided similar food aid support, however, to other governments it wished to retain in power. For example, the regime of South Korean President Syng Mahn Rhee received substantial shipments of US wheat following the Korean War in order to aid it in the consolidation of power. Food assistance is, in fact, a particularly attractive instrument for such purposes because the United States may either offer the aid on purely humanitarian terms (Title II), or permit the

regime to sell the food on the open market (Title I) for whatever purposes it deems appropriate for the maintenance of its base of political
support.

Military Support

In many situations where US allies were involved in military entangle-
ments, the common defense provisions of Title I have been used to
generate local currency which, in turn, released foreign exchange to purchase war material or to pay soldiers. In the case of South Vietnam, for
example, as the US involvement deepened during the Kennedy and Johnson administrations, Title I food aid was used to provide needed military
backup support.[16] PL 480 assistance actually began flowing to South
Vietnam during the Eisenhower era (1955). Early Title I agreements
were relatively small, never exceeding $10 million. But after the historic
Taylor–Rostow mission, dispatched to Vietnam by President Kennedy in
the fall of 1961,[17] US food aid agreements increased from a $2.5 million
agreement in March 1961 to a $15 million accord in December and a $14
million pact in November 1962.

A top-secret memorandum in 1962 from U. Alexis Johnson (Deputy
Under Secretary of State) to McGeorge Bundy (Special Assistant to the
President) indicated that, in clear recognition of the fact that the US government was in violation of the ceiling on aid set by the Geneva Ac-
cords, the White House had authorized US Ambassador Nolting to inform
South Vietnamese President Diem that "the United States would be willing to finance up to $160,000,000 commodity aid, including PL 480,
during FY 1961. . . . Additionally, we have offered and the GVN has accepted 50,000 tons of rice under Title I, PL 480, the purchase price to be
granted back to the GVN for their military budget."[18] The US food assistance effort never did approach the extreme figure emphasized in the
Johnson memorandum, but it does indicate the growing role of food aid
in strategic thinking. Apparently the US offer also had certain quid pro
quo conditions on the aid as well, because Under Secretary Johnson also
informed Bundy that "it is not yet possible to confirm whether the reported instructions by Diem to soften the newspaper campaign against
the United States were in fact issued or being carried out" [U. Alexis
Johnson (1961, p. 2)].

PL 480 agreements with South Vietnam passed the $30 million mark at
the beginning of 1964; four Title I agreements were signed totaling $68
million. At about the same time, the Johnson administration asked the

Congress to approve the use of PL 480 for "internal security" purposes in order to facilitate the so-called "strategic hamlet" program in Vietnam. Under this program, food aid was to be used to feed and (hopefully) to pacify inhabitants after a village had been "liberated" militarily. During the major buildup in American ground forces in 1965-1966, an unprecedented series of eight Title I PL 480 agreements were signed.[19]

It is clear that, as the executive branch became evermore inextricably committed to its political stand in Southeast Asia, food aid became a critical element of the US-financed military effort. The incredible succession of Title I agreements signed during the 1965-1966 period reinforce the validity of the conclusion cited earlier that the fundamental value of food aid as a strategic firefighting weapon lies in its capacity to respond rapidly to crisis situations without the need for congressional oversight.

Mutual Assistance

The use of food to compensate another nation for its assistance in promoting US security objectives also deserves brief mention in this context, specifically the allocation of food aid to secure US access to military base rights. In most cases of this type, however, food assistance has been only one component of a larger package of mutual assistance arrangements.

The most recent examples of US food aid as an explicit quid pro quo for military base rights are food assistance offered to Iceland and Portugal. Iceland, although hardly qualifying as a less developed country, was the recipient of token amounts (i.e., approximately $800-900 thousand per year) in Title I aid each year from the start of the PL 480 program in 1953 through 1973.[20] In fact, it was the new 70:30 per capita income restrictions on Title I, instituted in 1973, that apparently precluded the continuation of this arrangement. Portugal, on the other hand, does not share Iceland's high per capita income, and it has therefore been a larger recipient of US aid.[21]

Aid to both countries shares a common strategic characteristic: the United States is permitted to maintain large military installations on their soil. These agreements are in no way covert, and the food aid—to the extent that it is given for strategic purposes—is allocated as a form of payment in kind for the considerations extended to the United States. It might be noted, however, that since both countries are also US allies within NATO, each also derives a double benefit from its involvement under the US military umbrella.

LEVERAGE IN DIPLOMATIC NEGOTIATIONS

The previous examples of the strategic uses of food aid have conformed to an established pattern whereby certain foreign policy objectives are achieved by the threatened or actual withdrawal of aid, while others are promoted by the promise or actual addition of resources. A similar trend is also discernible in *diplomatic* uses of the food aid instrument, i.e., in situations where the United States has been involved in international political negotiations either as a direct participant or as an intermediary. Food aid has functioned in this context as a bargaining chip through which the United States could help at various times both to speed the cessation of hostilities and to arrange the terms of peace agreements. Accordingly, two cases are here examined where the food aid resource played a discernible role in diplomatic negotiations: the 1965 dispute between India and Pakistan over the Kashmir border area and the 1974 effort to extend the interim peace agreement in the Middle East.

In the case of the Indo–Pakistani dispute, the United States was placed in an extremely difficult diplomatic position when hostilities erupted in August 1965. It was keeping India afloat during its successive crop disasters and, at the same time, it was providing Pakistan with economic and military assistance. When these two neighboring states clashed over the Kashmir area, it was almost inevitable that the United States would be caught squarely in the middle. Chester Bowles, then US ambassador to India, cabled the State Department shortly after the fighting began seeking guidance on the US position; he himself was recommending that "most new loan action . . . should be suspended at least for the duration of the fighting" [Bowles (1965)].

When no immediate response was forthcoming from Washington, Bowles began to suspect that the State Department and the White House were contemplating the manipulation of PL 480 aid in order to force India to cease hostilities. On September 16, Bowles again cabled urgently to Washington:

Ever since the fighting started on August 5, I and members of US mission in Delhi have been bringing every pressure to influence India towards course of moderation in regard to a Pakistan settlement while at the same time seeking to buttress their faith in the USA. Yesterday Indian government in spite of its growing military advantage agreed unconditionally to an immediate ceasefire. If following all-out effort of our mission . . . USA should hold up urgently needed food shipments, our influence in India will be grievously eroded and Soviet influence in-

creased. . . . Following GoI action yesterday in unconditionally accepting U Thant's proposal for cease fire this pressure will be redoubled. . . .
I assure you that I am not repeat not crying wolf.[22]

The best evidence, which is revealed in a secret, internal White House
memorandum,[23] is that Bowles's suspicions were quite correct; the White
House *was* indeed dragging its feet on releasing food aid to both Pakistan and India in hopes of speeding an end to the fighting. President
Johnson was being advised that, by releasing only very limited quantities of wheat, starvation could be avoided but the desired "psychological
effect" still achieved. Meanwhile, in its public pronouncements the administration was claiming that its short-term allocation policy had been
implemented *before* the outbreak of the Kashmir dispute.

While in terms of the historical progression of events, this official explanation does seem to square with the facts, the reality of the situation
was also a good deal more subtle and complex. Indian Agricultural
Minister Subramaniam subsequently defended the US role before the Indian Parliament in early November, pointing out once again that the US
had moved PL 480 onto a short-term basis *prior* to the outbreak of hostilities. Chester Bowles also defended the US policy in a speech before
the Laski Institute in Ahmedabad, stating that charges that PL 480 was
used "to somehow shape Indian political thinking" is "utter,
unadulterated nonsense," since the decision had been made "months
before the fighting began."[24]

It would seem, however, that, as the Indians themselves complained,
even if the decision on the use of food aid had been made months before, the timing of the *implementation* of that decision was extremely
suspect, given the prevailing political situation. The most reasonable explanation is that Lyndon Johnson, enthused as he was at that time with
the idea of employing food aid as a lever to speed Indian agricultural development, thought he might also seize the opportunity to make similar
use of PL 480 (and other foreign aid resources) as a diplomatic lever as
well. This policy was partially implemented by the administration before ultimately running afoul of the facts that neither party (i.e., India or
Pakistan) had ever *requested* Washington to mediate the dispute, and
that negotiations were already progressing through the good offices of
UN Secretary-General U Thant.

As a result, the US strategy of holding up food aid shipments had the
undesirable effect of appearing to involve the United States in a heavy-
handed manner in a situation already well on its way to resolution. The
fact that the United States felt compelled to defend itself so vocally from

the charges in the Indian press that it was manipulating its food aid to force an end to the fighting would appear further to reinforce the fact that such diplomatic manipulation of the aid resource *had* been contemplated up until the time that the larger, negative ramifications became apparent to the administration.

A contrasting example of food aid as a lever in diplomatic negotiations is the more recent example of its use by Secretary of State Henry Kissinger in 1974 as an element of persuasion to convince the Egyptians and Syrians to extend the Interim Middle East Peace Agreements.[25] In this case, however, the element of threatened coercion was apparently not present and the aid was offered instead as a "sweetener" in order to influence both countries not to renew hostilities as they were threatening in their public rhetoric. Kissinger had labored mightily through his "shuttle diplomacy" to conclude the original cease-fire agreement after the Arab–Israeli Yom Kippur War, and he was determined that his efforts would not disintegrate as a result of political intransigence on both sides.

The Secretary of State previously had shown himself adept at recognizing the diplomatic and strategic potential inherent in PL 480. For example, he was a principal architect—along with Richard Nixon—of the "food for war" strategy used in Southeast Asia.[26] In fact, it had long been an accepted fact of life within the Agency for International Development that some portion of the annual PL 480 budget would be held in reserve for use by the Secretary in his diplomatic initiatives.[27] The timing of Kissinger's efforts in late 1974 was propitious, however, due to the prevailing squeeze on available food resources during the 1972–1974 global food "crisis." Thus, both Arab countries were in genuine need of the food assistance, and Egypt was especially desperate because of its traditional price subsidy of retail wheat for the bread staple.

During his last round of shuttle diplomacy earlier in 1974, Secretary Kissinger reportedly promised both the Egyptians and the Syrians that substantial US aid would be forthcoming if they refrained from renewing hostile actions. Consequently, during the World Food Conference in Rome, Secretary of Agriculture Earl Butz, acting by prior agreement with Kissinger and Ford, embarked on a side trip to the Middle East. He signed agreements there committing the United States to supplying 300,000 tons of wheat to Egypt and 75,000 tons of wheat and 24,000 tons of rice to Syria. To many observers—especially those concerned with the deteriorating situation in other, more seriously affected food deficit countries, such as those in the Sahelian region—the Kissinger–

Butz commitment was an out-and-out bribe for continued Middle East peace. Many others, however, welcomed it as a positive and constructive diplomatic usage of the PL 480 resource.[28]

The Kissinger diplomatic initiative was, of course, successful, and the Interim Agreement with Israel was extended by both the Egyptians and Syrians. Although the promise of additional food aid will not always be an appropriate diplomatic response, it is clearly preferable—in a nonstrategic sense—to the threatened withdrawal of aid. Thus, in those cases where additional food resources are valued by one or more parties to a negotiating process, the promise of food assistance may offer one source of diplomatic leverage to generate movement toward a mutually desired foreign policy objective.

FOOD POWER IN INTERNATIONAL DIPLOMACY

Although the United States has long been the predominant agricultural exporter, change in at least two factors since World War II has served to increase the attractiveness of food as a diplomatic and strategic instrument. The first of these is illustrated below in table 6.2. The data reveal that, whereas all geographic regions except Western Europe were net agricultural exporters before World War II, this situation had changed dramatically by the war's end. Since 1948, North American grain exports have more than quadrupled while the net grain balance for other geographical areas has declined severely, entering serious deficit situations in the last two decades. The United States and Canada have now become near-oligopolistic suppliers of grain, a fact which has enhanced greatly the potential economic and political leverage of their exportable food resources. Rothschild has noted that US dominance in grain trade with the developing world is even more pronounced than in grain trade as a whole. The United States provides one-third of the imports for the Western industrialized countries, but almost two-thirds of the LDC imports [Rothschild (1976, p. 288)].

The second significant new factor is of more recent origin. It concerns the declining availability of *other* economic instruments through which the United States can influence the policies and actions of other governments. For example, direct military assistance is often inappropriate on account of other political considerations. At the same time, Congress has grown increasingly skeptical of the value and effectiveness of foreign aid and has thus become less and less willing to spend freely for uncertain payoffs. The US has also failed to maintain its near-monopolistic

Table 6.2
The Changing Pattern of World Grain Trade[a] (Millions of Metric Tons)

Region	1934–1938	1948–1952	1960	1970	1976[b]
North America	+5	+23	+39	+56	+94
Latin America	+9	+1	0	+4	-3
Western Europe	-24	-22	-25	-30	-17
Eastern Europe and USSR	+5	–	0	0	-27
Africa	+1	0	-2	-5	-10
Asia	+2	-6	-17	-37	-47
Australia and New Zealand	+3	+3	+6	+12	+8

Source: Brown (1975, p. 11).
a. Plus sign indicates net exports; minus sign, net imports.
b. Preliminary estimate of fiscal year data.

position on the export of technological expertise and processes; it competes now with Japan, Germany, and a number of other developed countries. The combination of these factors now makes the food resource extremely attractive as a foreign policy instrument.

Precedents exist from as early as the post-World War I era for the diplomatic manipulation of food commodities.[29] But, in the modern, interdependent world, such actions are not quite so simple. For one thing, it is impossible today to divorce political actions from economic actions in international affairs, as was often the case previously. For another, the line between aid and trade, particularly with regard to food, has become blurred by extreme fluctuations in supply and demand. Thus, whereas food may offer substantial diplomatic and commercial leverage in periods of shortage, the long-term manipulation of the response in this fashion may well have substantial negative trade ramifications when the food production pendulum swings back toward a period of abundance.

Under these circumstances, it is necessary to identify and to separate explicitly two distinct manifestations of "food power" in international affairs: *bilateral* applications within specific political contexts and *multilateral* applications within the international arena. Subsequent chapters in this part will address many of the more explicit examples of the bilateral manipulation of US food aid, for example, the relatively well-publicized Indian short-tether policy.

Bilateral food power strategies generally can be categorized under three principal rubrics: *punishment actions*—delaying, obstructing, or prematurely terminating aid shipments; *reward actions*—initiating new

shipments amidst much publicity or increasing aid shipments above
agreed-upon levels; and *mixed actions*—threats or promises during aid
negotiations (Wallensteen (1976, p. 288)]. American bilateral food aid
policy has demonstrated examples of all three types of manifestations.[30]
Lester R. Brown (1975, pp. 36–43) of the World Watch Institute has even
argued that it will become necessary at some point for the United States
and Canada to establish a "Joint U.S.–Canadian Commission on Food
Policy" which would judge the assistance requests of food deficit countries on the basis of their agricultural development and population control efforts. While the chances of such bilateral application of food
power seem rather remote, it is indicative of the serious attention which
the concept engenders in many circles.

In the aftermath of the 1972–1974 food "crisis" period, the bilateral,
diplomatic use of food power has demonstrated a new third-party application as well. For example, according to claims made by former Secretary of Agriculture Earl Butz, US capacity to supply grain badly needed
by the Soviet Union (as a result of poor harvests) perhaps persuaded
Moscow to pressure the North Vietnamese into accepting the terms for a
negotiated cease-fire in 1972–1973.[31] The link between the availability of
US grain and the application of Soviet pressure on the North Vietnamese
was probably not as significant as the Butz perspective on these but the
former Secretary of Agriculture also argues that the temporary US sus-
pension of grain shipments to the Soviet Union in the summer of 1975
was, in some part, responsible for Russian noninterference in the delicate, US-sponsored negotiations between the Egyptians and the Israelis
for an Interim Sinai Peace Agreement.[32]

Apparently, the United States also considered—but later rejected—the
possibility of again withholding Soviet grain shipments in 1976 in retaliation for Russian involvement in the Angolan civil war, deciding that
attempts to link the two most likely would be ineffective and counterproductive.[33] The third-party application of food power is not specifically related to food *aid* per se, but it does represent an intriguing, and
perhaps, far less controversial, means of employing food resources for
diplomatic purposes while avoiding many of the potentially negative effects of similar manipulations in food deficient countries.

United States food power policy within the *multilateral* context has
been used primarily in order to influence the public pronouncements and
voting behavior of food deficient states within the United Nations. Such
diplomatic uses of foreign aid are, of course, not a particularly recent

phenomenon, and they have received substantial attention in the political science literature.[34] The general notion is simply that the closer the degree of congruence between a country's UN voting record and stated policy to that of the United States, the greater the volume of American economic assistance which will be directed to it. Conversely, those nations which criticize the United States consistently or oppose its positions on matters of substance will be most likely to have their aid curtailed or eliminated.

In the more contentious political climate of the seventies, the caucus of less developed countries, known commonly as the Group of 77, emerged as a vocal and active force, highly critical of the United States and other Western developed countries. The Group of 77 put forth a set of demands embodied in what they termed the New International Economic Order (NIEO). But the United States reacted strongly to its continued criticism by the Group of 77 and to the fact that it was being outmaneuvered by bloc voting within the very institution it had been largely responsible for creating. In March 1975, then Harvard Professor Daniel Patrick Moynihan published an influential article entitled "The United States in Opposition" [Moynihan (1975, pp. 35, 44)], in which he argued that the reason why the United States had dealt so unsuccessfully with the Group of 77 and the NIEO was that "we have not seen the ideology as distinctive; not recognizing it, we have sustained no effort to relate ourselves to it." Moynihan thus recommended that the United States no longer maintain its passive and compliant posture in the face of severe Third World criticism and punitive voting actions.

Moynihan soon had the opportunity to implement his philosophy when Gerald Ford appointed him the new US Ambassador to the United Nations. In January 1976, *The New York Times* obtained a cablegram from Ambassador Moynihan to Secretary of State Henry Kissinger (and all US embassies) in which he reiterated that "the new tactic at this mission [i.e., the UN] on the instructions of the President and the Secretary of State has been to respond to attack [i.e., by the Group of 77] with counterattack."[35] Moreover, at about the same time, Secretary Kissinger reportedly initiated a formal policy of selecting for cutbacks in American aid those nations that voted against the United States in the United Nations. In some cases the cutbacks involved food and other humanitarian relief [Gelb (1976, p. 1].

The Kissinger initiative extended into the State Department bureaucracy as well. An Office of Multilateral Affairs (OMA) was established within the Bureau of International Organization, where computers were employed to study and analyze the voting patterns of nations within the United Nations and other international forums; the results were used as one factor in the formulation of US foreign policy. Food aid to both Tanzania and Guyana was, in fact, suspended temporarily in 1976 because these countries voted in the United Nations to condemn "Zionism as racism" and to oppose the Ford administration's position on Korea [Gelb (1976, p. 1)].

The Senate reacted sharply to the Kissinger-Moynihan policy, however, and, with a presidential election approaching, the Secretary of State took steps publicly to downplay the punitive nature of the new State Department Office, emphasizing instead its "informational" role. Moreover, neither the OMA nor the punitive counterattack policy of the Ford administration was continued by President Jimmy Carter, although Carter has made clear his intention to enforce previous congressional mandates linking the continuation of foreign aid with positive action on human rights in recipient countries.

It is difficult to determine whether the recent softening in Third World approaches to its NIEO demands and to its relations with the United States and other developed countries is due to a realization that the United States does have at its disposal certain instruments—such as food aid—with which it can retaliate when attacked, or if it simply reflects a more mature, low-key approach to international relations. Most likely, the improving climate is a result of these and other factors as well, but it is clear that the food deficit countries have been offered a none too subtle reminder that, despite their contention that global interdependence is a two-way street, the *United States* still grows the food. Given the necessary provocation, the United States has demonstrated its willingness to use food and other economic leverage to protect its vital interests within both the bilateral and multilateral contexts.

ASSESSMENT OF POLICY OBJECTIVES

This chapter has covered a broad array of diplomatic and strategic uses of food aid as an instrument of political leverage. Each of the case examples encompassed a unique set of factors and conditions which demanded a new and original application of the food aid resource. At least two common threads are discernible in these cases, however, which bear directly on the appropriateness and effectiveness of food as a foreign policy instrument. The first such characteristic is that the *conception* of food aid in all the examples was either (1) as a short-term instrument designed to accomplish a discrete policy objective or (2) as a longer-term symbol of US power and influence. The second common denominator is that the *implementation* of the food aid instrument was accomplished either (1) through the threatened withdrawal of the resource or (2) through the promise of additional resources.

It was frequently the case that the apparent failure of policymakers to think through clearly the foreseeable obstacles in moving from policy conception to policy implementation was responsible for the ineffective, and in some cases, counterproductive application of food aid as a foreign policy instrument. Thus, for example, in the cases of the UAR and India, where the threat to withdraw food aid was employed, officials had not fully considered either the timing of their action in relation to other ongoing events or the impact of their decision in relation to the personalities of the recipient country's leadership. Similarly, when the United States acted to implement the Kissinger–Moynihan doctrine of using food and other aid to "punish" those who voted against it in the United Nations, public reaction both at home and abroad soon forced a modification of this policy.

At the root of the problem is not only the apparent inability of policymakers to understand the likely ramifications of their decisions but also a more fundamental problem related to the nature of the food aid resource itself. From the case examples examined here, it would appear that food aid is ill suited to most strategic and diplomatic applications because it is not a "clean" foreign policy instrument. That is, while food assistance has been perceived increasingly since 1961 as a foreign aid resource to be allocated in support of US global objectives in much the same manner as capital loans and grants, the fact of the matter is that the food resource differs *substantially* from capital or technical assistance.

Whereas capital and technical resources are useful for a wide variety of purposes which affect individuals only indirectly (e.g., industrialization, bridge and road construction), food maintains at least the appearance of intended use to *feed* malnourished human beings.[36] Thus, when the United States threatens to withhold food to coerce certain actions from a recipient government, it is vulnerable to attack as callous, immoral, and exploitative. At the same time, when an administration employs food aid politically by promising additional aid in return for certain recipient government behavior, it is again subject to criticism for diverting the food from more important humanitarian and developmental applications in countries with critical food deficits. It is, in some respects, a no win proposition for the United States, and there would appear to be little justification for, or likelihood of, a change in world reaction to American manipulation of the food resource as long as serious hunger and malnutrition continues to exist.

An appreciation of this fundamental difficulty with food as a diplomatic and strategic instrument lends a new aspect to the consideration of the two common policy characteristics outlined earlier. It suggests, for example, that conceptually, food aid is a poor instrument for the pursuit of short-term policy objectives whose implementation involves the threatened or actual withdrawal of resources. As former US ambassador to Egypt John Badeau correctly noted regarding the withdrawal of food aid to the UAR, "The guillotine can only be used but once per victim." That is, after a threat is made, there ensues almost immediately a loss of donor credibility and a deterioration in bilateral relations.

Food aid has also been criticized even when used as a positive (i.e., additional) tool for encouraging certain recipient government behavior. The evidence examined here indicates, however, that conceptually the enticement strategy is far more appropriate in the context of food than the coercive approach. Thus, although the offer of additional food aid had mixed but generally positive results in the case of Yugoslavia, it was of *substantial* value in the 1974 Middle East peace negotiations.

In situations where the policy goal is primarily to symbolize the power and influence of the United States, either food aid application may be effective depending on the context. For example, the enticement strategy is far better suited to quid pro quo arrangements involving military base rights—or even simply to maintain a US diplomatic presence in a particular country—while the threatened withdrawal of assistance is more effective under conditions in which vital US interests are at stake and the application of food power therefore represents an appropriate political response (e.g., multilateral applications within the United Nations). It should be reiterated, however, that the negative, long-term effects of the indiscriminate use of food power may well outweigh its short-term diplomatic benefits, because of the destructive effect on US bilateral and multilateral relationships.

Finally, it is appropriate to assess food aid in a more comprehensive fashion as an instrument of strategic and diplomatic leverage. From a strategic perspective, selective deployment of the aid resource has accomplished a wide variety of objectives, such as buying base rights, stabilizing volatile political situations within strategically critical countries, contributing directly to US military initiatives, and currying favor with Communist bloc nations. From a diplomatic perspective, however, the use of food has not demonstrated as consistently positive a record. Accurate assessment in this case is complicated by the fact that food aid relationships between countries cannot be considered in isolation from other major components of international relations. But, in general, the experience documented here would suggest that, when employed *selectively* and with restraint, food aid does offer certain advantages as an instrument of foreign policy leverage.

The promotion of US agricultural exports had its conceptual roots in policies formulated long before the existence of a formal US food aid program. This is the legacy of America's historic record of agricultural abundance. Food aid has served most commonly either as a temporary pressure release mechanism when surpluses grew insufferably large or as a means of introducing a taste for American wheat (and other products) among new consumers. In recent years, however, the trade promotion functions of food aid have been expanded considerably.

Food is now used in a wide variety of applications that relate only tangentially to the development or expansion of US agricultural markets abroad. This chapter will consider the nature of these broader international trade interests, which, in the present context, shall be defined as all activities designed to expand the volume of US exports or to protect commercial markets already established. The application of PL 480 resources in such an eclectic fashion is a far cry indeed from its original conception in 1954.

AGRICULTURAL MARKET DEVELOPMENT

Recent efforts to develop new agricultural export opportunities through PL 480 are, of course, an evolutionary outgrowth of the surplus disposal–market development objectives embodied in the original food aid legislation, the Agricultural Trade Development and Assistance Act of 1954. The notion was that countries might be "traded up" from the status of aid recipient to that of full paying customer. The line between market development and outright commodity dumping, however, has

become difficult to define, and the food aid program has often functioned more as a means of moving commodities on terms below prevailing world market prices (to relieve immediate domestic storage
pressures) than for establishing solid, long-term commercial trade
relationships.

Since the midsixties, the USDA has made a practice of pointing to certain market development success stories whenever the effectiveness of PL
480 has been questioned by Congress or the President. These examples
are most often countries that originally were substantial food aid recipients but have since graduated to a commercial agricultural trade relationship with the United States. Foremost among these successes, in the
USDA's estimation, is the case of Taiwan.

The United States began to pour millions of dollars of economic assistance into this island enclave shortly after the expulsion of the Nationalist Chinese forces from the mainland at the end of World War II.
Initially, the object was to prevent Taiwan's imminent economic collapse, but later efforts were designed to establish a showcase of anti-
Communist resistance. According to Jacoby (1966, pp. 39–42), US foreign aid to the Nationalist government totaled $1,462 million between
1950 and 1965, and consisted of defense support (64 percent), direct
forces support (9 percent), and PL 480 food aid (27 percent). During the
late 1950s, nonfood economic assistance fluctuated between $70 and
$130 million per year, while PL 480 shipments were valued at between
$4–18 million annually. In 1961, defense support was terminated, how-
ever, and nonfood assistance declined significantly thereafter, re-
stabilizing at a new level of $20–30 million per year. But, at the same
time that capital assistance was shrinking, Title I aid under PL 480 was
expanding to between $30–40 million annually—partially in order to
compensate for the loss of direct military assistance. The Taiwanese
economy was sufficiently robust by 1964 that David Bell, US AID administrator, was able to announce that *all* nonmilitary assistance, except
for limited volumes of PL 480, would be terminated at the end of fiscal
1965. Limited amounts of food aid continued to be allocated on a sporadic basis through fiscal 1971, but it was no longer considered necessary
for the nation's survival.[1]

The United States had clearly succeeded in creating a vigorous economic trading partner in East Asia, which furthered both its foreign
policy objective of containing Chinese Communist expansion and its
agricultural market development interests as well. Significantly, the
Taiwanese had acquired an enduring preference for US wheat (which

could not be grown locally) over the twenty-year period of US food assistance, and now they could well afford to spend foreign exchange to purchase their requirements. Consequently, between 1967 and 1974, US agricultural exports to Taiwan climbed by a staggering 531 percent,[2] thereby justifying the USDA claims of success for the "trade up" strategy.

Some instances of US agricultural market development employing food aid have been a good deal more aggressive than the example of Taiwan. There the United States has used PL 480, for example, as a means of forcing the Soviet Union out of the lucrative vegetable oil seed market in Iran. According to Morgan (1975, p. 1), the USDA had regarded Iran as its "domain" in the world oil seed trade throughout the 1960s. But then the Iranians discovered that they could purchase lower-priced sunflower seed oil from the Soviets, and by 1968, the US share of the Iranian market had begun to decline. In order to counteract this situation, the USDA made available $19.5 million in long-term, low-interest Title I credits, which apparently helped to convince an Iranian bank and private corporation to purchase an additional 83,000 tons of American soybean and cottonseed oil.

The Soviet Union could not possibly compete with the concessional terms on which the PL 480 commodities were sold, and it was soon forced to withdraw from the Iranian market. Shortly thereafter, in 1969, the availability of the PL 480 subsidy was terminated almost as suddenly as it began, and the Iranians were asked once again to pay full value for their vegetable oil. It is not known why the Soviets did not attempt at this point to reenter the Iranian market, but the result was that food aid had been used to develop—or, in this particular case, to protect—US agricultural markets by undercutting the competition, driving it out, and then returning the trade relationship to a straight commercial basis.

Morgan[3] has also suggested that PL 480 has been mobilized for the benefit of American agriculture in other ways as well. He notes that, in 1975 alone, the US rice industry received more than $200 million in contracts through PL 480. These purchases were particularly critical for California growers who have almost no other market for the short-grained variety which they produce.

COMMERCIAL MARKET ACCESS

There is a second market development strategy which employs US food aid, and it is also, in many respects, an outgrowth of the more traditional export objectives embedded in the original PL 480 concept. Under this conception, Title I food aid resources have been employed as a means of obtaining, or creating de novo, access to LDC markets by US-based multinational corporations. These markets are most often for the export of US agricultural products, although there have also been efforts made to use food aid as a quid pro quo for gaining or protecting nonfood commercial markets as well (see also the section following). Two examples of food aid as a market access mechanism are considered here, one dealing with an ongoing (agriculturally related) market for fertilizer in India and the other involving the creation of an agricultural import market in South Korea.

United States involvement in the domestic production of fertilizer in India was significant both for what it did and did not represent as a policy precedent. The adequacy of Indian fertilizer supplies first became an issue of major significance in 1965 during the period of India's serious monsoon failures. These climatic aberrations caused major crop failures and the subsequent reorientation of Indian agricultural development policies. One of the centerpieces of this new development strategy was the establishment of ambitious goals for increasing the rate of domestic fertilizer output.

In October 1965, John A. Schnittker, Under Secretary of Agriculture, prepared a candid memorandum for President Johnson in which he emphasized the direct connection between India's insufficient fertilizer production capacity and its growing food deficit:

We delude ourselves and the people of India if we continue to treat the month-to-month and year-to-year symptoms of India's food problem by shipping ever-growing quantities of food on concessional terms while neglecting the basic causes of these growing shortages. The central issue for the future of food production in India is fertilizer production. . . . India's nitrogen fertilizer needs to meet food production goals by 1970/71, are 2.6 million tons. This represents a *nine-fold increase* from 1965 production levels [emphasis added].[4]

Schnittker underscored the nature of India's fertilizer production problem and made a series of recommendations for the President's consideration:

The record of the Indian Government and the Indian economy in managing the fertilizer industry is tragic. It takes chemical engineers to operate a fertilizer industry. India has been operating largely with clerks. The fertilizer record is one of plants planned but never built, of plants which were built but did not function properly; of a *negative attitude toward outside capital; of an unwillingness to provide the incentives required for profitable foreign private investment. . . .* India's cultivators are asking for 2–3 times as much fertilizer as is available. To meet these demands and her own food needs, *India must turn to private foreign investment to do the job* [emphasis added]. [Schnittker (1965, p. 2]

India must improve the climate for foreign private investment, so that foreign capital with its accompanying managerial and technical know-how can supplement India's resources. Ministerial platitudes are not enough. Something must be done so that the bone-crushing bureaucracy of the Indian Government does not stifle the prospects for the future. . . . Corporations, consortiums, and individuals are ready to move into a *favorable* investment climate in India [emphasis added]. [Schnittker (1965, p. 2)]

Schnittker's eloquent but blunt message found a receptive audience in Lyndon Johnson, who, by 1965, was prepared to do whatever might be necessary to get India *off* the permanent US food dole. Consequently, one of the conditions[5] which the President attached to the release of any furthur US grain shipments to India was a change in official government policy regarding the regulation of companies owned by foreign private interests. The United States also demanded that, henceforth, foreign fertilizer companies—not the Indian government—be given full control over product pricing and distribution so that production could be moved onto a profitable basis.

The government of India thus was faced with a difficult decision. On the one hand, it was incapable of purchasing enough fertilizer on world markets because it lacked the necessary foreign exchange; nor could it hope to meet its needs through foreign aid, because few countries were in a position to give fertilizer as aid. Yet, on the other hand, the Indians clearly had little choice but to increase domestic production, since the United States had stated specifically that it would not be willing to continue indefinitely as the residual supplier of India's food and fertilizer needs. Ultimately, India was forced to accept the US conditions, which included freedom for private corporations to set their own marketing and distribution schemes; division of ownership of fertilizer plants between the government, private Indian investors, and private foreign companies; and permission for private companies to use the large, US-owned reserve of Indian currency as Cooley loans to help finance the involvement of US companies.

The measures taken by the Gandhi government found little favor in domestic political circles.[6] But the change in official policy slowly began to have the desired effect. During 1966, for example, two US companies, Standard of Indiana, Inc., and the International Minerals and Chemicals

Co., Inc., announced plans to invest in new Indian fertilizer production facilities.[7] It has been argued that India was not actually *forced* to accept these plants by the threat that food aid would be restricted or eliminated, but that "U.S. policy in this case seemed to be marked by nothing so much as a paternalistic, 'do it because it's for your own good,' attitude" [Weaver (1971, p. 29)]. The evidence reviewed by the author, however, would seem to suggest otherwise.

While there *was* clearly a strong element of paternalism in the US position, the policy was not quite this simple or benign. The Johnson administration was saying essentially, "Do it because it's good for you *and* because you *must* do it in order to obtain the grain you need to prevent further starvation and continued deterioration of political conditions." This is not meant to imply, however, that the US position was completely insensitive to the Indian's plight, nor that there was some covert profit motive hidden in the action. The Johnson administration was aware no doubt that private US corporations would profit substantially under the new arrangement, but in this particular instance, it was more than simply a case of government–industry "cooperation."

The policy was motivated, instead, by the realization that, without a rapid increase in fertilizer production and availability, the US approach to India's food problem would be a failure. Since there was generally wide agreement at the time that India was unwilling to take the necessary steps *on its own* to expand indigenous fertilizer production sufficiently, the Johnson administration determined to compel it to do so anyway. This approach ultimately offered three major benefits: (1) it helped Indian leaders to confront the hard and unpopular decisions necessary to increase domestic agricultural output; (2) it gained access to new commercial fertilizer markets for US companies; and (3) it saved the United States from the embarrassment of committing its food aid resources heavily to an unsuccessful policy. In light of the remarkable improvements in Indian domestic agricultural production, which were helped in no small measure by the parallel "green revolution" during the late sixties and early seventies, the US policy of withholding food aid as a means of forcing India to permit entry of foreign fertilizer companies was an important and positive initiative both from commercial trade and foreign policy perspectives.

The second example of commercial market access did not involve the manipulation of food aid resources in order to force penetration against the host government's will, but rather, the creation of completely new commercial opportunities for US multinational corporate interests. This case concerns the efforts by South Korean subsidiaries of the Ralston-Purina company and the Cargill and Peavy grain companies to use local currency credits under PL 480 to establish poultry raising and animal feed operations in South Korea. The object was both to establish profitable foreign subsidiaries and, at the same time, to generate additional demand for US wheat and corn exports.

The South Korean initiative was facilitated by a relatively new feature of the PL 480 legislation, known as private trade entity (PTE) loans, under which the US government grants credits to American subsidiaries overseas to buy Title I commodities. These companies, in turn, use the local currency proceeds from the sale of the commodities in order to generate necessary operating capital. According to Morgan (1975, p. 1), PL 480 dollar credits in 1975 to the three aforementioned private companies totaled $12 million, and they financed the importation of 193,000 metric tons of corn, animal fat, and wheat flour. The US government also financed portions of the ocean freight for these commodities and provided terms of credit at what one company official called "better than commercial rates" [Morgan (1975, p. 1)]. The availability of the PTE loans helped to finance highly profitable egg-laying and broiler operations in Korea as well as an unsuccessful effort to establish an American-style cattle feedlot operation.[8]

But this was only part of the reason why the market creation initiative in South Korea was so successful. At the same time that the United States extended the PTE loans, it also used its PL 480 leverage in order to obtain guarantees from the government of South Korea that no restrictions would be placed on the flow of feedgrain imports from the United States for at least three years. This action, in effect, *ensured* the existence of necessary grain supplies for the new commercial operations while, at the same time, it guaranteed a ready market for US feedgrain exports to Korea. The net effect was a double set of benefits for the United States: the profitability of US multinational overseas subsidiaries was promoted, and the demand for US agricultural exports and technological expertise was increased.

The contrast between the Indian and Korean examples is substantial. Whereas the former represented a large, well-orchestrated US effort to shift the pace and focus of Indian agricultural development efforts, it apparently involved little or no coordinated, government–private sector activity (although each was surely aware of the other's needs and interests). In the latter case, however, a more comprehensive US policy objective was not in evidence. But the level of government–private sector interaction was apparently quite high in that the public and private sectors cooperated in mobilizing resources for their mutual benefit. The final outcome in the case of South Korea was, in relative terms, at least as effective as the Indian example, although achieving a different type of result. The South Korean initiative also offered the additional advantage of being implemented *with* the apparent cooperation (or at least compliance) of the host government and *without* the element of coercion that later encumbered US relations with India.

COMMERCIAL MARKET PROTECTION

It has been established that the flexible terms of Title I, PL 480 food aid has facilitated a wide variety of commercial applications, many of which are virtually unrelated to the context of food aid used *as* food, i.e., as an essential human resource. When used for nonfood purposes, Title I commodities cease in most respects to have a recognizable function as *food* aid and become instead simply another form of capital resource transfer which can be employed in support of US policy interests.[9] The current case example illustrates yet another of the nonfood, economic objectives pursued through the manipulation of Title I food aid resources: the protection of US textile markets from encroachment by lower-priced exports from South Korea.

Since the shift from cotton to man-made synthetic fibers in the 1960s, the US textile industry and organized labor have pressed vigorously for the establishment of import quotas on foreign-made goods that can be produced far more cheaply due to substantially lower labor costs. The US government had, in fact, tried but failed in 1969 to negotiate an international agreement on synthetic textiles (similar to the long-term agreement extant for cotton) within the General Agreement on Tariffs and Trade (GATT). As a result of this failure, the United States initiated direct bilateral negotiations with its four major competitors, Japan, Hong Kong, Taiwan, and South Korea.

These countries opposed individual quota agreements ostensibly on the grounds that they were inconsistent with the provisions of the GATT. They demanded instead that negotiations be carried forward on an item-by-item basis only *after* the United States had demonstrated that the specific import had injured similar domestic production. But the Nixon administration came under heavy congressional and private pressure in 1970–1971 to protect the struggling US textile industry. Due to South Korea's long-standing dependence on US food aid programs, the administration perceived an opportunity to negotiate a mutually beneficial quid pro quo arrangement.

Accordingly, David Kennedy, an Ambassador-at-Large dealing primarily with economic matters, was dispatched to Seoul in 1971 to make South Korea "an offer it could not refuse." The substance of the US proposal was for $100 million in development loans and an additional $275 million in Title I PL 480 commodities over a three-year period if the government of Park Chung Hee would agree "voluntarily" to restrict its export of synthetic textiles to the United States. A later investigation by the US General Accounting Office found that "this $375 million increase was planned to offset an estimated 5-year $325 million net trade loss to Korea based on an anticipated loss in exports of between $600 and $700 million attributable to the quota restraint. This anticipated loss was reduced by 50 percent to account for a related reduction of imports [US GAO (1974, p. 29)]. Over the course of the next two fiscal years, South Korean "reverse aid" to the US textile industry was rewarded by over 500,000 tons of Title I rice aid [Morgan (1976, p. 10)].

The United States–South Korean agreement was concluded in secret in 1971 and kept from public disclosure until 1974. According to a report appearing in the magazine, *Korea Commentary*, the restrictions were intended to benefit "the heads of the textile industry in the southern U.S., [and] were reportedly important for Nixon's strategy to win over the Southern States in the 1972 elections."[10] Certain difficulties were encountered subsequently in the implementation of the agreement, due to cutbacks in PL 480 in 1973–1974 at the height of the domestic and international grain shortages, and the Office of Management and Budget concluded (somewhat ironically in view of the importance of fiscal restraint in the Nixon administration) in 1975 that "in any case it [the agreement] tends to contribute to inflationary pressures in the U.S. by possibly exerting upward pressure on the prices of textiles and food" [OMB (1976, p. 27)].

Yet, the final outcome of the United States-Korean agreements contained substantial benefits for both parties. The South Koreans were well compensated for their loss of American export markets and in a form which permitted the Park government to maintain its policy of subsidized rice prices. The Nixon administration, for its part, obtained the protection it desired for the US commercial textile industry, curried favor with important southeastern political interests, and managed to move large volumes of surplus rice in the process. It was, from the perspective of both governments, a highly advantageous application of the

Title I resource. This view was not shared, of course, by the individual South Korean farmer, for whom the massive influx of US rice resulted in low market prices for his domestically produced commodities. This, in turn, meant a continued inability to break out of the basic conditions that gave rise to his impoverished conditions.

RESPONSE TO EXPROPRIATION

The range of food aid uses that have been examined so far in this chapter have dealt primarily with American efforts to promote, develop, or defend access to agricultural and other commercial markets. These initiatives can generally be characterized as *active* in orientation; each employed food aid to accomplish a specific objective that was established more or less independently of the policies or actions of other governments. The current case, however, offers an example of a *reactive* policy initiative, i.e., one undertaken primarily in response to actions (anticipated or actual) by another government—specifically, the US decision to withdraw food and other economic assistance from Chile during the period from 1970 to 1973 in partial retaliation for the decision by the government of Salvador Allende Gossens to expropriate, without compensation, the vast holdings of certain American multinational corporations in Chile.

It is important to emphasize that the withdrawal of food aid was merely *one component* of a larger anti-Allende economic and political strategy. Moreover, even in the specific case of food aid, the decision to suspend assistance affected only the Title I concessional sales program and *not* the small, humanitarian Title II programs operated under the auspices of the private voluntary agencies. The crisis atmosphere that developed around the question of continued aid to Chile was also not a new issue when leftist candidate Salvador Allende was elected President in 1970. Ever since Allende first ran for President in 1958 against Jorge Allesandri, the US Central Intelligence Agency (CIA) had been active in trying to prevent a leftist victory. According to Fagan, "Directly and indirectly, perhaps a billion dollars in public funds had been committed by the United States during this period to the 'battle to preserve democracy in Chile,' largely defined as a battle to prevent the Left from coming to power" [Fagen (1975, p. 304)].

After running, again unsuccessfully, against Eduardo Frei in 1964, Allende was finally able to engineer a minority victory in 1970. The outcome of the Chilean elections sent shock waves through the private sector of the entire western world, but it raised particularly intense fears in the United States among private companies, such as the giant copper firms Anaconda and Kennecott, which had major capital assets invested in Chile. The basis for their concern was Salvador Allende's oft stated position that the holdings of foreign companies should be nationalized. The multinational companies realized, however, that their large inventories and capital investments precluded the possibility of either a sudden withdrawal from the Chilean economy or an open confrontation with the new government.

Such private sector apprehension also had parallels within the Nixon administration; Secretary of State Henry Kissinger took a particularly dim view of Allende's victory, reportedly remarking that "I don't see why we need to stand by and watch a country go Communist due to the irresponsibility of its own people" [Fagen (1975, p. 304)]. In fact, the State Department did not just "stand by"; according to Barnet and Müller, the Department instructed American Ambassador Edward Korry on 15 September 1970 " 'to do all possible short of a Dominican-type situation' to prevent Allende's inauguration. But gunboat diplomacy was ruled out" [Barnett and Müller (1974, p. 82)]. Salvador Allende did assume office, however, and, in September 1971, he formally announced the Allende Doctrine regarding the expropriation of foreign investments with generally little or no compensation.[11]

It was at this point that the manipulation of food and other economic instruments came under direct consideration by the Nixon administration. In August 1971, an economic warfare strategy was formulated under the direction of Treasury Secretary John Connally, apparently at the President's request, which included the following options: (1) cut Export–Import Bank credits for vital US imports; (2) pressure multilateral lending institutions such as the World Bank and the Inter-American Development Bank not to approve further loans to Chile; (3) encourage private banks to cut off credit (short-term credit shrank from $220 million in 1970 to $35 million in the first year of the Allende regime); and (4) terminate other foreign aid programs—including Title I food aid—except military assistance (which was reportedly maintained in order to facilitate conditions for a possible coup d'etat). The private corporations were also to be involved in the retaliation strategy through their refusal to sell Chile spare parts for trucks and other machinery. (The Kennecott Corporation later even initiated legal proceedings unsuccessfully in the International Court of Justice against the Chilean nationalization action.)

Questions also arose at this time as to whether the Chilean expropriation did not also constitute a violation of the terms of the Hickenlooper
Amendment to the Foreign Assistance Act of 1961, which prohibited US
aid to countries that expropriated American property without adequate
compensation. In a major policy statement,[12] President Nixon indicated
that, according to international law, the United States had a right to
expect that the expropriation of private property would be "nondis-
criminatory," i.e., that it would not apply *only* to US investments. He
warned that if prompt, adequate compensation were not forthcoming,
the United States "will not extend new bilateral economic benefits to the
expropriating country unless and until it is determined that the country
is taking reasonable steps to provide adequate compensation or that
there are major factors affecting US interests which require continuance
of all or part of these benefits" [Hart (1973, p. 164)].

Privately, however, Nixon's reaction was a good deal more blunt. He
announced that he intended "to make Chile's economy scream," and he
indicated "that unless there were strong considerations on the other side,
wherever we [have] a vote [i.e., in multilateral institutions] where Chile
[is] concerned, we [will] vote against them . . . since they [are] expropriating American property."[13] The Nixon administration decision to cut
off public and private sector credit was particularly harsh for consumers
because of agrarian reforms, enacted previously under the Frei administration, and efforts by some of the more conservative landowners to
limit agricultural production in order to damage the Allende regime. The
resulting reduction in food production made Chile even more dependent
on foreign imports, which doubled in 1971 to $261 million and increased
to an estimated $383 million in 1972.

Chile's foreign exchange reserves soon were nearly exhausted, but the
Nixon economic warfare policy prevented the Allende regime from obtaining additional relief through the multilateral lending institutions. The
true extent of the decline in US and multilateral economic assistance
during the 1971-1973 period is revealed in table 7.1. Whereas total economic aid through all channels for the two-year period 1968-1970 was
$414.5 million, total aid dropped to only $52.9 million from 1971 to
1973, or an 87 percent reduction. The sharpest reduction (90.7 percent)
was actually registered in aid from the principal multilateral lending institutions, but the cut in bilateral assistance (85.7 percent) was also substantial. The most massive downturn within the bilateral aid channel
was in capital loans and grants (97 percent), while food aid fell by 67.4

Table 7.1
United States and Multilateral Aid Authorizations to Chile: 1969–1970 and 1971–1973
(Millions of US Dollars)

	1968–70	1971–73[a]	Difference
I. US Assistance			
AID	111.3	3.3	−108.0
Peace Corps	4.3	1.7	−2.6
PL 480	45.2	14.7	−30.5
ExImBank[b]	128.8	21.6	−107.2
Subtotal	289.6	41.3	−248.3
II. Multilateral Assistance			
IBRD	30.9	0	−30.9
IDB	94.0	11.6[c]	−82.4
Subtotal	124.9	11.6	−113.3
Total	414.5	52.9	−361.6

Source: Schneider (1976, P. 16).
a. In general, up to 11 September 1973.
b. Includes credit guarantees and insurance.
c. Two credits totaling $11,600,000 were authorized by the IDB for two Chilean   univer-
sities.

percent. In fact, the only reason why food assistance did not decline as
sharply as general economic aid was that Title II contributions were not
suspended both for humanitarian reasons and in order that the United
States could continue to maintain a token presence within Chile.

The private sector credit squeeze was at least as devastating as the
public sector actions. Five major US banks—Chase Manhattan, Chemical, First National City, Manufacturers Hanover, and Morgan Guar-
anty—cut off short-term credit almost completely after the 1970
election. Whereas before the advent of the Allende government US
banks had supplied 78.4 percent of Chile's short-term credit, this figure
dropped to a mere 12 percent after 1970. In view of the fact that nearly
30 percent of these foreign exchange credits had been used to import
food, the impact was extremely serious [Barnet and Müller (1974, p.
142)]. With all but Title II food aid shipments suspended and with credit
unavailable from either public or private sources, food commodities
soon began to grow scarce. This, in turn, caused rising prices and
mounting discontent among the middle class, the political base that
Allende needed to retain in order to stay in power.

The Chilean government became increasingly desperate. In early

September 1973, just prior to the coup d'etat, it even sought to purchase wheat from the United States on a straight *cash* basis. This bid was rejected, however, reportedly "because of a political decision of the White House" [Rosenfeld (1974, p. 22)]. Three days later, on 11 September 1973, Salvador Allende was overthrown and subsequently murdered. The administration's coordinated strategy of economic retaliation had achieved its principal objective: to help bring about the downfall of the left-wing government. As if to underscore this fact, less than a month after the coup, the United States approved a large Title I credit sale of wheat to the new, right-wing junta which was *eight times* as large as the total food aid credits provided during the entire Allende period [Rosenfeld (1974, p. 22)].

The net change in US food aid flows to Chile during and after the period of the Allende government provides ample demonstration of the manner in which food can be utilized, along with other economic aid resources, to retaliate for the expropriation of commercial property and for other anti-US political actions. While the withdrawal of food aid was only one component of coordinated, public and private sector effort to bring about the downfall of the Allende regime, it was of central importance because of the ripple effect which it had on the political situation within the country. A government may be able to maintain itself in power when its people are starving and therefore too weak to fight, but it will be far more difficult for it to do so when its people are hungry—and often also angry. The curtailment of Chilean domestic agricultural production meant that the American cessation of food aid made a critical difference in terms of the overall adequacy of supplies and the resulting attitude of the people.

Perhaps the most striking feature of the Chilean case, however, is the extent to which public and private sector actions were orchestrated in order to achieve the results desired, namely, the overthrow of the Allende government. The degree to which these initiatives interlocked and the effectiveness with which they were promoted suggests a significant blurring of the distinction between public and private modes of action and responsibility. Although there are certain points of similarity to be found between the government–private sector "cooperation" in this case and that which occurred in the example involving South Korea, the two are not truly comparable. Whereas the South Korean initiatives were designed to develop or protect US markets, the Chilean case represented a far more comprehensive effort to mobilize public and private sector resources for punitive economic and political purposes.

FOOD POWER AND INTERNATIONAL TRADE

There is an additional use of food aid in the context of agricultural trade which demonstrates the problems encountered when mixing the economic and political policy applications inherent in food aid. In 1974, Title I food aid to Bangladesh was reduced at the very point when domestic crop failures had left the new country virtually without the means to feed itself. The official reason given for the cutback in US grain aid was the unprecedented demand—both trade and aid—for US commodities caused by the global supply problems that had developed since 1972.[14]

The failure of the Bangladesh to obtain the necessary wheat as aid to avert the impending famine forced them to enter the commercial market to *purchase* its requirements, expending extremely scarce foreign exchange in the process. Reportedly, 80 percent of Bangladesh's agricultural imports from the United States during 1974, totaling over $160 million, were obtained on commercial terms [Rothschild (1977a, p. 21)]. This shift from aid to trade was, of course, very much in keeping with the "free market" philosophy of Secretary of Agriculture Earl Butz. But, by the summer of 1974, when world grain prices had reached record levels, Bangladesh could no longer afford to buy the grain it needed. As Rothschild relates, the immediate result was that "one week in July, Bangladesh was obliged to cancel its contracts to buy 230,000 tons of United States wheat. . . . The wheat was ready . . . but there was no money. . . . If the grain had been shipped it would have arrived in Bangladesh at the time of the famine, in October" [Rothschild (1977a, p. 21)].

The USDA was monitoring these events closely, but it chose not to act. One reason it did not was that a related foreign policy problem had developed at the same time between the two countries. In the spring of 1974, Bangladesh had sold Cuba approximately $3 million worth of jute gunny sacks, thereby violating the terms of the PL 480 legislation which prohibited the allocation of US food aid to any nation trading with Cuba and North Vietnam. The US commenced a protracted series of legal negotiations with Bangladesh in order to obtain a cessation of this trade relationship. In the interim, it signed no new food aid agreements through October—when the last of the jute was shipped—despite the fact that the threat of massive famine was well known to the local AID mission.

McHenry and Bird report that the Bengalis "expressed surprise and shock that the United States would actually insist that a destitute Bangladesh should restrict its exports. The government of Bangladesh canceled further exports of jute to Cuba at a time when competition from Indian jute and low world market prices had substantially eroded its foreign exchange earnings [McHenry and Bird (1977, p. 82)]. After the Cuban sale was canceled, the US did agree finally to increase its food aid shipments, but no wheat was shipped until mid-November. Thus, the food did not arrive in Bangladesh until Christmas, *after* the worst effects of the famine had already been felt [Rothschild (1977a, p. 21)].

The Bengali case presents a clear example of the impact on food deficit countries of superimposing foreign policy imperatives on agricultural trade relationships. Food aid is often the only effective buffer between these two competing forces. Thus, the reduction or termination of concessional food exports will have a devastating impact when both food and foreign exchange are in short supply. Moreover, the explicit manipulation of food aid by the United States as strategic leverage for political and economic objectives (i.e., food power) is a dangerous, short-sighted policy under most conditions and is generally incompatible with the broader US role in promoting a more stable world political and economic order.

ASSESSMENT OF POLICY OBJECTIVES

This chapter has examined a wide array of US trade-related interests that have been promoted to some degree through utilization of the food aid resource. Certainly the one characteristic that all of these cases share in common is an interest in promoting or protecting the US international economic position. Richard N. Cooper (1972–1973, pp. 18–19) has noted the traditional distinction that has existed between what he terms "high foreign policy" and "low foreign policy": the former concerns matters of national security and survival, and the latter the large number of secondary issues relating to other matters between countries. He suggests that, in the past, trade policy was not a factor in matters of "high foreign policy," although "high" policy did at times intervene in the nature of trade arrangements. But trade issues have now assumed an increasingly prominent position as a component of "high foreign policy," and thus the role of food aid in promoting trade objectives is *not* insignificant from a foreign policy perspective.

Taken as a whole, these policy initiatives fall generally under two broad rubrics: *active* policies and *reactive* policies. That is, the development of new or expanded markets for US agricultural exports or the promotion of new or expanded market access for US agriculturally related technology were positive activities in which the United States took the initiative, employing food aid in order to promote trade and foreign policy objectives it considered important to its interests. By the same token, many of these case examples were reactive policies wherein the United States utilized food aid as a lever to protect traditional markets, to drive out trade competition, or to respond to the expropriation of US private overseas investments.

Both policies have achieved the results desired under favorable conditions. This raises the question whether there are any identifiable patterns in each policy's success. In general, the *active* policy has demonstrated a more consistent record of successful implementation than has the reactive policy. This may be explained partially by the fact that most of the examples of active policy dealt with limited, commercial situations in which the exploitation of comparative advantage was an accepted part of "the rules of the game." Even under these circumstances, however, the actions were subject to international criticism to the extent that American food aid was being used to benefit private agricultural and industrial interests at the expense of social welfare and economic growth in the developing world. If LDC domestic agricultural production was discouraged or if recipients were forced to accept types or volumes of commodities which they did not really want—or, in some cases, even need—then larger political and economic development goals were simply being sacrificed for short-term trade advantages. This does not, of course, constitute a satisfactory moral or political justification for the use of aid in a manner which is not in the best interests of the recipient. This issue, however, lies at the heart of the development debate and cannot properly be addressed in this context.[15]

The examples of *reactive* policy initiatives, on the other hand, have without exception been of a punitive nature—either economic, political, or both. As such, they are controversial in their own right. But it would be incorrect to issue a blanket condemnation of these actions simply because they sought to punish or retaliate against a nation for some action or policy considered inimical to US interests; this, too, is an accepted part of "the rules of the game" in international trade and political relations. Thus, for example, when US property is expropriated without compensation, the United States is obliged—indeed, even expected—to take some action to protect its national interest and/or the interests of American companies.

There are, however, at least two problems inherent in using food as an instrument of reactive policy. First, food occupies such a unique and essential position in human affairs that, while the threat to withhold supplies may, in some cases, be a reasonable form of leverage in foreign policy, the actual *interruption* of the commodity pipeline is clearly an extreme political statement. Under such circumstances, unless the precipitating event is at least of an *equally* serious nature (and few can possibly be), the cessation of food aid shipments will be an inappropriate and overreactive response. The second difficulty with employing food aid as a part of a reactive strategy is that, to the extent that the punitive measure is motivated by political (i.e., an eye for an eye) rather than strictly economic concerns (i.e., loss of profits, investments, and so on), the exploitation of the food resource will be likely to elicit a further, undesirable escalation of actions by the offending actor. This will, of course, require the donor to escalate its retaliatory measures once again. If unchecked, this process can lead ultimately to full-scale economic (if not political) warfare.

As in the case of the strategic and diplomatic applications examined in the previous chapter, the fundamental difficulty with food aid used to promote US international trade interests is that it is an imprecise instrument. Despite the fact that Title I of PL 480 is not explicitly a humanitarian, grant-type feeding program, the fact remains that, in the eyes of the rest of the world, all American food aid is given in order to *feed* people. When it is diverted for other purposes—no matter how well justified by surrounding or precipitating events—substantial, negative foreign policy ramifications are likely to result. It is evident from this varied case experience that, while the use of food aid as an *active* element of trade promotion may represent a generally effective means of attaining immediate commercial objectives, the manipulation of food as a *reactive* instrument will only rarely be an appropriate response, since it often creates as many problems as it solves.

Chapter 8
Food Aid and International Burden-Sharing

Since the end of World War II, the United States has been the world's largest supplier of economic assistance in absolute terms, particularly in the form of food. The United States has not carried this burden of responsibility lightly, however, or, for that matter, even willingly. Rather, the aid mantle was assumed largely by default as a result of the disintegration of the European colonial relationships after the war and the gradual shift of the global ideological struggle from Europe to the developing world. In effect, the United States saw little alternative to its new role; its European allies were either incapacitated or indisposed and its ideological rival, the Soviet Union, was becoming increasingly aggressive in promoting its influence and political hegemony.

By the end of the decade of the fifties, however, the other major developed countries of the free world could no longer evade sharing the foreign aid burden by claiming still to be in the process of economic reconstruction. Most had already reached, if not surpassed, their prewar levels of affluence. At the same time, the US Congress was demonstrating a mounting degree of frustration over the apparent inability of the Eisenhower administration to obtain the same type of tangible (and highly visible) results from the assistance offered to the LDCs as had been produced under the European Marshall Plan. As a result, the situation faced by John F. Kennedy in 1961 was characterized by growing congressional resistance to foreign aid expenditures, unabated recipient country need, and the restored economic vigor of the Western European countries. The combination of these factors provided an ideal opportunity for the new administration to examine and rethink the basic tenets of US foreign economic assistance policy.

Moreover, as the huge agricultural surpluses of the fifties gave way to a more limited agricultural carryover in the sixties, food itself was no longer so much a commodity to be dumped on recipients wherever possible as a valuable aid resource to be used to augment, and even in some cases to replace, scarce capital resources. Along with the competing demands on available food stocks in the sixties came the realization that neo-Malthusian predictions concerning world population growth were correct in some respects. Under these circumstances, the United States came to adopt the view that, unless the LDCs demonstrated a willingness to address comprehensively their population problems and to expand their emphasis on agricultural development, and unless the other developed countries made substantially increased contributions in proportion to their means, there was little likelihood that the long-term food needs of the developing world could be met.

Two specific foreign aid policy objectives evolved from this recognition in the midsixties of the altered state of the world food–population balance: to increase international food aid burden-sharing and to expand the level of recipient self-help. In particular, this chapter will be concerned with the types of benefits that were (and are) sought through the promotion of burden-sharing as a means of relieving the heavy dependence of food deficit countries on the United States as the residual supplier of food aid. This is, quite obviously, a rationale of self-interest motivated by the desire of the United States to shed a portion of the burden that it has carried almost unilaterally since World War II. But the United States also championed the concept of burden-sharing in order to strengthen the capacity of the international system to respond effectively whenever acute food emergencies occurred in the developing world.

American interest in promoting longer-term approaches to world food problems (i.e., as opposed to more parochial objectives such as surplus disposal, diplomatic and strategic objectives, and so on) can be traced to its support of the 1958 proposal by B.R. Sen, the Director-General of FAO, for a Free the World from Hunger Year, which was modeled ostensibly after the highly successful International Geophysical Year. The Sen proposal was compatible both with the ongoing FAO programs and with US bilateral aid initiatives, and it was thus approved by the Tenth FAO Conference in 1959. The result was the so-called Freedom from Hunger Campaign (FFHC), which was established as a five-year effort

(1960–1965) financed strictly through voluntary contributions. Its objectives were to achieve wider global awareness of the food supply problem precipitated by rapid population increases and to stimulate countries to take action to help bridge this gap.

The FFHC was endorsed by seventy-six countries, and privately funded Freedom from Hunger Committees were established in most subscribing nations. But the FFHC included no operational responsibilities, and its most visible and successful activity was to sponsor, jointly with the United States, a World Food Congress in 1963 marking the twentieth anniversary of the creation of the FAO at Hot Springs, Virginia, in 1943. Thus, while the FFHC served as a useful basis for launching other, more applied schemes to address long-term global food needs, it did little to actually facilitate global involvement in meeting world food needs.

THE WORLD FOOD PROGRAMME PROPOSAL

After the demise of the UNRRA food aid program, American interest in multilateral food aid was related primarily to its need to move additional surplus commodities. The first publicly documented US proposal for such an international aid entity appears to have come from then Vice-President Richard M. Nixon. During the 1960 presidential campaign, Nixon suggested that the United States should support the creation of a multilateral surplus food distribution mechanism since "it [the proposed multilateral program] will not be harmful to our friends and allies since they will participate in the program. It will not be subject to the criticism directed against unilateral US aid since it will be administered through the UN" [Department of State BIR (1970, p. 1)]. This statement was more than a bit ironic in view of Nixon's own subsequent unilateral uses of food aid in countries such as Chile, South Korea, South Vietnam, and Cambodia.

According to Don Paarlberg, then coordinator of the White House Food for Peace Program, Nixon wished to lay an innovative proposal before the UN and the FAO that would project a positive US international image and would circumvent the surplus disposal charges of Canada and Australia by coopting them in a joint undertaking. Nixon also apparently felt that a multilateral program might get food to needy people in places where bilateral aid could not reach due to political constraints.[1] A fourth Nixon objective might also be added to this list: the desire to "outinnovate" his presidential opponent, John F. Kennedy, who was also then calling for new US food aid initiatives (see chapter 9).

The multilateral aid concept was even of some interest, however, to Dwight Eisenhower, who directed Secretary of Agriculture Ezra Taft Benson and Don Paarlberg to conduct an interagency feasibility study prior to the election campaign in the summer of 1960. According to Paarlberg, the most substantial opposition to the plan surfaced among officials of the USDA, "who were basically suspicious of international institutions," and who consequently feared that "internationalizing the operation [i.e., of food aid] would result in bureaucratizing it, with much delay, and the volume of product moved might therefore be reduced."[2] There was also a genuine concern that, if food aid were multilateralized, the Congress might not support the program on as large a scale, and it was therefore decided that the President should obtain bipartisan congressional support before proceeding with a formal proposal to the United Nations.

Thus, on 8 August 1960, a special message was sent to Congress requesting approval of a concurrent resolution in support of an administration proposal with two distinctive new features: that the United Nations should act both as a coordinating and advisory body for bilateral programming and as a multilateral conduit for the actual donation and allocation of food resources. The concurrent resolution was approved a short time later in the Senate,[3] but the House adjourned without acting on the measure.

In order to circumvent congressional opposition, the multilateral food aid proposal was limited ultimately to a small, international undertaking, with the majority of US resources remaining committed to bilateral programming. This modification pacified anti-UN forces in both the executive and legislative branches, but the hoped for congressional resolution was never reintroduced. The final US proposal was presented in a speech to the UN General Assembly by President Eisenhower on 22 September 1960. The plan was then referred to the UN Economic and Finance Committee, which reported on it favorably. On 27 October 1960, the UN General Assembly voted to adopt a resolution calling on the FAO to establish "without delay procedures by which the 'largest practicable quantities of surplus food may be made available on mutually agreeable terms as a transitional measure against hunger.' "[4]

Less than a month later, however, US voters denied Richard Nixon the opportunity then to see his proposal through to fruition as President. But the Democrats were also left in an awkward position, as explained to Orville L. Freeman, the Secretary of Agriculture-designate: "The difficulty and embarrassment are that the United States, having initiated all this activity, has no policy whatsoever, and it is necessary to develop one without delay."[5] In reality the Kennedy administration had two practical alternatives: either make the FAO merely an information clearinghouse regarding surpluses and world food needs, or actively launch the FAO on a positive food distribution program.

George S. McGovern, Kennedy's choice as the first Director of his White House Office of Food for Peace,[6] soon became involved in the ongoing discussions concerning the new administration's position on the multilateral concept. In April 1961, McGovern headed the US delegation that met at FAO headquarters in Rome to consider the findings of an ad hoc expert group on the feasibility of establishing a multilateral food aid mechanism. The report expressed support for the concept but proved not to contain any concrete proposals. Disappointed and frustrated at the lack of progress on what seemed to them such a worthwhile and timely initiative, McGovern and his delegation retired to their hotel to discuss the possibility of placing a specific plan before the meeting.

The delegation agreed ultimately upon a scheme that called for an initial fund of $100 million, with the United States contributing 40 percent ($40 million). But neither interagency consultation nor final presidential approval had been obtained for such an American commitment. McGovern thus placed a transatlantic telephone call to the White House, and, within twenty-four hours, had obtained official permission to introduce the proposal.[7] The subsequent proposal to the FAO meeting stated,

1. The US favored the creation of a multilateral approach, as a supplement to bilateral arrangements, with the widest possible participation by member countries.
2. The US was ready to contribute $40 million in commodities with the possibility of a supplementary cash contribution.
3. The primary function of the program should be to meet emergency needs with possible other uses including school feeding and labor-intensive projects. [McGovern (1964a, pp. 108–109)]

The US initiative was so unexpected and so *specific* that the other delegates were unprepared to act on it. Consequently, the Rome meeting was adjourned while officials returned home for consultation. In the interim, President Kennedy received a full report from McGovern and gave the plan his public endorsement at a press conference on 22 April 1961 [McGovern (1964b, p. 31)].

As finally approved by the UN General Assembly and the FAO Conference, the structure of the World Food Programme (WFP) paralleled closely the general principles of the McGovern proposal. Haas has argued that the United States chose to support the creation of the WFP as an alternative to a rival scheme for a comprehensive commodity plan, to be administered through the UN Special Fund, that was advocated by Canada, the Third World countries, and the FAO Secretariat [Haas (1969, p. 155)]. There is little evidence, however, that this alternative plan ever received serious consideration, particularly after US opposition became known.

Despite the fact that the United States was still beset in 1962 with a massive burden of surplus agricultural stocks held at public expense, there were now indications of a shift in the motivation for developing the multilateral food aid channel. The narrow surplus disposal emphasis favored by the Eisenhower administration was replaced, in the public rhetoric at least, by a new concern for international economic development. There was, of course, no reason why these two objectives were necessarily incompatible, but, significantly, the United States began to make a more visible commitment to LDC development problems, proposing in November 1961 the creation of a UN Development Decade.

The American commitment to the concept of using multilateral food aid for development was also emphasized before the United Nations by Richard N. Gardner, then Deputy Assistant Secretary of State for International Organizational Affairs:

My Government sees in the program [i.e., the WFP] which we are now discussing another potentially very important expansion of our efforts at international cooperation. . . . In taking this approach we trust that the program of multilateral food aid will become an important vehicle in strengthening the trend toward more effective forms of multilateral assistance for economic and social development.[8]

But Gardner also reiterated the US demand for the widest possible sharing of food aid burden, emphasizing "that one of the principal concerns which will influence us in any future decisions will be the willingness and ability of other countries to contribute food to the program and to make contributions in cash and services. We should like to see the broadest possible participation in this global effort" [Gardner (1962)]. Thus, the Kennedy multilateral food aid policy was marked by a dual set of concerns: a unilateral interest in redistributing the international responsibility for food aid while retaining the capacity to dispose of US agricultural surpluses, and a broader interest in building an international institutional capacity to allocate food aid for economic and social development.

Although the Kennedy presidency was cut short just as the WFP began its maiden year of operation, Lyndon B. Johnson did not substantially alter the slain President's policy while serving the remainder of his term. After his own election in 1964, however, Johnson became increasingly frustrated with the inequitable division of the international food aid burden, particularly in view of the sharp decline in US surplus stocks. In 1964, he ordered a change in US policy, just as the three-year experimental period of the WFP was nearing its end. The US pledge was henceforth to be tied to a 50:50 matching formula whereby American food aid would be contributed only on a one-to-one basis with the total resources made available by all other donors.

The new policy was designed to underscore the seriousness with which the United States viewed the need for wider multilateral sharing. Moreover, much to the dismay of many other WFP members, the United States announced in April 1965 that it was planning to reduce its food aid share still *further* by adjusting its matching formula to 40:60.[9] Thus, by 1966, the US desire to promote international food aid burden-sharing had become a predominant theme of the Johnson administration's food aid policy.

THE FOOD AID CONVENTION OF 1967

The United States moved to further its burden-sharing policy through other multilateral channels as well. Negotiations had been underway since the Kennedy period under the auspices of GATT—what therefore came to be known as the Kennedy Round of negotiations—on a broad range of international trade issues; one element of these discussions was a possible new arrangement on grain trade and food aid.[10] The burden-sharing concept assumed a prominent role in these negotiations because the United States had made it abundantly clear to the other developed countries that their wider participation in food aid was a sine qua non for additional US concessions on international grain trade and, indirectly, on the entire range of international trade and tariff issues.

The US position was actually more the result of a gradual evolution in its policy on international trade than of a radical new initiative by the Johnson administration. As early as November 1961, Orville Freeman (upon returning from an around-the-world fact-finding trip) had urged President Kennedy that

the participation of other agriculturally well developed, surplus producing nations in multilateral programs for food aid in cooperation with the United States would have many advantages. . . . Such a program could . . . contribute to the development of working mechanisms, procedures and attitudes that would facilitate the development of international commodity agreements on agricultural products, and thus contribute toward the expansion of trade among friendly nations.[11]

In November 1963, just prior to the assassination, Freeman was again counseling Kennedy about the important relationship between aid and trade:

It is clear that trade competiton and potential trade wars between the agricultural surplus nations are dangerous. We need then to follow a basic principle, such as market sharing, and to look forward to the goal of expanding markets in developing nations. . . . Therefore, as part of commodity agreements, we ought to strongly advocate provisions for sharing the task of meeting the deficit which must be met in those nations if their economic development is to continue.[12]

The resulting American strategy for the Kennedy Round of GATT negotiations thus sought to link a broad range of US trade concessions to changes in at least two agricultural policies of the European countries: a modification of the EEC Common Agricultural Policy to permit wider US access to European markets, and a more equitable sharing of responsibility for international food aid in the form of grains. While the latter demand did not find great favor among the Europeans, the former quickly became the linchpin of the entire cereals negotiations. The European delegates were adamant in their opposition to any significant modification of the variable price levy provision contained in the EEC Common Agricultural Policy.

The position of both sides remained intransigent through 1966 and neither showed much inclination to compromise as the deadline for a new agreement approached. At literally the final moment, in May 1967 (only thirty-six hours before the ultimate end of the negotiations), the United States dramatically dropped its central demand for guaranteed access to European grain markets,[13] thereby facilitating new movement, which led eventually to the International Grains Agreement of 1967. The agreement required the European countries to undertake substantial new commitments to provide wheat as food aid on an outright grant basis. But the agreement also had the effect of removing European grain from the international market, thereby providing more room for the commercial export of additional American surplus stocks.

Negotiation of the Food Aid Convention furthered a number of US interests concerning the promotion of longer-term solutions to world food problems. Because food aid under the convention continued to be allocated bilaterally, it represented a desirable and complementary alternative to aid given through the World Food Programme, as well as a substantial donor response to US demands for international burden-sharing. At the same time, the concessions wrought from the Europeans during the Kennedy Round benefited the United States by reducing its unilateral food aid burden while also creating additional room in international grain markets for commercial exports. The net result has been the development of more equitable and orderly system of international food aid.

INDIAN FOOD AID BURDEN-SHARING

Lyndon Johnson was not a President of great diplomatic finesse, but he *was* a President who knew how and when to manipulate the levers of power. During 1966, India's dire food emergency had forced it to seek assistance—food, fertilizer, and capital—from more than twenty different countries.[14] But Johnson became increasingly annoyed with the lack of substantive responses from these other countries, all of whom seemed quite content to sit back and let the United States bail India out of its food crisis unilaterally. The Australians announced a token contribution of wheat, but the input from most other donors remained inconsequential in comparison to the US undertaking. With presidential patience at an end, Johnson decided that the United States would no longer "go it alone" as India's sole source of support.

Action taken as a result of Johnson's decision represented yet another type of initiative designed to promote burden-sharing in international food aid. In the case of the Indian food crisis, there was no intention of creating an additional institutional mechanism similar to the World Food Programme or Food Aid Convention. Rather, the American objective was to urge other countries to respond to the needs of food deficit countries by expanding the volume of their bilateral aid contributions. But the United States clearly stood to gain at least as much from country-specific burden-sharing as it did from the existence of international institutions such as the WFP. Not only would the emergence of additional donors decrease India's absolute dependence on the United States, but it would also free additional quantities of American grain for sale through commercial channels.

Concern about the failure of other donors to respond to India's famine-induced crisis had been growing since the summer of 1965, when US development policies were reoriented to emphasize recipient self-help. In this context burden-sharing was viewed as the natural complement to India's own internal efforts. By the beginning of 1966 the United States and India had developed a dual strategy to support this objective. India would bring direct, high-level pressure on the Canadians and Australians to divert commercial shipments (already en route) for use as food aid, while similar pressures were to be exerted on the Japanese, Germans, and British regarding the procurement of desperately needed supplies of chemical fertilizer. At the same time, the United States would mobilize support within the United Nations for an international appeal for greater donor country response to India's food need. As to the latter, it was agreed that the United States offer to match the contributions of the other donors, as it did for the WFP, on a two- or three-to-one basis.[15]

At the January 1966 WFP pledging conference, Orville Freeman seized the opportunity to launch the American part of the strategy during a luncheon attended by UN Secretary-General U Thant and WFP Executive Director Boerma; both leaders reacted favorably to the US proposal. In subsequent meetings in New York and Washington, it was agreed that U Thant would issue an appeal for international response and would call a meeting of donor nations under UN auspices to review resources and to urge cooperation. The Indians also fulfilled their responsibilities regarding the direct approach to other major donors, but neither channel elicited any significant new commitments.[16]

President Johnson pressed his initiative during a visit to the United States by Prime Minister Indira Gandhi in late March 1966, urging her to renew the efforts of her predecessor to obtain aid from other donors. In addition, Johnson's special congressional message concerning India's food crisis was forwarded by the State Department to all embassies and legations with the directive that it be brought immediately to the attention of the host government. Twenty countries responded to the Johnson speech but none offered more than token assistance. Slowly, however, other donors did begin to come to India's assistance; some on their own initiative (e.g., Canada, Denmark, and West Germany) and others only after intense diplomatic pressure by India and the United States (e.g., Australia). By December 1966, Canada had announced a grant of nearly 200,000 tons of wheat and Australia grudgingly provided an additional 150,000 tons.

But no end was in sight to India's continuing food crisis, and the President remained dissatisfied with the unreliable and ad hoc nature of international burden-sharing. Consequently, on Christmas eve, 1966, Johnson asked George Woods, then the President of the World Bank, to attempt to persuade the other donors to participate in a more formal food aid consortium for India. At the same time, the President dispatched two of his top advisers on food matters, Eugene Rostow, Under Secretary of State for Political Affairs, and John Schnittker, Under Secretary of Agriculture, on an around-the-world trip to marshall additional food aid support for India.

The Rostow–Schnittker mission was successful in obtaining new aid pledges worth nearly $200 million. Moreover, at the initiative of George Woods, a comprehensive assessment of India's immediate food and economic needs was undertaken under the auspices of the World Bank India Aid Consortium.[17] The object of Woods's efforts was not only to identify the nature of India's current need but also to determine what steps should be taken to move the country toward a self-sustaining basis in food production.

The success of the Rostow–Schnittker mission and the preliminary efforts by Woods enabled Lyndon Johnson to report to Congress on 2 February 1967 that "the problem of international cooperation has steadily improved. . . . In an unprecedented display of common concern, governments, private organizations and individuals in 42 other nations have joined in providing $180 million in food and other commodities."[18] The President reiterated the three basic principles of his War on Hunger as they applied to the case of India, namely, self-help, multilateral burden-sharing, and comprehensive planning, and he articulated the current US policy on burden-sharing in the continuing Indian food crisis: "The United States cannot—and should not—approach this problem alone or on an ad hoc improvised basis. We must support the Indian Government's efforts to enlist the aid of other nations in developing a systematic and international approach to the problems of Indian agriculture" [Department of State *Bulletin*, 20 February (1967, p. 299)].

Seven specific policies were recommended in the Johnson message, but the only real departure from previous practice was the proposed utilization of the World Bank India Aid Consortium as the principal food aid coordinator. The plan called for the consortium to accept formal responsibility for mobilizing resources to meet India's emergency food needs, coordinating the emergency aid through the consortium mechanism, and ensuring that the aid was *additional* to other resources previously committed for Indian economic development. The consortium was also called upon to undertake detailed projections of India's food production and food aid requirements, to prepare an equitably shared program for nonfood imports necessary for the production of food, to review India's self-help efforts, and to identify areas of future activity.

Under the new burden-sharing proposal, the United States offered to continue bearing the brunt of the food aid burden through the first half of 1967, after which point the members of the World Bank India Aid Consortium[19] were to begin to match 50 percent of the US effort. In March 1967, Orville Freeman and Eugene Rostow reemphasized the US demand for a 50:50 aid matching formula during congressional testimony, and in April, Rostow was able to obtain specific matching pledges, amounting to $122.2 million, from Britain, France, West Germany, Japan, and the Scandinavian countries during a Paris meeting of the India Aid Consortium [Lyndon B. Johnson (1971, p. 230)].

With the commitment of these resources, a new era of international food aid cooperation seemed to be dawning. In August 1967, however, Secretary Freeman urged the President to delay delivery of one-third of the 1.5 million tons of emergency food aid authorized by Congress due to uncertainties regarding the actual nature of the pledges made by other donors. At a news conference in September, Johnson confessed that "in all frankness, we do not know precisely how much of the $122 million meets the *additional* criteria. There is strong evidence that much of it does [emphasis added]."[20] The President explained that, in order to be meaningful,

the new aid must be a real increment to Indian resources and it must be *additional* to regular contributions to the India Aid Consortium. No one's interests are served by a charade in which real American wheat is "matched" by meaningless financial transactions or by funds which would otherwise be provided through the Consortium anyway and are merely earmarked for this purpose [emphasis added]. [Department of State *Bulletin*, 2 October (1967, p. 431)]

Despite these initial difficulties, the consortium approach did begin to take effect, and by the end of 1967, an important precedent had been established concerning food aid burden-sharing at the country-specific level. The significance of this precedent was that, when combined with institutional burden-sharing initiatives embodied in the FAC—which was also established in 1967—and the WFP, the United States had succeeded in using its food aid leverage to contribute to the development of a more orderly system of international food aid. The consortium approach to burden-sharing was particularly attractive in that it contained benefits both for the recipient, in terms of a larger net inflow of resources, and for the United States, in the form of relief from its solitary burden as the commodity lifeline for a desperately food-short nation.

ASSESSMENT OF POLICY OBJECTIVES

With the exception of the period of India's critical food emergency (1965–1967), the promotion of international food aid burden-sharing as a response to world food problems has often been obscured by other, more pressing aid objectives. The burden-sharing principle never disappeared, however, after its introduction in the midsixties; it was simply pursued with declining vigor as the crisis environment eased and agricultural surpluses reappeared temporarily in the United States. Yet, particularly since the elimination of publicly owned stocks of surplus grain, debate over the proper use of American food resource transfers has grown steadily.

Food aid in the world food "crisis" environment of the Nixon and Ford administrations had become a scarce and valuable resource. The United States—already under severe criticism from the Group of 77 caucus for the declining relative share, as a percentage of GNP, of its Official Development Assistance—could not afford to reduce its food aid for fear of further antagonizing its Third World relations. Recognition of this fact motivated renewed American efforts to promote an even wider and more equitable sharing of the food aid responsibility. The importance of this policy was underscored, for example, in a 1974 congressional hearing by Ambassador Edwin M. Martin, US Coordinator for the World Food Conference: "In the future, when we don't expect to have these kinds of surplus stocks, then it becomes a more direct burden on the United States and the U.S. taxpayer to provide aid in the form of food than it has been in the past so that this justifies, I think, the effort which we are making to get others to bear a larger share of the burden."[21]

It would make little sense, of course, to assess the unilateral benefits of burden-sharing apart from those advantages which are external to the United States; the two are symbiotic to a large extent. Yet the reality of recent policies adhered to by the United States presents a rather paradoxical record: burden-sharing has been championed strongly in rhetoric but given less than enthusiastic support in practice. The United States has maintained its support for the Food Aid Convention, which has been extended by protocol since 1971. The succeeding conventions have served American aid and trade objectives well. As a result, the United States continues to view the FAC as probably the single most effective instrument for maintaining a guaranteed annual volume level of food aid contributions from the other agricultural exporters, especially the EEC.

In terms of multilateral programming, however, US participation in the WFP has been more problematic in that it has consistently tended to view the WFP as an *extension* of its own bilateral program. Thus, while the United States has urged an expanded level of donor participation within the UN food aid agency, it has also demonstrated an extreme reluctance to support WFP projects or policies that place multilateral food aid in competition with the US bilateral program. This has been particularly true in situations where the United States desires to maintain bilateral control in order to gain leverage in support of foreign policy objectives.[22]

The United States has also demonstrated other hesitancies about shifting additional resources from the bilateral to the multilateral channel.[23] For one thing, AID officials continue to have substantial doubt about the organizational and managerial effectiveness of the WFP. In addition, the contentious political environment that has often characterized relations within the UN arena has caused many US policymakers to fear that an expanded multilateral food aid involvement would simply substitute the international politics of the United Nations for the domestic politics of the United States. Obviously, when food aid burden-sharing within the WFP becomes politicized in ways that run contrary to established American policy—for example, the question of whether food aid should be offered to liberation movements such as the PLO or to countries not belonging to the United Nations (e.g., Angola)—there is little incentive for the United States to shift policy emphasis decisively toward multilateralism.

Finally, contradictory US support for multilateral food aid may be seen, from the congressional perspective, to result from the fact that there is no organized, identifiable constituency that speaks effectively on behalf of a greater US commitment to the WFP or, for that matter, that stands to benefit directly from such a decision. The Inter-Religious Task- · force on US Food Policy, a nonprofit Washington-based sectarian group concerned with all aspects of US food policy is the closest approximation to a multilateral food aid lobby. But the Taskforce, which has been the most active on these matters, is constrained by the fact that it must also support the private voluntary agencies (many of which are also sectarian) which actually *compete* with the WFP for scarce Title II PL 480 resources.

The only other likely source of support for multilateral food aid is the

FAO North American Liaison Office. But it is apparently precluded by its mandate from adopting an advocacy role. Thus, there remains no unified source of support in Washington capable of lobbying for enlarged US participation in food aid multilateralism.

It must be noted, however, that the conflicting, paradoxical nature of US policy is not quite as irrational as it might seem. Prior to 1967, the United States was, in fact, forced to carry an inordinately large share of the international food aid burden. Moreover, the United States continues to support the concept of country-specific aid consortia. It would seem, therefore, that the question of expanded American involvement in multilateral food aid efforts is related not so much to the absolute level of food aid resources it is willing to make available, as is the case with most other donors, as to a profound reluctance to relinquish bilateral political and managerial control over the destination and end use of its aid resources.

The United States is no longer deluded about the seriousness or likely duration of world food problems. It has fully recognized the fact that, in order to develop viable longer-term solutions, it will be necessary to obtain the cooperation of other potential donors as well as the full participation of the aid recipients themselves. The United States has also taken a number of significant and fairly successful steps to promote such activities. But long-term burden-sharing objectives still must compete along with other, more pressing foreign policy uses of American food resources. Consequently, except in periods of acute food emergencies such as the 1965–1966 food shortages in India, the comparatively low political importance of longer-term goals tends to relegate them to a secondary position in the ordering of US food aid priorities. The evidence presented here suggests an apparent inconsistency in American policy: the United States has demanded wider donor involvement when that has served its purposes, but then has failed subsequently to give its wholehearted support to these efforts. It is unlikely, therefore, that further development of multilateral burden-sharing arrangements involving food aid will occur until some of the internal conflicts within American policy have been resolved.

The majority of the foreign policy objectives pursued by the United States through the allocation of its food assistance occurred either at the direction or with the approval of the President. Most also reflected the influence of powerful forces—both individual personalities and bureaucratic structures—within the administration. As suggested frequently throughout this analysis, this is both the strength and the weakness of the US food aid program: it can and does function in the simultaneous pursuit of so many divergent policy objectives.

There is another aspect to the use of food aid in support of foreign policy, however, which relates neither to the influence exerted on the President by other actors within the executive branch nor to the pursuit of larger programmatic goals such as international burden-sharing. Food aid has, from time to time, served as a specific discretionary tool through which, in coordination with other means of influence, the President could achieve certain immediate foreign (and domestic) policy objectives. Some of these uses have been closely related to the features inherent in food as a form of foreign aid, while others have been concerned more with the specific domestic and international policies adhered to by each President. Thus, food aid will be examined here both as a symbolic and instrumental tool of short-term presidential policymaking.

KENNEDY: POLITICAL PROMOTION

Claims to the specific authorship of the "Food for Peace" slogan for the PL 480 program are numerous, but the evidence would seem to support

attribution to the late Senator Hubert H. Humphrey. Whoever the orig-
inator, the idea was soon coopted by the Eisenhower administration and
a Food for Peace Coordinator was appointed in 1960. But the evidence
also indicates that the Republican initiative was primarily an effort to
repackage old programs under a new name in order to preempt the
Democrats in an election year.

Presidential candidate John F. Kennedy and his campaign staff had a
different vision of the program, however. They viewed it more in terms
of its potential as an instrument of foreign policy than as a pressure
release valve for farm surpluses. Moreover, the Kennedy people considered the issue of food aid to be an ideal element of their innovative
New Frontier image. They believed that if the Democratic candidate
could be associated in the voters' minds with solid, humanitarian causes
like food assistance, it would serve both to improve his election chances
and to promote the development of bold new programmatic thrusts once
in office. Candidate Kennedy therefore announced in October 1960 the
appointment of a "committee of distinguished citizens"[1] to formulate
recommendations on how the new administration might transfer the
Food for Peace slogan into "a truly effective long-range use of our food
abundance to build foundations for durable peace and progress"[2]

In their report to the then President-elect on 19 January 1961, the
committee recommended, among other things, that "to insure that the
program functions vigorously, it is necessary to have a central point of
responsibility and initiative (i.e., an Office of Food for Peace) . . . and
an officer (i.e., a Food for Peace Director) . . . to be responsible to the
President and serve as his principal adviser and agent in connection with
the Food for Peace program."[3] This advice paralleled closely the recommendations of a number of other Kennedy staffers including Arthur M.
Schlesinger, Jr., who also recognized the political and public relations
potential of such a high-visibility program coordinated at the White
House level.[4] Consequently, by executive order (the second such directive of his presidency), Kennedy established the position of Director of
Food for Peace and directed that the Office of Food for Peace (OFFP) be
located within the Executive Office of the President. But the President
also had a secondary reason for his decision that was related far more to
partisan political concerns.

As a presidential hopeful in 1959, Kennedy had traveled to South
Dakota to campaign for his friend and congressional colleague, Repre-
sentative George S. McGovern, who was then running for the Senate.
McGovern lost his election bid, however, by less than 1 percent of the

vote and Kennedy felt that somehow he had been partly responsible for the loss. Immediately after the results became known, Kennedy telephoned McGovern expressing his regret and urging that McGovern contact him again before making any future plans. The implication of the message was clear, and McGovern subsequently expressed his tentative interest in some food-related post in the new administration.[5]

After the election, Kennedy was determined to make good on his pledge. Some have suggested that Robert Kennedy and Sargent Shriver wanted McGovern for Secretary of Agriculture. But the President-elect apparently was convinced that McGovern had a good chance of gaining election to the Senate in 1962, and some of his advisors argued that the agriculture post was traditionally ruinous to a political candidate—particularly one from the Midwest.[6] Largely on this basis, John Kennedy decided to appoint George McGovern as the Director of the Office for Food for Peace, promising him enhanced responsibility and a high degree of public visibility in preparation for a second campaign bid.

McGovern seemed tailor made for the position, possessing both a strong concern for agriculture and a deep feeling for the humanitarian aspect of the world hunger problem. The task as set out by Kennedy also needed doing since the Food for Peace concept had never actually been implemented under Eisenhower, due to the lack of political commitment and to interagency jealousies. McGovern was charged specifically with eliminating these bottlenecks. He became both coordinator and expediter, not administering the food aid program in an operational sense but acting as the focal point within the administration for all food aid-related issues and discussions.

The object of his efforts was to modify the operational focus of the PL 480 program in order to reflect the new approach to foreign aid then being developed within the administration and to mobilize public opinion in support of food aid and in economic assistance in general.[7] In order to pursue the public relations aspect, an American Food for Peace Council was created by Presidential invitation in June 1961. Over one hundred representatives from agriculture, labor, industry, commerce, and civic groups were invited to participate. The council was requested to develop public information on world hunger, to enlist public support for the "attack" on world hunger, and to advise the Food for Peace director.[8] McGovern also initiated additional promotional efforts early in 1962 by enlisting the services of the US Advertising Council to mount a public information campaign—similar in many respects to that undertaken on behalf of the newly established Peace Corps—to raise the level of citizen awareness concerning the humanitarian and *ideological* importance of food aid.

As expected, George McGovern announced his resignation as Director of Food for Peace in July 1962 in order to run once again for a Senate seat from South Dakota. He was replaced by Richard Reuter, then President of CARE, Inc., and the White House was careful to emphasize its desire to take "no action that would seem to downgrade the Food for Peace function [of] Mr. McGovern's service as Director of Food for Peace or in any way impair his chances in the fall election. The President's deep personal interest in Food for Peace must be clearly recognized."[9] Kennedy did, in fact, continue to maintain an interest in the food aid program, and he ordered Reuter to mount a major effort to end the interagency squabbling over the PL 480 program and to shift thinking at the operational level from surplus disposal philosophy to a recognition of the political and economic value of food aid.

Reuter also undertook to make good on the Kennedy campaign pledge to convene an international food conference commemorating the twentieth anniversary of the FAO. The proposal for a World Food Congress was approved by the President in October 1962 and the meeting was scheduled for June 1963. Over twelve hundred international participants were invited, including private citizens, academicians, representatives of nongovernmental organizations, and the like.

From the White House perspective, convening such a conference fulfilled a number of the administration's goals and interests simultaneously. First, it made good on the Kennedy campaign pledge, and it emphasized the President's *personal* interest and commitment to the problem of world hunger. Second, it focused international attention of the problems of hunger and population and emphasized the need for coordinated global action. John Kennedy personally delivered the keynote address of the congress, and with typical rhetorical flourish, he underscored the importance of the hunger problem:

For the first time in the history of the world we do know how to produce enough food now to feed every man, woman and child in the world, enough to eliminate all hunger completely.

So long as freedom from hunger is only half achieved, so long as two-thirds of the nations have food deficits, no citizen, no nation, can afford to be satisfied. We have the ability, as members of the human race. We have the means, we have the capacity to eliminate hunger from the face of the earth in our lifetime. We need only the will.[10]

It is interesting to speculate on the direction US food aid policy might have taken had John Kennedy lived to complete his first term and, perhaps, to serve for a second. But, five months after his World Food Congress speech, he was gone. Although Lyndon Johnson attempted to carry on Kennedy's programs and policies for the remainder of the term, the role and functions of the OFFP—as well as the overall application of American food aid—began to undergo a perceptible change (see chapter 3), particularly after the start of Johnson's own elected term. This is not to suggest that the new President was any less commited to the problem of world hunger and malnutrition; in fact, in many respects Lyndon Johnson became more *personally* involved than Kennedy had ever been (see section following). But, by 1965, Johnson and his staff had come increasingly to view the OFFP as a vestige of the Kennedy period (and the Kennedy "people") and as somewhat antithetical to his own highly-centralized style of administration.

The result was the active reconsideration of a plan, which had been debated on and off since George McGovern's resignation in 1962, for consolidating the OFFP into either the State Department or the USDA. Reuter and other food aid advocates argued strongly against the idea, but the decision was finally made in October 1965 to transfer the OFFP out of the White House into the State Department, with its director, Richard Reuter, now reporting as a Special Assistant to the Secretary of State. In his executive order, the President stressed the continuing importance of the Food for Peace program and his own personal interest in it. Privately, however, Mr. Johnson was said to feel that there was no reason to maintain a bureaucratic structure which was created, he believed, primarily in order to elect George McGovern to the Senate.[11]

Richard Reuter remained in his new post for another year, resigning in December 1966 amidst an interagency power struggle between the USDA and the State Department over control of the PL 480 program that had developed in the absence of White House coordination and leadership. After Reuter's resignation, the OFFP was soon absorbed completely with the AID bureaucracy. Lyndon Johnson *did* continue to maintain an intense, personal involvement with the US food aid program, but it was orchestrated henceforth directly from the Oval Office.

During its five-year existence, the OFFP had served a valuable *symbolic* function in demonstrating the personal commitment of the President to the problem of world hunger and malnutrition. This support came at a time when the use of food aid and all economic assistance as a foreign policy instrument was in a period of critical transition. The existence of the OFFP thus served to increase the public visibility of the PL 480 program, to further the political career of its first director, George

McGovern, and to facilitate, at least to some degree, the coordination of agency efforts in the allocation of food aid.

JOHNSON: POLITICAL LEVERAGE

During the period from 1965 to 1968, the Johnson administration undertook a widely-publicized policy, known as the "short tether," wherein food aid shipments to India were allocated only on an extremely short-term basis (often month-to-month) as dictated by certain corresponding actions by the aid recipient. The short tether policy was actually a code word, however, for two distinct initiatives: the first was the effort to employ the continued flow of food as a lever to force the reorientation of Indian development policy from its primary focus on industrialization to a greater emphasis on expanding agricultural output; and the second was the use of food aid to indicate presidential displeasure with specific political actions of the government of India.

The former aspect of the short-tether policy, i.e., the encouragement of agricultural development through self-help, is of particular interest. It represented the first, explicit recognition of the futility of pouring millions of tons of food aid each year into food deficit countries such as India without addressing the underlying economic, agricultural, and social (e.g., population control and health) problems that were at the root of the growing shortfalls. The self-help aspect of the short-tether policy was designed, in the theory at least, both to help the Indians help themselves and, in the process, to help the United States as well by reducing long-term Indian dependence on US concessional food assistance.

Since the closing years of the Eisenhower administration, India had developed an increasing dependence on US food aid as its population–food production capacity imbalance worsened (between 1957 and 1960, $1.3 billion worth of American food aid was allocated to India). As a result of Eisenhower's successful visit to the subcontinent, the single largest Title I food aid agreement in the history of the PL 480 program up to that time was signed on 4 May, 1960, calling for the four-year shipment of 17 million tons of grain valued at almost $1.3 billion. It must be noted, however, that this situation of growing dependency was not altogether troublesome for the United States, since surplus agricultural stocks held at government expense had also reached an all-time record at this time. Nor did the Indians themselves object. The availability of the grain permitted them to concentrate their scarce foreign exchange resources on the development of heavy industry. In fact, when a member of Secretary of Agriculture Orville Freeman's staff inquired about India's emergency food reserve stocks on a 1961 fact-finding trip, the official reply was reportedly, "Oh, our reserves are in Kansas."[12] Consequently, as Westwood concludes, "India's massive need came as a 'Godsend' to surplus disposal, and PL 480 became a 'Godsend' to those concerned with India's economic development" [Westwood (1966, p. 71)]. It is therefore significant, although highly ironic, that the United States later became such a vocal critic of the Indian development policy when it had helped indirectly to shape that policy in the first place.

Through 1964, Indian development policies continued to be characterized by heavy emphasis on industrial development and equally heavy reliance on the United States as a residual source of food commodities. Just as the results of these development policies were becoming evident, however, things fell apart: food shortages, caused by the failure of the monsoon, were the worst in the history of independent India. This led quickly to soaring prices, inflation, food hoarding, and food riots. The Shastri government undertook emergency countermeasures, which were largely unsuccessful, and was soon forced to issue an urgent appeal to the United States for additional food aid. Consequently, in September 1964, a new PL 480 agreement was concluded which resulted in the shipment during fiscal 1965 of 6.78 million tons of wheat—fully one-fifth of the entire US wheat crop for that year—and 350,000 metric tons of rice [CIA (1965, p. 2)].

Once again, in April 1965, India was forced to submit a request for another large PL 480 food aid agreement. When no immediate response was forthcoming, the new Indian Food and Agriculture Minister, Chidambara Subramaniam, called in US Ambassador Chester Bowles to underscore the urgency of the situation. There was a reason for the delay, however; a comprehensive reassessment of US food aid policy regarding India was then under way in Washington. It seems that the Indian food emergency had motivated Secretary of Agriculture Orville Freeman to act on his long-held belief that "negotiation of new Public Law 480 agreements represents an opportunity to induce the recipient nations to take steps which they would not take on their own in improving their food situation."[13] Freeman continued, in a memorandum to the President, by warning of the threat of widespread famine throughout the developing world unless steps were taken to use food aid as "a 'lever' in economic development, not only in India but in Ceylon, Brazil and Pakistan as well" [Freeman (1965a, p. 3)].

The Freeman memorandum sparked further policy deliberations, within both the White House and the USDA during the summer of 1965, concerned with the identification or specific steps that India should take to improve its food situation.[14] The extreme political sensitivity of the United States pressing such measures on the Indians was also noted, however, as well as the value of seeking specific congressional support.

One particular memorandum, produced within the USDA, also provided the conceptual groundwork for what eventually became the short-tether approach. It called for the United States to

agree to supply food aid to India through a series of short-run extensions of our present PL 480 agreement or some similar arrangement. No commitment or performance from the GoI would be written into an agreement and subject to enforcement. However, it would be made crystal clear to the GoI that agricultural performance would weigh heavily in determining the terms of future food assistance.[15]

The result of this intense policy reformulation process was the emergence of a new dual strategy in the fall of 1965 designed to elicit both the desired alterations in Indian development policies and the necessary support from Congress. The new food aid policy contained three major elements: (1) a strong emphasis on recipient self-help measures to increase their own agricultural production; (2) an explicit tieing of future food aid to the introduction of self-help policies; and (3) a modification of the PL 480 legislation to reflect the shift away from surplus disposal and toward a new emphasis on economic development.

Secretary Freeman pursued the first two objectives at the November FAO Conference in Rome. He met with Indian Agricultural Minister Subramaniam and spelled out clearly what India would have to do in order to maintain its US food aid supply pipeline. Surprisingly, the Indian official offered far less resistance to Freeman's hard-line approach than had been anticipated, indicating that the US pressure would provide him with the leverage he needed to convince the Indian Cabinet and Parliament to shift development priorities in favor of agriculture.[16] On 7 December, 1965, India officially announced its new and expanded agricultural program, and seven days later President Johnson ordered an additional 1.5 million tons of wheat shipped and *routed* "directly to the stomachs of those who need it."[17]

Conditions deteriorated on a number of fronts at the beginning of 1966: the monsoon failed again, bringing another meager harvest and, in early January, Prime Minister Shastri died of a heart attack. The latter event was considered a major blow to the US self-help strategy because it was Shastri's political support that had enabled Subramaniam to weather the storm of controversy aroused by the US pressure tactics. Moreover, Shastri had been scheduled to visit the United States in order to discuss overall Indian economic development and US foreign aid, and now such a trip would be delayed at least until a new Prime Minister was selected.

It was decided subsequently to renew the presidential invitation to Shastri's successor, Indira Gandhi, for a Washington visit in late March. In the interim, Johnson's new food aid policy was packaged as a Food for Freedom program (see chapter 3), emphasizing the need for economic development through agricultural self-help and international burden-sharing, and sent up to Congress on February 10 as part of his dual strategy for dealing with India's food crisis.

Gandhi visited the United States in March and held private talks with the President. According to Johnson memoirs, "We discussed her country's food problem and our considered judgement of the best ways to meet it. She expressed full understanding and support for the principle of self-help and international sharing on which our policy was based" [Lyndon B. Johnson (1971, p. 227)]. Johnson expressed public admiration for his new Indian counterpart, likening her to "a cross between Barbara Ward and Lady Bird," and vowing to his staff "to help that girl," but Bjorkman maintains that, in private, "He (Johnson) reportedly had also concluded that she was a 'typical woman in politics' who tended toward the opaque if not the vacuous" [Bjorkman (1974, p. 34)].

Immediately after Mrs. Gandhi's departure, President Johnson sent a special message to Congress on emergency food aid to India. The President proposed that the United States allocate an additional 3.5 million tons of food aid with a matching volume to be provided by other donor nations. (He announced that Canada had already agreed to offer a million tons of wheat and flour to India.) Johnson stated further that "the United States interferes neither in the internal politics nor the internal economic structure of other countries. The record of the last fifteen years is a sufficient proof that we ask only for results."[18] Yet, professions of such innocent and altruistic intent hardly seemed to square with the facts concerning the administration's short-tether policy.

Lyndon Johnson had also become increasingly aware of the potential value of food as a *political* lever as well. In September 1965, capital assistance to both India and Pakistan had been suspended in an attempt to force an early end to the Kashmir border conflict (although food aid was not included explicitly because it was considered an overly drastic step). Moreover, once the short-tether policy had been established in order to force the pace of agricultural development and self-help, it was a relatively simple—and, in some respects, almost unavoidable—step to transform it from a relatively benign developmental tool to a political instrument.

In late November 1965, a new administrative procedure was developed at the President's request whereby all new economic aid program loans of over $5 million and all project loans of over $10 million were to be submitted for *direct* presidential review and approval. The plan was developed by Budget Director Charles L. Shultze and it included the PL 480 program. Shultze estimated that Johnson would be involved directly in approximately 85 percent of all new project aid decisions, and he informed Johnson that "in addition to submitting all loans and grants above the proposed dollar magnitudes, AID would submit through Bundy any new commitments which involved special foreign policy issues, e.g., loans to India, Pakistan, Indonesia, UAR."[19] The new procedure was implemented swiftly. It marked both the beginning of a long, tortuous procession of aid proposals through the Oval Office and the emergence of the Bureau of the Budget as a major actor in the formulation of food aid policy—much in the same way that the (renamed) Office of Management and Budget gained influence during the early seventies.

Lyndon Johnson had thus gained personal control over the critical decisions concerning when and in what quantities US aid would flow to recipient countries.[20] As Johnson himself admits in his memoirs, his short-tether decision was profoundly unpopular both in New Delhi and among India's defenders in the United States, and he describes his action as "one of the most difficult and lonely struggles of my Presidency" [Lyndon B. Johnson (1971, p. 275)].

The domestic impact of Johnson's decision to hold up Indian grain shipments was mounting bureaucratic frustration and paralysis; AID officials became unwilling to make even the most minor aid allocation decisions for fear that their actions might be countermanded by the President. The international impact was even more profound. Although there is probably no explicit point at which the short-tether policy was transformed from an instrument for eliciting expanded recipient self-help to an instrument of political sanction, Bjorkman (1974, p. 33) suggests that a critical event may well have been a communique signed by Indian Prime Minister Indira Gandhi during a state visit to Moscow.

Political relations between the United States and India had become problematic in many respects as early as the spring of 1965 when the

United States canceled abruptly the planned visit of Prime Minister Shastri. Although there is no specific evidence that the cancellation was related directly to India's position regarding the war in Southeast Asia, the action was apparently perceived that way by officials in New Delhi.[21] Indo–American relations became increasingly hostile, however, during 1966 as India reacted with growing resentment to its dependency on US aid and to the humiliating nature of Johnson's heavy-handed control. As a result, in order to reassert symbolically its sovereign prerogatives, as well as to make a favorable impression in domestic politics, Mrs. Gandhi signed an Indo–Soviet communique criticizing the "imperialists in South East Asia."

Such statements had not had much effect on Indo–American relations prior to 1966. This may be explained largely by the fact that the failure of US policy in Southeast Asia had not yet become apparent, and thus Lyndon Johnson was not yet excessively sensitive regarding his Vietnam policy. Moreover, relations between the two countries were still friendly in many other respects (i.e., in matters not pertaining to food), and, since the food crisis in India was just beginning, India's vulnerable dependency relationship had not yet developed.

But in 1966 presidential reaction was swift and predictably severe: Johnson, who was fast losing patience with his Vietnam critics, was reportedly furious with Mrs. Gandhi's action and, according to Bjorkman, "Descriptions of his reaction range from the violent to the obscene" [Bjorkman (1974, p. 33)]. He viewed the Prime Minister's remarks as a blatant slap in the face to the very nation that was helping India through its worst food crisis since 1948.

Political relations continued their steady deterioration through the remainder of 1966. In November, Johnson ordered a temporary freeze on grain shipments which the Indian government had been counting on to arrive just prior to the February 1967 national elections. This raised the possibility of a serious political setback for the Congress party. In addition, the President *still* remained sufficiently unsure of Indian compliance with the self-help policy that he directed Secretary Freeman to send an expert team to India to assess the current harvest and the extent of self-help actions taken to increase agricultural output. In addition, Freeman was instructed to form a congressional inspection team[22] to make an independent assessment of the situation in early December. In the meantime, Johnson maintained the freeze on new PL 480 shipments that had already been in effect since August 1966. By Christmas, the President had received both reports.

The USDA team analyzed Indian self-help efforts within eight categories: investment in agriculture, incentives to farmers, fertilizer production, fertilizer availability, availability of high-yielding seed varieties, agricultural credit, soil and water management, and the creation of a Food Corporation of India, as well as the overall food situation within the country. They concluded that, while the record was somewhat uneven, India had made a generally sincere effort to meet the commitments it had agreed to in the November 1965 meeting between Freeman and Subramaniam.[23]

On the basis of the expert group's report, Secretary Freeman gave his own evaluation to the President, stating that the Indians *had* indeed made a sincere effort, and that the food situation was grave. "Two million tons of grain must come from somewhere between mid-January (1967), when the pipeline runs out and April, when the spring crop comes in."[24] The congressional study mission reported a similar finding, recommending that the President authorize an additional 1.8 million tons of grain on an interim basis through April 1967.

Based on these firsthand reports, Johnson approved an additional authorization of 450,000 tons of wheat and an equal volume of other grains, but he kept the short-tether policy in effect. As he recalled in his memoirs, "I kept the 'short tether' on. No one would starve because of our policies. India would receive the grain needed, but on a month-to-month basis rather than a year-to-year basis. What happened in the next months, I told Freeman, would depend on two things: what Congress would do and what other countries would do" [Lyndon B. Johnson (1971, p. 229)]. India, for its part, sought indirect retribution against the United States by severely criticizing Israel, a close US ally, during the 1967 Six Day War. Mrs. Gandhi also sent greetings to Ho Chi Minh, the leader of North Vietnam, on his seventy-seventh birthday, and, in November, she attended the fiftieth-anniversary celebrations of the Russian revolution in Moscow. As former US ambassador to India Chester Bowles reports, "Cables from Washington burned with comments about 'those ungrateful Indians,' and the shipments of wheat were delayed still further" [Bowles (1971, p. 526)].

Again in May 1967, Johnson delayed approving an agreement for 1.5 million tons of grain, despite repeated urging to the contrary by Secretaries Rusk and Freeman. They counseled that to delay shipments further would accomplish little and would be likely to create much additional ill will. For the year 1967 as a whole, grain reached Indian ports at a monthly rate some 200,000 tons lower than in 1966 [Lelyveld (1967, p. 3)].

As the President's food aid decisionmaking became more unpredictable, the Indian outcry also grew louder. As a result, Lyndon Johnson's media image, already battered from Vietnam, received further damage. As Johnson himself later recalled,

> During this period our policy was the target of a heavy propaganda barage. Through official and unofficial channels, the Indians pressed us to change our position. . . . In the press and at Washington cocktail parties, I was pictured as a heartless man willing to let innocent people starve. . . . I decided I would have to live with the noisy but superficial criticism and do what I believed was right. [Lyndon B. Johnson (1971, p. 228]

Ignoring Johnson's outburst of self-congratulation, it is possible to read between the lines in his statement the fundamental difficulty with *political* use of the short-tether policy. The President had so consolidated the reins of power in the allocation of food aid that each decision came to depend almost entirely on Johnson's own personal inclination at the time.

The problem though was that Lyndon Johnson had *never* understood the Indians (although he was remarkably conversant with the nature and extent of their food problem), and he would accept no advice from those in the government who did. His misapprehension prevented him from realizing that much of India's public reaction to the short-tether policy (e.g., Mrs. Gandhi's statement in Moscow) was political posturing meant more for domestic consumption in India than as a meaningful foreign policy statement. But, by this time, Johnson was increasingly obsessed by his own personal demon, the War in Southeast Asia, the war which was consuming his presidency and overshadowing his very real achievements in domestic affairs. Consequently, he could only view India's statements against the war from a narrow, defensive perspective.

It is difficult, even in retrospect, to place the Johnson policy in its proper perspective, since the short-tether policy did serve overlapping development and political goals which were (and are) impossible to separate completely. Purely in terms of the *agricultural* aspects of the short-tether approach, the initiative must be judged a success. In the late sixties and early seventies India substantially improved its capacity to meet its own food needs. This, in turn, reduced the burden on the United States after 1968. In purely political terms, however, there was no parallel story of success.

In spite of his own humanitarian instincts, Johnson continued to delay, and occasionally even to halt, food aid as a form of political sanction against his weak Indian client. Under the terms of PL 480 in 1967, however, there was little that either the Congress or others in the executive branch could do to deter Johnson from his ill-fated action once initiated. Thus, the damage was done. Once the President had decided to begin his *political* manipulation of the short-tether policy, many of the most positive and beneficial aspects of his agricultural self-help program were negated in the process. Moreover, Indo–American relations were damaged for many years to come.

NIXON: "FOOD FOR WAR"

In some respects, it can be argued that the inability of the Congress to react quickly and effectively to Lyndon Johnson's use of PL 480 aid in India returned eventually to haunt his successor, Richard M. Nixon, in the context of Southeast Asia. It is unnecessary to review in great detail the intense domestic political resistance in the early seventies to the continuing US military involvement. Richard Nixon had won the election in 1968 promising that he had a "secret plan" to end US participation, but he was unable to conclude a peace agreement with the North Vietnamese prior to the 1972 elections. Despite the large plurality of the Nixon victory margin, national political sentiment soon began to swing heavily against the war. This shift was, of course, reflected also in Congress, where new efforts were made to limit the total volume of military assistance allocated to Vietnam and Cambodia.

But the Nixon administration perceived the congressionally imposed restraints as a direct impediment to the ongoing peace negotiations, fearing that they would strengthen the enemy's resolve to outwait the American side. Moreover, the Vietnamese army was totally dependent on uninterrupted resupply by the United States simply to hold its ground against the Vietcong and the North Vietnamese. Under these circumstances, the decision was made to substitute, to the extent practicable, food aid resources under Title I of PL 480 for direct military aid. This policy was carried out under the so-called "common defense" provision which had actually been in use in Vietnam since the earliest days of US involvement (see chapter 6). Proceeds derived from the sale of Title I commodities could be used by the Vietnamese and Cambodian governments to free foreign exchange in order to *purchase* desperately needed war materiel.

For a number of years, this new "food for war" strategy went virtually unnoticed—or at least, unchallenged—by the Congress and the citizen antiwar movement. But, by one account, between 1968 and 1973, South Vietnam alone received twenty times the value of food aid that the five African countries of the Sahelian drought region received *jointly* during this same period [Lappé and Collins (1977, p. 339)]. Figure 9.1 provides an overall indication of the enhanced role of food as an aid resource for South Vietnam and Cambodia after 1970. It reveals that direct military aid climbed steadily (as a result of commitments already in the pipeline) through fiscal 1973, but then plummeted sharply until the US withdrawal. Other loans and grants, known as security supporting assistance, remained relatively static after 1970 and also began a gradual decline after 1971. Food aid, however, increased substantially in 1971 and, after an interruption in 1972, continued its sharp upward movement in 1973, when most other aid was declining. During the critical year of 1973–1974, when direct military support fell by more than 61 percent, food aid grew by fully 53 percent. Thus, up until shortly before the collapse in Southeast Asia, food aid had assumed a major role in bolstering the failing regimes in South Vietnam and Cambodia.

Congress and the general public finally became aware of the true extent of the Nixon evasion strategy in 1972 with the advent of major LDC food shortages. But, despite the severe global food need, 67 percent of Title I PL 480 aid programmed in fiscal 1973 was targeted for South Vietnam, Cambodia, and South Korea; for fiscal 1974, South Vietnam's share alone had jumped to 40.1 percent and Cambodia's to 29.3 percent. The administration had clearly chosen to place strategic, political considerations ahead of humanitarianism in its food aid policy.

From the White House perspective, the attractiveness of food aid lay in the fact that Congress had no direct means of controlling either the destination or the specific volume of food programmed in any given year. Moreover, even if Congress *did* choose to cut back the PL 480 budget, the huge volume of accumulated dollar credits under the control of the Commodity Credit Corporation meant that any limitation on the President's freedom of action would not be felt until many years in the future. The Nixon administration was successful in this fashion in using the insulation of the PL 480 program to circumvent the intent of Congress regarding the level of military aid flowing to South Vietnam and Cambodia.

Once the actual nature of the Nixon strategy did become apparent, congressional action was soon forthcoming. In 1973, Congress passed an

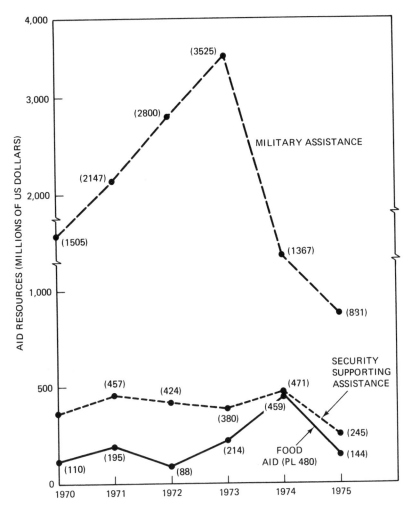

Figure 9.1
Aid resources to South Vietnam and Cambodia: 1970–1979. Horizontal axis gives fiscal year, vertical axis gives aid resources in millions of US dollars. Source: US AID (1977, pp. 69, 82).

amendment to the Foreign Assistance Act of 1961 (as amended), forbidding the use of local currencies generated from the sale of Title I commodities for common defense purposes without specific congressional approval. But, as Lappé and Collins (1977, p. 339) have pointed out, the effect of this modification on the use of PL 480 as "food for war" was almost negligible since proceeds from the resale of Title I food aid often go into the general treasuries of the recipient countries, thereby making it impossible to monitor how they are spent.

World food shortages continued in 1974, but the administration again programmed more than half of all PL 480 resources for Southeast Asia in its new fiscal 1975 budget. Congress, for its part, was now under heavy public pressure to take meaningful action to halt the "abuse" of the food aid program. Thus, in its next session (1974), a different approach to the problem was adopted.

Congress directed the President, in Section 55 of the Foreign Assistance Act of 1974, that no more than 30 percent of Title I food assistance for fiscal 1975 was to be allocated to countries *not* appearing on the UN "most seriously affected" list unless it could be demonstrated that the food would be used solely for humanitarian purposes. This new limitation was more successful in obtaining the desired restraint on executive branch policymaking. However, the administration then proceeded to announce a last-minute increase in total *dollar* level budgeted for PL 480 in fiscal 1975, which enabled it once again to evade congressional intent by making additional resources available for *all* categories of food aid. Congress, in turn, tightened the new categorical control provisions still further in 1975, reducing to 25 percent the portion of Title I resources that could be allocated to countries with a per capita GNP over $300 per year and requiring that at least 1.3 million tons of food commodities be programmed through the Title II grant-type aid mechanism.

Of course, by 1975 the US involvement in Vietnam and Cambodia was past history. But the Congress had succeeded through its actions in 1974 and 1975 in reasserting some degree of oversight regarding presidential manipulation of food aid resources. It is interesting to note, however, that even the new limitations of PL 480 did not entirely eliminate the basic feature of Food for Peace as a back-door means of financing foreign policy initiatives when other types of aid were unavailable for one reason or another. The congressional action succeeded merely in placing limits on the total quantity of funds that could legally be employed for such purposes.

The use of "food for war" in Southeast Asia provides an interesting contrast with the two previous policy initiatives examined here. It would be inaccurate to suggest that the notion of manipulating aid resources in this manner originated with Richard Nixon himself, or that Nixon necessarily controlled such decisions in the same way that Lyndon Johnson immersed himself in the details of the Indian short-tether policy. Yet, the fact remains that the massive diversion of Title I commodities to South Vietnam and Cambodia between 1973 and 1975 provided an effective means of evading congressional restraints on the flexibility of the Nixon–Kissinger foreign policy initiatives. In a larger sense, therefore, this use of food aid was just as much an element of presidential discretion as either the Kennedy Food for Peace initiative or the Johnson short-tether political sanctions.

FORD: FISCAL RESTRAINT

The final example of food aid used as an element of presidential discretion departs in many respects from the two previous examples, in which instrumental actions taken by the President (or on his behalf) had specific domestic and/or foreign policy ramifications. The present case, which occurred near the height of the world food "crisis" period and against the background of the 1974 World Food Conference, concerns Gerald R. Ford's decision *not* to increase the volume of US food aid commitments in spite of unprecedented world demand. By choosing to emphasize domestic fiscal restraint over urgent international food needs, the Ford food aid policy, like that of John Kennedy, was intended primarily as a symbolic indication of the administration's priorities.

Three critical background facts are relevant to the case, each of which served to reinforce the symbolic importance of the President's ultimate decision. First, Gerald Ford assumed the presidency, unelected, under the most bizarre and unprecedented conditions in the history of the office. He was relatively unknown outside of the House of Representatives and untested as a leader of national stature. Moreover, substantial doubt had been expressed in many quarters concerning his basic ability to function effectively as President. Second, Gerald Ford became President during the third year of a global food supply "crisis" in which the United States, as the largest agricultural producer and exporter, had been generally conspicuous for its lack of a coordinated policy response. His predecessor had waged a long and largely unsuccessful battle against the ravages of inflation, which had included a comprehensive policy of fiscal restraint and a brief flirtation with wage and price controls. Thus, both the US voting public and the international community were asking the same questions in the fall of 1974: "Who is Gerald Ford? What does he plan to do about current US and international food and economic problems?"

Certain other factors also figured prominently in Gerald Ford's decision concerning the level of US food aid programming. The President had inherited Earl L. Butz as his Secretary of Agriculture, a man firmly committed to a "free market" agricultural export policy and the individual who had convinced Richard Nixon to approve the elimination of government-owned food reserve stocks. This association became extremely significant not only because the United States no longer retained its food reserve cushion but also because Butz held the PL 480 program in low esteem, believing that it should not be paid for out of the USDA budget. In 1973, for example, Secretary Butz had dramatized his position by sending the annual USDA budget request to the OMB with a zero line item figure entered for PL 480, stating that, with commercial agricultural exports at an all-time high, he no longer "needed" the food aid outlet. The Butz policy reflected, of course, the farmers' own interests in maximizing commercial exports, which meant that the food aid program had lost—at least temporarily—a portion of its most powerful constituency, the farm lobby.

Two other powerful interests were ready to fill the vacuum left by the abdication of agriculture, and it was the policy debate that ensued between these forces that the President was called upon ultimately to resolve. The first was the foreign policy interest as articulated by Secretary of State Henry Kissinger. In Southeast Asia, and again in the Middle East, Kissinger had skillfully utilized the food aid resource as a means of pursuing larger diplomatic and strategic objectives. As the world food situation deteriorated after 1972, the task also fell to Kissinger to develop the US response. Acting then in his capacity as National Security Advisor to the President, Kissinger ordered the preparation of a National Security Study Memorandum on food, which was completed late in the year. Later, in September 1973, shortly after his appointment as Secretary of State, Kissinger proposed that a World Food Conference be convened under UN auspices in 1974 in order to coordinate global action on pressing LDC food needs.[25]

Another competing interest in food aid policy grew out of the serious and worsening international economic situation. Unprecedented increases in the price of OPEC oil, combined with poor world harvests and fertilizer shortages, had created a soaring LDC debt burden and

double-digit inflation. All of this enhanced the influence of fiscally oriented actors within the Nixon and Ford adminstrations, including the
Office of Management and Budget (OMB), the Council of Economic Advisors (CEA), the Council for International Economic Policy (CIEP), and
the Treasury Department. Their message was clear: controlling inflation
must be the administration's number one priority if economic disaster
was to be avoided. As Gelb and Lake concluded,

The prevailing idea in the Nixon Administration that fiscal restraint was
the answer to inflation was as important as the Butz free enterprise arguments. Food aid was a billion-dollar program, and if various agencies of
government were being called upon to show restraint, why not cut back
food aid as well? Food aid was caught in a budgetary squeeze. [Gelb and
Lake (1974–1975)]

Secretary Kissinger, meanwhile, was fast becoming a convert to the
need for a substantially expanded US effort to address the real food and
agriculture needs of the Third World. Kissinger reportedly hoped that
the OPEC nations might also be convinced to make a parallel gesture by
rolling back crude oil prices for the LDCs. But Kissinger's approach ran
headlong into the opposition of Treasury Secretary George P. Schultz,
who argued for fiscal restraint and the importance of using food exports
in commercial trade in order to improve the US balance of payments position. Moreover, by this time (spring, 1974), Richard Nixon was so
deeply preoccupied with the growing Watergate scandal that he was
never more than a peripheral actor in this ongoing policy debate.

Secretary Kissinger was scheduled to give a speech before the special
session of the UN General Assembly called to deal with the international
economic crisis, and he wanted very much to make a typically broad
proposal for action by the United States and other developed countries.[26] But Secretary Schultz still objected on fiscal and economic
grounds, and, with Richard Nixon immobilized by Watergate, there was
no presidential arbiter to resolve the interagency dispute. Kissinger thus
decided to include in his speech a carefully worded statement promising
"a major effort to increase the quantity of food aid over the level we
provided last year."[27]

As Gerald Ford assumed the presidency in August 1974, there was
some reason to believe that a strong US harvest might ease the pressure
on available supplies and permit the United States to meet fully both its
aid and trade commitments. But a summer drought afflicted the corn-
belt, and, although the rice crop was strong, the wheat harvest was
below the record levels projected by the USDA. The result was that high

domestic food prices continued while the debate between the State and Treasury Departments over the appropriate level of food aid programming intensified still further.[28]

When Gerald Ford entered the picture directly, he was confronted with a wide variety of pressing, unresolved problems besides the food issue. There was, of course, the rapidly deteriorating situation in Southeast Asia, as well as the twin problems of high inflation and a stagnant economy (termed by many "stagflation"). Moreover, with the World Food Conference only three months away, certain major policy issues remained undecided. The President was also committed to deliver an address before the UN General Assembly, during which some statement on US food aid commitments would have to be made.

A mere two days before his UN appearance, Ford received a final decision memorandum from Budget Director Roy L. Ash warning that "a major increase in outlays in support of foreign policy objectives at a time when you are calling upon government and the American people to employ restraint in spending, will be inconsistent with our program to combat inflation and subject to considerable criticism."[29] Ash nevertheless presented the President with three funding options[30] which set out clearly the fundamental policy dilemma facing the new President.

Ford's basic choice, therefore, was between maintaining consistency in his domestic fiscal restraint initiative and contributing on a much larger scale to the short term needs of the food deficient countries. Table 9.1, included originally with the Ash presidential memorandum, indicates the likely impact of each of the three funding options on PL 480 programming. It was apparent that the President's ultimate decision would be of utmost significance both in terms of his domestic anti-inflation campaign and in terms of the US foreign image. With the World Food Conference about to commence, the United States was clearly vulnerable to severe criticism if Ford chose not to increase food assistance.

On September 17, the President met with Secretaries Kissinger and Butz, Budget Director Ash, and Alan Greenspan, Head of the Council of Economic Advisers. The decision facing the group was extremely delicate in view of the pressing urgency of both the domestic and international problems. It was concluded that a position somewhere in between the two extremes outlined in the OMB memorandum was required; the President should announce in his UN speech that US food assistance would be increased, but reserve final judgment on the specific dollar figure until the actual size of the American wheat harvest was known. Thus, the decision to increase the dollar figure budgeted for food aid

Table 9.1
Distribution of Optional PL 480 Funding Levels: 1975–1976 (Millions of US Dollars)

Priority/Country programs	Option I	Option II	Option III
Southeast Asia			
Cambodia	146	146	146
Vietnam	107	107	107
Subtotal	253	253	253
Middle East			
Egypt	93	93	93
Israel	15	21	21
Jordan	3	8	8
Syria	14	18	18
Subtotal	125	140	140
Traditional recipients			
Chile	18	35	65
Korea	–	110	121
Indonesia	1	65	70
Pakistan	8	42	42
Subtotal	27	252	298
Asian subcontinent			
Bangladesh	49	67	91
India	–	83	82
Subtotal	49	150	173
Other countries and flexible reserve			
Other countries	6	6	58
Flexible reserve	127	–	90
Total Title I commodities	587	801	1,012
"Humanitarian" purposes:			
Title II donations	285	291	339
Total commodities	872	1,092	1,351
Freight costs	124	140	178
Receipts from repayment	-254	-254	-254
PL 480 — Total	742	978	1,275

Source: memorandum from Roy L. Ash (Director, Office of Management and Budget) for the President, 16 September 1974 (Ash, 1974, p. 4)

(but *not* tonnage—which still remained below fiscal 1973 due to the increased price of wheat) was depicted as a "substantial" new US commitment.

There were many, however, both in the United States and abroad, who did not agree with the administration's view. A World Hunger Action Coalition, composed of church and charitable groups, the private voluntary agencies, and certain liberal senators, continued to lobby actively prior to the start of the World Food Conference for an increase in the *volume* of US food aid for the 1975 fiscal year. Henry Kissinger, too, was urging the President to modify his decision on the PL 480 volume level. The Secretary of State was scheduled to deliver a major address at the November 5 session of the Rome Conference, and he wished to present a positive image of the US food aid program. Much subsequent behind-the-scenes maneuvering[31] occurred over the wording of the Kissinger speech, but once again the advocates of fiscal restraint prevailed and President Ford stood by his decision. In his speech, Secretary Kissinger acknowledged only that "an expanded flow of food aid will clearly be necessary," without stating specific dollar or volume levels.

The World Hunger Action Coalition made one last-ditch effort during the World Food Conference to force the President's hand. A cable was sent to the President, signed by Secretary Butz at the behest of the coalition, urgently requesting a minimum *volume* increase of 1 million tons of food aid for the 1975 fiscal year. Caught in the glare of wide media coverage, Ford huddled once again with his top economic advisors and, for yet a third time, decided to stand by his policy of fiscal restraint. This was, perhaps, the most difficult of the three Ford decisions because it could not be made in the secluded, protective environment of high-level White House policy groups. But the President apparently had decided that the inevitable international criticism of his decision would be outweighed in the long run by the domestic benefits of restraining federal spending.

It is ironic that the prolonged agony of the food aid programming decision proved ultimately to have been unnecessary. Grain prices declined in December and into January 1975 and the rate of domestic inflation also began to slow. This made it possible for Secretary Butz to announce a substantial increase in the final food aid budget for the 1975 fiscal year. But the symbolic importance of the Ford initiative remained: the President had used the food aid programming decision as an effective means of underscoring the need for fiscal restraint. This initiative did not include the same kind of unilateral exercise of power demonstrated by Lyndon Johnson in the case of the Indian short-tether policy because the options in this case had been filtered through a complex process of bureaucratic debate. Yet, in the final analysis, it was only through the direct intervention of the President that the fierce interagency competition for influence was resolved.

ASSESSMENT OF POLICY OBJECTIVES

It was suggested at the outset of this chapter that the use of food aid as an instrument of presidential discretion has been manifested in both symbolic and instrumental applications. Similarly, the intent of these presidential initiatives has also varied, with the aid at some times serving domestic political objectives, and at other times promoting US foreign policy goals. It is also possible to differentiate in the cases examined here between active and passive approaches.

The two instrumental presidential actions, the Johnson short-tether policy and the Nixon evasion strategy, present perhaps the sharpest contrast. The manipulation of food aid by Lyndon Johnson was clearly an active policy designed to achieve specific political and development objectives with respect to India. By contrast, Richard Nixon's use of food aid in order to avoid congressional limitations on his freedom of action in Southeast Asia was a generally passive approach. The Nixon "food for war" policy was adopted in *reaction* to the congressional restraints and was ostensibly a short-term, temporary expedient while a peace accord was being negotiated. At the same time, while the Nixon initiative had an obvious underlying foreign policy motivation, its immediate intent was to manuever around domestic political obstacles.

The two symbolic uses of food aid also demonstrate the active–passive and foreign–domestic dichotomies, although the motivations in these cases are somewhat less explicit and straightforward. John Kennedy's support for the White House Office of Food for Peace was largely an active public relations scheme based on sincere, altruistic motivations. It was meant primarily to enhance the new conception of food aid as more than just another means of surplus disposal. In this sense, the Kennedy policy was conceived at least as much for domestic political consumption as it was for the benefit of aid recipients and other potential food donors overseas. Its most visible and significant accomplishment, however, was to emphasize the need for global solutions to the problems of hunger and malnutrition.

Gerald Ford's involvement in food aid programming was, by contrast, a *passive* symbolic action designed to demonstrate, through his *lack* of action, the heavy emphasis he placed on the need for fiscal restraint as a means of combatting inflation. Here again, however, presidential action was characterized by a mixed domestic–foreign intent, as is so often the case. The principal concern at this time was clearly with the domestic economic impact of increasing food aid expenditures. But, when the Ford policy is examined in the larger context of the 1972–1974 food "crisis" and the World Food Conference, the foreign policy ramifications of the President's decision are also significant.

Comparisons between the effectiveness of using food aid in symbolic versus instrumental applications are somewhat difficult, and perhaps spurious, due to the unique circumstances surrounding each case. It appears that, while the two instrumental actions attained the immediate objectives desired by the President, they had substantial negative repercussions in both the domestic and international contexts. The two symbolic actions are less amenable to comparison. Both were also relatively successful in demonstrating the President's personal approach to the use of food aid, but the foreign policy message of the Ford initiative, at least, was subject to extensive negative interpretation in the international community.

Thus, a number of specific conclusions can be drawn regarding the use of food aid as a personal instrument of presidential discretion. First, it is undeniable that the most intense, individual involvement by a President was Lyndon Johnson's implementation of the short-tether approach; in no other case did policy originate so markedly with the Chief Executive. Yet, food aid was not well suited for use either as a means of political sanction or as a means of political evasion because of the strong humanitarian motives inherent in the program. The result was that both the Johnson short-tether and the Nixon "food for war" policies were subjected inevitably to substantial domestic and international opposition. A similar difficulty befell the Ford fiscal restraint policy as well. The United States was portrayed in the media as callous and insensitive to the pressing food needs of the developing world. It appears, therefore, that only when food assistance was employed by the President as a positive public relations instrument did it obtain the desired political benefits *without* creating an undesirable negative fallout.

The sum of the experience reviewed here suggests that food aid does *not* offer significant advantages as an instrument of presidential discretion, except under extremely limited conditions. It is in the nature of the resource that food aid will always serve both humanitarian needs and political objectives, and in most cases, it will be impossible to separate the two in explicit fashion. Where the food resource can be employed in the pursuit of positive, humanitarian goals, the President's purposes will be well served by doing so. But, where more controversial foreign policy objectives are involved, it generally will be difficult—if not impossible—for the President to attain his goals while still avoiding negative international reaction.

The evidence presented in the preceding chapters has offered a varied demonstration of the manner in which food aid has served the cause of US foreign policy. The sum of this analysis, however, raises the question whether, and how, a useful distinction may be drawn between acceptable and unacceptable foreign policy applications of the food resource; or, phrased somewhat differently, under what conditions (if any) does a particular food aid application constitute a political "abuse" of the PL 480 program? The attempt to draw such a distinction inevitably will be a highly subjective and somewhat conjectural undertaking. But it also strikes at the heart of the ongoing policy debate over the underlying purpose of the US food assistance program.

A second question raised in the process of evaluating the foreign policy objectives inherent in food aid is whether, and how, such uses of the food resource are compatible with the development of an organized system of international food aid. That is, can the United States realistically expect to use its aid to fulfill bilateral political and economic objectives and still promote a coordinated, international approach to global food needs? This concern leads logically to yet a third set of foreign policy questions regarding the current US approach to international food aid delivery—both operational multilateralism and coordinated bilateralism—and the manner in which the United States perceives its role and responsibilities in that system.

FOOD AID AND FOREIGN POLICY

The specific foreign policy objectives considered here in relation to food aid have offered relatively few surprises. In general, they have tended to parallel the overall priorities of American foreign aid, with political, economic, and security-related goals receiving the highest priority. It is important to reiterate, however, that the broad applicability of food aid from a foreign policy perspective is due both to the essential nature of the food resource in the maintenance of human welfare and to the fact that food can be readily converted to a form of general assistance. That is, commodity assistance can be either employed directly as food aid or resold by the recipient government in order to free foreign exchange for other purposes.

When aid can be given either for its propaganda value in feeding hungry people or for its value as a support for a regime, the foreign policy flexibility of the asset is increased dramatically. Moreover, since food assistance has both symbolic and instrumental value, the propaganda aspects of the aid may often have as much impact as the more explicit quid pro quo uses. The manipulation of food resources as a symbol of food power is dangerous, however, in many respects. It is subject to easy misinterpretation by the recipient and to substantial negative international reaction.

Specific instrumental objectives, on the other hand—whether political, strategic, or economic—are, perhaps, more easily attained, but can also be problematic. They tend to portray the donor as callous, heavy-handed, and insensitive to the real food needs of the recipient. It would seem, therefore, that the successful use of food aid as an instrument of foreign policy will most often be achieved by pursuing those objectives which either divorce the aid entirely from the food context (e.g., the Korean textile agreement) or make the application so highly food specific (e.g., the Johnson short-tether policy) that it is not subject to misinterpretation.

It is also in the nature of the food aid resource that its application in a foreign policy context can be equally effective as a reward or as a punishment. Consequently, the two most ubiquitous actions involving food aid are *preferential access* and *denial*. In the former case, the promise of additional food is employed as a sweetener in order to promote policies favorable to the US position (e.g., aid to Yugoslavia, aid to the Middle East, aid to Korea); in the latter case, the threatened or actual denial of assistance is employed as an attempt to coerce a recipient to comply with the dictates of US policy (e.g., Johnson short tether, aid to the UAR, aid to Chile). There are also cases that combine both features, where US food resources are used to match the participation of other countries while the threat of reduced American participation is em-

ployed as an additional prod (e.g., the Food Aid Convention or food
aid burden-sharing in India).

Food aid has also had *domestic* applications both as a straightforward
propaganda instrument (e.g., the Kennedy Office of Food for Peace) and
as a symbolic demonstration of federal spending restraint (e.g., the Ford
food aid policy). Employed in a more instrumental, domestic context,
the manipulation of the aid resource permitted the Nixon administration
to outflank Congress temporarily on the "food for war" issue. But, aside
from its basic value in promoting American agricultural strength, most
domestic initiatives involving food aid have been inconsequential, accru-
ing only limited political and economic payoffs.

When the viability and effectiveness of the denial strategy is compared
to that of preferential access, it is apparent that the leverage potential of
denial is constrained by the finality of the act. That is, as former US
Ambassador to the UAR John Badeau warned President Johnson, "The
guillotine can only be used but once per victim." However, the denial of
food need *not* be an absolute action in all cases. At the same time, the
preferential access approach is often a less direct and less effective means
of obtaining the same (or similar) objectives since the capacity of the
donor to enforce a quid pro quo when giving resources is not as great as
when withholding them.

In general, selection of the proper food aid instrumentality will depend, to a large extent, on the conditions prevailing at the time (e.g., the
degree of food deficit or surplus, the nature of the prior food aid relationship) and on the importance of the foreign policy objective pursued
relative to the action contemplated. Thus, for example, the United States
is unlikely to withdraw food aid over a minor propaganda incident,
while it may be more inclined to do so after repeated anti-American
provocations (e.g., the withdrawal of food aid to the UAR under
Nasser). There is also, of course, a large middle ground wherein the flow
of food aid shipments may be reduced (but not withheld entirely) in ac-
cordance with specific recipient government policies and actions (e.g.,
aid to Yugoslavia, the Indian short tether). In many of the cases, in fact,
it was the failure of the government to examine fully the potential ramifications of the instrumentality selected that resulted in the incomplete
attainment of the policy objective.

As indicated in table 10.1, most food aid applications fit rather neatly
into a dichotomous foreign policy orientation. In the vast majority of
situations, the assistance represented an American initiative directed
toward a recipient country and was therefore active in focus. That is,

Table 10.1
Assessment of Policy Applications

Nature of policy				Policy setting		Policy outcomes	
Foreign policy instrument	Policy Focus	Instrumentality	Policy orientation	Arena	Actors	Benefits	Relation to foreign aid rationale
1. Diplomatic and strategic leverage	★ Political ★ Security	★ Denial ★ Preferential access	★ Active	★ Internat'l-bilateral-multilateral	★ White House ★ State Dept.	★ Cold War ★ US security ★ Peace ★ US influence	★ Enhance US political and security interests ★ Promote world order
2. Promotion of US international trade interests	★ Economic ★ Security	★ Dumping ★ Preferential access ★ Denial	★ Active ★ Reactive	★ Domestic ★ Internat'l-bilateral	★ USDA ★ Multinat'l corps. ★ White House	★ Market dev., access, protection ★ Retaliation ★ US security	★ Promote US trade ★ Enhance US security
3. International burden-sharing and recipient self-help	★ Political ★ Economic development	★ Denial ★ Matching	★ Active ★ Counteractive	★ Internat'l-bilateral-multilateral	★ White House ★ State ★ USDA ★ World Bank ★ WFP	★ Internat'l burden-sharing ★ LDC econ. development ★ Internat'l institution-building	★ Promote US economic interests ★ Enhance US security ★ Promote world order ★ Respond to moral obligation
4. Presidential discretionary initiatives	★ Political ★ Fiscal	★ Propaganda ★ Denial ★ Diversion ★ Restraint	★ Active ★ Reactive ★ Counteractive	★ Domestic ★ Internat'l-bilateral	★ White House ★ State ★ USDA ★ Treasury ★ OMB	★ US influence ★ Retaliation ★ Foreign policy flex. ★ Fiscal restraint	★ Promote US political/security interests ★ Contribute to US economic interests

the decision to give or withhold aid was most often made on the basis of the requisites of US foreign policy and not simply as a result of external events. Food aid applications indicative of a reactive policy orientation were those in which the government was *responding* to actions directed toward the United States by other actors (e.g., the Chilean expropriation case, the UN activities of the Group of 77). There was also a third type of approach which, though far less common, was nonetheless important. Under this counteractive policy, the government signaled its intentions either by *not* acting, as in the Ford policy of fiscal restraint, or by reducing the level of its participation, as in the American matching formula for the World Food Programme.

The process of extending foreign aid of any kind is, almost by definition, an active and long-term undertaking. Reactive policies, therefore, have most often tended to be punitive in nature and short term in application. They are generally a more precise form of food aid initiative, particularly when implemented through the strategy of denial. From a foreign policy perspective, however, the principal danger of a reactive policy is that it permits other actors and external events to shape and control American actions.

The advantage of the counteractive policy focus, on the other hand, is that it conveys a highly symbolic message regarding US intentions and interests but that is not as likely to cause damage to bilateral or multilateral relations. But a counteractive food aid policy has only limited application since there is little leverage to be gained by giving *less* aid or by doing nothing at all. Thus, except under certain extraordinary economic and political circumstances, active food aid policy is generally the most expeditious means of attaining US foreign policy objectives. It might be noted, however, that the capacity of the executive branch to maintain an active posture will be constrained to some extent by domestic political considerations, including congressionally imposed limitations and possible secondary impacts of the contemplated application.

POLICY SETTING

It is significant that many of the most salient characteristics of the US food aid program are conditioned as much by priorities within the domestic context as by foreign policy considerations. It is, in fact, an oft overlooked feature of US economic assistance in general that most of the resources, perhaps as much as 80 percent, are actually spent *within* the United States. This is particularly true in the case of food where the production, transport, and marketing of the commodity is a multibillion dollar business. There are, of course, many domestic interests that attempt to influence the overseas allocation of American food aid, and this continuing struggle has played itself out within both the domestic and international arenas (see table 10.1).

Domestically, conflicting pressures on the use of food in US foreign policy have been generated both from the private sector and Congress. Agribusiness interests such as the large grain exporting companies tend commonly to view the PL 480 program as an instrument for foreign market access and development, and they have often employed Title I commodities for such purposes (e.g., the cases of Taiwan and South Korea). This trend was given increased emphasis by the shift to a "free market" agriculture policy in 1972 during the Nixon administration.

While Congress is also concerned about the US international trade position, it has an additional role to play as overseer of US foreign policy. Consequently, Congress has scrutinized and restructured the features of the PL 480 legislation from time to time in response to its changing conception of the purposes of American foreign aid. Its activist role in food aid policy did not really begin, however, until 1972, when it discovered how the Nixon administration had been manipulating Title I resources in order to evade restrictions on the flow of military aid to Southeast Asia. There is now little doubt that the new allocation criteria imposed by Congress as a result of the Nixon "food for war" strategy have had a profound impact on the flexibility and availability of food aid for other types of uses in foreign policy.

A word is also in order concerning the matter of international food aid burden-sharing. When the US government decided finally to alter the perception long held by other developed country donors that the United States would continue to function as the world's residual supplier of food, a perception which it had done very little to discourage during the period of massive surpluses in the fifties and early sixties, it chose to do so in a rather interesting way. Rather than simply prevailing upon other potential donors to expand the level of their individual participation, the United States chose instead to establish entirely new multilateral institutions in order to elicit the desired response.

For example, the UN–FAO World Food Programme was established in 1961 largely at American initiative. Moreover, beginning late in the Kennedy term, discussions on food aid were undertaken within GATT, resulting ultimately in the Food Aid Convention of 1967. Finally, the Johnson administration took a number of steps to enable the World

Bank-sponsored India Aid Consortium to function as a vehicle for in-creased burden-sharing. By the early 1970s, substantial success had been achieved in making the distribution of the international food aid burden more equitable.

A number of actors may be identified in relation to the use of food by the United States as a foreign policy instrument, and a schematic repre-sentation of these is presented in figure 10.1. The bureaucratic sphere is clearly the largest and most important, and, in the context of foreign policy, the White House (or, more accurately, the Executive Office of the President) functions at the center in almost all these cases. However, except in those circumstances in which the President has employed food aid for his own short-term discretionary purposes (e.g., the Johnson short-tether policy), most policy decisions have been influenced heavily by the advice of at least four line agencies. As the issues and the political and economic conditions have changed, each of the organizational ac-tors within these competing spheres of interest (i.e., foreign policy, agriculture, economic development, and fiscal policy) has each gained primacy in the formulation of foreign policy. The two most immediate factors responsible for this shifting pattern of influence generally have been the adequacy of food supplies and economic conditions both in the United States and abroad.

As a result, in periods of domestic surplus, agricultural interests have been successful in securing market development objectives. Conversely, in periods of poor US harvests and/or when other domestic economic factors have required fiscal restraint, as in the case of the Ford food aid decision, the advice of an entirely different set of fiscally oriented actors has dominated. Overlaid also on these two groups is the input of other interests concerned with the need to promote agricultural and economic development in food deficient countries and with the growing attractive-ness of food as an instrument of strategic and diplomatic leverage.

Food aid decisions are also influenced, of course, by other actors. The multinational corporations (particularly agribusiness) have a substantial interest in the availability of food aid for market access and develop-ment. American merchant shipping interests also have a multimillion dollar stake in the PL 480 program since this legislation requires that at least 50 percent of all food aid commodities be shipped in American bot-toms. Finally, despite the fact that most international institutional mech-anisms dealing with food were created originally at the initiative of the United States, they are now semiautonomous political forces in their own right. The United States is now constrained, therefore, to some de-

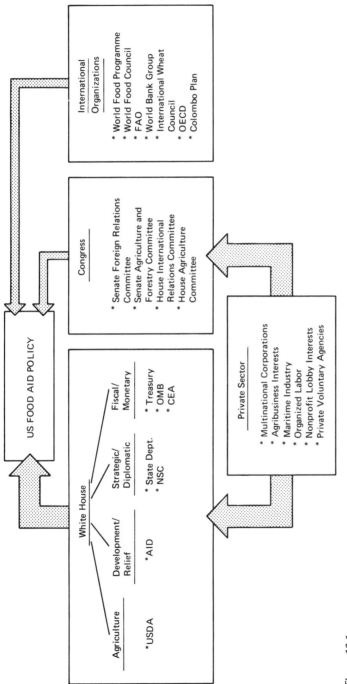

Figure 10.1
Institutional participants in US food aid policy formation.

gree in the manipulation of its food aid for foreign policy purposes by the policies of these international organizations.

It was argued previously that it is at once both an asset and a liability that the American food aid program contains sufficient flexibility to encompass and respond to so many competing interests and demands. In the context of foreign policy, however, this flexibility has most often appeared as an asset. That is, except perhaps during the 1972–1974 "crisis" period, the food aid pie has been able historically to accomodate most of the demands placed upon it. Barring some sudden, unforeseen climatic disaster, there seems little indication that this arrangement is likely to change greatly in the near future.

POLICY OUTCOMES

The four policy applications considered in the preceding chapters have encompassed a variety of benefits, ranging from those which were short term and highly situation specific to those which were of a broader, more enduring nature (see table 10.1). Each also demonstrated the links between food aid and the larger rationale for American foreign aid. The intention here is both to evaluate the overall effectiveness of each policy application and to consider its longer-term ramifications (if any) for US foreign policy.

When used an an instrument of *diplomatic and strategic leverage*, food aid has served at least two major foreign aid objectives: enhancing the political and security interests of the United States and promoting a more stable world order. But these two objectives are not necessarily congruent, and the United States has employed its food aid resources most often either directly in support of its *own* security interests (i.e., for base rights and the like) or as a balance mechanism to maintain the political status quo (e.g., the Cold War uses of food aid, US support for strategic regimes). On some occasions, the United States has managed to use its food aid in an innovative fashion to promote the search for peace and world stability (e.g., in the Middle East); on other occasions, the aid has functioned more as a retaliatory mechanism, demonstrating the strength of US food power. The particular advantage of food as a strategic and diplomatic instrument relates, of course, to the fact that it is a universal human need. Moreover, since agricultural commodities are relatively abundant in the United States, food aid is less expensive in comparison to most other types of aid resources (e.g., military aid, capital).

The United States has achieved considerable success also in exploiting its food aid in pursuit of its perception of world order. This policy has encountered difficulty, however, in those cases where the manipulation of the aid proved unacceptable to the recipient, as in the case of the UAR under Nasser, or where it was found to violate generally accepted norms of international behavior, as in the explicit use of food power within the United Nations. Food aid inevitably is destined to continue as a strategic and diplomatic instrument, but the evidence reviewed here would indicate the need to apply the instrument with intelligence and with an awareness of its potential ramifications.

The application of food aid in support of US *international trade interests* is less problematic in many respects, primarily because the promotion of markets for food exports has long been a traditional element of international relations. Promoting exports is also congruent with the rationale for American foreign aid since the United States generally offers economic assistance as much to create demand for its own goods and services as to transfer resources to the recipient country. Specific benefits from the trade promotion policy have ranged from agricultural market development and protection (e.g., the case of vegetable oil in Iran) to the use of aid in order to gain access to, or protect other nonfood markets (e.g., the Korean textile agreement).

But trade-related food aid applications also have not been entirely without difficulty. Under the Nixon administration, for example, the withdrawal of food aid suddenly took on aspects of a retaliatory weapon in response to the expropriation of US property. While it is conceivable that the Chilean case may have represented nothing more than an anomalous policy of the Nixon administration, this explanation does not seem fully satisfactory. Rather, the experience would appear to reflect a new recognition of the way trade is promoted in an interdependent world.

There can be little doubt that, where food aid is employed directly in the promotion of US agricultural trade, it is serving a purpose that has been at the heart of the PL 480 program since its inception. Whether or not one agrees with this motivation for food assistance, it can well be argued that, if the market development function were eliminated, a substantial portion of the domestic support for PL 480 would disintegrate. Where food aid is employed for nonfood purposes, however, the impact is less clear. Because the United States is now so heavily dependent on food as a primary export product, it will no doubt wish to continue to employ this asset in a variety of commercial applications. But there is a fundamental difference between quid pro quo applications of food aid in the context of commercial trade and the coercive use of food power, either as a retaliatory weapon or as a means of preferential access.

The promotion of *international burden-sharing* as a longer-term approach to world food problems contains the greatest number of explicit links with the traditional rationale for US foreign aid. By demonstrating its support for an international approach, the United States has helped to encourage a more rational response to the problem of world hunger. Moreover, it has fulfilled a perceived moral obligation as a wealthy develped country to help reduce the pervasive poverty of the Third World. But in the process, the United States has also enhanced its own economic and security interests—truly a policy of enlightened self-interest. Significantly, this aspect of American food aid is the only one of the four food aid applications considered here that contains specific benefits for actors other than United States (namely, the developing country recipients).

The United States had a number of reasons for supporting international approaches to the issue of world hunger. It was apparent even at the outset of the Kennedy administration, when the United States still maintained large food surpluses, that the world food problem was (or soon would be) too large for one donor nation to handle unilaterally. Moreover, there was already an awareness of the fact that food aid in itself solved nothing; it simply met the food deficit of the moment and re-created the status quo ante. Yet another reason for the shift in US policy was that Lyndon Johnson was seriously concerned about the enormity of India's food dependence during its food emergency of 1965–1967. If US policymakers had ever seriously thought that, by shipping a certain volume of food aid each year to food deficient states, they would be able to avoid addressing the root causes of the food supply problem, the experience in India disabused them of this notion.

The immediate response was to develop a variety of bilateral and multilateral channels to meet the immediate need to feed the hungry and simultaneously to mobilize new efforts to address the longer-term problems of agricultural development and population control. Through a combination of enticement, threat, and old-fashioned "horse trading" (e.g., the Food Aid Convention), the United States was reasonably successful in convincing other donor countries to increase substantially their annual commitments. Success on a more limited scale was also achieved regarding LDC agricultural development, but only through the application of a political and morally controversial short-tether approach.

Recent changes in US food aid legislation have served to underscore the increasing urgency of the need for recipient countries to derive their own internal solutions to the problems of food production and distribution as well as population control. Under this new conception, food aid is recognized more explicitly as a limited, short-term measure that can best be used to facilitate broader economic and social development efforts. But the political reality of food aid has meant that concepts such as international burden-sharing and agricultural development have tended mostly to become rhetorical constructs with very little policy substance. It is therefore difficult to foresee how food aid can be used more effectively to promote development objectives unless a substantially increased portion of annual aid resources are identified and targeted explicitly for this purpose alone. These aid resources must, in addition, be insulated thereafter from diversion for other, short-term political expedients.

The final application of food aid concerns its widely varied use in support of specific, *presidential initiatives*. The case examples considered were dissimilar in many of their particulars, and thus the actual links with US foreign aid doctrine were much more tenuous and controversial. What ultimately binds these cases together is not the specific benefits they produced—although these were often fairly significant—but the flexibility of action they provided the Chief Executive in implementing his particular conception of US foreign policy.

Because the US food aid program is insulated to a certain degree from direct congressional oversight, it has long been an attractive policy instrument for presidential manipulation. Each president since John F. Kennedy has chosen to employ the resource for a different purpose, which has often reflected a deeply felt personal bias—for example, Lyndon Johnson's personal anger over Indira Gandhi's anti-US statements on Vietnam or Gerald Ford's deep commitment to the need for restraint in federal spending.

In terms of foreign policy outcomes, these examples of presidential discretionary power did not often produce beneficial results. With the exception of the Kennedy Food for Peace initiative, each case led ultimately to a *negative* reaction, whether in the form of the Indian backlash to the heavy-handed Johnson short-tether approach, the congressional backlash to the Nixon "food for war" strategy, or the international backlash to Ford's temporary refusal to increase the level of food aid programming. On the other hand, it should be noted that only the most blatant of presidential food aid initiatives ever receive sufficient publicity to become visible outside of the White House. Moreover, those cases which *do* receive media attention tend generally to be representative of the more questionable, political uses of food aid.

The capacity of food aid to fulfill specific presidential foreign policy needs probably cannot and, in any case, should not be legislated out of existence. Rather, it is the responsibility of Congress to exercise a reasonable degree of oversight regarding executive branch food aid initiatives in order to prevent the kind of periodic excesses documented here. In the absence of such oversight, a substantial portion of food aid resources becōmes subject, for better or worse, to each President's *personal* view of international affairs and to his assessment of the exigencies of US foreign policy.

FOOD AS A FOREIGN POLICY INSTRUMENT

The foregoing is *not* meant to suggest that all—or even most—policy initiatives involving food aid have been in any way improper or inappropriate to the normal exercise of US foreign policy. Furthermore, it would be utterly unrealistic (if not unconstitutional) for Congress to become more deeply involved in the operational aspects of the food aid policy process, which is properly the concern of the executive branch. But it has been argued here that, when food is used as an instrument of foreign policy, it automatically involves a number of additional concerns and counterpressures not normally encountered in more traditional forms of foreign assistance.

As a result, when food aid is considered *solely* as a foreign policy resource apart from its other functions in surplus disposal or market development and so on, a fundamental conflict arises between aid given primarily for the benefit of the donor and aid given for the benefit of the recipient. The importance and attractiveness for the United States of food as a policy instrument has grown steadily as the availability of other forms of aid has declined (see chapter 3). But its *ostensible* function nevertheless continues to be that of feeding hungry and malnourished populations. This creates a fundamental political and moral dilemma, particularly when the aid is employed as a diplomatic, economic or strategic lever.

It is true, of course, that, in an imperfect political world, nations rarely undertake initiatives affecting other nations based on narrow, unidimensional objectives. Moreover, food aid is, as we have noted previously, perhaps the preeminent example of a program capable of serving *multiple* objectives simultaneously. Under most circumstances, however, it is still possible to define a rough demarcation between acceptable and unacceptable uses of food in support of foreign policy. If so, then the elusive notion of a political "abuse" of the food aid program remains a valid and useful concept.

At least two questions are raised immediately by this assertion. First, according to what standards or criteria is the "abuse" to be defined: moral or political, absolute or relative? Second, what individual or institution is realistically capable of passing judgment on such matters? These are complicated and weighty questions, but they are also central to the notion of food aid used as a foreign policy instrument.

While the *moral* imperatives of food aid obviously can never be ignored, the evidence presented in this study would indicate that they have played a relatively minor role in the Realpolitik of US foreign policy. Thus, we are dealing basically with *political* criteria for separating acceptable from unacceptable uses of food aid, and such political standards are rarely, if ever, absolute. Rather, they evolve slowly in relation to the changing values and requirements of society, just as the purposes and applications of food aid shift over time. This would suggest that the assessment of food aid in the context of foreign policy clearly must be conducted according to *relative* political standards.

The question then becomes, "How and by whom are such decisions to be made?" The American judicial system does not appear to be the appropriate vehicle except, perhaps, for those few cases which involve fundamental constitutional issues. Yet, while the executive branch is the traditional policy implementer, it is also the source of the most troublesome difficulties of the food aid resource. It thus falls to the legislative branch to interpret prevailing political will by establishing dynamic, workable policy guidelines.

The difficulty is, however, that Congress itself has often been at cross purposes regarding its priorities for the food aid program (i.e., whether emphasis should be given to surplus disposal, foreign policy, economic development, etc.); and in any case, the PL 480 legislative instrument is so broad and imprecise as to offer any President a wide degree of policy latitude. In fact, it can be argued that it was the *inconsistency* of the foreign policy signals emanating from Congress in the late sixties and early seventies that both forced and encouraged the executive branch to turn to food aid as an alternative, and less visible, means of achieving the same political and economic objectives.

When Congress did finally become aware of how food aid resources were being used by Lyndon Johnson in India and by Richard Nixon in Southeast Asia, it *overreacted* in many respects. That is, when Congress finally moved in 1973 to impose limitations on the political uses of food aid, it failed to discriminate adequately between specific *types* of applications, assuming that *all* foreign policy involving food must in some sense be an "abuse" of the resource.

The specific food aid application that came under most severe congressional attack was, of course, the use of "food for war" in Southeast Asia in order to circumvent existing limitations on military aid to that region. It can be argued, however, that this was, in many respects, an anomalous outgrowth of a long and complicated US military involvement. Furthermore, it can be demonstrated that, if the "food for war" uses are segregated, the vast majority of other food aid applications will be found to conform quite closely to traditionally accepted notions regarding the role of foreign aid within the larger foreign policy framework. In this paradigm, the United States provides economic assistance to those nations which it supports (which are generally those that support it), and it withholds or withdraws aid from those nations which it opposes (or that choose to attack or oppose the United States).

This explanation does not, of course, resolve the basic dilemma regarding the conception of food aid as *food* versus its conception as a resource similar to any other form of foreign assistance. But, the unique nature of the commodity in question may render this basic conflict unresolvable. The problem could be ameliorated substantially, however, by the explicit *separation* of food aid intended to address the problem of hunger and malnutrition from assistance meant to support US foreign policy concerns. Based on recent proposals for modification of the PL 480 legislation, there is some evidence that Congress is slowly coming to accept this view.

UNITED STATES FOOD AID IN THE INTERNATIONAL SYSTEM

Another fundamental difficulty with using food aid to promote foreign policy objectives—both political and economic—is that it tends to complicate relations between the United States and other nations. For example, Third World recipients argue, particularly when the aid is tied in some way by the donor, that it represents simply another form of neocolonialist intrusion into their internal political and economic affairs. At the same time, other food aid donors are critical of American demands for wider international aid burden-sharing when the United States continues to employ its comparative advantage in agriculture for its own political and economic benefit. Here again, the conflict emerges between food aid used as *food* versus food aid used as any other form of foreign aid.

Typically, the US government might respond to such criticism by countering that America was for many years the *sole* supplier of food to countries with acute or chronic food deficits; that the United States continues to do more than its fair share to provide food on grant or concessional terms; and that the majority of US aid is programmed for distinctly *nonpolitical* purposes. In general, the United States sees no basic incompatibility between its efforts to promote wider international participation and its own foreign policy uses of food aid so long as its share of humanitarian and developmental contributions is not reduced. But, while this rationale may justify to some extent the deployment of US bilateral food aid, it certainly does *not* respond adequately to criticisms concerning the level of US multilateral participation.

In order to understand fully the nature of the problem involved here for the United States, it may be useful first to reiterate the foreign policy objectives that have impelled the United States to support the development of multilateral alternatives: (1) a desire to vest other wealthy nations with additional responsibility for providing greater quantities of food aid resources; (2) a need in the early years of the program to find new outlets for surplus commodities and later, to make more room in international commercial markets for US grain by forcing competitors to commit a greater portion of their exportable supplies as aid rather than trade; (3) an interest in developing an institutional capacity within the United Nations in the food area; and, more recently, (4) an effort to be more accommodating to Third World demands (embodied in the NIEO doctrine) for a greater distribution of resources through the less overtly political, multilateral channel.

The above explanation offers some indication of the reasons why the United States has supported multilateralism in the past, but it fails to account for the present division of resources between the two aid channels. It will be recalled, however, that the United States has often tended to view the WFP and certain other multilateral mechanisms merely as extensions of the American food aid program. For many years, in fact, when American food represented more than 50 percent of WFP resources, this *was* actually the case. But now, largely as a result of its *own* demands for increased international efforts, US food aid contributions represent less than 25 percent of total WFP resources.

However, the overwhelming impression to be gained from examining US policy in this regard is that the official American perception of the viability and effectiveness of the World Food Programme is out of phase with present institutional realities. Moreover, the United States no longer dominates the multilateral arena through the sheer weight of its resource contribution. As a result, it now finds its proposals outvoted—and its wishes ignored—within the WFP governing council, the CFA, although this situation is also a function of the polarized international political environment as well. In the absence of an organized and effective domestic interest group constituency supporting the notion of food aid multilateralism, the United States has chosen to maintain its multilateral involvement at a fairly static level (in real dollars), while pursuing other policy initiatives that contain greater potential for influence and unilateral benefits.

It is possible to argue that with the exception of the Canadian input, the framework of the international food aid system was created largely at US initiative. Yet, while the United States has now relinquished its position of absolute dominance (although still clearly the largest food aid provider in total volume), its policy has not been adjusted to reflect this altered state of affairs. Whether or not the fact has been recognized explicitly in Washington, US food aid policy has entered a period of transition. The days of "rugged individualism" and surplus dumping have more or less ended—despite the current reappearance of grain surpluses—and other developed countries, net exporters *and* importers alike, have assumed a substantially larger share of the global food aid burden. Under these circumstances, it has become incumbent upon the United States to review its international food assistance role and the manner in which it employs food aid in support of its various foreign policy objectives.

These contrasting uses of food aid resources are the response to America's changing needs and responsibilities in an interdependent world. For example, humanitarian relief and LDC economic development are intended to present a more favorable US image in world affairs and to reduce the dangerously high level of LDC food dependency. These food aid applications are clearly as much a part of US foreign policy as the more controversial diplomatic and strategic applications. Interestingly, however, only those benefits relating directly to the enhancement of US economic or strategic advantages are incompatible with the *multilateral* channel of delivery.

This does not mean that the two modes of delivery will be equally effective in attaining a specific policy goal. In fact, in many situations the pursuit of one channel will work to the detriment of—if not negate entirely—objectives promoted through some other channel. But in terms of the fundamental decisions that determine the distribution of American food resources, the relationship between aid delivery channels becomes critically important. In theory at least, it would suggest that many of the foreign policy benefits the United States now derives from its bilateral program could be derived as well from a broader, multilateral commitment that would facilitate also strictly bilateral goals. It also suggests, however, that US expectations regarding its food aid program have entered a period of intensive scrutiny and reevaluation which parallels, in many respects, the changing perception of the larger American role in international affairs.

Particularly since the 1974 World Food Conference, there has been substantial new interest in expanding both the responsibilities and political effectiveness of the international institutions dealing with food. What began largely as a unilateral US effort has now developed into a network of ongoing relationships between developed and developing countries, food exporters and importers. It is undeniable that this network is still neither consistently effective nor consistently employed by aid donors; nevertheless, it represents a significant new trend in the politics of international food aid.

At the same time, however, the distribution of global food production capacity remains highly skewed, with the United States and a limited number of other exporters providing the vast majority of resources. Thus, although the United States no longer maintains the same overwhelming position of dominance in the WFP and other international food organizations that it did a mere ten years ago, it still makes the single largest resource contributions of any donor and retains a substantial role in the policy process.

The significance of this continuing imbalance in global agricultural output is that food cannot be treated like the other resources that are transferred between rich and poor nations. The United States has been able to maintain wide freedom of choice with regard to the nature and uses of its food aid program precisely because it continues to occupy such a commanding (although not monopolistic) position relative to total world agricultural production. Thus, whereas developing countries can turn to a large number of potential donors for capital or technical assistance, there are simply very few other grain exporting countries capable of meeting LDC food needs.

It was suggested previously that the other participants in international food aid—donors and recipients—receive far greater benefits from American participation than the United States receives from being part of this network of relationships. Those benefits which *do* accrue to the United States are clearly related to the broader international economic and political context, for example, the benefits that follow from making a favorable impression on nations considered critical, either for political or economic reasons, to American foreign interests. Consequently, the United States will be encouraged to expand the level of its participation in international food aid to the extent that the politics of international food aid is concerned with broadening the relationship between the provision of food and the requisites of international relations.

There are those who have argued that PL 480, the Food for Peace program, has finally outlived its usefulness after almost thirty years of existence and should therefore be abolished or completely restructured. Beyond the profound political and economic disruptions that would inevitably result, proposals of this kind run counter to the basic American strength in world affairs. Due to its expanded economic and political ties with the developing world, the United States has little choice but to be responsive to legitimate LDC demands. But, in a time of deteriorating balance of payments, soaring energy costs, and rising inflation, there is neither the domestic political will nor the popular sentiment for increasing the level of capital assistance efforts. Thus, the continuation and expansion of *food* resource transfers remains one of the enduring American aid assets. Food is available. It is relatively cheap to produce, and it is appropriate in many cases to the basic needs of the recipient populations.

Given the myriad of policy applications and controversies that have surrounded the US food aid program over the years, frequently it has been easy to lose sight of the real achievements of Food for Peace. It is true, of course, that, on some occasions, food aid resources have been employed for the narrow political advantage of the donor or in ways that have disrupted local food production incentives. But in the aggregate, it is yet to be proved that recipient countries would have fared better had they not accepted food assistance from the United States (or from any other donor country, for that matter).

In fact, given the tremendous volume of resources committed under PL 480, it is a matter of serious concern how few systematic studies have been conducted regarding the positive and negative effects of food aid. Obviously, such investigations might well generate results which neither the United States nor the various recipient governments would wish for political reasons to confront. But, in the *absence* of conclusive data, it is clear that the specific ordering of food aid priorities will continue to be shaped by the political and economic exigencies of US foreign policy.

PART IV
IMPLICATIONS FOR THE INTERNATIONAL FOOD AID SYSTEM

Chapter 11
The Nature of the Multilateral Food Aid Debate

The distribution of food aid through a neutral, international distribution mechanism has frequently been suggested as the best means of circumventing the variety of political, economic, and other problems which have beset the international food aid system. Despite the fact that multilateral food aid operations have existed since the creation of UNRRA in 1943, however, serious interest in a common international food distribution mechanism (for purposes other than immediate disaster relief) did not really begin until the UN–FAO World Food Programme (WFP) was proposed in the late 1950s. Even then, however, the limited size and scope of the program meant that, in practice, multilateral food aid represented little more than an additional outlet for the agricultural surpluses of the major exporters, principally the United States. In fact, it was only when a combination of declining food surpluses and the lack of international aid burden-sharing motivated the United States to impose a matching formula on its WFP contributions in the mid-1960s (and to conclude the International Grains Arrangement, which included the Food Aid Convention) that aggregate multilateral resources began to represent a viable alternative to bilateral food aid.

Tables 11.1 and 11.2 provide an indication of the trends in multilateral aid donations, the former in the aggregate and the latter in relation to food as a specific aid resource. It may be observed that overall multilateral aid contributions were rather inconsequential from 1964 to 1966, averaging only about 6 percent of total Official Development Assistance (ODA). A significant upward trend, however, is in evidence beginning in 1971. By 1973, multilateral aid comprised nearly one-fourth of all economic assistance offered by the OECD countries, and, by 1977, this figure was approaching one-third of total ODA. But, if general multilateral

Table 11.1

Capital Contributions to Multilateral Agencies As a Percentage of Total Official Development Assistance of DAC Countries: 1964–1977 (Millions of US Dollars)

Aid channel	1964–1966[a]	1971	1973	1975	1977
Bilateral assistance	5,550.0	6,322.5	7,109.6	9,815.5	10,083.7
Multilateral assistance	363.1	1,338.2	2,268.1	3,769.9	4,611.9
Total official development assistance	5,913.0	7,660.5	9,378.0	13,585.3	14,695.7
Multilateral aid as a percentage of total aid	6.1	17.4	24.1	27.7	31.4

Sources: OECD (1975, p. 217), OECD (1976, pp. 216–217), and OECD (1978, pp. 202–203).
a. Average capital assistance per year.

Table 11.2

Food Aid Contributions to Multilateral Agencies As a Percentage of Total Food Aid Contributions of DAC Countries: 1964–1977 (Millions of US Dollars)

Aid Channel	1964–1966[a]	1969	1971	1973	1975	1977
Bilateral food aid	1,375.0	1,084.3	1,050.2	850.4	1,581.4	1,405.4
Multilateral food aid	14.8	89.7	166.9	279.3	498.0	507.1
Total food aid	1,389.8	1,174.0	1,217.1	1,129.7	2,079.4	1,912.5
Multilateral food aid as a percentage of total food aid	1.0	7.6	13.7	24.7	23.9	26.5

Sources: OECD (1974, p. 92), OECD (1975, p. 217), OECD (1976, pp. 216–217), and OECD (1978, pp. 202–203).
a. Average food aid per year.

assistance was inconsequential during the mid-1960s, the *food* component of this aid was practically nonexistent. The average of food resources allocated through international channels from 1964 to 1966 amounted to a mere $14.8 million (of an average annual total ODA for the OECD countries of $5,913 million), which represented only 1 percent of total food aid contributions.[1]

Multilateral food aid increased at a very slow rate through the remainder of the decade; but then, between 1971 and 1977, it doubled. By 1973, multilateral food aid represented a larger relative percentage of total food aid resources (24.7 percent) than the percentage of total ODA represented by multilateral *capital* assistance (24.1 percent). Further scrutiny of the data for 1973 reveals, however, that, in dollars terms, multilateral food aid was only about 12 percent of *total* multilateral assistance and that this figure had risen only to about 15 percent by 1974.

Taken together, the data suggest that, until the early 1970s, multilateral *food* aid was a negligible component of total multilateral aid. Since that time, multilateral food aid resources have constituted a small but growing portion of total multilateral economic assistance. Moreover, since 1972, the relative volume of food resources contributed multilaterally has tended to parallel to some degree trends in overall multilateral ODA.

The political significance of these data appears rather straightforward. The level of multilateral food aid commitments is meaningful, in spite of its small absolute size, both as an indication of donor commitment and as a means of promoting other desirable bilateral policies.

Because food aid trends have follwed general multilateral aid trends so closely since 1972, it may be concluded that donors have come to view multilateral food assistance as a viable component of their total ODA contribution. Yet, in absolute terms, the total volume of multilateral food aid continues to be inconsequential in comparison to the total volume of foreign aid donated by all OECD countries (4 percent of total ODA).

This suggests that, in most cases, the donors still perceive food aid resources basically as a *bilateral* policy instrument. Moreover, it reflects the fact that, while total world food aid contributions (expressed in dollars) has stabilized at about $2 billion since 1975, total ODA has continued to increase each year. This would tend to indicate a general turning away from *food* aid in favor of other forms of foreign assistance, including greater support for international financial institutions such as the World Bank.[2]

Both tables, in fact, reveal a general increase in multilateral contributions since 1971, a period characterized by heightened donor sensitivity to Third World demands for a New International Economic Order (NIEO). While it is not possible to substantiate a cause and effect relationship, it nonetheless seems reasonable to suggest that many aid donors have increased their multilateral aid contributions as one relatively moderate response to the NIEO doctrine. This general upward trend may signal not only a growing donor commitment to the use of multilateral aid channels but also a recognition of the need to alter underlying aid policies in an era of global interdependence.

In the remainder of this chapter, the arguments both favoring and opposing the wider multilateralization of food aid[3] will be explored and analyzed within five substantive areas: *donor-related issues*—factors concerning the positive and negative aspects of donor participation in multilateral food aid, particularly from the US perspective; *recipient-related issues*—a similar treatment of the advantages and disadvantages of obtaining needed food resources through the multilateral channel from the recipient's point of view; *resource issues*—topics concerning the composition, source, terms, volume, and availability of multilateral food aid resources; *organizational and management issues*—questions involving the structure and administrative capacity of the international bureaucracy to procure and to distribute food aid resources; and *conceptual issues*—characteristics relating directly to the fundamental nature of aid multilateralism and to its impact on the operation of food aid programs.

DONOR ISSUES

Perhaps the oldest reason for donors to participate in multilateral food aid arrangements of any sort relates to the value placed on enhancing the effectiveness of international institutions and developing a more rational approach to global problems. Numerous precedents, beginning with the creation of UNRRA during World War II, have reinforced this lofty, if somewhat idealistic, goal. In the case of food, the notion is that, by transferring responsibility for the allocation of food aid from the bilateral to the multilateral sphere, a more sustained and equitable short-term response to world hunger is facilitated.

As principal donor, the United States has clearly derived the most tangible benefits from the existence of a multilateral food aid institution since it has been able both to move additional surplus commodities through the WFP and to spread the food aid burden more widely among other developed countries.[4] Clearly, the surplus disposal function has become less important in recent years as government-owned food stocks have been virtually eliminated. But, where multilateral food assistance represents a net addition to the amount of aid that would otherwise be allocated (i.e., where donors do not simply substitute aid given previously through bilateral channels), agricultural exporters such as the United States, Canada, and the EEC do benefit from the existence of an additional outlet through which to move surplus stocks during periods of overproduction.

A unique feature of the multilateral mechanism is its capacity to include both exporters and importers in the aid giving process since resources may be donated to the WFP either in the form of commodities, cash, or services (e.g., ocean transportation). As a result, the multilateral mechanism includes both food *importing* developed nations and food exporting nations that are otherwise characterized as less developed, thereby permitting others who are less well endowed to share—to the extent of their agricultural and cash resources—in meeting global food needs. In the case of nations rich in oil or other natural resources (e.g., Saudi Arabia), or those which are potentially rich in food (e.g., the Sudan), this may represent a fairly substantial and largely untapped resource.

Donors are often attracted to the concept of multilateral food aid as a means of improving their foreign image, since past political "abuses"[5] of bilateral food assistance have tarnished substantially the reputation of the United States and certain other donors in many Third World countries. When multilateral channels are employed, however, donors agree to contribute some portion of their resources *without* extracting an explicit quid pro quo in return from individual recipients. Moreover, to the extent that poor donor–recipient relations are a function of the "psychological effect"[6] of aid dependency, a policy of multilateralizing food aid eliminates a major source of tension and ill feelings from the developed-developing country relationship.

Depoliticizing a greater portion of the aid relationship offers donors additional advantages, particularly in the changed international economic and political climate of 1970s. For example, food aid employed bilaterally in order to gain specific political or strategic benefits (i.e., the so-called food power uses of aid) can, in some cases, be damaging to donor interests guaranteed access to supplies of vital raw materials. In addition, the multilateral food aid mechanism can provide donors with an acceptable, although somewhat less direct means, of influencing recipient development policies *without* becoming vulnerable to charges of unjustifiable interference in LDC internal affairs.

Finally, donors have long complained about the disparities between each country's food aid policies, which have resulted in an unnecessarily high degree of program overlap, redundancy, and waste of scarce resources. The existence of an international aid mechanism with adequate capabilities for setting criteria and evaluating projects would eliminate most causes of this common problem. In fact, donors frequently oppose wider food aid multilateralization due to the degree of political influence and leverage they must sacrifice in the process.

For established food aid providers such as the United States, the foreign policy flexibility afforded by the bilateral allocation of foreign assistance has become an integral component of relations with developing countries. In some cases, donors have employed their bilateral leverage to facilitate positive, long-term changes in recipient development policies. In others, bilateral aid leverage has been used solely to support the donor's own foreign policy objectives. In every bilateral application, however, the donor has been in the position to exercise unrestricted influence over where and under what circumstances its food aid was used.

Even under current multilateral food aid arrangements, donors retain the right in extreme cases to indicate that they do not wish their resources utilized in countries with which they have strained (or nonexistent) political relations.[7] But political objections are only one aspect of donor concern about the loss of influence and flexibility. In theory at least, once resources have been pledged to the WFP, donors cease to retain any special influence over the ultimate destination or end use of the aid (other than as noted above). On occasion, the threatened withholding of multilateral aid pledges may be used to manipulate WFP allocation policies, but the only *formal* recourse the donor may use to affect the course of WFP food aid allocations is its single, unweighted vote in the governing council, known as the Committee on Food Aid Policies and Programs (CFA). Informally, of course, there is much that the United States and other donors can do behind the scenes to shape the selection of aid recipients and the design of food aid projects.

Matters are complicated further by the fact that some donors (again notably the United States) have attempted to compensate to some degree for the loss of direct leverage by regulating the size of their multilateral food contributions. The strategy here is to apply indirect pressure on the WFP to accede to the donor's wishes or face the possible reduction—or outright withdrawal—of pledged food resources. Donors have occasionally been forced to resort to this strategy in self-defense against what they considered the tyranny of bloc voting by the Group of 77.[8] The threatened loss of resources has proved rather effective in countering the effects of unweighted voting procedures, although the extreme nature of this approach underscores the degree of political impotence that donors must accept when participating in multilateral food aid.

Certain other types of donor sacrifice are also involved in the wider multilateralization of food aid. For one thing, the kind of agricultural market development activities undertaken by the United States through Title I of PL 480 are virtually precluded under the terms of multilateral food aid. Moreover, substantial increase in grant-type food aid would be unlikely to gain wide support among US farm interest groups, who tend to view food aid more as a market development mechanism than as an instrument of humanitarian relief or economic development.[9]

Donors also fear that wider use of the multilateral food aid channel would increase the competition between bilateral and multilateral aid agencies for recipient allegiance. Tendencies in this direction have been noted among the private voluntary organizations, such as CARE and CRS, and the World Food Programme. In some cases, recipient countries have chosen to seek increased assistance from the WFP in preference to aid offered bilaterally either through the voluntary agencies or directly by the donor.

Finally, many donors—the United States foremost among them—retain serious reservations about the resource management and food aid delivery practices of the UN multilateral program. They criticize the slow call forward (i.e., the actual request for shipments of aid pledged by the donor) of pledged commodities as well as ineffective project formulation, monitoring, and evaluation. Further negative reaction has been directed toward the WFP's slow reaction time in emergency situations and especially to the serious in-country storage problems the program has encountered.

The bulk of donor concern about food aid delivery is related to the fact that, under the current charter of the WFP, responsibility for the delivery of food aid commodities to individual recipients is transferred to the host government immediately upon arrival at the port of entry. Thus, unlike bilateral programs, in which the aid is normally managed and monitored from source to end use, the multilateral agency can only *advise* recipients on how to manage the resources themselves. While, in the long run, this self-administration policy undoubtedly builds an in-

creased LDC capacity to deal with indigenous food distribution bottlenecks, donors fear that the short-term result—particularly in countries
suffering from substantial infrastructural and/or managerial deficiencies—is more likely to take the form of an unacceptably high level of
food spoilage, diversion, and waste. The nutritional impact of such aid
on populations most directly at risk is therefore questionable.

RECIPIENT ISSUES

Based on the previous discussion, it appears that recipients tend to favor
multilateral food aid because of the *absence* in this form of aid of the
political and economic conditions that have so often accompanied bilateral assistance. This is not to suggest that all—or even most—bilateral
aid is used to obtain concessions from recipients, nor, conversely, that
the multilateral channel is entirely *free* of such machinations. The principal difference is that, when dealing in the multilateral context, recipients
have clear, a priori knowledge of the conditions and terms on which the
aid is given, while the strings attached to bilateral aid tend to shift
according to prevailing political exigencies. Multilateralism can also
eliminate or substantially reduce recipient vulnerability to major changes
in donor food policy,[10] which can cause sudden, unanticipated reductions in the availability of food.

Recipients also tend to find multilateral food aid more desirable because it is allocated on a straight grant basis, meaning that none of it is
sold on concessional credit terms as it is in the case with Title I of PL
480.[11] As a result, LDC governments are not forced to assume additional
debt service burden, which is, in many cases, already onerous. Moreover, the use of grant-type food aid ensures that commercial quid pro
quo arrangements, such as demands for preferential access to LDC
markets, play no part in the aid relationship. Multilateral aid delivery
can also help to eliminate or reduce greatly the agricultural price
disincentive effects often encountered when food aid is sold in LDC
markets. In fact, the WFP has established specific criteria under which
multilateral food aid may be sold when, for one reason or another, it
cannot be used directly as food.

Because multilateral food aid reduces the "psychological effect"[6] of aid
dependency, officials in recipient countries tend to be less mistrustful of
donor motives and actions. In fact, multilateral aid can often represent a
less controversial and more palatable means of assisting the LDC
governments to formulate their economic and social development

policies. Properly trained and situated, development experts working under multilateral auspices can advise governments and evaluate programmatic effectiveness with a greater degree of local cooperation and trust.

It is not particularly surprising, therefore, that, ceteris paribus, recipient governments tend generally to favor the multilateral food aid channel. Those aspects of multilateralism which they do find problematic relate almost exclusively to the question of resource availability. That is, some recipients have concluded that they may be better off in the long run by dealing with a greater number of food aid donors (preferably each using its own allocation criteria) than with a single, comprehensive food aid agency employing a standardized set of project selection criteria and commanding a limited amount of resources. These countries believe that, by skillful shopping around and fast political footwork, they can obtain a larger net volume of resources than under a fully multilateralized system.

Recipients have also expressed the fear from time to time that the total volume of global food aid might actually level off—and, perhaps, even decline—if all assistance were multilateralized. They reason that, if donors are no longer able to obtain the collateral market development, foreign policy, and trade benefits which they now gain in the process of giving aid bilaterally, future expansion of aid resources might occur only through bilateral nonfood channels.

Finally, recipients find fault with the fact that all multilateral food aid is currently of the *project* type. The WFP is prohibited from offering the kind of comprehensive program assistance provided by some bilateral donors; such aid is attractive because it can be sold for a variety of budgetary purposes. Thus, recipients fear that without a future broadening in the terms of WFP food aid, expanded multilateralism may do substantial damage to their net foreign exchange positions, thereby slowing the pace of development efforts.

RESOURCE ISSUES

The more diverse food resource basket available to the WFP offers, at least in theory, an enhanced capacity to provide recipient populations with a more nutritionally adequate diet. The actual experience, however, has been mixed in this respect; until 1969, only a limited number of donors provided the bulk of WFP resources. Although most donors do now take some account of the nature of their anticipated agricultural output when making their WFP pledges, it would be inaccurate to state that food resources are produced in all cases specifically for use as aid.

When donor contributions do consist of surplus agricultural commodities, the multilateral mechanism facilitates resource pooling so that commodities may be employed in a manner more appropriate to recipient needs and food habits. Having the resources of a greater number of donors to draw upon also enhances the security and reliability of multilateral food aid commitments, particularly when a particular donor is unable to meet its resource pledge. The multilateral food agencies have not always enjoyed secure resources. When available, however, secure resources can encourage greater innovation and flexibility in resource programming and improved planning by recipients.

There is one additional resource advantage of multilateral food aid. Certain developed countries actually have the agricultural and/or financial capacity to become limited food aid donors; but, due to the small size of their resources and to their lack of an aid delivery capacity, they are unable to offer food aid bilaterally. Under such circumstances, the economics of scale attainable through joint distribution mechanisms can encourage their involvement.

Perhaps the most serious resource shortcoming of the WFP as it is now constituted is that it can offer only food. This is neither an obvious nor a trivial point. For most bilateral donors, food is only one component of a more comprehensive package of assistance, which may also include capital resources and technical advice; but economic assistance within the UN system is fragmented among a number of specialized agencies. Since few (if any) food aid projects—even those involving food-for-work—are composed *solely* of a labor input, the multilateral channel becomes less attractive, due to its inability to supply needed supporting resources such as tools, seeds, and so forth. Some cooperative projects have been undertaken along these lines between FAO and the World Bank, but the WFP so far has been isolated from these activities.

The need to maintain some semblance of geopolitical balance in multilateral food aid distribution is also a difficult, resource-related problem. Since the 1972–1974 "crisis" period, efforts have been made to reorient WFP food aid toward the so-called *least* developed countries. But, in order to satisfy its heterogeneous economic and geographic constituency, the WFP is under continual pressure to spread food aid resources among the widest number of recipients.[12] Besides the obvious logistical difficulties of such a global undertaking, there are also legitimate questions regarding the cost effectiveness of spreading resources so thinly. This problem would no doubt be mitigated to some extent by a significant increase in the total volume of multilateral resources, but it is difficult to determine the exact point at which resources become sufficient to support this type of allocation strategy.

It is in the nature of the joint international aid approach that successful operations will be dependent on the responsiveness of the principal resource contributors, namely, the United States, the EEC, and Canada. On the operational level, this raises questions about the capacity of the system to respond to unexpected, severe food deficit situations such as that which occurred in the period from 1972 to 1974. There are also questions about the capacity of the WFP to raise the necessary volume of *cash* to cover the costs of ocean transportation, storage, and supporting services. Donors who are net agricultural exporters clearly find it more expedient to donate resources in the form of food.[13] But, more importantly, the critical dependence of the WFP on a relatively small number of countries that produce a food surplus raises fundamental questions regarding the capacity of any multilateral food aid organization to establish policy independent of the wishes of its largest contributors.

ORGANIZATION AND MANAGEMENT ISSUES

Although the level of food resources programmed annually through the WFP remains below the total resources allocated bilaterally by the United States alone,[14] few other individual donors (perhaps only the EEC and Canada) offer a sufficiently large volume of food aid to match the management economics of scale of the WFP. This advantage is negated to some degree, however, by structural shortcomings related to the absence of WFP ocean transportation capabilities or in-country storage facilities. But, to the extent that moderate-to-small-size donors are forced to expend limited cash resources on prosaic and largely duplicative administrative procedures, the multilateral mechanism can offer the promise of substantial savings in administrative overhead.

For example, one particular type of administrative procedure that all food aid programs must undertake, no matter what their size, is the evaluation of aid project requests. Multilateral administration of food aid programming can eliminate, or at least reduce, the need to duplicate this time-consuming process, especially for donors who do not or cannot maintain adequate foreign agricultural or economic aid missions. But, even in the case of large donors such as the United States, who operate extensive overseas field missions and who neither need nor desire to participate in combined project evaluation efforts, multilateral coordination offers the possibility of greater standardization in project selection criteria and increased rationality in the terms, conditions, and objectives of the aid projects themselves.

We have noted previously the deep involvement of some donors in the operational aspects of the World Food Programme, which is due primarily to a felt need to compensate for the loss of direct, bilateral political influence. But some donors also fear that the management shortcomings of the UN system will result in the misuse or outright waste of food resources. During its early "experimental" period (1963–1965), problems encountered by the World Food Programme provided substantial cause for such donor anxiety.

Multilateral food aid has been characterized as slow, cumbersome inefficient, and ineffective.[15] One explanation for such criticism is that the WFP does not possess an extensive foreign service like the large bilateral donors. In fact, the program relies primarily on the Resident Representatives of the UN Development Program (UNDP) in order to avoid the extreme administrative costs a larger field staff would entail. But the UNDP is involved in a wide variety of development programs, and its personnel can therefore devote only limited amounts of time to the food aid effort.

The absence of a large, in-country presence also means that the WFP is often slow to react to immediate food emergency situations. It is hampered further by the fact that, by definition, a multilateral food aid mechanism is one step removed from its sources of supply. That is, in crisis situations, the WFP must first receive an official aid request from the affected country before then seeking a donor from which to obtain the necessary commodities. This added bureaucratic layer can slow reaction time considerably, although the recent establishment of an International Emergency Reserve—administered by the WFP—should solve this problem to some extent.

One other commonly raised criticism of the WFP (and the UN system as a whole) relates to general level of competence of its bureaucracy. UN officials are appointed as a rule according to preestablished country quotas, and the highest-level positions are generally apportioned to achieve geopolitical balance. As a result, multilateral programming is frequently conservative and lacking in imagination. In addition, since most UN career advancements are made on the basis of seniority rather than competence, there is no effective means either of rewarding innovation or penalizing poor performance.

CONCEPTUAL ISSUES

Perhaps the most attractive feature of food aid multilateralism is that, unlike bilateral relationships, in which the recipient is placed in the role of supplicant, internationalized distribution involves providers and receivers jointly in the process of establishing aid criteria and overseeing project management. This arrangement has worked to the advantage of both, since donors are shielded from charges of capriciousness in their aid decisions and recipients are provided with an opportunity to identify and ameliorate those conditions which they find particularly burdensome or damaging to their interests. In the process, an institutionalized capacity to deal with the problems of hunger and malnutrition within an international context is strengthened and legitimized.

From the recipient's perspective, a major advantage of multilateral food aid is that (supposedly) it is free from political manipulation for bilateral foreign policy purposes by the donors. This is *not* to suggest, however, that multilateral aid decisions are made on a perfectly objective, apolitical basis; donors often simply shift the focus of their control to more indirect instrumentalities (see the section following). But distributing food aid multilaterally *does* remove many of the more explicit types of political manipulation,[16] and it focuses efforts more narrowly on economic development and emergency relief priorities. Moreover, since multilateral food aid is not normally used to develop markets, it tends not to provide the same kinds of incentives as bilateral, concessional credit sales.

The multilateral channel also has the capacity to provide added flexibility in emergency situations, such as the Sahelian famine, that overlap geopolitical boundaries. For example, a common international effort can obviate the need for bilateral donors to conclude individual food aid agreements with each country in an afflicted area. Furthermore, a multilateral instrumentality potentially could serve as an informational and managerial focal point for the coordination of emergency relief measures by all food aid donors in the event of a major natural or man-made disaster (e.g., earthquakes, wars).

Despite its obvious assets, the multilateral form of food aid delivery poses conceptual difficulties that are among the most problematic of the entire bilateral–multilateral debate. While the heterogeneous composition of WFP membership (with both donors *and* recipients represented) provides the program with a broad base of international political support, it also increases the difficulty of reaching consensus on the most appropriate policy priorities. In addition, the composition of the WFP membership has itself been subject to criticism due to the absence of substantial Communist bloc participation.

Communist nations have chosen, by and large, to extract the maximum propaganda value from their limited food aid by extending it almost exclusively on a bilateral basis. The very concept of food aid is also troubling to Communist countries from an ideological perspective, since they tend to view such efforts as a palliative offered in lieu of the fundamental social, economic, and political changes which they consider essential to improve basic social and economic conditions in the developing world. Eastern European countries have also chosen not to participate in the WFP because of what they see as the continued dominance of the United States and the other large food exporters among the Western nations.

The inability of the WFP and other multilateral food aid agencies to deviate substantially from the policies and funding priorities of the largest donors have been noted previously; so, too, have been the attempts by donors to compensate for the loss of bilateral leverage by exerting heavy influence on the course of multilateral aid policy. These matters obviously are related, and both are central to the conceptual difficulties involved in wider multilateralization of food aid. At the root of the matter are the degree to which *donors* are willing to forego the direct political and economic benefits of bilateral food aid without receiving partial compensation through some form of weighted voting in the CFA, and the degree to which *recipients* are willing to tolerate an unequal role in decisionmaking in order to receive a larger volume of food through the less blatantly political, multilateral channel.

Many countries have also voiced disagreement with the philosophy adhered to in the actual delivery of WFP food commodities. Whereas, in the case of bilateral aid programs, the food commodities are managed and monitored down to the level of the individual recipient, the World Food Programme does not—and, under the terms of its charter, cannot—operate in the same fashion. The WFP has chosen to avoid the politically sensitive sovereignty issues arising from in-country management of the aid by terminating its operational responsibility for the commodities at the recipient's port of entry.

In one sense, structuring the multilateral aid mechanism in this fashion almost *guarantees* that the WFP will be ineffective in those developing countries lacking in managerial expertise and related infrastructure. Yet, given the difficulty of obtaining policy consensus among donor countries, there seem to be few other options that would not result in some degree of political conflict, programmatic paralysis, and reduction in aid flows. While many argue that forcing the recipient to develop an indigenous capacity to administer and distribute food aid is more consistent with the long-term objectives of LDC food self-sufficiency, it is also true that this policy tends to increase the likelihood of food diversion, spoilage, and mismanagement. On the basis of the operational record, however, it would appear that the doubts held by donors about the effectiveness of allocating additional food aid through the multilateral channel are justified to the extent that structural barriers now preclude a more substantial in-country management role for the World Food Programme.

THE REALITY OF MULTILATERAL FOOD AID

Much of the preceding discussion has concerned the role of multilateral food aid as it exists in *theory* and has not addressed the reality of developing an expanded multilateral channel given the nature of existing political and economic constraints. It is most expedient to begin such a recapitulation from the recipient's perspective since it is easiest to weigh the arguments in this case. Virtually all the recipient's apprehensions about multilateral aid are resource related (e.g., net volume of aid, type of aid available); but these apprehensions have been overshadowed by the substantially larger number of benefits resulting from this method of food aid delivery. To the extent that the multilateral channel can reduce the host country's vulnerability (to political pressure by the donor or to sudden reductions in resource availability), minimize foreign involvement in LDC internal development policies, and expand opportunities for recipients to participate in the formulation of international food aid policy, it would appear to be in the long-term interest of such countries to favor this channel of assistance.

From the donor's perspective, the weight of the arguments presented do not permit such a positive conclusion. There is little argument over the fact that the multinational alternative has proven valuable to the United States in encouraging additional developed countries to participate in sharing the international food aid burden. Moreover, in the present economic environment, expanded participation in the WFP has offered one definite way by which donors may appear responsive to Third World demands for a reduction in "aid imperialism" and adherence to the NIEO doctrine while still retaining some capacity to influence the course of LDC development policies. Donors are also attracted naturally to the possibility of reducing unnecessary program duplication and wasteful, counterproductive competition between donor governments, private voluntary organizations, and UN agencies. Multilateral mechanisms thus have the potential to respond to the need for improved coordination of food aid delivery.

At the same time, donors have been reluctant to support wider deployment of multilateral food aid due to continuing questions about management effectiveness. This is, to a large extent, an issue of the donors' own making, however, since WFP operations are generally constrained by the limits placed on it by its members—particularly the largest contributors. While a substantial portion of these difficulties is no doubt endemic to the nature of international organizations, many are also caused by the unwillingness of the principal donors to permit greater programmatic flexibility.

Beyond these procedural difficulties, there exists a series of difficult political trade-offs which are at the very heart of the multilateral aid debate. For example, to what degree are such undertakings designed to benefit the aid recipient rather than the aid donor? Moreover, if the giving of aid is intended to be *mutually* beneficial, which party's needs are to be met more fully? Despite an increased awareness of the requisites of global interdependence, it is apparent that the major donors have not yet reached the point where they are willing to forego the immediate advantages of bilateralism. It would, of course, be politically naive to expect such a fundamental change in donor policies to occur over a relatively short period of time. But it is difficult to anticipate a significant enlargement of the multilateral food aid channel until and unless such a change in political perspective occurs.

Resource-related issues are somewhat paradoxical in nature. On the one hand, the existence of a multilateral alternative facilitates certain types of resource pooling that otherwise would be impossible; on the other hand, constraints on use and the absolute dominance of a few major donors limit the effectiveness of WFP assistance. Undeniably, however, the most significant resource advantage of the multilateral channel is that it facilitates the participation of small aid donors, who almost certainly would not otherwise become involved.

The negative aspects of the resource issue are also significant. The inability of the WFP to provide critically needed nonfood resources and pressures on the program to maintain a wide geopolitical distribution pattern reduce substantially the aid's impact on development. It must also be reiterated, in this context, that it does *not* necessarily follow that a wider multilateralization of food aid, combined with a concurrent reduction in bilateral assistance, would automatically result in a larger total volume of food assistance, since donors might choose instead simply to reduce or reprogram aid from one channel to another.

Thus, the reality of the multilateral food aid resource situation contains a certain degree of ambiguity. The development of a joint distribution capacity has doubtless made possible a wider level of donor participation and a more nutritionally adequate resource mix. But many of the most beneficial developments have been offset by constraints on use and lack of collateral nonfood inputs. As a result, the existence of a multilateral alternative has not had a major impact in recipient countries—in terms of either resource use or availability—beyond that already attainable through the bilateral channel.

No other aspect of the multilateral food aid debate has engendered greater controversy than the argument over the organization and management of the delivery mechanism. Where proponents of the international approach are quick to point to a wide array of benefits inherent in joint food distribution—for example, the potential economies of scale, the elimination of duplicative procedures, and the standardization of terms, conditions, and objectives of aid—detractors are equally quick to emphasize the considerable WFP administrative shortcomings, particularly, questions about the competence of the personnel, the lack of field staff, and the slow emergency response time. It is interesting to note, in fact, that most of the arguments advanced in support of multilateral food aid consider the program's operation *in theory*, while most of the arguments critical of multilateral assistance are based on the programs' *actual* operation.

It is difficult, on this basis, to conclude that the multilateral food aid mechanism currently represents a viable organizational alternative to bilateral food aid, much less an administratively superior mode of delivery. This is not to suggest that the claims made in support of the WFP are necessarily fallacious. Rather, it is indicative of the fact that a real opportunity to test the program's organizational effectiveness has been precluded by the refusal of the principal donors to provide necessary operating latitude. Consequently, until such time as the donors choose to allocate a greater portion of their resources through the multilateral channel and to relax their rigid oversight and control, it is doubtful that the organization and management debates will be resolved.

We come, finally, to a consideration of the viability of the multilateral food aid channel as an operational concept. The international administration of food assistance clearly does offer a number of advantages not readily available through bilateral channels; these include, for example, the joint involvement of providers and receivers in establishing program policy, the easier allocation of aid in situations transcending political boundaries, the greater freedom from the direct manipulation of aid for political purposes, and the strengthened international institutional capacity to deal with global food problems. Arrayed against these positive features, however, are a certain number of operational problems: the questionable effectiveness of food aid delivery, the lack of participation by the Communist bloc countries, the vulnerability of the program to the wishes of the principal donor countries, and the difficulties involved in reaching policy consensus among a politically and economically heterogeneous membership.

Since, from the recipients' perspective, the apparent gap between the *promise* of multilateralism and its less than satisfactory *performance* is the result of the pivotal role played by the few large donors, to what degree have these donor countries supported the concept and practice of multilateral food aid? To answer this we must examine whether the donor countries have shown (1) theoretical acceptance of the multilateral concept, (2) political support for the multilateral concept, and (3) administrative implementation of the multilateral concept through expanded resource commitments.

There seems little doubt that the concept of multilateralism as a viable channel of economic assistance, and food as a specific component of that channel, has now gained general *theoretical* acceptance among donor governments. In fact, due to increasing donor sensitivity to the requisites of global interdependence and to LDC political activism, developed countries have frequently given rhetorical support to this type of comprehensive international approach.

At the *political* level, however, the contrast between rhetoric and action begins to become apparent. It is one thing for donors to advocate the notion of multilateralism in the abstract, but it is quite another thing for them to advocate the idea in practice. Yet, for the United States at least, political support for multilateral food aid has helped to promote a number of America's foreign policy objectives. The existence of an international food aid channel has thus fulfilled both the explicit role of an alternative means of food delivery (and surplus disposal) and also what Krause and Nye have termed certain "latent roles,"[17] relating in this case to an enhanced capacity to bring pressure on other actors to behave in a particular fashion.

But if food aid multilateralism has been accepted in theory and also has received some political endorsement, it is in the actual *implementation* of the policy that it has failed to gain widespread support. Thus, when the multilateral food resource contributions of the United States or the EEC are compared with the volume of food aid flowing bilaterally from these donors, it becomes apparent that political will and programmatic commitment are, in this case, far from identical. Because the major food aid donors possess the agricultural capacity to make resource contributions to the multilateral program while continuing, at the same time, to operate large bilateral programs, there is little to motivate or compel them to shift the balance of resource distribution. Consequently, donors are able, under the current arrangement, to maintain the appearance of political support for multilateral food aid while also retaining a maximum degree of bilateral foreign policy flexibility.

Barring some major, unforeseen reduction in donor agricultural output, or some change in foreign aid policies, it is impossible to anticipate more than incremental increases in the total volume of resources committed through the multilateral food aid channel. More than to a failure of political will, this situation may be attributed to the sheer lack of political or economic incentive. There is, in the final analysis, simply no overriding reason why donors should alter the current distribution of their food aid resources, since the current arrangement facilitates the simultaneous pursuit of multiple foreign policy goals.

It would seem far more productive, therefore, to accept the current level of multilateral food aid programming as more or less a given and to focus attention instead on alternative institutional arrangements which might accomplish many of the same objectives. For example, the modalities of aid coordination and standardization as represented in the Food Aid Convention of the International Wheat Agreement may offer far greater short-term opportunities for effective international cooperation than any significant expansion of the WFP. In fact, this notion of "multilaterally coordinated bilateralism" may ultimately represent a *more* viable means of obtaining the desired mobilization of global food aid resources while at the same time avoiding the many conceptual difficulties inherent in the more traditional multilateral approach.

Prior to the decade of the sixties, there was no coherent framework of international food aid. With the exception of the United States, donors operated food aid programs largely on an ad hoc basis, with involvement predicated upon the volume and nature of surpluses and the specific geographic location of the food deficit (i.e., whether the country or countries in question fell within a particular donor's sphere of interest). After 1961, the prevailing arrangement was changed by the slow evolution of the US food aid program from its preoccupation with surplus disposal and by the creation of a small but nonetheless significant multilateral food aid mechanism, the UN–FAO World Food Programme. Even as late as 1966, however, there was still no identifiable international food aid framework. The United States was far and away the largest bilateral donor, and it was also contributing more than half of the food resources of the WFP.

At the same time, with the exception of Canada, the programs of the other bilateral donors tended to be sporadic and inconsequential. But the Johnson administration placed increased emphasis on international burden-sharing both at the *macrolevel*, through the creation of the Food Aid Convention, and at the *microlevel*, through country-specific applications such as the India Food Aid Consortium. The ultimate result was a substantial increase in the level of participation by other aid donors. For example, by 1970, the European Economic Community had grown from an inconsequential contributor to the second largest overall supplier of aid.

The simple fact that the total volume of food commodities moving internationally as aid has increased is not in itself as significant as three other new factors which now suggest the beginning of a more coordinated international approach. First, the United States—which is, of course, the single most important agricultural exporter—is no longer as dominant as in the past. Its bilateral food aid program is still by far the largest, but its contributions to the WFP now represent less than 25 percent of the program's total resources. Second, other food providers have finally recognized that the United States is neither willing nor able to function as the world's residual food aid supplier. These countries have therefore had to adjust their own policies in order to reflect the new demands placed upon them. Third, a number of international mechanisms have been created as a result of the 1974 World Food Conference to deal explicitly with the need to coordinate and promote the transfer of food resources.

There are, therefore, definite indications that the individual donors have become more interactive and less isolated operationally from each other and that the basic elements of a coordinated, international food aid framework have begun to evolve. Its coordinative function is still somewhat uneven and ineffective, however, because many donors—the United States foremost among them—have not yet indicated a willingness either to consult on all aspects of food aid programming or to abide fully by established international policy on the specific uses of their food resources. But the fact remains that there *are* now a substantial number of individual elements which function together with far greater effectiveness than is generally realized.

IMPACT OF UNITED STATES POLICY

It is apparent that the most salient characteristic of the international food aid system is the pivotal role played by the United States. There is probably no other natural resource, except petroleum, required by and traded between virtually every nation for which the comparative advantage is held so disproportionately by a single nation. The result is that US policy has had a profound influence on the actions of other donors and on the system as a whole.

American food aid policy can be divided roughly into four phases. The first was primarily an inward-looking period during the fifties and early sixties, when the motivation to give food assistance was conditioned almost exclusively by the need to dispose of surpluses. Whatever negative impact this had on the markets of other exporters or on the agricultural development of the aid recipients were considered secondary to the principal concern, which was to relieve domestic agricultural pressures.

This narrow policy focus gave way slowly during the Kennedy administration to a more international approach, which was further reinforced under Lyndon Johnson. By the late sixties, the reorientation of agricultural policy succeeded finally in gaining some degree of control over domestic production, and hence, the level of surplus carry-over. As the need for surplus disposal was reduced, the United States was forced to confront the fact that it could not—and in any case, should not—continue indefinitely in the role of residual food aid supplier. Heavy aid dependency relationships, such as that which held between the United States and India, were recognized not only as counterproductive to the solution of world food problems, but also as unhelpful in many respects to US foreign relations. In addition, other nations—both exporters and importers—had persisted in their demands that the United States cease its unilateral dumping of food commodities on LDC markets and adopt a more rational agricultural export policy.

The third phase of US policy began during the first Nixon term and was characterized by renewed US demands for more equitable participation by other developed countries in the provision of food aid. Food was no longer viewed as the cheap, throw-away resource of a decade earlier, and the fiscally conscious Nixon administration was determined that the food aid program would not contribute to the already serious domestic inflation. During the first Nixon term, food also took on more explicit, political uses as an instrument of US foreign policy.

Richard Nixon's second term was marked by the further politicization of food aid and by a new interest in *commercial* food exports as a major source of balance of payments support. Food was in short supply worldwide during the 1973–1974 period, but the United States was still attempting to curb inflation through rigorous fiscal restraint. It chose, therefore, not to expand the volume of its food aid shipments. But the United States was sensitive to vocal Third World criticism and, under the terms of the Nixon Doctrine, the American overseas profile was subsequently reduced.

This temporary tactical retreat permitted the United States to reexamine many aspects of its foreign policy toward the developing world, particularly as it related to foreign aid. Eventually, this led to a fourth policy phase wherein the concept of global interdependence has become a more significant element of US strategic thinking. There is now also evidence of a more conservative approach to the political manipulation of food and other economic assistance. At the same time, however, the United States continues to employ its food aid leverage to promote its view of the world on such issues as basic human rights.

The net impact of American policy behavior must be considered in relation to the fact that the nature of the international food aid system has changed dramatically since 1967. With the creation of the World Food Programme, and the signing of the first Food Aid Convention, the United States had successfully backed away from the role of residual food supplier, a role it had actually *encouraged* during the heavy surpluses of the fifties and early sixties. More recently, it has also developed new commercial priorities for its food resources, while altering the conceptual basis of its foreign aid policy to emphasize the need for more explicit attention to "basic human needs." Moreover, as a result of the 1972–1974 food shortage period, and the World Food Conference that followed, the United States and other donor countries have slowly begun to move toward a new international accommodation regarding the division of food assistance responsibilities, including an explicitly stated annual food aid target which has been set by the UN World Food Council at 10 million metric tons.

IMPACT OF OTHER DONORS' POLICIES

In comparison to the complex, multiple objectives of the United States, the food aid policies of the other major donor countries have been relatively straightforward. Prior to the midsixties, donors such as France, West Germany, and Great Britain offered food assistance only on a sporadic, ad hoc basis and with a substantial degree of geopolitical bias. In general, however, this aid tended to be far more outward looking in intent than the American initiative because few of these countries (Canada is the principal exception) were forced to deal with the kind of massive, and seemingly intractable, commodity surplus burden that originally motivated the US program. In many respects the very *existence* of these continuing agricultural surpluses in the United States effectively neutralized whatever sense of responsibility these other donors may have felt for the need to provide food assistance on a regular and continuing basis.

This situation began to change gradually in the early sixties as a result of the new international approaches adopted by the Kennedy administration and the perceptible decline in the US surplus stocks. The first significant policy shift for many donors was the agreement to participate in the World Food Programme in 1961. But these contributions remained rather inconsequential until much later in the decade. Thus, it was really not until 1967 and the signing of the Food Aid Convention that the other donor countries became a major factor in international food aid, once again due to a policy initiative of the United States.

The principal focus of US concern, which led directly to its quid pro quo offer within the GATT cereals discussions, was the Common Agricultural Policy (CAP) of the European Economic Community. Canada and Australia, the other major exporters, were also a part of the GATT negotiations, but the United States found no fault with their positions because they had not imposed the type of structural barriers in their agricultural markets maintained by the Europeans. Moreover, besides questions of tariff and nontariff trade barriers, CAP also resulted in the creation of substantial EEC surpluses in dry skim milk and butter oil, which the EEC endeavored to dump just as the United States did, although with less regularity.

By compromising on other issues, the United States did succeed ultimately in convincing the Europeans and other donor countries to regularize their aid contributions (although, significantly, it failed in its attempt to overcome the CAP market barriers) by acceding to the Food Aid Convention (FAC) of 1967. The signing of the FAC changed symbolically—if not also instrumentally—the nature of international food aid. For the first time, other donors besides the United States were formally committed by international agreement to provide a stated annual volume of food assistance. In terms of comparative policy, however, the developments of real significance were those which occurred *after* the FAC agreement had been reached.

An analysis of individual donor country efforts indicates that a substantial portion of the food aid has been provided largely for humanitarian and developmental purposes. This has not been true universally, however, since countries such as West Germany, France, and Australia have, on occasion, used the selective allocation of their aid for purposes of foreign policy and trade leverage. But, as a result of the Food Aid Convention of 1967, the European countries have created a unique form of food aid; it is contributed individually by each of the Common Market countries but is administered jointly through the Commission of the European Communities. This joint aid can, in turn, be allocated either bilaterally through the commission to a specific country or multilaterally through the WFP or the International League of Red Cross Societies.

The existence of this so-called communitarized food aid capability—
which, presumably, is *not* to reflect the political biases of the member
states—has resulted both in a substantial increase in European food
aid and in the expansion of aid to countries not normally within the traditional spheres of European influence. The food aid program operated
by the commission has also functioned as an alternative surplus disposal
outlet for unmarketable dairy products created by the EEC Common
Agricultural Policy. While surplus dumping still continues to a limited
extent, the EEC has now begun to reorient its food aid policy toward an
emphasis on development.

By contrast, the food aid policies of other bilateral donors have been
far less controversial. Canada, for example, which is the second-largest
individual donor, has maintained steady bilateral and multilateral contributions since the early sixties, featuring a strong humanitarian and developmental orientation. In addition, countries such as Japan and the
United Kingdom, which historically have been net food *importers*, have
agreed to participate by contributing resources either in cash or in kind.
The willingness of developed countries that are food importers to help
provide international food aid offers a further indication of the important role that food transfers now play in the developed country response
to Third World demands for a substantial increase in efforts to meet
basic human needs.

IMPACT OF THE MULTILATERAL MECHANISMS

It has been suggested that, until the creation of the UN–FAO World
Food Programme in 1961, there was no coherent framework of international food assistance. Thus, for many aid donors, the pledge of resources to the WFP—however limited—represented the first, *regularized*
commitment to address global food problems. Although most of these
early pledges were more symbolic than instrumental, such symbolism
later proved extremely important as a precedent for subsequent multilateral initiatives.

Three distinct forms of food aid multilateralism have been examined
here: *operational programs*—the World Food Programme and UNICEF;
bilateral aid coordinating mechanisms—the Food Aid Conventions; and
political and consultative organizations—the Subcommittee on Surplus
Disposal and the World Food Council. Although only the first category
involves the actual allocation of multilateral food aid, all three types of

mechanisms have contributed to (and increased the complexity of) the international aid framework.

Operational Programs

In considering the operational impact of multilateral food aid programs, it is reasonable to focus solely on the World Food Programme because it is considered—even by the other UN agencies dealing with food—to be the principal international aid delivery channel. WFP operations can be divided into two discrete historical periods. During the first phase (1961–1968), the institution was promoted and sustained largely through the support of the United States, which underwrote most of the costs at first in order to create an additional surplus disposal outlet and to encourage other potential donors to participate. WFP resources in the early years were extremely modest in comparison to the PL 480 program, and the multilateral undertaking fulfilled mostly a symbolic role.

Since the start of the second phase (1969–present), however, food resources have increased to the point where total WFP aid is now nearly commensurate with the individual operations undertaken by the United States, the EEC, or Canada. Moreover, as the contributions by other donors have increased, the WFP has become more truly multilateral in character. Thus, from an operational standpoint, it has really only been during this later phase of its existence that the WFP has represented a viable alternative to traditional bilateral food aid.

Although some have argued that contributing food through the multilateral channel represents a depoliticized form of assistance, this is not actually the case. In most situations, multilateral aid simply substitutes the politics of decisionmaking within the United Nations and other international organizations for the politics of bilateral foreign relations. It is also not possible to argue that the WFP offers a superior organizational structure. Due to the operational constraints inherent in the nature of the multilateral approach, profound—and, in some cases, unresolved—problems have developed in the administration of the aid (e.g., the fact that food shipments cannot be managed beyond the recipient's port of entry). Yet, the fact that the WFP continues to exist, and even to expand, suggests that, for a variety of reasons, member countries value this organizational approach.

It may be argued, of course, that the mere fact that the WFP continues in operation is not necessarily indicative of its political importance in the international system, since imbedded bureaucratic structures often demonstrate a surprising capacity to sustain themselves long after they have outlived their usefulness. In this case, however, there are a number of important features that result directly from the continued existence of WFP food aid.

First, through its governing council, the CFA, the WFP functions as a forum for international efforts to consult, coordinate, and act upon common food aid problems and objectives. Second, despite the existence of political problems within the multilateral arena, WFP food aid is insulated from most bilateral political manipulation and generally does represent a *net addition* to the level of food aid resources that would otherwise be available. Third, the existence of the WFP facilitates the participation of donors whose resources are too limited to justify a separate bilateral program. As a result, the multilateral program is one of the few—if not the only—international aid initiatives that has actually grown in recent years. Finally, the WFP represents the *only* formally constituted international forum in which donors and recipients participate jointly in the formation and implementation of food aid policies and programs.

It may be concluded on this basis that the impact of multilateral food aid, as embodied principally in the WFP, has been substantially positive. Despite this fact, however, there is no indication that the obstacles which so far have prevented wider deployment of multilateral food aid will be overcome in the foreseeable future.

Bilateral Aid Coordinating Mechanisms

The coordination of bilateral food aid contributions within a multilateral framework is a relatively recent development. Nevertheless, agreements such as the Food Aid Convention (FAC) hold perhaps the greatest promise for the future and have attracted a substantial amount of international attention and political support. Donors respond positively to coordination under the FAC for many of the same reasons they choose *not* to participate more widely in the WFP; the FAC permits a wider degree of international burden-sharing but does not require donors to relinquish any of their foreign policy flexibility. Donors are obligated only to make specific volume commitments, while the decisions as to *where* the food will be programmed (i.e., which countries will receive it) or *how* it will be programmed (i.e., through the bilateral or multilateral channel) are left entirely to their individual discretion. The existence of the FAC has thus resulted in a net increase in the total volume of food moving as aid, particularly on account of the expanded commitments made by the European countries under the auspices of the EEC.

While "multilaterally coordinated bilateralism" under the FAC does offer significant advantages over the WFP, it too has certain drawbacks. For example, because the FAC exists as part of the International Wheat Agreement, it is tied to the continued existence of the accord, a fact which becomes apparent each time the International Wheat Agreement must be renegotiated (as in 1978–1979). Moreover, the FAC is limited only to countries acceding to the agreement. Consequently, the world's largest wheat producer, the Soviet Union—which is not a signatory— does not participate; nor do a number of other potential or actual exporters such as New Zealand and Brazil. Second, there is no provision for representation of food aid *recipients* in FAC policy deliberations (as in the case with the WFP), meaning that decisions on programming levels and so on are made by the donors alone.

This suggests yet a third difficulty with the FAC mode of coordination: donors have so far refused to enter into substantive discussions in that forum regarding their individual food aid policies and programs, that is, which countries get how much. The convention is viewed purely as a means of obtaining a stated annual level of donor aid commitments, *not* as a vehicle for examining what each donor does with the aid it agrees to provide.

The foregoing critique of the coordinated bilateral approach cannot be dismissed lightly. On the other hand, the fact that succeeding FAC agreements have represented the first—and, to date, the only—effort to solidify and regularize the level of donor aid commitments has had a profound impact on the international food aid framework. It signifies a break with the old surplus disposal philosophy of the past and suggests a new perception of food aid as a regular component of international resource transfers between developed and developing countries.

The reality of the matter is that FAC-type food aid offers many of the same advantages as pure multilateral assistance while acknowledging the Realpolitik of foreign aid, namely, that donors give food and other economic assistance as much to fulfill their *own* foreign policy objectives as to meet the needs of the recipients. Thus, the multilateral coordination of bilateral assistance enables donors both to attain their goals and priorities and to provide a greater volume of resources for those countries suffering food deficits.

Political and Consultative Organizations
In some respects, political interaction and consultative dialogue represent opposite extremes in the spectrum of international relations: consul-

tation is generally orderly and bureaucratic while political dialogue is often disorganized and contentious. Both have contributed to the viability of international food aid. In general, more success has been achieved in promoting consultation on food aid issues than in developing effective political interaction. In fact, the Consultative Subcommittee on Surplus Disposal (CSD) predates the creation of any of the other current multilateral food aid mechanisms.

Interestingly, the multilateral organization which has demonstrated perhaps the greatest capacity to operate on *both* the consultative and political levels is the Committee on Food Aid Policies and Programs (CFA), the governing council of the World Food Programme. This is due in part to the fact that the WFP has a highly specific mission: supplying food aid to hungry people. Consequently, member countries are aware that, if political debate becomes too rancorous, it will quickly become impossible to fulfill the program's mandate. On the other hand, the CFA was constituted in its present form directly as a result of the World Food Conference of 1974, where it was decided that a new forum was needed which would facilitate discussion of a broad range of policy issues relating to food aid. In fact, the WFP just recently has established a policy unit within its secretariat ostensibly for this very purpose.

Thus, it is possible to draw a further distinction between *mission*-oriented entities such as the World Food Programme and *policy*-oriented entities such as the World Food Council. While both types of organizations are clearly necessary, the evidence suggests that the most successful international food initiatives will occur in the context of mission-oriented organizations.

THE FUTURE MIX OF AID CHANNELS

It was noted previously that the current agricultural productive capacity of the largest exporters provides little motivation for a substantial alteration in the current mix of food aid programming. At present, donor countries have sufficient resources to give both bilateral and multilateral food aid; consequently, they are able to maintain the *appearance* of political support for the international distribution mechanism while also retaining the foreign policy flexibility afforded by bilateral food assistance.

The success of this policy is, of course, contingent upon the continued availability of abundant food supplies in the donor countries. If these supplies were to be threatened seriously as a result of drought or other natural or human-made events, donors would be forced to make their allocation decisions on a more narrow, self-serving basis. The prospects for food aid multilateralism in this situation would be considerably diminished.

Barring any major change in donor food production capabilities, however, it is probable that the major suppliers will maintain the capacity and will to allocate food aid through *both* delivery channels. Moreover, there is likely to be little fundamental change in the prevailing mix of policy objectives that food aid is intended to fulfill. That is, it is as naive to assume that donors such as the United States will forego the foreign policy and market development benefits of bilateral aid as to assume that they will be inclined to give *all* of their aid for humanitarian and developmental purposes. While some marginal readjustment of aid priorities may be anticipated, the basic programmatic objectives are likely to remain more or less the same.

It follows logically that, if the basic objectives of food aid continue essentially unchanged, there is no real motivation for donors to alter their present resource allocation formulas. Although it is conceivable that this situation could be altered by a major restructuring of the operational format of the World Food Programme, there is no indication at present that any such modification is likely. The WFP has, undeniably, made substantial progress in increasing the efficiency and effectiveness with which it administers the food resources at its disposal, but it has been unable to overcome the basic problem inherent in the multilateral approach, which is related to the process of decisionmaking and power-sharing within the multilateral arena and to the ambiguous role of the multilateral agency within the recipient country. Even assuming an increased donor commitment—which is also not now evident—it is far from certain that these obstacles are even amenable to successful resolution.

Thus, the only conclusion that may be stated with confidence in the present circumstances is that, ceteris paribus, there is no persuasive reason to foresee any substantial expansion in the multilateral channel. Rather, multilateral resource contributions are likely to increase only very slowly, and then merely to compensate for inflation or specific crises. This is *not* meant to suggest, however, that there will be no further modifications in the policies of the WFP, but only that such changes probably will represent limited tinkering with the existing structure and will not attract any major new commitment of donor resources.

If the WFP does not offer the promise of becoming a more viable alternative, then the question may legitimately be asked, "Is there any *real*

prospect for change in the current framework of international food aid?"
The sum of the evidence considered here—including the opinions of a
substantial number of key policymakers in the United States, Canada,
Europe, and the multilateral food agencies in Rome—does not indicate
the existence of any significant support for major alterations in the current channeling of food aid resources. The longer-range prospect (i.e.,
beyond the next three to five years) is obviously a good deal more difficult to predict. Assuming, however, that the International Wheat Agreement does not disintegrate into a new and dangerous round of myopic,
commercial protectionism, there is some reason to believe that the kind
of coordinated bilateral approach embodied in the FAC might have even
wider application in the future.

Given the close and continuing relationship between food aid and foreign policy, from the donor's perspective there is little or no advantage
in expanding such operational mechanisms as WFP. While this assessment might look vastly different from the aid recipient's perspective, such
views have never figured prominently in the Realpolitik of international
food aid. What may be expected, instead, is a gradual increase in the
willingness of donors to conclude new multilateral agreements that
follow the general policies by which they *bilaterally* allocate their food
aid resources. Such agreements would permit aid recipients to obtain
food assistance under more regularized terms and conditions but would
be unlikely to alter the subjective, political criteria that govern foreign
aid programming decisions.

TOWARD GLOBAL FOOD SECURITY

The fundamental question underlying all of these issues is not, "What
sort of marginal changes can be made in the international food aid
system in order to make it work more effectively?" but, "What action
can be taken to alter the basic social, political, and economic factors that
make food aid necessary in the first place?" Full consideration of this
matter is, of course, far beyond the scope of this study, but it is important to maintain a sense of perspective when examining various food
aid policy options. Otherwise, even under the best of circumstances, it
becomes difficult to retain sight of the fact that food aid is a means and
not an end in itself, and that, unless carefully programmed, it is most
often a problematic and temporary solution to the problems of hunger
and malnutrition.

A great number of policy recommendations—most of them still unful-

filled—have been advanced in recent years for modifying specific operational components of international food aid. The vast majority of these
proposals, however, have fallen short of the mark. The need at this
juncture is *not* to create new institutional constructs, or even necessarily
to alter the basic policies of existing programs. Rather, the need at present is to understand fully the basic motivations for donor involvement in
the food aid process and then to use that knowledge in order to promote
the objective of global food security.

As employed here, global food security is meant to connote that state
of affairs in which every nation is assured of adequate food resources,
under all conceivable conditions, to meet the basic food requirements of
its population. What is new in this conception is that it accepts surplus
disposal, market development, and foreign policy applications as an inevitable—and, perhaps, even necessary—part of the basic donor motivation to give foreign aid in the form of food.

In addition, it recognizes that the effort to remove or further constrain
these objectives would lead almost inevitably to a substantial reduction—and possible elimination—of support among interest groups
within the donor countries (e.g., the alienation of the agricultural community). That is, it accepts the priorities which donors have established
and ceases the seemingly futile attempt to force policy changes that are
unlikely to be forthcoming in the foreseeable future. This is essentially
why the paradigm of "multilaterally coordinated bilateralism," embodied in the succeeding Food Aid Conventions, is so fundamentally attractive. Commitment to FAC does not in any way restrict the donors'
policymaking flexibility; it simply formalizes the donors' commitment to
provide a predetermined volume of assistance each year. In fact, wider
use of the multilateral coordination model would encourage donors to
offer food aid on a more regularized, longer-term basis.

Greater reliance on FAC-type coordination might also help to avoid a
good deal of the conscious mislabeling of bilateral food aid (i.e., assistance given ostensibly for one purpose but meant actually to achieve
another, unrelated objective) that still occurs with disturbing frequency.
The mislabeling of food assistance is, without question, one of the most
serious, recurring obstacles to global food security. Such actions tend to
create false expectations on the part of recipient countries, and they can
result in food aid being reduced or withdrawn suddenly, often with a
devastating impact on the recipient's agricultural development. By contrast, improved coordination and integration among bilateral programs,

and between bilateral and multilateral channels, under the global food security paradigm would reduce substantially the risks posed by this problem.

The basic approach suggested here does not really differ greatly from the existing configuration of the international food aid framework. In fact, the *principal* difference is related not so much to the instruments of aid delivery as to the basic philosophical approach to world food problems. The global food security philosophy begins with the notion that freedom from hunger is among the most basic of human rights. It further posits that matters of *greater* social complexity, such as world order and stability or global economic interdependence, cannot be resolved without first addressing the more basic question of the availability of adequate supplies of nutritious food. Global food security is viewed here as a sine qua non for the world's future economic and political development. Thus, only when donor countries come to recognize the interconnectedness of their food policies and other aspects of their foreign policies will it be possible to progress toward the kind of world that all nations profess to desire.

At the same time, however, it may be apparent that the kind of philosophical approach suggested here will do little in the short term to avoid the steadily growing world food deficit. Insofar as donors among the developed countries continue to adhere to their present aid delivery systems and foreign policy priorities, it will be necessary both to expand the total volume of food moving as aid and to improve the developmental impact of the resources available. Current efforts to create an international grain reserve—although fraught with extreme complexity and uncertainty due to its impact upon international agricultural trade—represent a major step toward ensuring a reliable flow of food commodities under a stable price structure. It is significant, although hardly surprising, that many of the problems encountered in the negotiations on the reserve mechanism are similar to the original concerns that motivated the development of an international food aid system. For example, questions have emerged such as: Who is to pay for the purchase, storage, and distribution?; How is the burden to be shared among the developed countries?

The problem of global food security will not be solved through noble-sounding rhetoric in international forums; nor, for that matter, will it be eliminated through a continuation of the pattern of ad hoc responses to particular crises (e.g., the Sahelian drought and famine). By maintaining a short-sighted crisis mentality toward the ever worsening world food problem, donor countries simply avoid confronting the difficult but necessary sacrifices that each must ultimately make. In the process, they damage their own long-term prospects for continued economic growth.

Notes

Introduction

1. According to statistics compiled by the Agency for International Development (AID), the total US overseas assistance effort in capital loans and grants during the period from 1946 through 1976 was $62.8 billion. Source: US AID (1976).

2. According to the same AID statistics [US AID (1976)] total aid under PL 480 in 1976 represented 33.5 percent of total economic assistance for that year.

3. The term "food priority country" came about as a result of a recommendation made to the Second Ministerial Session of the UN World Food Council. The countries were identified on a set of criteria based on per capita income, present and projected food gaps, balance of payments situation, extent of malnutrition, agricultural performance, and potential for food production. An *illustrative* (i.e., unofficial) list of forty-three "food priority countries" was approved by the council in 1976.

4. For example, there have been a variety of suggestions, both in the United States and abroad, concerning the use of food power in a manner analogous to the use of petro power leverage employed by the OPEC nations.

Chapter 1

1. In fact, it was the Commodity Credit Corporation (CCC)—created by Executive Order No. 6340 on 16 October 1933— that eventually bore the brunt of managing the surplus problem. The CCC was authorized to buy, sell, and make loans to farmers on agricultural commodities in order to increase production or to stabilize prices or to assure adequate supplies.

2. In fact, a Congressional Research Service study concluded that [US Congress HCIR (1977, p. 23)] "from a level of only 56 million bushels . . . in 1945, exports jumped to 318 million bushels in fiscal year 1946, 367 million bushels in fiscal 1947, 479 million bushels in fiscal year 1948, and peaked at 505 million bushels in fiscal year 1949."

3. Humanitarianism had also continued to be an element of the program as, in 1950, and again in 1951, the Congress passed special bills to earmark funds, previously appropriated under the European Recovery Act, for use in shipping commodities to relieve famines in Yugoslavia (1950) and India (1951).

4. The political exigencies that had required Truman to endorse the maintenance of agricultural price supports at 90 percent of parity continued to exist, thereby guaranteeing the price to farmers for unmarketable production through 1954.

5. Between 1951 and 1954, US wheat carryover jumped from 256 million bushels to 1,036.2 million bushels, or almost a 500 percent increase. The peak year for surpluses was 1954, until they once again began to increase in 1958. Cited in Cochrane and Ryan (1976, p. 203).

6: For a complete description of the Principles see FAO (1972, p. 1).

7. The work of the CSD continues to the present day, although the nature of its responsibilities has changed and expanded substantially. See also the discussion of the CSD in chapter 5.

8. In the words of Don Paarlberg, then Special Assistant to the President and Coordinator of the Food for Peace Program, "We do not need an export program to bail out our unwise price-support laws; we need farm programs that accomodate the present needs of our farmers. . . . We have a workable export law; we need more appropriate domestic programs." Paarlberg's speech also provided an early indication of the changing perception of US food aid in terms of domestic and foreign policy objectives: "There are some who view the food needs of the developing parts of the world simply as a safety valve to permit the continuation of unsound price support legislation in the U.S. What I am suggesting is something far different: the conscious reorientation of our farm policies with respect to the needs and opportunities of our foreign policy." Address of Donald Paarlberg, quoted in Department of State *Bulletin*, 9 November 1959, p. 675).

9. The situation with regard to feedgrains had, in fact, become so acute that, as of 1 January 1961, an additional bushel of feedgrain taken over by the government would have incurred a storage cost *greater* than the original value of the commodity itself. This necessitated an emergency feedgrain program in March 1961 in order to reduce the level of government-owned stocks. Cited in Cochrane and Ryan (1976, p. 79).

10. This decision altered the apportionment of seats in the US House of Representatives.

11. The Agricultural Act of 1962 required an unprecedented, national referendum to be held so that farmers could decide for themselves between two separate systems of price supports. In what was considered a major domestic setback for the new administration, the alternative associated with the Kennedy–Freeman position was defeated.

12. Year-by-year data, extending from 1955 to 1966 (inclusive), give the following figures, in millions of metric tons, for (respectively) wheat and feedgrains (now consisting largely of corn and sorghum): 1955—28.2 and 35.5 = total 63.7; 1956—28.1 and 39.2 = total 67.3; 1957—24.7 and 44.3 = total 69.0; 1958—24.0 and 53.5 = total 77.5; 1959—35.2 and 61.2 = total 96.4; 1960—35.8 and 68.6 = total 104.4; 1961—38.4 and 76.8 = total 115.2; 1962—36.0 and 65.1 = total 101.1; 1963—32.5 and 58.0 = total 90.5; 1964—24.5 and 62.3 = total 86.8; 1965—22.3 and 49.3 = total 71.6; and 1966—15.1 and 46.3 = total 61.4. Source: Freeman (1966c, p. 8).

13. Memorandum from Orville L. Freeman for the President, 19 November 1964 [Freeman (1964, p. 1)].

14. Memorandum from Orville L. Freeman for the Vice-President and others [Freeman (1966a, p. 1)].

15. There was eventually enough interest in the reserve stocks concept within the White House to consider floating a trial balloon with the Congress. Such a bill was actually introduced, but it was killed in subcommittee in November 1967.

16. Draft memorandum from Orville L. Freeman for the President, 23 June 1967 [Freeman (1967, p. 2)].

17. As Earl Butz himself has writen [Butz (1976, p. 137)], "I lean toward an economic decision-making process whereby people vote daily with their dollars . . . markets transmit signals from the public farm more quickly, clearly and impartially and more for the good of all than the slower, more institutionalized bureaucracy, which is the action of the political process."

18. Adapted from table compiled by the National Farmers Union, 1012 14th St. N.W., Washington, DC, 1 October 1974.

19. Butz proclaimed that the act represented "an historic turning point in the philosophy of farm programs in the United States," with its emphasis on full production and the elimination of any form of acreage restrictions. Government intervention would occur only when market prices fell below previously established target levels. Cited in US Congress SCAF (1976b, p. 195).

20. For further elaboration on the events which precipitated the world food crisis, see Schertz (1974).

21. Data calculated in Destler (1978, p. 634).

22. Address to the UN General Assembly by Secretary of State, Henry Kissinger, September 23, 1973. Cited in Department of State *Bulletin*, 15 October (1973, p. 472).

23. The issue of global climatic change and its possible impact on the United States and other grain exporting countries has been addressed in CIA (1974) and also in Schneider (1976).

24. These issues are considered further in chapter 9.

25. Statement of Mark Hatfield, cited in Destler (1978, p. 638).

26. In September 1975, the United States formally proposed the creation of a 30-million-ton reserve of wheat and rice, which was to be nationally held but internationally regulated. The proposal evoked some interest but many reservations from the countries represented on the International Wheat Council, and it failed to gain approval.

Chapter 2

1. For a more recent treatment of the problem, see Singer (1975).

2. In fact, up until the 1966 changes in PL 480 *all* commodities shipped under the law had first to be certified as surplus by the Secretary of Agriculture. As a result, countries such as Indonesia have undergone radical changes in their eating habits as basically rice-eating populations have been exposed to, and "force-fed", wheat.

3. At one point in the midsixties, for example, food aid absorbed fully 79 percent of the US wheat crop available for export. Computed from USDA statistics.

4. Between 1970 and 1975, food aid declined to about 26 percent of total US aid [US Congress SCANF (1977, p. 24)]. Also note that food and capital aid are authorized by different congressional committees.

5. Until 1970, local currencies were accepted for the sale of US Title I food aid. An amendment was also added to PL 480 in 1957 which provided that the local currencies could be loaned to American and foreign entrepreneurs for business development and trade expansion in recipient countries. Up until 1972, when the option was deleted, over three hundred private US businesses had acquired loans repayable in US-owned local currencies for projected expansion in LDCs.

6. The total of all food and other relief delivered during World War I and the reconstruction period (1914–1924) may be broken down by the following major relief operations: Committee for the Relief of Belgium (CRB)—4,988,059 metric tons (value $861,340,244) from November 1914 to August 1919; US Food Administration—23,103,266 metric tons (value $3,050,496,599) from April 1917 to August 1919; armistice period—1,571,534 metric tons (value $220,704,581) from August 1919 to July 1923. Total deliveries in the period from November 1914 to July 1923, therefore, came to 33,841,307 metric tons, valued at $5,234,028,208. Source: Surface and Bland (1931, p. 7).

7. No other sources of corroboration on these points were known or accessible to the author.

8. Cited in the first paragraph of UNRRA Resolution No. 7.

9. Almeida et al suggest that the lack of response in 1943 was due to the fact that UNRRA's activities were limited to war victims in liberated areas of countries that belonged to the United Nations; and in 1945-1946 the failure to respond was justified once again on the basis that India was not then "a priority anti-communist front zone." Cited in Almeida et al. (1975, p. 138).

Chapter 3

1. This point is noted in Benedict and Bauer (1960, pp. 34-35).

2. It will be recalled from chapter 2 that the United States had twice previously turned down similar Indian requests for assistance during World War II.

3. In fact, the Congress apparently attached some interesting political conditions on the aid. According to Lappé and Collins (1977, p. 328), the US government saw India's need for American food as an excellent source of leverage to force the lifting of the embargo which India had previously established on the export of monozite sands containing thorium. These sands were vital to the production of atomic weapons.

4. Garnett's role in the early years of the PL 480 program was indeed crucial. Not only was he primarily responsible for the wording of the original legislation, but he later became the first administrator of food aid as head of the USDA Foreign Agricultural Service from 1955 to 1958. Based on personal interview with Gwynn Garnett, Arlington, Virginia, 26 September 1977.

5. It is noteworthy that only one of these objectives involves *explicit* attention to hunger and malnutrition. In fact, of the five goals cited, three actually deal with benefits for the United States rather than for the recipients of food aid.

6. See "Benson is Pleased by Surplus Sales," *The New York Times*, 10 November (1955, p. 22).

7. Until 1972, the credit for the purchase of commodities under Title I could be repaid to the United States with local currency, that is, with currency which was not readily convertible into dollars. Because the money was good, therefore, only in the recipient country, it became known as "funny money" and the United States was often unable to conceive of sufficient uses for these vast sums.

8. Under the terms of the maintenance of value clause, US-owned local currencies generated from the sale of PL 480 commodities could be reloaned to the recipient government only if that government guaranteed that it would repay the loan at the *original* value of the currency (i.e., at the time of the loan) plus interest accrued.

9. The report found that "PL 480 had long since exhausted its function as a surplus disposal program. In order for it to function properly it must be regarded frankly as a foreign aid program, the test of value of which is not whether an equivalent amount of money accrues to the US in repayment . . . but whether our basic foreign policy objectives are in fact achieved." Cited in McClellan (1964, p. 39).

10. Thus, literally on the day before the measure was to be sent to Congress, Benson had inserted a special paragraph stating, in part,
Food can be a powerful instrument for all the free world in building a durable peace. We and the other surplus producing nations must do our best to make the fullest constructive use of our abundance of agricultural products to this end . . . I am setting steps in motion to explore anew with other agricultural surplus producing nations all practical means of utilizing the various agricultural surpluses of each in the interest of reinforcing peace and the well-being of friendly peoples throughout the world—in short, using *food for peace*. [emphasis added].
Cited in Benson (1962, p. 433).

11. Statement of John F. Kennedy, press release, 31 October 1960. [John F. Kennedy (1960, p. 1)].

12. Matters surrounding the establishment and operation of the White House Food for Peace Office are addressed in detail in chapter 8.

13. An example of the effect of this technological optimism is chronicled in Pariser et al. (1978, pp. 227–232).

14. Letter from Orville L. Freeman to David E. Bell, 26 June 1961 [Freeman (1961a)].

15. Toma (1967, p. 63) has suggested that 1961 marked the first, identifiable point at which the State Department offered any sort of public support for PL 480 as "an important factor in the foreign relations of the United States."

16. The issue of the US role in establishing the WFP is considered in chapter 9.

17. Memorandum from Orville L. Freeman for the President, 21 March 1967 [Freeman (1967a)].

18. Memorandum from Charles L. Shultze for the President, 16 November 1965 [Shultze (1965a)].

19. The change of the short title became an issue for two reasons: (1) a procedural problem, pointed out by Senator George McGovern, regarding the translation difficulties with the word "freedom" in such languages as Arabic, Urdu, and Portuguese; and (2) political resistance in the Conference Committee to changing the name of a well-established program.

20. Coming at the beginning of the massive US buildup in Southeast Asia, PL 480 inevitably became entangled in the raging political debate. But, as Orville Freeman told the Senate Agricultural Committee, "This language would set restrictions on other countries more severe than the restrictions we impose upon ourselves. We are able . . . to supply food and medicine to Cuba if we determine it is in our national interest to do so." Cited in Oudes (1966, p. 122).

21. Beginning in 1966, the Secretary had only to take into account domestic production capacity, domestic demand, and adequate carry-over stocks. Zachar (1977, p. 27) has suggested that this particular change was critical for two reasons: first, it demonstrated the "newly activist administration attitude on food aid"; moreover, it revealed that "America was running low on commodities it could call surplus."

22. In practice, self-help provisions have proven next to impossible to enforce and they have most often remained as vague, generalized promises within the food aid agreement. The self-help provision did, however provide the justification for the controversial, Johnson short-tether policy regarding food aid to India (see chapter 9).

23. Rothschild (1977b, p. 23) has suggested that it was this 1966 restriction on the allocation of PL 480 which precluded a timely US response to the critical food situation in Bangladesh in 1974.

24. Press release upon signing the Food for Freedom bill, 12 November 1966 (White House Central Files, Legislation GEN LE/PA 3, Box 147, File: EX LE/PC2, LBJ Library, Austin, Texas), p. 1.

25. Butz was reported to have stated at one point during the budget preparation process, "If Henry (Kissinger) wants the aid so much, let him (i.e., the State Department) pay for it." Whereupon, Butz submitted a zero line item figure for the PL 480 program. Cited in Destler (1978, p. 634).

26. Data adapted from Cochrane and Ryan (1976, p. 280), USDA (1977a, p. 8), and USDA (1975, p. 16).

27. Memorandum from Roy L. Ash, Director of OMB, for the President, 16 September 1974 [Ash (1974)]. For further details on the contexts of the Ash memorandum, see chapter 9.

28. In fact, during the remainder of the Ford administration, the predominant issue was related not to the allocation of the aid but to problems caused by the $300 per capita income limitation on Title I food aid agreements. Countries whose economies were suffering rapidly increasing inflation began to slip over the eligibility line, thereby qualifying only

for the limited assistance available under the 25 percent category of Title I. This problem was finally resolved by raising the per capita income criteria in 1977 to the IDA recommended level of $520.

29. This fact was underscored in an interview with a State Department official: "Food for Peace was based on an ethnocentric idea that we could pacify the world by food. Now our thinking is that feeding the world is an international problem, maybe one for the United Nations. The worst thing we could do for a country would be to put it on a permanent dole." Quoted in Rosenfeld (1974, p. 23).

30. For further details on the Food Aid Convention, see chapter 5.

31. Unlike the situation that prevails for certain other donors the United States pledge under the FAC represents food commodities that would have been given as aid in any event. Other donors, however, must divert commodities from commercial trade channels, and this aid is therefore additional to what otherwise would have been given.

32. On this point, see Rothschild (1977c) or Austin and Wallerstein (1978).

Chapter 4

1. Cereal food aid includes the items most consumed as the staple part of the diet of humans and animals, namely, food grains (mainly wheat), feed grains (including corn), and rice.

2. Significantly, this total for 1976–1977 was still short of the indicative World Food Council per year food aid target of 10 million metric tons.

3. Year-by-year Canadian food aid allocations (in millions of US dollars) in the period 1970–1977 are as follows. Bilateral food aid—$80.6; $71.8; $73.4; $75.1; $124.4; $119.3; $149.4; $139.1. Multilateral food aid—$18.6; $16.7; $14.4; $20.8; $18.1; $92.9; $87.3; $91.3. Sources: OECD (1974, p. 37) and data provided by the Canadian government.

4. Year-by-year Australian food aid allocations (in millions of US dollars) in the period 1969–1977 are as follows. Bilateral food aid—$14.3; $19.1; $11.0; $17.4; $18.7; $72.6; $57.9; $30.0; $20.1. Multilateral food aid (which was entirely through WFP in this period)—$0.8; $1.8; $1.5; $1.1; $0.9; $2.6; $3.1; $5.8; $4.1. Sources: OECD (1974, p. 29), OECD (1975, pp. 204–205), OECD (1976, pp. 216–217), and OECD (1978, pp. 200–203).

5. Year-by-year Japanese food aid allocations (in millions of US dollars) in the period 1969–1977 are as follows. Bilateral food aid loans and grants—$54.8 ($1.5 in grants); $99.5 ($23.3 in grants); $133.5 ($16.8 in grants); $23.9 ($1.4 in grants); $104.5 ($7.5 in grants); $71.2 ($9.9 in grants); $12.8 ($10.6 in grants); $4.7 (all in grants); 15.1 (all in grants). Multilateral food aid (which was entirely through WFP during this period)—$0.5; $0.5; $0.7; $0.7; $1.3; $2.8; $2.5; $3.5; $7.5. Sources: OECD (1974, p. 58), OECD (1975, pp. 204–205), and data provided by the Japanese government.

6. Japan has a unique and somewhat controversial arrangement within the FAC in that it is permitted to substitute rice and/or agricultural "material" (e.g., tractors) for wheat at a predetermined exchange value of $1.75 per bushel of wheat. See chapter 5 for further details.

7. Table 4.2 indicates that Japanese food aid represents only 1.1 percent of the nation's total ODA, the lowest among all OECD countries.

8. Year-by-year British food aid allocations (in millions of US dollars) in the period 1969–1977 are as follows. Bilateral food aid—$11.3; $10.6; $10.6; $1.0; none; $16.8; $20.1; $17.2; $14.3. Multilateral food aid—$6.1 (all through WFP); $5.3 (all through WFP); $6.9 (all through WFP); $1.7 (all through WFP); $14.3 ($1.5 through WFP, $12.8 through EEC); $32.4; $32.3; ($13.8 through WFP, $18.5 through EEC); $27.7 ($3.0 through WFP, $24.4 through EEC); $37.1 ($9.5 through WFP, $27.6 through EEC). Sources: OECD (1974, p. 66), OECD (1975, pp. 204–205), and data provided by the government of the United Kingdom.

9. Year-by-year French food aid allocations (in millions of US dollars) in the period 1969–1977 are as follows. Bilateral food aid (FAC)—$14.6; $13.7; $13.7; $5.2; $24.4; $21.2; $32.2; $20.8; $9.7. Multilateral food aid (FAC)—$6.1; $6.9; $5.2; $5.2; $21.0; $19.0; $51.0; $29.0; $42.0. Other EEC food aid (dairy produce, etc.)—none; $5.2; $15.0; $22.0; $14.6; $15.1; not available 1975–1977. Multilateral food aid (WFP)—$0.5; $0.5; $0.1; $0.1; $0.1; $0.1; $0.5; $0.4; $0.1. Emergency food aid (non-FAC)—none 1969–1972; $5.9; $5.2; not available 1975–1977. Sources: OECD (1974, p. 49), OECD (1975, pp. 204–205), OECD (1976, pp. 216–217), and OECD (1978, pp. 200–203).

10. Year-by-year West German food aid allocations (in millions of US dollars) in the period 1965–1977 are as follows. Bilateral food aid (FAC)—none for 1965–1968; $13.8 average per year for 1969–1971; $13.9; $31.7; not available; $47.9; $30.9; $43.4. Bilateral food aid (non-FAC)—$0.4 average per year for 1965–1968; $0.8 average per year for 1969–1971; $0.8; not available; $1.9; none; none. Multilateral food aid (German share of contributions to the WFP, which in 1973 was 29 percent of EEC contributions)—$2.7 average per year for 1965–1968; $3.4 average per year for 1969–1971; $8.8; $12.6; not available 1974–1977. Multilateral food aid (EEC)—none for 1965–1968; $18.3 average per year for 1969–1971; $21.0; $41.8; not available 1974–1977. Sources: OECD (1974, p. 51), OECD (1975, pp. 204–205), and data provided by the government of the Federal Republic of Germany.

11. Year-by-year Danish food aid allocations (in millions of US dollars) in the period 1970–1977 are as follows. Bilateral food aid—$0.9; $1.3; none; $2.6; $1.8; $2.6; $2.8; $8.1. Multilateral food aid—$5.8; $6.0; $8.0; $11.3; $19.1; $17.3; $19.7; $20.5. Sources: OECD (1974, p. 41), OECD (1975, pp. 204–205), and data provided by the government of Denmark.

12. Swedish ODA contributions for 1977 were 0.99 percent of GNP, making it the acknowledged leader among all other OECD countries. Source: OECD (1978, pp. 202–203).

13. Year-by-year Swedish food aid allocations (in millions of US dollars) in the period 1969–1977 are as follows. Bilateral food aid—none except for 1972 ($0.1) and 1974 ($14.9). Multilateral food aid (WFP)—$3.5; $3.6; $5.6; $4.1; $6.6; not available; $9.9; $9.9; $12.7. Multilateral food aid (FAC)—$4.5; $3.8; $3.8; $2.4; $4.6; not available; $6.5; $6.5; $5.6. Sources: OECD (1974, p. 80), OECD (1975, pp. 204–205), and data provided by the government of Sweden.

14. The International Emergency Reserve, operated by the WFP, amounted to approximately 100,000 metric tons in 1977, with Sweden's contribution to that total being 36,920 metric tons. Source: WFP (1977c, p. 2).

15. Year-by-year Norwegian food aid allocations (in millions of US dollars) in the period 1968–1977 are as follows. Bilateral food aid—$6.2; $2.2; $0.4; none; $0.2; $0.7; $0.3; $0.3; $2.0. Multilateral food aid (FAC)—none; $1.7; $1.1; $0.7; none; 1972–1977. Multilateral food aid (WFP)—$2.3; $2.4; $5.7; $4.1; $2.5; $3.7; $7.3; $6.2; $13.7; $17.5. Sources: OECD (1974, p. 64), OECD (1975, pp. 204–205), and OECD (1978, pp. 200–203).

16. Food aid allocations (in millions of US dollars) in 1977 of Switzerland, Italy, Belgium, and the Netherlands (respectively) are as follows. Bilateral food aid—$9.7; $21.9; $5.5; $19.1. Multilateral food aid—$6.8; $23.7; $17.9; $45.7. Source: OECD (1978, pp. 202–203).

17. For a complete description of the development of the EEC Common Agricultural Policy see CEC (1976, pp. 5–15). It should also be noted that, in October 1972, the six heads of state comprising the EEC, meeting in Paris, agreed on the responsibility of the community to help solve the world food problem. A new clause was added to Article 39 of the basic treaty reflecting this change.

18. In the case of cereal aid, food is given both by the EEC and by member states; in the case of dairy products, all aid is channeled through the commission. Personal communication, Thérèse Belot, Brussels, Belgium, 14 March 1978.

19. Personal interview, Adam Szarf, formerly Chief of the Division for Food Aid, Development Directorate, Commission of the European Community, EEC, Brussels, Belgium, 1 June 1977.

20. Personal interview, W. K. Davis, Acting Director, Resources Management Division, UN-FAO World Food Programme, Rome, Italy, 12 May 1977.

21. Personal interview, Adam Szarf.

22. Personal interview, Adam Szarf.

23. Year-by-year EEC food aid allocations (in millions of US dollars) in the period 1974–1978 are as follows. Bilateral food aid—$162.4; $206.1; $191.4; $130.0; $181.7. Multilateral food aid—$51.3; $72.4; $106.5; $78.6; $75.9. Data provided by the Directorate-General for Development, Commission of the European Communities, October 1978.

24. Personal interview, Livio Marinucci, Chief of Division, Agricultural Directorate, Commission of the European Communities, EEC, Brussels, Belgium, 1 June 1977.

25. See, for example, CEC (1974b).

26. Adapted from CEC (1974a, p. 6).

Chapter 5

1. The two proposed objectives of the WFB were these [Boyd-Orr (1964, p. 55)]:
1. To assist with credits, industrial products and technical assistance, countries asking for help to develop agriculture and ancillary industries.
2. To buy and hold in reserve storable food and other agricultural products, which, after a bumper harvest, or for other reasons, could not be marketed immediately; to release from this world reserve, the products in short supply after a bad harvest in any area; by these and other means to stabilize prices in the world market within given limits, and so provide a guaranteed world market for agricultural producers at a price fair to producers and consumers.

2. Truman's action was taken on the basis of State Department objections to the fact that the United States would not retain control over the use of its aid resources. In the face of the embryonic Cold War, food aid was becoming an increasingly important instrument of foreign policy.

3. The Food Council proposal later became the FAO Council, which is a smaller group of member countries that meets more frequently than the FAO Conference in order to deal with the ongoing affairs of the organization.

4. The Three Circles Plan was so-called because it proposed that donor countries might participate in multilateral action in one or more of three ways: (1) continuing commodity pledges; (2) continuing cash pledges; and (3) commodities or cash on an ad hoc basis.

5. UN General Assembly Resolution No. 1496 (XV), 27 October 1960.

6. The meaning of "resource diversion" here is situations in which proceeds from the sale of food are used not to benefit the most vulnerable target populations but for the political and economic benefit of the ruling elite.

7. By December 1976, this figure had climbed to 24 percent of total WFP aid or $680 million. Cited in Gongora and Shaw (1977, p. 15).

8. The food-for-work thrust of WFP development aid is indicative of the basic operating policies adopted by the program at the conclusion of its three-year "experimental" period in 1965. These so-called "criteria of preference," which were standards formulated to aid in project selection, include the following major guidelines:
1. Projects should be labor-intensive in character.
2. Projects should contribute to increasing local food production.
3. Projects should distribute food *qua* food, rather than selling the commodities for local currency (if at all possible).
4. Projects should be sufficiently large to make an impact in the recipient country.

5. Projects should be compatible and coordinated with other efforts already underway and should take account of other sources of aid available.
6. Projects should be capable of continuation with local resources after WFP aid is terminated.
Cited in Shaw (1970, p. 218).

9. The fact that 10 percent of WFP's resources are under the direct control of the FAO Director-General, rather than the WFP Executive Director, is the result of a fascinating power struggle between the head of the FAO at the time, B.R. Sen, and the leader of the WFP, A.H. Boerma. From its inception, Sen had wanted to make the WFP fully a part of the FAO. But because this proposal was not acceptable to a number of major donor countries, a deal was struck whereby 10 percent of the program's resources were to be under the direct control of the Director-General in order to appease Sen.

10. Boerma also noted that problems with WFP emergency aid were created by the fact that the WFP did not maintain its own shipping or storage facilities. (Comments of A.K. Boerma, Executive Director of the WFP, before the Third Session of the IGC, 13–17 May 1963, ICG/3/63/REP/2.)

11. During 1976, the WFP undertook twenty-six new emergency relief operations, meeting the acute food needs of about 6.9 million people in twenty-two countries; total cost amounted to $48 million of which $40 million was drawn from the WFP emergency allocation and the remaining $8 million from the International Emergency Food Reserve. (The International Emergency Food Reserve is a system of specially earmarked food aid resources set aside by certain donor countries for the express use of the WFP in the event of emergencies.) Natural disasters (e.g., earthquakes, floods, droughts, etc.) accounted for 47.6 percent of this total, while the remainder went to human-caused problems (e.g., refugees, war emergencies), of which almost 40 percent was for food aid to Lebanon, torn by civil war. (WFP (1977c, p. 1).

12. It should also be pointed out, in this regard, that donors do not wish the WFP to give program aid because that would place it indirect competition with the more political, bilateral aid efforts of the individual donors.

13. According to Dawson (1964, p. 127), the WFP does not accept project proposals of less than $200,000 because they simply are not cost effective.

14. In cases where a country is unable to meet its share of the costs of operating a food aid project either because of its financial (e.g., Yemen) or political (e.g., Lebanon during its civil war) situation, the WFP is currently precluded by its General Regulations from offering any direct assistance. In response to this dilemma, the IGC approved a policy of permitting the limited sale of WFP commodities to meet specific needs (such as inland transportation, etc.) in least developed countries.

15. For a detailed analysis of the prospects for multilateral administration of the program approach, see WFP (1966a, p. 14).

16. The WFP divides food aid projects involving sales into three distinct categories: (1) those where sales are inherent in the nature of the project in order to have a beneficial impact on the market itself (e.g., dairy development, price stabilization schemes; (2) those where sales are utilized only for groups insulated from the market (e.g., inland resettlement schemes); and (3) those where sales are made on the open market in order to provide seed capital for tools and other necessary infrastructure. It is really only this third category which has been of concern to the IGC–CFA even though, by current estimates, such sales have accounted for less than 2 percent of total WFP food aid commitments. See WFP (1969) and WFP (1977c).

17. In Afghanistan, for example, the WFP has conducted a multiproject effort at seven hundred work sites with seventy to eighty food distribution points.

18. WFP price stabilization schemes have been tried in Dahomey, Upper Volta, Ethiopia, Ghana, Turkey, and, most recently, in Ruanda.

19. The lack of food aid contributions from the Soviet Union is not particularly surprising in view of the fact that it is not even a member of FAO. The generally low level of Communist bloc participation is also discussed further in chapter 8.

20. UN General Assembly Resolution No. 2768 (XXVI), 18 November 1971.

21. It has been pointed out to the author, in this regard, that the 1973 Canadian resolution included only the least developed countries and did *not* account for the MSA countries "most seriously affected" by the economic crisis. Consequently, such key developing countries as India and Pakistan were entirely unaffected by the change in WFP allocation policy. (Personal interview, D. John Shaw, Evaluation Service, WFP, Rome, Italy, 12 May 1977.)

22. Any explanation for the limited size of their particular contributions would be highly speculative, but the reader's attention is directed to the food aid policies of these countries presented in chapter 4.

23. It is significant that the WFP has not been successful in obtaining substantial cash contributions from other OPEC nations. The Saudis have announced, however, a continuation of their substantial cash pledge through the 1979–1980 biennium.

24. The WFP has never been successful in obtaining the full 33 percent cash contribution from each donor recommended in its general policy. Most agricultural exporting donors find it more expedient to give commodities rather than cash. Consequently, the best cash percentage the program has ever obtained was 29 percent of total resources.

25. The "services" category represents pledges used primarily to cover the cost of ocean transportation.

26. At the May 1977 meetings of the CFA government council, major resistance to the $950 million figure was voiced by the United States and by certain other donors. These countries were concerned that the pledging target has been pushed up too rapidly, especially in light of the fact that the WFP encountered difficulty in meeting the $750 million target set of the 1977–1978 biennium. The fact remains, however, that the WFP is one of the few UN agencies whose resources have continued to expand substantially in recent years.

27. Contributions of the WFP under the 1967 and 1971 FACs and the 1974 extension (which includes contributions as of 31 December 1976) in terms of *commodity volume* (thousands of metric tons) and *cash value* (thousands of US dollars) respectively: 1968–1969 = 218.6 and $16,653; 1969–1970 = 228.8 and $16,887; 1970–1971 = 280.2 and $20,706; 1971–1975 (cumulative total for five-year period) = 730.7 and $46,984; 1975–1976 = 229.9 and $35,385. The grand total (including preliminary contributions for the 1976–1977 period) are 1,017.6 thousand metric tons and $114,847 million. Sources: WFP (1973a, p. 52) and WFP (1977a).

28. Noted in a personal interview, Anthony Dawson, Chief of the Evaluation Service, WFP, Rome, Italy, 12 May 1977.

29. It has also been suggested that the recipient countries cannot afford to alienate the donor countries too greatly within the CFA for fear that the donors will reduce the level of their contributions to the WFP in retaliation. (Personal interview, Thomas Robinson, Executive Director (a.i.), WFP, Manila, Philippines, 12 June 1977.)

30. The issue is addressed at length in chapter 11.

31. There is, however, a valid counterargument. Unlike the private voluntary agencies (e.g., CARE, CRS), which manage their food aid operations down to the individual recipient, the WFP purports to be more concerned with building a capacity in the recipient country to run such projects themselves and, thus, eventually to meet their own food needs.

32. Recently, the WFP Evaluation Service has been considering a new procedure which would integrate site visits with more in-depth project analyses conducted by academicians within the recipient country. (Personal interview, Anthony Dawson.)

33. In fact, it appears that many of the PVO criticisms which relate to the WFP are directed more at their principal aid supplier, the US AID, than at their competitor.

34. By letter of 11 July 1977, WFP Executive Director (a.i.) Thomas Robinson (1977, p. 1) informed the UNDP Resident Representatives and WFP Field Officers that "cases have occasionally occurred . . . in which governments have requested assistance from WFP for feeding programs previously assisted by organizations such as CARE, CRS and other voluntary agencies. While we cannot stop governments from making requests to WFP . . . we should tactfully avoid giving any encouragement to governments to the effect that WFP is ready to take over or replace assistance previously provided by another agency."

35. The United States has consistently been the largest donor of food aid to UNICEF, providing approximately 500,000 metric tons of commodities between 1959 and 1976. Other UNICEF donors have included Canada, the EEC, Belgium, Cuba, and Switzerland.

36. UNICEF declared its primary interest to be in assisting "long-term national programmes benefitting children" and in providing emergency relief only in immediate crisis situations when it was in a position to do so. WFP declared its primary interests to be in providing food aid in emergency situations, improving the nutritional status of vulnerable groups, and increasing LDC agricultural development and rural development. The two agencies agreed that "UNICEF will look to WFP as the first and main source of food supplies, with due regard to the special circumstances that may arise in emergencies." If, for some reason, the WFP was not in a position to supply the food needed, UNICEF would then make efforts to obtain the food from other sources.
Adapted from UNICEF/WFP Memorandum of Understanding, 14 May 1976, contained in UNICEF field memorandum from Charles A. Eggar to all Field Offices, EX PRO - 250, 21 June 1976.

37. For an excellent discussion of the Wheat Trade Convention and other issues surrounding the 1967 IGA, see Sanderson (1968, p. 591).

38. Minimum commodity contributions (in thousands of metric tons) by participants in 1967 Food Aid Convention: United States, 1,890 (42.0 percent of total); Canada, 495 (11.0 percent); Australia, 225 (5.0 percent); Argentina, 23 (0.5 percent); EEC, 1,035 (23.0 percent); United Kingdom, 225 (5.0 percent); Switzerland; 32 (0.7 percent); Sweden, 54 (1.2 percent); Denmark, 27 (0.6 percent); Norway, 14 (0.3 percent); Finland, 14 (0.3 percent); Japan, 225 (5.0 percent). Source: IWC (1967, p. 2).

39. All told, the WFP has received about 250,000 tons of pledged food aid under the FAC of 1971, or roughly 8 percent of total FAC commitments.

40. This provision has been used extensively by Japan, which has given rice and agricultural "material" (e.g., tractors and appropriate technology), and by Switzerland and the United Kingdom, which have given cash.

41. Subsequently enlarged to 35 percent for the 1971 FAC.

42. Denmark, the United Kingdom, and Ireland rejoined in 1973 upon entering the European Common Market.

43. Minimum commodity contributions (in thousands of metric tons) by participants in 1971 Food Aid Convention (contributions of Denmark and the United Kingdom are included under the EEC): United States, 1,890 (47.5 percent of total); Canada, 495 (12.4 percent); Australia, 225 (5.6 percent); Argentina, 23 (0.5 percent); EEC, 1,035 (26.0 percent); Switzerland, 32 (0.8 percent); Sweden, 35 (0.8 percent); Finland, 14 (0.3 percent); Japan, 225 (5.6 percent). Source: IWC (1971, p. 21).

44. Chapter 6 of the Bard book is devoted entirely to a consideration of the CSD, and it is recommended for further information.

45. But the Soviet Union *is* a member of the World Food Council, although the People's Republic of China is not.

46. UN General Assembly Resolution 3348 (XXIX), 15 December 1974.

47. The fact that the total volume of aid available, some two and a half years after this goal was established, was still almost 20 percent below the target figure (total world food aid provided in 1976 amounted to 8.3 million metric tons) was, in fact, of grave concern to the delegates at the Third Ministerial Session of the WFC, which met in Manila in June 1977.

48. On this matter, see, for example, Wallerstein and Austin (1978, pp. 191–201).

Chapter 6

1. This argument does not, of course, deny the questionable propriety of using food aid in such endeavors. But this matter will be discussed separately in chapter 10.

2. It is interesting to note that one of the specific instruments employed by the United States in order to transfer food aid to Yugoslavia (and Poland) was the private voluntary agency, CARE, Inc. According to Richard Reuter, former President of CARE, moving Title II food aid through the voluntary agency channel rather than directly government-to-government was considered more politically palatable for the United States. (Personal interview with Richard Reuter, Chicago, Illinois, 31 August 1977).

3. These conditions included (1) Yugoslavia was to remain independent of Soviet control, (2) Yugoslavia was not to participate in Communist efforts at world conquest, and (3) US national security interests would be served by providing such aid.

4. Secret memorandum from Dean Rusk for the President, 13 January 1962 [Rusk (1962, p. 6)].

5. Internal policy statement by President John F. Kennedy, undated [John F. Kennedy, 1961–1963)].

6. Statement by President John F. Kennedy in a press conference of 7 June 1963. Cited in Wszelaki (1964, p. 118).

7. Congressional opponents of aid to Eastern European countries were active in 1964 and again in 1966, attempting to introduce amendments to the basic PL 480 legislation prohibiting the sale or grant of food aid to Communist countries. In the 1966 debate, a rider was successfully attached to PL 480 that prevented agreements with any country trading or aiding Cuba or North Vietnam. Since Yugoslavia was then providing medical goods to North Vietnam and also maintaining trade with Cuba, Lyndon Johnson was compelled to terminate the food aid relationship late in 1966.

8. Memorandum from Dean Rusk for the President, 5 May 1961 [Rusk (1961)].

9. Report of Edward Mason on the economic survey mission to the UAR, 1–18 March 1962 [Mason (1962)].

10. William Gaud, former Director of US AID, has argued in an oral history interview [Gaud (1966)] that "as soon as Mr. Nasser got his three-year agreement under his belt, he embarked on a whole series of political activities which were inimical to us, and it was much harder for us to cut off the food to his people who needed it badly when we had an outstanding agreement than it would have been if we had had a series of short-term agreements."

11. State Department summary of letter from Ambassador John Badeau to the President, 3 January 1964, [Badeau (1964)].

12. Quoted from a cable by Ambassador Battle to the State Department, 24 December 1964, [Battle, (1964)].

13. Cable from the State Department to American Embassy, Cairo, 27 June 1965: National Security Files—UAR, File—UAR—Cables, Vol. III (11/64–6/65), LBJ Library, Austin, Texas.

14. Memorandum from Under Secretary John A. Schnittker to the Secretary of Agriculture et al., 21 November 1964 [Schnittker (1964, p. 1)].

15. See discussion in chapter 9.

16. Rothschild has calculated that somewhere near 80 percent of the funds generated by the sale of PL 480 commodities were "granted back" for strategic purposes in South Vietnam. Cited in Rothschild (1977, p. 44).

17. David Halberstam (1969) has suggested that this marked the critical watershed decision to commit significant US military forces in Southeast Asia in the vacuum left by the defeated French.

18. Top secret memorandum from U. Alexis Johnson to McGeorge Bundy, 28 November 1961 [U. Alexis Johnson, (1961, p. 2)].

19. According to Anderson (1970, p. 401), the $7 million food aid agreement signed in May 1965 was amended to $14 million in July, to $17 million in August, to $29 million in September, to $32 million in October, to $39 million in December, and to $40 million in January 1966. The final agreement during this period was signed in March 1966 for $52 million.

20. According to AID statistics, total food aid to Iceland for this period was $13.2 million [US AID (1976)].

21. AID statistics also indicate that food aid to Portugal totaled $104.9 million 1953–1976 [US AID (1976)].

22. Cable from Chester Bowles to the State Department [Bowles (1965)].

23. Secret memorandum from Robert Komer for the President, 16 September 1965 [Komer (1965)].

24. Quoted in an editorial appearing in the Calcutta daily newspaper, *Amrita Bazar Patrika*, 19 November 1965.

25. A detailed account of these events based on primary source documents is precluded by the currency of the matter and by the fact that most of the information is restricted by national security regulations.

26. See chapter 9.

27. Privileged communication to the author from an official of the Agency for International Development, Washington, DC, 14 December 1976.

28. For example, an editorial in *The Washington Post*, 29 November (1974, p. A30), noted that "the use of food for more overtly political purposes . . . has an undeniable merit of its own. There is no need to shy from it out of excessive fastidiousness. Food is not only a natural resource but a political one, and the proper policy question is not whether to use it but how." The editorial went on to applaud the diplomatic use of food aid in the Middle East: "The United States does not have to apologize for using every means at its disposal to facilitate its Middle East diplomacy. Indeed it is refreshing to find Food for Peace being used for once in the uplifting spirit of the program's name."

29. In fact, as George Kennan concluded in *Russia and the West* [quoted in Brynes (1966, p. 94)] concerning the offer of US food aid to the Soviet Union in the 1920s, "The idea of using food as a weapon . . . appealed to some of the most dangerous weaknesses in the American view of international affairs, and in my opinion had a pernicious influence on American thinking. . . . No use of troops was involved. . . . One simply defined one's conditions and left it to the other fellow to take it or leave it."

30. The Carter administration has also used the food aid instrument as a means of demonstrating its commitment to the human rights theme. The State Department apparently has established a "troublesome list" of countries that may be violating human rights, thereby making them ineligible for further aid. The list is said to have included South Korea, Indonesia, Bangladesh, and Zaire.

31. Reported in "Food as a Weapon—Will the U.S. Ever Use It?," *U.S. News and World Report*, 2 June (1975, pp. 50–51).

32. According to former Secretary Earl Butz, "They could have prevented that or made it very difficult had they wanted to. But they knew they had to come back in the American market for more grain. This was no time for them to rock the boat." Quoted from an interview with Earl L. Butz in "Food: Potent U.S. Weapon," *U.S. News and World Report*, 16 February (1976, 26–28).

33. See, for further elaboration, Shabecoff (1976, p. C1).

34. See, for example, Keohane (1966) or Wittkopf, (1973, pp. 868–888).

35. Quoted from text of a cablegram from Daniel P. Moynihan to the Secretary of State and all American Embassies and Legations, *The New York Times*, 28 January (1976, p. 8).

36. It is important, however, to underscore the fact that the majority of US food aid (about 70 percent) continues to move under Title I of PL 480. Since the basic Title I mechanism calls for the food to be allocated on concessional credit terms and then sold by recipient governments in order to generate needed local currency, it too responds only indirectly to the real food needs of recipient populations. This capital generating feature of Title I—which is so fundamentally attractive to most LDC governments—does not prevent the recipients from lumping all food aid together when such statistical manipulation suits their propaganda purposes, however.

Chapter 7

1. In fact Neil H. Jacoby, who undertook an assessment of US economic aid to Taiwan in cooperation with AID, found that food aid had been "overused." Jacoby (1966, pp. 208–209) concluded that "in 1965, Taiwan conformed more nearly to the case of a country in which PL 480 commodities could have counterdevelopmental effects. It was, on the whole, self-sufficient in food. It had a highly productive agriculture capable of further expansion. . . . In view of this, it is hard to avoid the conclusion that PL 480 imports of wheat and soybeans did seriously reduce domestic production of profitable crops."

2. Statement of Orville L. Freeman, former US Secretary of Agriculture, before Senate Foreign Relations Committee, cited in Lappé and Collins (1977, p. 333).

3. Adapted from an excellent series of articles which appeared in *The Washington Post* in March 1975. See in this regard, Morgan and Oberdorfer (1975, p. 1).

4. Memorandum from John A. Schnittker for the President, 23 October [Schnittker (1965, p. 2)].

5. The matter of conditions or "strings" on US food aid to India are taken up more fully in chapter 9.

6. For example, those on the Left attacked the Prime Minister during 1966 for abandoning the principles of socialism and neutralism by acceding to pressure from Washington. This criticism was considered serious enough for Mrs. Gandhi to go on All-India Radio on 24 April 1966 in order to respond to the charges, stating that the action had been necessitated by India's dire need and that the new policy would not reduce the country's economic or political flexibility or freedom. Cited in Weaver (1971, pp. 127–128).

7. "US Business vs. Malthus," *Forbes Reports*, 1 March (1966, pp. 24–25).

8. Morgan, (1975, p. 1) reports that "according to E.E. Hurst of Ralston-Purina's International Division, 'We wouldn't have put capital into that market without this arrangement. . . . What it did for us was provide for a capital influx at a time when the market was very small.' "

9. It is primarily on this basis, in fact, that many have argued for the explicit separation of the Title I and Title II features of the US food aid program, since one is purely humanitarian (and developmental) grant-type aid, while the other is characterized by the *sale* of food.

10. "PL 480 and the South Korea Lobby," *Korea Commentary*, (September–December (1977, p. 16).

11. Under the Allende Doctrine, the government stated that the compensation for nationalized properties would be reduced on the basis of an "excess profits" calculation. Subsequently, the US copper firms Anaconda and Kennecott were informed that *no* compensation would be offered since the book value of their properties was below the $774 million calculated as excess profits. In fact, these companies were actually informed by Chile that they *owed* that government money. Cited in Fagen (1975, pp. 307–308).

12. "Economic Assistance and Investment Security in Developing Nations," Statement by the President, 19 January 1972.

13. Excerpts from interview with Richard M. Nixon by David Frost, transcript from television program, 25 May 1977, *The New York Times*, 26 May (1977, p. 40).

14. Rothschild has suggested, however, that the unavailability of subsidized wheat for Bangladesh was actually due more to the fact that the United States attached a higher degree of political salience to aid for South Vietnam, Cambodia, South Korea, and Chile than for Bangladesh. Cited in Rothschild (1977a, p. 21).

15. For two differing views on this controversial subject, see Goulet and Hudson (1971) or Hayter (1971).

Chapter 8

1. Personal communication from Don Paarlberg, letter of 17 October 1977, p. 1.

2. Personal communication from Don Paarlberg, letter of 17 October 1977, p. 2.

3. Senate Concurrent Resolution No. 114.

4. UN General Assembly Resolution No. 1496 (XV), 27 October 1960.

5. Report from Meyer Feldman to Orville Freeman, 3 January 1961 [Feldman (1961, p. 12)].

6. For further elaboration on this appointment, see chapter 9.

7. Statement of George S. McGovern, 24 April 1964 [McGovern (1964b, p. 30)].

8. Statement of Deputy Assistant Secretary Richard N. Gardner before the Second Committee of the UN General Assembly, 22 January 1962 [Gardner (1962)].

9. As explained by the US delegate to the WFP pledging conference, "This multilateral program was only a small part of our food aid program, and . . . we felt that if it (the WFP) was to be truly multilateral 40 percent was a substantial share." Memorandum from Dorothy H. Jacobson to Orville L. Freeman [Jacobson (1965, p. 2)].

10. See chapter 5 for further details on the development of the resulting International Grains Arrangement of 1967.

11. Report to the President from the Secretary of Agriculture Orville L. Freeman, 30 November 1961 [Freeman, (1961b, p. 6)].

12. Memorandum from Orville L. Freeman for the President, 12 November 1963 [Freeman (1963, p. 5)].

13. John Schnittker, former Under Secretary of Agriculture and the chief US negotiator of the Grains Arrangement, suggests that the United States knew for many months that its demand for guaranteed access could not be met and that, if it persisted, the negotiations would fail. The strategy adopted, therefore, was to wait until the last possible opportunity before dropping the demand in order to open the way for further compromise by the other side. Oral History Interview with John A. Schnittker [Schnittker (1968)].

14. According to a USDA memorandum, India approached the following other governments for assistance during the crisis: Argentina, Austria, Australia, Belgium, Brazil, Burma, Canada, Denmark, France, West Germany, Greece, Iran, Italy, Japan, Netherlands, New Zealand, Norway, Pakistan, Sweden, Switzerland, Thailand, UAR, United Kingdom, USSR, and Yugoslavia. (From the files of the Office of the Secretary of Agriculture, 1966, Box 105, File: RG 16 Foreign Relations 2&3, NARC, Washington, DC).

15. Adapted from memoranda from Walt W. Rostow for the President, 6 January 1966 [Rostow (1966)] and from Orville L. Freeman for the President, 18 January 1966 [Freeman (1966b)].

16. Lyndon Johnson (1966) expressed his mounting irritation at this apparent donor intransigence in a letter to Pope Paul VI, confessing that "in all candor and confidence, we are disappointed that the other major producers of wheat have so far not contributed in proportion to the size of their stocks. Nor have those nations which enjoy substantial foreign exchange reserves done what we believe they could." (Letter from Lyndon B. Johnson to Pope Paul VI, 25 February 1966, (WHCF, Confidential IS 1 - IS 49, Box 58, File: IT 6 Food and Agriculture Organization (FAO), LBJ Library, Austin, Texas).

17. The World Bank India Aid Consortium was composed of those countries and international agencies providing development assistance to India. It had already been in existence for a number of years, but it had not been concerned previously with food aid.

18. Message from President Lyndon Johnson to the Congress, "The War on Hunger: Food for India," Department of State *Bulletin*, 20 February (1967, p. 297).

19. The member countries of the India Aid Consortium included Japan, Italy, France, the United Kingdom, the Netherlands, Belgium, West Germany, Austria, Canada, and, of course, the United States.

20. Statement by President Lyndon Johnson, 1 September 1967, Department of State *Bulletin*, 2 October (1967, p. 431).

21. Testimony of Edwin M. Martin before the House Committee on Foreign Affairs, 26 November 1974, US Congress HCFR (1974, p. 25).

22. This apparent dilemma was demonstrated quite clearly in an internal State Department position paper prepared in 1974 for the World Food Conference. According to Morgan (1974, p. A7) the paper reportedly *opposed* a wider US commitment to the WFP on the grounds that "we have not been able to influence appreciably the policies and procedures of the WFP or the distribution of aid to particular destinations. There would appear to be no advantage to the U.S. favoring a greater role and more resources for the WFP."

23. For an expanded treatment of this subject, see chapter 11.

Chapter 9

1. The members of Senator Kennedy's Food for Peace Committee included Murray Lincoln, then President of CARE; Senator Hubert H. Humphrey; Donald Murphy; George Forell; William Benton; and Mary Lasker.

2. Press release by "Farmers for Kennedy–Johnson," 31 October 1960 (Myer Feldman Papers, Box 9, File: Food for Peace Program (10/60–1/61), JFK Library, Boston, Massachusetts).

3. The committee also recommended that the surplus disposal philosophy of the program be ended and that US agricultural output should be reoriented to meet the specific food consumption needs of the developing world.

4. Schlesinger (1965, p. 556), for example, recalls that he wrote to Richard Neustadt, Senior Presidential Adviser, pointing out the need to maintain a separate identity for the Food for Peace Program and the Peace Corps: "The two programs have more political potential than anything else in the foreign aid picture. It seems to me that there is strong argument for holding them close to the President. Would F.D.R. ever ever have let such programs out of his immediate grasp?"

5. Oral history interview with George S. McGovern, 24 April 1964 (Oral History Collection, JFK Library, Boston, Massachusetts).

6. Personal interview with Herbert Waters, 18 October 1977, Washington, DC.

7. As emphasized in a memorandum for the President by Orville Freeman, dated 31 May 1962 [Freeman (1962, p. 2)],

Public understanding and support for the "Food for Peace" program is thus the major function of a White House "Food for Peace" office. . . . The Food for Peace office could mobilize public opinion . . . as part of an overall foreign aid program. . . . This great motivation (i.e., food aid) should be utilized as a take-off point to develop understanding of and support for much more complex and less understood reasons for a foreign assistance program that includes economic, social and political development of the emerging nations.

8. Letters of invitation, 9 May 1961 (Food for Peace Council, Box 197, File: FG 609 American Food for Peace Council (1/20/61–5/20/61), JFK Library, Boston, Massachusetts).

9. Notes of a meeting on the Food for Peace Program, 26 April 1962 (Myer Feldman Papers, Box 9, File: FFP Program (2/62–1/63), JFK Library, Boston, Massachusetts).

10. Remarks of the President at the opening ceremony of the World Food Congress, 4 June 1963 [John F. Kennedy (1963)].

11. Personal interview with Herbert Waters, 18 October 1977, Washington, DC.

12. Anecdote from personal interview with Dorothy Jacobsen, former Assistant Secretary of Agriculture, 18 September 1977, Washington, DC.

13. Memorandum from Orville L. Freeman for the President, 2 July 1965 [Freeman, (1965a)].

14. These included expanding importation of fertilizer, additional public works, increased buffer stocks, and other measures related to seed and pesticide availability and agricultural price incentives.

15. Memorandum from Martin E. Abel to Nathan M. Koffsky, Economic Research Service, USDA, 30 August 1965 [Abel (1965)].

16. According to Orville Freeman's own recollection of these events in an interview 21 July 1969 [Freeman (1969, p. 9)], "We had them over a barrel and we squeezed them, but he didn't object very much to being squeezed. And I found this true with other ministers of agriculture who in the last analysis had had such a difficult time getting any resources from the Finance Minister that they welcomed the fact that there was pressure from outside to help them to get some of the resources they needed. . . . He had a pretty wide mandate [i.e., Subramaniam], and he seemed fairly confident that if this [i.e., the US demands] did not leak that he could get it through the Cabinet and get it through the Parliament."

17. As reported by Freeman in a memorandum dated 14 December 1965 [Freeman (1965b)], Johnson, in fact, directed that "we should be prepared to use Army trucks if necessary, to fly it in if that's required and that if we needed submarines to blast something out of the way we should do that, that we should make it clear that once we made it available we are going to see to it that it gets there."

18. Special message to the Congress on the Indian food emergency, 30 March 1966 (White House Press Release, p. 4).

19. Memorandum from Charles L. Shultze for the President, 31 December 1965, [Shultze, (1965b)].

20. Rostow (1972, p. 423) provides an indication of the depth of Presidential involvement: "I helped him follow the fall of rain in India and Pakistan as closely as he did along the Pedernales. He knew the dates of shipment from American ports of grain required for timely arrival in Calcutta and the state of Indian grain stocks. He personally guided the negotiation of each tranche of food aid."

21. India's active involvement in the Vietnam issue had a long history. India had served as Chairman of the International Commission for Supervision and Control in Vietnam since 1955, and, in this capacity, it had periodically adopted positions inimical to US policy. For example, Weaver reports that, in July 1965, India supported inclusion of the National Liberation Front in a Geneva-type peace conference, a notion which the United States categorically refused to accept. Noted in Weaver (1971, pp. 108–109).

22. The congressional team was composed of Senators Jacob Miller (Iowa) and Gale McGee (Wyoming) and Representative Robert Dole (Kansas) and Robert Poage (Texas).

23. Report of the USDA Study Mission, 27 November 1966 (National Security Files—India, Box 4, File: India's Food Problem—Vol. II, LBJ Library, Austin, Texas).

24. Memorandum from Orville L. Freeman for the President, 28 November 1966 [Freeman (1966d)].

25. Address to the UN General Assembly by Secretary of State Henry Kissinger, 24 September 1973, cited in Department of State *Bulletin*, 15 October (1973, p. 472).

26. In this case, Kissinger conceived a $4 billion fund of concessional aid for the MSA countries.

27. Address of Secretary of State Henry A. Kissinger to the Special Session of the UN General Assembly, 15 April 1974.

28. "In June and July, State Department economists were saying that Agriculture [i.e., the USDA] greatly overestimated the inflationary effects of increasing food aid. Agriculture said that while the budgeted PL 480 program of about $900 million was not inflationary, anything above that figure would be. State wanted to increase the programmed total to at least $1.8 billion. After numerous studies, agreement was reached that an increase on the order of $500 million would lift the price of a loaf of bread by no more than about one cent" [Gelb and Lake (1974–1975, p. 182)].

29. Memorandum from Roy L. Ash for the President, 16 September 1974 [Ash (1974 p.2)].

30. *Option I*—called for budget outlays to be held constant at $742 million (recommended by OMB, CIEP, and USDA). Ash noted that "it is the only option consistent with your fiscal policy, and contributes to the credibility of fiscal discipline in other government programs and to a broad anti-inflationary policy. It meets fully requirements in Indochina, and provides adequately for humanitarian programs and the Middle East."
Option II—called for a budget outlay of $978 million, or $236 million over budget (recommended by Treasury). Ash suggested that this option "provides fully for requirements in Indochina and the Middle East, and distributes the balance of available funds among traditional political recipients, countries in the Asian subcontinent and humanitarian programs so that all requirements are met in a manner than [sic] can be characterized as minimal to adequate."
Option III—called for a budgeted outlay of $1.28 billion, or $533 million over budget (recommended by DoS, AID, and NSC). According to Ash, "It fully meets all major security, political, and humanitarian objectives, short of making a major gesture of leadership at the World Food Conference or responding massively to severe food shortages in India. It also permits modest programs for a number of small countries of political importance, and an adequate reserve to deal with unforeseen developments." But Ash also cautioned that "a program of this size would, however, seriously undermine your fiscal policy risks damaging chances of cooperation from Congress in reducing FY 1975 outlays elsewhere." See Ash (1974, pp. 4–5).

31. This occurred within the context of the newly created Economic Policy Board, established by President Ford on 30 September 1974 to advise him on the "formulation, coordination, and implementation of all economic policy, foreign and domestic" and "to serve as the focal point for all economic policy decision making" (Executive Order No. 11808); as part of the Board's supporting staff, a so-called Food Deputies Group was also established to deal specifically with food-related issues.

Chapter 11

1. These figures, too, must be qualified further. Because multilateral food aid contributions are pledged in cash rather than by volume, an increased capital level may not necessarily indicate an increase in actual food resources. In fact, as a result of inflation and other market factors, there may well be a net decline in food aid in real terms.

2. I am indebted to Professor Henry Nau for providing valuable supplementary analysis on this point.

3. A basic assumption in this discussion is that any future expansion of the multilateral food aid channel will be modeled generally along the same basic conceptual lines as the present World Food Programme. While there is no fundamental reason why this paradigm must necessarily be employed, it has been posited here for the purpose of effective comparison.

4. Although the United States is only one of many donors contributing to multilateral food aid programs, it remains the largest overall provider of food assistance and has thus been chosen as the model for considering those issues pertinent to the donor perspective.

5. Political "abuses" are defined here as the diversion of food aid resources for the specific political benefit of the donor, where such uses are perceived as improper either by food aid recipients or by other donors.

6. This "psychological effect" is manifested in the form of latent hostility of the aid recipient toward the aid donor arising from the need to rely on external sources of support.

7. The United States, for example, has indicated that it does not wish its WFP contributions utilized for food assistance to Cuba, the People's Republic of Vietnam, or Kampuchea.

8. The Group of 77, now numbering well in excess of one hundred countries, is an unofficial caucus of developing countries within the United Nations. It functions as a consensus-building mechanism for joint action on political and economic matters of particular concern to its membership.

9. Recipient populations have still been introduced through the WFP to new foods (e.g., CSM and WSB), however, which are only available commercially through a single source—the United States.

10. In the US context, this vulnerability was demonstrated by the shift to a "free market" agricultural policy under Secretary of Agriculture Earl L. Butz. In 1973, Title II food aid allocations were curtailed suddenly and without warning. The result was serious hardship for recipient populations dependent on this source of food supply.

11. Recipients also tend to find the composition of the multilateral food aid basket (i.e., the specific mix of commodities available as food aid) more varied than that of any single bilateral donor. While it cannot be said with certainty that the particular mix will necessarily be better or more appropriate to the food habits and needs of the recipient population, there is a greater likelihood that commodities will not simply be dumped on the recipient because the donor happens to have them in surplus.

12. Through 1972, the beneficiaries of WFP food assistance by region were distributed as follows: Africa (south of Sahara), 4.3 million; Asia and the Pacific, 13.8 million; Europe (southern), 0.3 million; Latin America and the Caribbean, 3.8 million; North Africa and the Near East, 4.6 million; grand total, 26.9 million participants. Source: WFP (1973a, p. 60).

13. This raised at one point an awkward situation for the WFP. As a result of a large $50 million cash contribution from Saudi Arabia, and the continued unwillingness of the United States to contribute a larger share of cash resources, the Saudi contribution was, in effect, used by the WFP to finance the costs of shipping the American wheat.

14. Total resources available to the WFP for the 1976–1977 biennial pledging period were roughly $750 million. This compared with a total budget for the US PL 480 program for the same period of approximately $1.3 billion.

15. See, for example, Smethurst (1969, pp. 205–219) and Wightman (1968).

16. While the United States has sometimes extracted political concessions from aid recipients in return for PL 480 assistance, it has been pointed out to the author that this strategy works both ways. That is, recipients can also apply pressure on donors to extract aid as the price of a favorable vote in the United Nations or a desired change in policy.

17. The three "latent roles" suggested by Krause and Nye (1975, p. 337) are (1) *arena*—the political process by which agendas are set, etc., (2) *instrument*—use of the international organization to bring pressure on other governments or transnational actors (this is the role of the most salience regarding multilateral food aid), (3) *actor* or *catalyst*—use of the international organization as a focal point for coalition building.

Selected Bibliography

A broad spectrum of literature was reviewed during the conduct of this research. Thus, in order to assist the reader, this list of selected references is subdivided into seven topical areas: (1) US foreign aid; (2) aid in the multilateral arena; (3) US food and agriculture policy; (4) theory and practice of food aid; (5) US food aid programs and policies; (6) non-US food aid programs and policies; and (7) selected public documents.

US Foreign Aid

Aspen Institute for Humanistic Studies. *The Planetary Bargain: Proposals for a New International Economic Order to Meet Human Needs.* Report of an International Workshop Convened in Aspen, Colorado. 7 July–1 August 1975.

Baldwin, David A. *Foreign Aid and American Foreign Policy.* New York: Frederic A. Praeger, 1966.

Banfield, Edward C. *American Foreign Aid Doctrines.* Washington: American Enterprise Institute for Public Policy Research, January 1963.

Center for International Policy. *Human Rights and the U.S. Foreign Assistance Program—Fiscal Year 1978. Part 1—Latin America.* Washington: Center for International Policy, 1977.

Feis, Herbert. *Foreign Aid and Foreign Policy.* New York: St. Martin's Press, 1964.

Frank, Charles R., and Mary, Baird. "Foreign Aid: Its Speckled Past and Future Prospects." In *World Politics and International Economics.* C. Fred Bergsten and Lawrence B. Krause, eds. Washington: The Brookings Institution, 1975.

Fulbright, J. William. *The Arrogance of Power.* New York: Random House, 1966.

Fulbright, J. William. "Foreign Aid? Yes, But With a New Approach." *The New York Times Magazine* Sunday, 21 March 1965.

Hart, Judith. *Aid and Liberation—A Socialist Study of Aid Policies.* London: Victor Gollancz, Ltd., 1973.

Hayter, Teresa. *Aid as Imperialism.* Baltimore: Penguin Books, 1971.

Hero, Alfred O. "Foreign Aid and the American Public." *Public Policy* 14 (1965), 72–116.

Huntington, Samuel P. "Foreign Aid: For What and For Whom?" In *Development Today.* Robert E. Hunter and John E. Reilly, eds. New York: Frederick A. Praeger, 1972, 21–60.

Jacoby, Neil H. *U.S. Aid to Taiwan—A Study of Foreign Aid, Self-Help, and Development.* New York: Frederick A. Praeger, 1966.

Lowenthal, Abraham. "Foreign Aid As a Political Instrument: The Case of the Dominican Republic." *Public Policy* 14 (1965), 140–159.

Mason, Edward S. *Foreign Aid and Foreign Policy.* New York: Published for the Council on Foreign Relations by Harper and Row, 1964.

Millikan, Max F. *American Foreign Aid: Strategy for the 1970s.* New York: American Foreign Policy Association, August 1969.

Montgomery, John D. *Foreign Aid in International Politics,* Englewood Cliffs, New Jersey: Prentice-Hall, 1967.

Morgenthau, Hans. "A Political Theory of Foreign Aid." *APSR* 57 (1962), 301–309.

Morrell, James R. "Foreign Aid: Evading the Control of Congress." *International Policy Report.* Vol. 3, No. 1. Washington: Center for International Policy, January 1977.

Nelson, Joan M. *Aid, Influence, and Foreign Policy.* New York: The Macmillian Company, 1968.

O'Leary, Michael K. *The Politics of American Foreign Aid.* New York: Atherton Press, 1967.

Packenham, Robert A. *Liberal America and the Third World.* Princeton: Princeton University Press, 1973.

Pearson, Lester B., et al. *Partners in Development—Report of the Commission on International Development.* New York: Praeger Publishers, 1969.

Taskforce on International Development. *U.S. Foreign Assistance in the 1970s: A New Approach.* Report to the President, 4 March 1970.

Thorp, Willard L. *The Reality of Foreign Aid.* New York: Praeger Publishers for the Council on Foreign Relations, 1971.

Weissman, Steve, and Members of Pacific Studies Center and the North American Congress on Latin America. *The Trojan Horse—A Radical Look at Foreign Aid.* San Francisco: Ramparts Press, 1974.

Westwood, Andrew F. *Foreign Aid in a Foreign Policy Framework.* Brookings Staff Paper. Washington: The Brookings Institution, April 1966.

White, John. *The Politics of Foreign Aid.* New York: St. Martin's Press, 1974.

Aid in the Multilateral Arena

Asher, Robert E. "Multilateral versus Bilateral Aid: An Old Controversy Revisited." *International Organization* 16 (1962), 697–719.

Auerbach, Kenneth D. "The Distribution of Multilateral Assistance: Who Gets What and Why." Ph.D. Dissertation, Indiana State University, May 1974.

Balough, T. "Multilateral versus Bilateral Aid." In *Foreign Aid.* Jagdish Bhagwati and Richard S. Eckaus, eds. Baltimore: Penguin Books, 1970, pp. 203–222.

Cleveland, Harlan. "The U.S. versus the U.N.?" *The New York Times Magazine* Sunday, 4 May 1975, 78.

Cleveland, Harlan. "The Management of Multilateralism." In *Report of the Commission on the Organization of the Government for the Conduct of Foreign Policy, Vol. 1, Appendix C: Multilateral Diplomacy.* Washington: US GPO, 1974, pp. 262–271.

Gelb, Leslie H. "U.S. Linking Aid to Votes at U.N." *New York Times* 9 January 1976.

Keohane, Robert O. "The Study of Political Influence in the General Assembly." In *International Organization: Politics and Process.* Leland M. Goodrich and David A. Kay, eds. Madison, Wisconsin: University of Wisconsin Press, 1973.

Krause, Lawrence B., and Joseph S. Nye, Jr. "Reflections on the economics and politics of international organizations." In *World Politics and International Economics.* Lawrence B. Krause and Joseph S. Nye, Jr., eds. Washington: The Brookings Institution, 1975, pp. 322–342.

McVitty, Marion H. "Should U.S. Aid be Channelled Through the UN?" *Current History* (August 1966), 102, 107–116.

Maynes, Charles W. "A U.N. Policy of the Next Administration." *Foreign Affairs* 54, 4 (July 1976), 804–819.

Moynihan, Daniel P. "The United States in Opposition." *Commentary* 59, 3 (March 1975), 31–44.

Raichur, Statish, and Craig Liske, eds. *The Politics of Aid, Trade and Investment.* New York: John Wiley and Sons, 1976.

Rosenstein-Rodan, Paul. "The Consortia Technique." In *Foreign Aid.* Jagdish Bhagwati and Richard S. Eckaus, eds. Baltimore: Penguin Books, 1970, pp. 223–231.

Weiss, Thomas G. and Robert S. Jordan. "Bureaucratic Politics and the World Food Conference: The International Policy Process." *World Politics* 28, 3 (April, 1976), 422–239.

Wittkopf, Eugene. "Foreign Aid and United Nations Votes: A Comparative Study." *APSR* 67 (September 1973) 868–888.

Yost, Charles W. "Conduct of Multilateral Diplomacy by the U.S. Government." In *Report of the Commission on the Organization of the Government for the Conduct of Foreign Policy, Vol. 1, Appendix C: Multilateral Diplomacy.* Washington: US GPO, 1974, 283–295.

US Food and Agriculture Policy

Brown, Lester R. *The Politics and Responsibility of the North American Breadbasket.* Worldwatch Paper No. 2. Washington: October 1975.

Butz, Earl L. "Agripower." *Saturday Evening Post* 248 (May–June 1976), 37, 88–89, 120.

Cochrane, Willard W. *Feast or Famine: The Uncertain World of Food and Agriculture and Its Policy Implications for the U.S.* Report No. 136. Washington: The National Planning Association, February 1974.

Cochrane, Willard W. and Mary E. Ryan. *American Farm Policy, 1948–1973.* Minneapolis: University of Minnesota Press, 1976.

Destler, I.M. "United States Food Policy 1972–1976: Reconciling Domestic and International Objectives." *International Organization* 32:3 (Summer 1978), 617–654.

Gelb, Leslie H. and Anthony Lake. "Less Food, More Politics." *Foreign Policy,* 17 (Winter 1974–75), 176–189.

Green, Stephen Keith. *United States Agricultural Policy and World Food Production.* Discussion Paper No. 3, C/75–12. MIT International Nutrition Program, April 1975.

Hopkins, Raymond F. "How to Make Food Work." *Foreign Policy* 27 (Summer 1977), 89–107.

Hopkins, Raymond F. "Lessons of Food Diplomacy." Unpublished Paper, April 1977.

Hopkins, Raymond F., and Donald Puchala, eds. "The Global Political Economy of Food." *International Organization* 32:3 (Summer 1978), 581–616.

Lancaster, Carol. "Can Food Resources be Used Beneficially for Non-Food Diplomatic Purposes?" Unpublished Paper, April 1977.

Lappé, Francis Moore, and Joseph Collins. *Food First—Beyond the Myth of Scarcity.* Boston: Houghton Mifflin Company, 1977.

Morgan, Dan. "Our Newest Weapon: Food—American Agripower and the Future of a Hungry World. *Saturday Review,* 13 November 1976, 7–12.

North American Congress on Latin America. *U.S. Grain Arsenal.* 9:7, (October 1975).

Paarlberg, Don. *American Farm Policy—A Case Study of Centralized Decison-Making.* New York: John Wiley and Sons, 1964.

Peterson, Trudy H. "The Agricultural Trade Policy of the Eisenhower Administration." Ph.D. Dissertation, University of Iowa, 1975.

Rosenfeld, Stephen S. "The Politics of Food." *Foreign Policy* (Spring 1974). 17–29.

Rothschild, Emma. "Food Politics." *Foreign Affairs 54* (January 1976), 285–307.

Sanderson, Fred H. "The International Grains Arrangement." Department of State *Bulletin* 6 May 1968, 590–594.

Schnittker, John A. "Grain Reserves—Now." *Foreign Policy* 20 (Fall 1975), 225–231.

Tresize, Philip H. *Rebuilding Grain Reserves: Toward an International System.* Washington: The Brookings Institution, 1976.

"U.S. Food Power - Ultimate Weapon in World Politics." *Business Week,* 15 December 1975, 54–58, 60.

Wallensteen, Peter. "Scarce Goods as Political Weapons: The Case of Food." *Journal of Peace Research.* 4 (1976), 277–298.

Warley, T. K. "Agriculture in International Economic Relations." New York: The Agricultural Development Council, Inc., 29 (February 1977).

Theory and Practice of Food Aid

Allen, G.R., and R.G. Smethurst. *The Impact of Food Aid on Donor and Other Food Exporting Countries.* World Food Program Studies No. 2. Rome: FAO, 1965.

Almeida, Silvio, et al. "Analysis of Traditional Strategies to Combat World Hunger and Their Results." *International Journal of Health Services* 5 (1975), 121–141.

Austin, James E., and Mitchel B. Wallerstein. "Reformulating U.S. Food Aid Policy for Development." *World Development* 7 (June 1979), 635–646.

Bard, Robert L. *Food Aid and International Agricultural Trade.* Lexington, Massachusetts: D.C. Heath and Company, 1972.

Chakravarty, S., and P.N. Rosenstein-Rodan. *The Linking of Food Aid with Other Aid.* World Food Programme Studies No. 3. Rome: FAO, 1965.

Dessau, Jan. *The Role of Multilateral Food Aid Programs.* World Food Programme Studies NO. 5. Rome: FAO, 1965.

Field, John O., and Mitchel B. Wallerstein. "Beyond Humanitarianism: A Developmental Perspective on American Food Aid." In *Food Policy.* Peter G. Brown and Henry Shue, eds. New York: The Free Press, 1977, pp. 234–258.

FitzGerald, D.A. *Operational and Administrative Problems of Food Aid.* World Food Programme Studies No. 4. Rome: FAO, 1965.

Food and Agriculture Organization. *Development Through Food.* Basic Study No. 2. Rome: FAO, 1962.

Isenman, Paul J., and H.W. Singer. *Food Aid: Disincentive Effects and Their Policy Implications.* AID Discussion Paper No. 31. Washington: U.S. A.I.D., October 1975.

Maxwell, J.J., and H.W. Singer. "Food Aid to Developing Countries: A Survey." *World Development* 7 (March 1979), 225–247.

Organization for Economic Cooperation and Development. *Food Aid: Its Role in Economic Development.* Paris: OECD, 1962.

Organization for Economic Cooperation and Development. *Food Aid.* Paris: OECD, 1974.

Rogers, Keith D. "Theory and Application of Food Aid in Economic Development." Ph.D. Dissertation, Iowa State University, 1971.

Rogers, Keith D., Leo V. Mayer, and Earl O. Heady. *Utilization of U.S. Farm Surpluses for Welfare and Development Programs at Home and Abroad.* CARD Report No. 41, Center for Agricultural and Rural Development. Ames, Iowa: Iowa State University, June 1972.

Schneider, Hartmut. *Food Aid for Development.* Paris: Development Centre of OECD, 1978.

Shuman, Charles B. "Food Aid and the Free Market." In: *Food Policy.* Peter G. Brown and Henry Shue, eds. New York: The Free Press, 1977, pp. 145–163.

Srivastava, Uma, Earl O. Heady, Keith D. Rogers, and Leo Mayer. *Food Aid and International Economic Growth.* Ames, Iowa: The Iowa State University Press, 1975.

Stephens, Christopher. *Food Aid in the Developing World.* New York: St. Martin's Press, 1979.

Wightman, David R. "Food Aid and Economic Development." In *International Conciliation,* No. 567. New York: Carnegie Endowment for International Peace, March 1968.

Food Aid Policies and Programs

Anderson, William D. "The Intersection of Foreign and Domestic Policy: The Examples in Public Law 480." Ph.D. Dissertation, University of Illinois, 1970.

Balz, Daniel J. "Agriculture Report/Food for Peace Program Comes under Congressional Scrutiny." *National Journal Reports,* 7 June 1975, 857–860.

Balz, Daniel J. "Agriculture Report/Politics of Food aid Presents U.S. with Policy Dilemma." *National Journal Report* 23 November 1974, 1760–1766.

Benedict, Murray, and Elizabeth Bauer. *Farm Surpluses: U.S. Burden or World Asset?* Berkeley: University of California Press, 1960.

Bjorkman, James Warner. "Public Law 480 and the Policies of Self-Help and Short-Tether: Indo–American Relations, 1965–68." Prepared as part of the study *Coordination of Complexity in South Asia* for the Commission on the Organization of the Government for the Conduct of Foreign Policy, 30 September 1974.

Buckley, Bren LuRee. "Public Law 480: A Study of Shifting Priorities." B.A. Thesis, Radcliffe College, March 1975.

Mcgovern, George S. *War Against Want—America's Food for Peace Program.* New York: Walker and Company, 1964.

McHenry, Donald F., and Kai Bird. "Food Bungle in Bangladesh." *Foreign Policy* 27 (Summer 1977), 72–88.

McClellan, David S. "Public Law 480: The Metamorphosis of a Law." New York: Eagleton Institute Case Studies, September 1964.

Oudes, Bruce. "Food for Freedom: The Paradox of Foreign Aid." *Nation* 203 (9 August 1966), 120–124.

Rothschild, Emma. "Is it time to end Food for Peace?" *The New York Times Magazine* Sunday, 13 March 1977, 15, 43–48.

Saylor, Thomas R. "A New Legislative Mandate for American Food Aid." In *Food Policy—The Responsibility of the United States for the Life and Death Choices.* Peter G. Brown and Henry Shue, eds. New York: The Free Press, 1977.

Shaughnessy, Daniel E. "The Political Uses of Food Aid: Are Criteria Necessary?" In *Food Policy–The Responsibility of the United States for the Life and Death Choices.* Peter G. Brown and Henry Shue, eds. New York: The Free Press, 1977, pp. 94–102.

Stanley, Robert G. *Food for Peace—Hope and Reality of U.S. Food Aid.* New York: Gordon and Breach, 1973.

Surface, Frank M., and Raymond L. Bland. *American Food Aid in the World War and Reconstruction Period.* Stanford, California: Stanford University Press, 1931.

Toma, Peter A. *The Politics of Food for Peace.* Tucson, Arizona: The University of Arizona Press, 1967.

Weaver, David R. "P.L. 480, India, and the Objectives of U.S. Foreign Aid 1954–1966." Ph.D. Dissertation, University of Cincinnati, 1971.

Zachar, George. "A Political History of Food for Peace." Document No. 246. Ann Arbor, Michigan: Nutrition Planning Information Service, 1978.

Non-US Food Aid Programs and Policies

Dawson, Anthony. "Food Development: The World Food Programme." *International Labour Review* 90, (1964), 99–129.

European Economic Community. *The European Community and the developing countries* AND *Memorandum on EEC Food Aid Policies.* Brussels: Commission of the European Communities, 1974.

Little, I.M.D., and J.M. Clifford. *International Aid.* London: George Allen and Unwin, Ltd., 1965.

Mettrick, Hal. *Food Aid and Britain.* London: The Overseas Development Institute, Ltd., 1969.

Shaw, D. John. "The Mechanism and Distribution of Food Aid—Multilateral Food Aid for Economic and Social Development." *Journal of World Trade Law* (1970) 207–238.

Smethurst, Richard G. "Direct Commodity Aid: A Multilateral Experiment." *The Journal of Development Studies* 5,3 (April 1969), 205–219.

Wickwar, Hardy. "Distribution is Social: Some Aspects of International Food Programs." *Social Service Review* 38, (March 1964), 51–56.

Selected Public Documents

Central Intelligence Agency. "Potential Implications of Trends in World Population, Food Production and Climate." OPR–401. Washington: US GPO, August 1974.

Congressional Budget Office. *Food and Agriculture Policy Options—Budget Issue Paper.* Washington: US GPO, 1977.

Congressional Budget Office. *Bilateral Development Assistance: Background and Options—Budget Issue Paper.* Washington: US GPO, February 1977.

Congressional Budget Office. *U.S. Food and Agriculture Policy in the World Economy.* Washington: US GPO, April 1976.

Congressional Research Service. "Food Power: A Review of the Options and Arguments on the Potential Use of U.S. Grain Exports as an Instrument of Foreign Policy." Janice Baker, Analyst. 77–42 EP. Washington: US GPO, 1977 1 April 1977.

Council on International Economic Policy. "U.S. Policy on National and International Stocks of Agricultural Commodities." CIEP/SM 30. Unpublished Paper, 13 May 1974.

Council on International Economic Policy. "U.S. Food Aid Policy Alternatives." CIEP/SM 31. Unpublished Paper, 29 April 1974.

General Accounting Office. *Greater U.S. Government Efforts Needed to Recruit Qualified Candidates for Employment By U.N. Organizations.* ID–77–14. Washington: US GPO, 16 May 1977.

General Accounting Office. *The United States Should Play a Greater Role in the Food and Agriculture Organization of the United Nations.* ID–77–13. Washington: US GPO, 16 May 1977.

General Accounting Office. *The World Food Program—How the U.S. Can Help Improve It.* ID–77–16. Washington: US GPO, 16 May 1977.

General Accounting Office. *U.S. Participation in International Food Organizations: Problems and Issues.* ID–76–66. Washington: US GPO, 6 August 1976.

General Accounting Office. *Channeling Foreign Aid Through Private and Voluntary Organizations.* ID–76–58. Washington: US GPO, 5 May 1976.

General Accounting Office. *Impact of U.S. Development and Food Aid in Selected Developing Countries.* ID–76–53. Washington: US GPO, 22 April 1976.

General Accounting Office. *Grain Reserves: A Potential U.S. Food Policy Tool.* OSP–76–16. Washington: US GPO, 26 March 1976.

General Accounting Office. *Need for an International Disaster Relief Agency.* ID–76–15. Washington: US GPO, 15 May 1976.

General Accounting Office. *The Overseas Food Donation Program—Its Constraints and Problems.* ID–75–48. Washington: US GPO, 21 April 1975.

General Accounting Office. *Economic and Foreign Policy Effects of Voluntary Restraint Agreements on Textiles and Steel.* B–179342. Washington: US GPO, 21 March 1974.

U.S. Congress, House, Committee on Agriculture. *Hearings on the Extension of the Food for Peace Program.* 93d C., 1st S. 4–5 April 1973. Washington: US GPO, 1973.

U.S. Congress, House, Committee on International Relations. *Use of U.S. Food Resources for Diplomatic Purposes—An Examination of the Issues.* Report Prepared by the Congressional Research Service. 95th C., 2nd S., January 1977. Washington: US GPO, 1977.

U.S. Congress, House, Committee on International Relations. *Implementation of Recommendations of the World Food Conference.* A Report Submitted by AID. 94th C., 2nd S., December 1976. Washington: US GPO, 1976.

U.S. Congress, House, Committee on International Relations. *United States Grain and Oil Agreements with the Soviet Union.* Hearings, 28 October 1975. Washington: US GPO, 1975.

U.S. Congress, House, Committee on International Relations. *The U.S. Proposal for an International Grain Reserve.* Report of a Staff Study Mission to the IWC Preparatory Group Meeting. 94th C., 1st S., November 1975. Washington: US GPO, 1975.

U.S. Congress, House, Committee on International Relations. *Food Problems of Developing Countries: Implications for U.S. Policy.* Hearings before the Subcommittee on International Resources, Food and Energy. 94th C., 1st S., 21 May and 3,5 June 1975. Washington: US GPO, 1975.

U.S. Congress, House, Committee on International Relations. (Formerly House Committee on Foreign Affairs.) *Report on the World Food Conference.* Hearings, 93rd C., 2nd S., 26 November 1974. Washington: US GPO, 1974.

U.S. Congress, House, Committee on International Relations. (Formerly House Committee on Foreign Affairs, Subcommittee on International Organization and Movements.) *International Food Reserves: Background and Current Proposals.* Report Prepared by the Congressional Research Service. 93rd C., 2nd S., October 1974. Washington: US GPO, 1974.

U.S. Congress, House, Committee on International Relations. (Formerly House Committee on Foreign Affairs.) *Data and Analysis Concerning the Possibility of a U.S. Food Embargo as a Response to the Present Arab Oil Boycott.* Report Prepared by the Congressional Research Service. 93rd C., 1st S., 21 November 1973. Washington: US GPO, 1973.

US Congress, House and Senate, Committees on International Relations and Foreign Relations. *Legislation on Foreign Relations, with Explanatory Notes.* 94th C., 2nd S., April 1976. Washington: US GPO, 1976.

US Congress, Senate, Committee on Agriculture, Nutrition, and Forestry. *Future of Food Aid.* Hearings before the Subcommittee on Foreign Agriculture Policy on S. 1164. 95th C., 1st S., 4–5 April 1977. Washington: US GPO, 1977.

US Congress, Senate, Committee on Agriculture and Forestry. *Farm and Food Policy, 1977.* 94th C., 2nd S., 15 September 1976. Washington: US GPO, 1976.

US Congress, Senate, Committee on Agriculture and Forestry. *American Foreign Food Assistance—Public Law 480 and Related Materials.* 94th C., 2nd S., 13 August 1976. Washington: US GPO, 1976.

US Congress, Senate, Committee on Agriculture and Forestry. *Who's Making Foreign Agricultural Policy?* Hearings before the Subcommittee on Foreign Agricultural Policy. 94th C., 2nd S., 22–23 January 1976. Washington: US GPO, 1976.

US Congress, Senate, Committee on Agriculture and Forestry. *Implementation of World Food Conference Recommendations.* Hearings before the Subcommittee on Foreign Agricultural Policy. 94th C., 1st S., 1 May 1975. Washington: US GPO, 1975.

US Congress, Senate, Committee on Foreign Relations. *World Food Grain Situation.* Hearings before the Subcommittee on South Asian Affairs and African Affairs. 93rd C., 1st S., 5 October 1973. Washington: US GPO, 1974.

US Congress, Senate, Committee on Foreign Relations. *Alternatives to Bilateral Economic Aid.* Report Prepared by the Congressional Research Service. 93rd C., 1st S. June 18, 1973. Washington: US GPO, 1973.

US Congress, Senate, Select Committee on Nutrition and Human Needs. *The United States, FAO, and World Food Politics: U.S. Relations with an International Food Organization.* A Staff Report. 94th C., 2nd S., June 1976. Washington: US GPO, 1976.

US Congress, Senate, Select Committee on Nutrition and Human Needs. *U.S. Participation in the Food and Agriculture Organization of the United Nations.* Hearings. 94th C., 2nd S., 4–5, March 1976. Washington: US GPO, 1976.

US Congress, Senate, Special Committee to Study the Foreign Aid Program. *The Objectives of United States Economic Assistance Programs.* Report Prepared by the Center for International Studies, MIT. 85th C., 1st S., January 1957. Washington: US GPO, 1957.

Technology Assessment Board of the Office of Technology Assessment. Congress of the United States. *Food Information Systems.* Hearings. 94th C., 1st and 2nd S., September, December 1975 and February 1976. Washington: US GPO, 1976.

References

Abel, Martin E. (1965). Memorandum from Martin E. Abel to Nathan M. Koffsky, Economic Research Service, USDA, 30 August. Office of the Secretary of Agriculture, 1965, Box 104, File: Foreign Relations RG 16, NARC, Washington, DC.

Almeida, Silvio et al. (1975). "Analysis of Traditional Strategies to Combat World Hunger and Their Results." *International Journal of Health Services* 5.

Anderson, William D. (1970). "The Intersection of Foreign and Domestic Policy: The Examples in Public Law 480." Ph.D. Dissertation, University of Illinois.

Ash, Roy L. (1974). Memorandum from Roy L. Ash for the President, 16 September. Processed.

Austin, James. E., and Mitchel B. Wallerstein (1978). *Towards a Developmental Food Aid Policy.* Cambridge: MIT INP Discussion Paper.

Badeau, John (1964). State Department summary of letter from Ambassador John Badeau to the President, 3 January. National Security Files—U.A.R., File: UAR—Cables, Vol. I (11/63-5/64), LBJ Library, Austin, Texas.

Bard, Robert L. (1972). *Food Aid and International Agricultural Trade.* Lexington: Heath and Co.

Barnet, Richard, and Ronald Müller (1974). *Global Reach.* New York: Simon and Schuster.

Battle, L.D. (1964). Cable from Ambassador L.D. Battle to the State Department, 24 December. National Security Files—U.A.R. File: Cables, Vol. II (6/65), LBJ Library, Austin, Texas.

Benedict, Murray, and Elizabeth Bauer (1960). *Farm Surpluses: U.S. Burden or World Asset?* Berkeley: University of California Press.

Benson, Ezra Taft (1962). *Cross Fire—The Eight Years with Eisenhower.* New York: Doubleday and Co.

Bjorkman, James W. (1974). "Public Law 480 and the Policies of Self Help and Short Tether: Indo-American Relations, 1965-68." Prepared as a part of the study, *Coordination of Complexity in South Asia* for the Commission on the Organization of the Government for the Conduct of Foreign Policy, 30 September.

Bowles, Chester (1965). Cable from Ambassador Chester Bowles to the State Department, 9 September. NSF—India, Box 2, (File: India, Cables, Vol. V), LBJ Library, Austin, Texas.

Bowles, Chester (1971). *Promises to Keep: My Years in Public Life, 1941–1969.* New York: Harper and Row.

Boyd-Orr, John (1964). *The White Man's Dilemma.* London: George Allen and Unwin, Ltd.

Brown, Lester R. (1975). "The Politics and Responsibility of the North American Bread-basket." *Worldwatch Paper* 2 (October).

Brynes, Asher (1966). *We Give to Conquer.* New York: W.W. Norton and Co.

Butz, Earl L. (1976b). "An Emerging, Market-Oriented Food and Agriculture Policy." *Public Administration Review* (March–April), 137.

CEC (1974a). Commission of the European Communities, "Food Crisis and the Community's Responsibilities Toward Developing Countries." Memorandum on Food Aid Policy of the European Economic Community, 6 March, COM (74) 300 final.

CEC (1974b). Commission of the European Communities, "Development Aid: Fresco for Community Action Tomorrow," *Bulletin of the European Communities* (Supplement August).

CEC (1976). Commission of the European Communities, "The Agricultural Policy of the European Community." European documentation, 1976/5.

CEC (1977). Commission of the European Communities. "The European Community and the Developing Countries." European documentation, 1977/1.

CFA (1977). Committee on Food Aid Policies and Programs, "Food Aid Policies, Including in Particular a Review of the Implementation of Recommendations Adopted." WFP/CFA: 3/7-A, March.

CIA (1965). US Central Intelligence Agency, "India's Food Shortage: Causes and Consequences," 19 February. National Security Files—India, Box 1, File: India—memos & misc., Vol. IV, LBJ Library, Austin, Texas.

CIA (1974). US Central Intelligence Agency, "Potential Implications of Trends in World Population, Food Production and Climate." OPR-401, August.

CIEP (1974a). Council of International Economic Policy. "U.S. Food Aid Policy Alternatives." CIEP/SM 31, Unpublished, 29 April, Section A.

CIEP (1974b). Council on International Economic Policy, "Study of Food Aid." CIEP/SM, 29 April, unpublished.

Cochrane, Willard W, and Mary E. Ryan (1976). *American Farm Policy 1948–1973.* Minneapolis: University of Minnesota Press.

Cohen, Walter (1974). "Herbert Hoover Feeds the World." In Weissman et al., *The Trojan Horse—A Radical Look at Foreign Aid.* San Francisco: Ramparts Press.

Cooper, Richard N. (1972–1973). "Trade Policy is Foreign Policy," *Foreign Policy* 9 (Winter), 18–36.

Department of State BIR (1970). Bureau of Intelligence and Research, Department of State, " 'Food-for-Peace' and 'Freedom from Hunger.' " Intelligence Report No. 8331, 23 August. RG 59 General Records, National Archives and Records Center.

Destler, I.M. (1978). "United States Food Policy 1972–1976: Reconciling Domestic and International Objectives." *International Organization* 32 (Summer).

Ezekiel, Mordecai (1954). "Proposed New Directions in World Agricultural Policy." *Journal of Farm Economics* 36, 402–414.

Fagen, Richard R. (1975). "The United States and Chile: Roots and Branches." *Foreign Affairs* 53 (January), 304.

FAO (1961). Food and Agricultural Organization, *Development through Food—A Strategy for Surplus Utilization.* Rome: FAO, Basic Study No. 2.

FAO (1972). Food and Agricultural Organization, "Principles of Surplus Disposal and Consultative Operations of Member Nations." Rome: FAO.

FAO (1978). *Food Aid Bulletin* 1 (January).

US Congress HCIR (1977). United States Congress, House, Committee on International Relations, 93rd C., 2nd Sess., *Use of U.S. Food Resources for Diplomatic Purposes—An Examination of the Issues.* Report prepared by the Congressional Research Service, Library of Congress, January 1977. Washington: US GPO, 1977.

Feldman, Meyer (1961). Report from Meyer Feldman to Orville Freeman, 3 January. Meyer Feldman Papers, Box 9, File: FFP Program (10/60–1/3/61), JFK Library, Boston, Massachusetts.

Field, John O., and Mitchel B. Wallerstein (1977). "Beyond Humanitarianism: A Developmental Perspective on U.S. Food Aid." In *Food Policy—The Responsibility of the United States in the Life and Death Choices,* Peter G. Brown and Henry Shue, eds. New York: The Free Press, 1977, pp. 234–258.

Freeman, Orville L. (1961a). Orville Freeman to David E. Bell, 26 June. USDA Microfilm, Food for Peace Program, Roll No. 3, JFK Library, Boston, Massachusetts.

Freeman, Orville L. (1961b). Report to the President from the Secretary of Agriculture, Orville L. Freeman, 30 November. President's Office Files—Depts & Agencies, Box 68, File: Agriculture (6/61–12/61), JFK Library, Boston, Massachusetts.

Freeman, Orville L. (1962). Memorandum from Orville L. Freeman for the President, 31 May. President's Office Files—Departments and Agencies, Box 68, File: Agriculture (6/61–12/61), JFK Library, Boston, Massachusetts.

Freeman, Orville L. (1963). Memorandum from Orville L. Freeman for the President, 12 November. President's Office Files—Depts. & Agencies, Box 69, File: Agriculture (9–11/63), JFK Library, Boston, Massachusetts.

Freeman, Orville L. (1964). Memorandum from Orville L. Freeman for the President, 19 November. Folder: EX FO 3-2, Box 22, File: EX FO 3-2 (10/1/64–12/31/64), LBJ Library, Austin, Texas.

Freeman, Orville L. (1965a). Memorandum from Orville L. Freeman for the President, 2 July. White House Central Files—Confidential FO 3-2, Box 47, File: CONFO 3-2 Mutual Security (Aug.-Dec. '65), LBJ Library, Austin, Texas.

Freeman, Orville L. (1965b). Memorandum for the Files, Orville L. Freeman, 14 December. Office of the Secretary of Agriculture—1965, Box 104, File: RG 16 Foreign Relations, NARC, Washington, DC.

Freeman, Orville L. (1966a). Memorandum from Orville L. Freeman for the Vice President and others, 4 January. Folder: White House Central Files FO 3-2 (Jan.-Mar. 1966) Confidential, Box 48, File: FO) 3-2 Mutual Security (Jan.-Mar. 1966), LBJ Library, Austin, Texas.

Freeman, Orville L. (1966b). Orville L. Freeman for the President, 18 January. National Security Files-India, Box 4, File: India's Food Problem—Vol. I, LBJ Library, Austin, Texas.

Freeman, Orville L. (1966c), "The U.S. Wheat Situation: Implications for Concessional Food Aid," 9 July. White House Central Files—Confidential/ CM (Agriculture), Box 5, File: CM (Wheat), Papers of the President, LBJ Library, Austin, Texas.

Freeman, Orville L. (1966d). Memorandum from Orville L. Freeman for the President, 28 November. White House Central Files, GEN FO 3-2 (9/2/65), Box 26, File EX FO 3-2/CO 62–121, LBJ Library, Austin, Texas.

Freeman, Orville L. (1967a). Memorandum from Orville Freeman for the President, 21 March. White House Central Subject File, EX CM/Food, Box 4, File: CM/Food (1/1/67-6/20/67), LBJ Library, Austin, Texas.

Freeman, Orville L. (1967b). Draft memorandum from Orville L. Freeman for the President, 23 June. Folder: EX AG7 (11/23/67), White House Central Files, Box 10, File: EX AG7 (11/13/66), LBJ Library, Austin, Texas.

Freeman, Orville L. (1969). Interview with Orville L. Freeman, 21 July. Oral History Collection, Interview with Orville Freeman, Tape No. 3, LBJ Library, Austin, Texas.

Gardner, Richard N. (1966). Statement of Deputy Assistant Secretary Richard N. Gardner before the Second Committee of the UN General Assembly, 22 January. Arthur M. Schlesinger, Jr. Papers, Box 9, File: FFP (1/29/62-10/14/63) & Undated, JFK Library, Boston, Massachusetts.

Gaud, William (1966). Oral History Collection, Interview with William Gaud, First Tape, 16 February, LBJ Library, Austin, Texas.

Gelb, Leslie H., and Anthony Lake (1974–1975). "Washington Dateline: Less Food, More Politics." *Foreign Policy*, 17 (Winter), 176–189.

Gelb, Leslie (1976). "U.S. Linking Aid to Votes at U.N. *The New York Times*, 9 January, p. 1.

Gongora, J., and D.J. Shaw (1977). "World Food Programme Assistance for Supplementary Feeding Programmes." *Food and Nutrition* 3, 15.

Goulet, Dennis, and Michael Hudson (1971). *The Myth of Aid*. Maryknoll: Orbis Books.

Haas, Ernst (1969). *Tangle of Hopes*. Englewood Cliffs: Prentice-Hall, Inc.

Halberstam, David (1969). *The Best and the Brightest*. New York: Random House, Inc.

Hart, Judith (1973). *Aid and Liberation—A Socialist Study of Aid Policies*. London: Victor Gollancz, Ltd.

Hayter, Teresa (1971). *Aid as Imperialism*. Baltimore: Penguin Books.

Isenman, Paul J., and H.W. Singer (1975). "Food Aid: Disincentive Effects and Their Policy Implications." AID Discussion Paper No. 31 (October).

IWC (1967). International Wheat Council, "International Grains Arrangement 1967 and Rules of Procedure." London: I.W.C.

IWC (1971). International Wheat Council, "International Wheat Agreement, 1971, and Rules of Procedure." London: IWC.

Jacobson, Dorothy H. (1965). Memorandum from Dorothy H. Jacobson to Orville L. Freeman, 24 May. Office of the Secretary of Agriculture, 1965, Box 104, File: RG Foreign Relations, NARC, Washington, DC.

Jacoby, Neil H. (1966). *United States Aid to Taiwan: A Study of Foreign Aid, Self-Help, and Development*. New York: Frederick A. Praeger.

Johnson, Lyndon B. (1966). Letter from Lyndon B. Johnson to Pope Paul VI, 25 February. WHCF, Confidential IS 1—IS 49, Box 58, File: IT 6 Food and Agriculture Organization (FAO), LBJ Library, Austin, Texas.

Johnson, Lyndon B. (1971). *The Vantage Point: Perspective on the Presidency 1963-1969*. New York: Holt, Rhinehart and Winston.

Johnson, U. Alexis (1961). Top secret memorandum from U. Alexis Johnson to McGeorge Bundy, 28 November. President's Office Files—Countries, Box 128, Vietnam Security—1961, JFK Library, Boston, Massachusetts.

Kennedy, John F. (1960). Press Release, October 31. Meyer Feldman Papers, Box 9, File: Food for Peace Program (10/60-1/3/61), John F. Kennedy Library, Boston, Massachusetts.

Kennedy, John F. (1961-1963). Internal policy statement by President John F. Kennedy, undated. President's Office Files—Countries, Box 128, File: Yugoslavia (1961-1963), JFK Library, Boston, Massachusetts.

Kennedy, John F. (1963). Remarks of the President at the opening ceremony of the World Food Congress, 4 June. President's Office File—Speeches, Box 44, File: Speech Files (5/1/63-6/9/63), JFK Library, Boston, Massachusetts.

Keohane, Robert (1966). "Political Influence in the General Assembly." *International Conciliation*, No. 557 (March).

Komer, Robert (1965). Secret memorandum from Robert Komer for the President, 16 September. National Security Files—India, Box 2, File: India—memos & misc., Vol. V (6/65-/9/65), LBJ Library, Austin, Texas.

Krause, Laurence, and Joseph S. Nye, Jr. (1975). "Reflections on the economics and politics of international economic organizations." In *World Politics and International Economics*, L. Krause and F. Bergsten, eds. Washington: The Brookings Institution, pp. 323-342.

Lappé, Francis Moore, and Joseph Collins (1977). *Food First—Beyond the Myth of Scarcity*. Boston: Houghton Mifflin Co.

Lelyveld, Joseph (1967). "U.S. and India—Some Mutual Irritations Over Food." *The New York Times*, 11 June, Section IV, p. 3

McClellan, David S. (1964). "Public Law 480: The Metamorphosis of a Law." New York: The Eagleton Institute Case Studies (September).

McGovern, George S. (1964a). *War Against Want—America's Food for Peace Program*. New York: Walker and Co.

McGovern, George S. (1964b). Statement of George S. McGovern, 24 April. Oral History Collection, JFK Library, Boston, Massachusetts.

McHenry, Donald, and Kai Bird (1977). "Food Bungle in Bangladesh." *Foreign Policy* 27 (Summer), 72-88.

Markovich, Stephen C. (1968). "The Influence of American Foreign Aid in Yugoslav Politics, 1948-1966." Ph.D. Dissertation, University of Virginia.

Mason, Edward (1962). Report of Edward Mason on the economic survey mission to the U.A.R., 1-18 March. President's Office Files—Countries, Box 127, File: U.A.R. (Security), JFK Library, Boston, Massachusetts.

Morgan, Dan (1974). "U.S. Farmers Stockpile World Grain." *Washington Post*, 26 October, p. A7.

Morgan, Dan (1975). "Opening Markets—Program Pushes Produce." *The Washington Post*, 10 March, p. 1.

Morgan, Dan (1976). "Rice: The Diplomatic Crop." *Saturday Review*, 13 November, p. 10.

Morgan, Dan, and Don Oberdorfer (1975). "Impact of United States Food Heavy on South Korea." *The Washington Post*, 12 March, p. 1.

Moynihan, Daniel Patrick (1975). "The United States in Opposition." *Commentary* 59 (March), 31-44.

OECD (1974). Organization for Economic Co-operation and Development, *Food Aid.* Paris: OECD.

OECD (1976). Organization for Economic Co-operation and Development, *Development and Cooperation—1975 Review.* Paris: OECD.

OECD (1977). Organization for Economic Co-operation and Development, *Development and Cooperation—1976 Review.* Paris: OECD.

OECD (1978). Organization for Economic Co-operation and Development, *Development and Cooperation—1977 Review.* Paris: OECD.

OECD (1979). Organization for Economic Co-operation and Development, *Development and Cooperation—1978 Review.* Paris: OECD.

OMB (1976). Office of Management and Budget, Internal discussion paper prepared on PL 480 programming levels for fiscal 1976, undated.

Oudes, Bruce (1966) "Food for Freedom: The Paradox of Foreign Aid." *Nation* 203 (August), 120–124.

Pariser, E.R., Mitchel B. Wallerstein, Christopher J. Corkery, and Norman L. Brown (1978). *Fish Protein Concentrate: Panace or Protein Malnutrition?* Cambridge: MIT Press.

Peterson, Trudy H. (1975). "The Agricultural Trade Policy of the Eisenhower Administration." Ph.D. Dissertation, University of Iowa.

Robinson, Thomas C.M. (1977). Letter from Thomas C.M. Robinson to Resident Representatives, 11 July. WFP/RR/142.

Rogers, Keith D., Leo V. Mayer, and Earl O. Heady, (1972), *Utilization of U.S. Farm Surpluses for Welfare and Development Programs at Home and Abroad.* Center for Agricultural and Rural Development, Iowa State University, C.A.R.D. Report No. 41, June.

Rosenfeld, Stephen S. (1974). "The Politics of Food." *Foreign Policy* (Spring), 17–29.

Rostow, Walter W. (1966). Memoranda from Walter W. Rostow for the President, 6 January. National Security Files—India, Box 2, File: India-memos & misc.—Vol. VI, LBJ Library, Austin, Texas.

Rostow, Walter W. (1972). *The Diffusion of Power.* New York: The Macmillan Co.

Rothschild, Emma (1976). "Food Politics." *Foreign Affairs* 54 (January), 285–307.

Rothschild, Emma (1977a) "For Some a Feast of Crumbs." *The New York Times,* 10 January, p. 21.

Rothschild, Emma (1977b). "The Rats Don't Starve." *The New York Times,* 11 January, p. 23.

Rothschild, Emma (1977c). "Is it time to end Food for Peace?" *The New York Times Magazine,* 13 March, pp. 15, 43–48.

Rusk, Dean (1961). Memorandum from Dean Rusk for the President, 5 May. Presidential Office Files—Countries, Box 127, File: U.A.R. (Security), JFK Library, Boston, Massachusetts.

Rusk, Dean (1962). Secret memorandum for the President, 13 January. Office of the Secretary of Agriculture—Correspondence, 1961, Box 91, File: RG 16 Foreign Relations, 2, N.A.R.C., Washington, DC.

Sanderson, Fred (1968). "The International Grains Arrangement." Department of State *Bulletin,* 6 May, pp. 590–594.

Saylor, Thomas R. (1977). "A New Legislative Mandate for American Food Aid." In *Food Policy: The Responsibility of the United States for the Life and Death Choices."* Peter G. Brown and Henry Shue, eds. New York: The Free Press, pp. 199–211.

Schertz, Lyle P. (1974). "World Food: Prices and the Poor." *Foreign Affairs* 52 (April), 511–537.

Schlesinger, Arthur M, Jr. (1965). *A Thousand Days*. Boston: Houghton Mifflin Co.

Schneider, Stephen H. (1976). *The Genesis Strategy: Climate and Global Survival*. New York: Plenum Press.

Schneider, William (1976). *Food, Foreign Policy, and Raw Materials Cartels*. New York: Crane, Russak and Co.

Schnittker, John A. (1964). Memorandum from Under Secretary John A. Schnittker to the Secretary of Agriculture et al., 21 November. Office of the Secretary of Agriculture, 1964, Box 90, File: RG 16 Foreign Relations 3, N.A.R.C., Washington DC.

Schnittker, John A. (1965). Memorandum from John A. Schnittker for the President, 23 October. NSF—India, Box 2, File: India, Memos & Misc. Vol. VI (Continued), LBJ Library, Austin, Texas.

Schnittker, John A. (1968). Oral History Interview with John A. Schnittker, Oral History Collection, Tape No. 2, 21 November 1968, LBJ Library, Austin, Texas.

Shabecoff, Philip (1976). "Ford Bars Cutoff of Grain to Soviet in Angola Dispute." *The New York Times*, 6 January, p. C1.

Shaw, D. John (1970). "The Mechanism and Distribution of Food Aid—Multilateral Food aid for Economic and Social Development." *Journal of World Trade Law* 207–237.

Shultze, Charles L. (1965a). Charles L. Shultze for the President, 16 November. White House Central Files—Confidential, FO 3-2 (Jan–Mar. 1965) Box 47, File: CONF FO 3-2 Mutual Security (Aug–Dec. 1965), LBJ Library, Austin, Texas.

Shultze, Charles L. (1965b). Memorandum from Charles L. Shultze for the President, 31 December. GEN FO 3-2 (9/2/65), Box 26, File: EX FO 3-2/CO 61, LBJ Library, Austin, Texas.

Smethurst, Richard G. (1969). "Direct Community Aid: A Multilateral Experiment." *The Journal of Development Studies* 5 (April), 205–219.

Surface, Frank M., and Raymond L. Bland (1931). *American Food Aid in the World War and Reconstruction Period*. Stanford: Stanford University Press.

Toma, Peter A. (1967). *The Politics of Food for Peace*. Tucson: Arizona Press.

US AID (1976). United States Agency for International Development, *U.S. Overseas Loans and Grants—Obligations and Loan Authorizations, July 1, 1945—September 1976*. Washington: US GPO.

US AID (1977). United States Agency for International Development, *Overseas Loans and Grants, July 1, 1945–September 30, 1976*. Washington: US GPO.

US Congress HCIR (1974). United States Congress, House, Hearings before the Committee on Foreign Affairs. 93d C. 2nd Sess., *Report on the World Food Conference*, 26 November, Washington: US GPO.

US Congress HCIR (1977). United States Congress, House, Committee on International Relations, 93d C., 2nd Sess., *Use of U.S. Food Resources for Diplomatic Purposes—An Examination of the Issues*. Report prepared by the Congressional Research Service, Library of Congress, January.

US Congress SCAF (1976a). United States Congress, Senate, Committee on Agriculture and Forestry, 94th C. 2nd Sess., *American Foreign Food Assistance*, 13 August. Washington: US GPO.

US Congress SCAF (1976b). United States Congress, Senate, Committee on Agriculture and Forestry, 94th C., 2nd Sess., *Farm and Policy, 1977,* September 15. Washington: US GPO.

US Congress SCANF (1977). United States Congress, Senate, Committee on Agriculture, Nutrition and Forestry, Hearing before the Subcommittee on Foreign Agricultural Policy on S. 1169, 94th C. 1st Sess., *Future of Food Aid,* April 4–5. Washington: US GPO.

US Congress SCFR (1958). United States Congress, Senate, Committee on Foreign Relations, *Hearings,* Mutual Security Act of 1958, C. 85th 2nd Sess. Washington: US GPO.

USDA (1974). United States Department of Agriculture, Economic Research Service, "U.S. Agricultural Exports Under PL 480." ERS-Foreign 395 (October).

USDA (1975). United States Department of Agriculture, *Foreign Agricultural Trade of the United States* (FATUS) (December).

USDA (1977a). United States Department of Agriculture, *Foreign Agriculture* 15 (March).

USDA (1977b). United States Department of Agriculture, *Food for Peace-Fiscal Year 1975.* Washington: USDA.

US GAO (1974), United States General Accounting Office, *Economic and Foreign Policy Effects of Voluntary Restraint Agreements on Textiles and Steel,* 21 March, B-179342. Washington: US GPO.

US GAO (1975). United States General Accounting Office, "The Overseas Food Donation Program—Its Constraints and Problems." ID-75-48, April 21. Washington: US GPO.

US GAO (1977). United States General Accounting Office, *The World Food Program— How the United States Can Help Improve It.* Report to the Senate Committee on Governmental Affairs, May 16, ID-77-16.

Wallensteen, Peter (1976). "Scarce Goods as Political Weapons: The Case of Food." *Journal of Peace Research,* 13, 287–298.

Wallerstein, Mitchel B., and James E. Austin (1978). "The World Food Council at Three Years: Global Food System Manager?" *Food Policy* (August), 191–201.

Weaver, David R. (1971). "P.L. 480, India, and the Objectives of United States Foreign Aid, 1954–1966." Ph.D. Dissertation, University of Cincinnati.

Westwood, Andrew (1966). *Foreign Aid in a Foreign Policy Framework.* Washington: Brookings Staff Paper, April.

WFC (1974). World Food Council, "General Review of Food and Policies and Programmes." WFC/CFA: 7/6–B March.

WFC (1977). World Food Council, "Food Aid: Progess Report and Recommendations for Further Action." WFC/38, 24 March.

WFP (1966a). World Food Programme, "Report of the Jamaica Mission (Study on the Feasibility of Multilateral Food Aid for National Development)." WFP/IGC: 9/18, 16 February.

WFP (1966b). World Food Programme, "The Selection of Projects." WFP/IGC: 9/14, 18 February, p. 2.

WFP (1969). World Food Programme, "WFP Sales Policy." WFP/IGC: 15/17. 21 March.

WFP (1973a). World Food Programme, *Ten Years of World Food Programme Development Aid, 1963–1972.* Rome: WFP.

WFP (1973b). World Food Programme, "Canadian Proposal for Special Measures in Favour of Least-Developed Countries in the Utilization of Multilateral Food Aid." WFP/CFA: 24/12, August.

WFP (1977). World Food Programme, "Sale and Exchange of Commodities." WFP/CFA: 4/9, September.

WFP (1977a). World Food Programme, "Annual Statement of the Executive Director on the Development of the Programme." WFP/CFA: 3/4, March. Annex IV.

WFP (1977b). World Food Programme, "Resources of the Programme," WFP/CFA: 4/4, July, Annex I, p. 8.

WFP (1977c). World Food Programme, "Emergency Operations." Report by the Executive Director, March, WFC/CFA, 3/6.

WFP (1977d). World Food Programme, "Emergency Operations, Including Adequacy of Provisions, on Emergency Food Aid." WFP/CFA: 4/6, September.

Wightman, David R. (1968). "Food Aid and Economic Development," *International Conciliation*, No. 567. New York: Carnegie Endowment for International Peace (March).

Wittkopf, Eugene (1973). "Foreign Aid and the United Nations Votes: A Comparative Study." *APSR* 67 (September), 968–888.

Wszelaki, Jan (1964). *John F. Kennedy and Poland—Selection of Documents, 1948–1963.* Jan Wszelaki, ed. New York: Polish Institute of Arts and Sciences in America.

Zachar, George (1977). "A Political History of Food for Peace." Ann Arbor: Nutrition Planning Information Service, Document No. 246, p. 27.

List of Acronyms

AFBF
American Farm Bureau Federation

AID
Agency for International Development

ARA
American Relief Administration

CAP
Common Agricultural Policy

CARE
Cooperative for American Relief Everywhere

CCC
Commodity Credit Corporation

CCP
Committee on Commodity Problems

CEA
Council of Economic Advisors

CEC
Commission of the European Communities

CFA
Committee on Food Aid Policies and Programmes

CIA
Central Intelligence Agency

CIDA
Canadian International Development Agency

CIEP
Council for International Economic Policy

CRB
Commission for the Relief of Belgium

CRS
Catholic Relief Service

CSD
Consultative Subcommittee on Surplus Disposal

DOS
Department of State

ECOSOC
UN Economic and Social Council

EEC
European Economic Community

FAC
Food Aid Convention

FAO
Food and Agriculture Organization of the UN

FFHC
Freedom from Hunger Campaign

FFP
Food for Peace Program

FFW
Food for Work

GAO
US General Accounting Office

GARIOA
Government and Relief in Occupied Areas

GATT
General Agreement on Tariffs and Trade

HCA
House Committee on Agriculture

HCIR
House Committee on International Relations

ICCH
International Commodity Clearinghouse

IER
International Emergency Reserve

IFAP
International Federation of Agricultural Producers

IGA
International Grains Arrangement

IGC
Inter-governmental Committee

IWA
International Wheat Agreement

IWC
International Wheat Council

JFK
John F. Kennedy Presidential Library

LBJ
Lyndon B. Johnson Presidential Library

LDC
Less Developed Country

MSA
Mutual Security Act

NARC
National Archives and Records Center

NATO
North Atlantic Treaty Organization

NIEO
New International Economic Order

NSC
National Security Council

ODA
Official Development Assistance

OECD
Organization for Economic Co-operation and Development

OMA
Office of Multilateral Affairs

OMB
Office of Management and Budget

OPEC
Organization of Petroleum Exporting Countries

OSRO
FAO Office of Special Relief Operations

PAG
Protein Advisory Group

PTE
Private Trade Entity

PVO
Private Voluntary Organization

QAP
Quick Action Procedure

SCAF
Senate Committee on Agriculture and Forestry

SCANF
Senate Committee on Agriculture, Nutrition and Forestry

SCFR
Senate Committee on Foreign Relations

SIDA
Swedish International Development Agency

SSCNHN
Senate Select Committee on Nutrition and Human Needs

UAR
United Arab Republic

UNDP
UN Development Program

UNDRO
UN Disaster Relief Office

UNHCR
UN High Commission for Refugees

UNICEF
UN International Children's Emergency Fund

UNIDO
UN Industrial Development Organization

UNRRA
UN Relief and Rehabiliation Administration

UNRWA
UN Relief and Works Agency

USDA
US Department of Agriculture

USIA
US Information Agency

USGPO
US Government Printing Office

WFB
World Food Board

WFC
World Food Council

WFP
World Food Programme (UN-FAO)

WHO
World Health Organization

WMO
World Meteorological Organization

Index

Agricultural Adjustment Act of 1933, 4
Agricultural Adjustment Act of 1962, 264n11
Agriculture and Consumer Protection Act of 1973, 11
Agricultural Trade Development and Assistance Act of 1954 (PL 480)
  aid to Communist countries, 43
  Cooley loans, 37
  effect of LDC food habits, 265n2
  Food for Freedom program, 44
  goals of, 266n5
  local currency accumulation under, 37
  market development objectives of, 147–148
  original configuration of, 36
  passage of, 6, 34–36
  prohibition of Title I sales, 43
  program antecedents, 31–33
  restrictions on aid to Cuba or North Vietnam, 274n7
  signing of by Eisenhower, 35
  specific purposes of, 35
  survival of, 3
  Title I, 25–26
    as a strategic instrument, 130–132
    capital generating feature of, 276n36
    impact of Cooley loans, 265n5
    local currency provision, 266n7
    maintenance of value clause, 266n8
    private trade entity loans, 153
    self-help provisions, 267n22
  Title II, 25–26
Allende Doctrine, 277n11
American Farm Bureau Federation (AFBF), 34

American Food for Peace Council, 182
American Relief Administration (ARA), 28
Ash, Roy L., 50–51, 200
Australian food aid, 74–75, 268n4

Badeau, John
  advice on aid to UAR, 127
  as ambassador to UAR, 125
Bangladesh, 161–162
Belgian food aid, 81–82, 269n16
Bell, David, 148
Benson, Ezra Taft, 6, 34–35
  impact of policy on multilateral programs, 93
  position on Humphrey Food for Peace proposal, 39
  role in creation of FFP, 266n10
  role in WFP proposal, 168
Boerma, A.H., 174
Bowles, Chester
  as Ambassador to India, 136–138
  and India food crisis, 186, 191
  mission to UAR, 126
Boyd-Orr, Sir John, 91
Brannan, Charles, 91
British Food Aid, 76–77, 268n8
Bundy, McGeorge, 43, 124
Burden-sharing and international food aid, 248–249
  assessment of, 177–179
  current US position on, 278n22
  factors in, 165–167
  FAC of 1967, 171–173
  India food aid, 174–176
  matching formula, 277n9
  WFP proposal, 167–171